Recent Studies on Indian Women

Recent Studies on Indian Women

Empirical Work of Social Scientists

EDITORS
KAMAL K. MISRA
JANET HUBER LOWRY

RAWAT PUBLICATIONS
Jaipur • New Delhi • Bangalore • Mumbai • Hyderabad • Guwahati

ISBN 81-316-0049-1

Published by
Prem Rawat for **Rawat Publications**
Satyam Apts., Sector 3, Jawahar Nagar, Jaipur 302 004 (India)
Phone: 0141 265 1748 / 7006 Fax: 0141 265 1748
E-mail: info@rawatbooks.com
Website: www.rawatbooks.com

New Delhi Office
4858/24, Ansari Road, Daryaganj, New Delhi 110 002
Phone: 011-23263290

Also at Bangalore, Mumbai, Hyderabad and Guwahati

Typeset by Rawat Computers, Jaipur
Printed at Chaman Enterprises, New Delhi

Contents

1

Travails of the Indian Woman

From *Purdah* to Modernity

JANET HUBER LOWRY AND KAMAL K. MISRA

If the recently promulgated Hindu Succession (Amendment) Act, 2005 is any indication of India's commitment to bridge the gender gap in tune with the international trend, it is certainly a welcome step forward. The amendments have been recently approved by both houses of the Indian Parliament and have received the Presidential assent through which the Indian Government after 50 years has finally addressed some of the vexing questions of gender inequalities enshrined in the 1956 Hindu Succession Act. Despite some anomalies still persisting, the Act seeks to cover gender inequalities on many fronts, viz., inheritance of agricultural land, *Mitakshara* joint family property (see Chapter 10 in this volume), parental dwelling house, widows' rights, etc. Yet the question is still often asked in academic and human rights circles in India today whether the amended Act would give Indian women the minimum security they seek? Could the amended Act move ahead any change in the obstinate mindset of a staunchly patrilineal society to grant any concession to its women notwithstanding the law in their favour? Is the ideal-typical cultural construction of the Indian woman, *Bharatiya Nari*, traditionally characterized by "a large *bindi* on her forehead, wearing a *saree* and fair in complexion... sexually passive, gentle and self-sacrificing, monogamous, looking upon the face of the only one man in her life, her husband, and ... the repository of the honour of the family" (Channa, Chapter 2 in this volume), paving the way for identifying an Indian woman who is educated, assertive, and conscious of her rights and responsibilities, by the promulgation of this amended Act? All the chapters in this volume address these issues tangibly or intangibly, sometimes with deep empirical insights of the authors. The chapters are divided into four sections, viz., the socio-cultural context, issues of marriage and family, empowerment of the marginalized, and women in new roles. All these sections together present a very broad spectrum of Indian women as they are perceived temporally and spatially with all their variability.

The Socio-Cultural Context of Gender

The social construction of a pan-Indian ideal woman has indeed prompted scholars like Channa to probe into the background of such a monolithic construction, though in reality, India possesses a rich variety of socio-cultural formations, ethnicities, religions and religious sects. She attributes such monolithic social construction to the unification of identities by the colonial administration in India in its own interest, or owing to a resistance to this attempt. She invokes how the emergence of an elite and educated class of Brahmins and Kayasthas with its exposure to English education in the colonial period, the beginning of women's writings belonging mostly to this class in Indian print media, and the spread of a variety of reform movements with the upper caste Hindu woman as its focus, have culminated in the construction of the ideal Indian woman engendered in the class and caste structure of India that favoured a particular elite point of view.

The process of monolithic social construction of gender, Channa observes, was not only influenced by the colonial rule and western patriarchy of the British in the name of 'objectification', but was also complemented by the Indian male intellectualism and elite hegemony of the upper castes having access to reading and interpreting Sanskrit texts. The ideal image of woman in India, was therefore, filtered by innumerable isms, viz., casteism, male chauvinism, colonialism, regionalism, and so on, and finally what was construed as Indian woman "was the wife of the elite Indian man, the Brahmin *Pandit*, the Kshatriya ruler, or at best, the Vaishya householder". Channa, therefore concludes, "Left out was the woman, who was the labourer, the potter's wife, the washerwoman, the tribal woman and those who were not within the folds of high caste Hindu households". In other words, the image of an ideal Indian woman was portrayed in tune with its Great Tradition enshrined in the Hindu religious texts and not in its innumerable Little Traditions or folk versions as practiced by the majority of rural and tribal Indians. The image of an Indian woman, therefore, is confined to the minority elite stereotypes, leaving aside the cultural construction of women by a large majority of non-elite Indian population.

Channa cites many examples of the stereotypes of an ideal Indian woman with the image of a *devi* or the goddess, contrasting her image as a *dasi* or a servant. In popular culture, while the former conforms to the self-sacrificing and virtuous woman fit to be married and adored as a wife, the latter image is about the woman who is desirable and is an object of love. Both the images run parallel to each other; one symbolized by her submissiveness to patriarchal norms and codes of conduct, and the other as independent, self-sufficient and assertive. Channa aptly remarks how the mainstream Indian television has been reinforcing and rather strengthening the gender stereotypes already present in Indian society. The *devi* is projected in these popular serials as docile, traditional, adjustable, emotional, sentimental, sacrificing, eager to please and gain acceptance, an archetype of feminine perfection. On the other hand, the working or ambitious woman (the boardroom woman) is portrayed as having a plunging neckline, short hair, being bold, conniving, heartless, ruthless, and perfect in the art of seduction, popularly addressed as a power hungry villain. Such stereotypes convey confused messages which have a negative effect on impressionable young minds. Channa, therefore, recommends "a quiet revolution to reinstate the *dasi* on the throne of the *devi*, to recognize the power of womanhood and to admire its potency, to recognize the creative force of the universe as a part of the household and not only as a part of the temple".

Channa suggests analyses similar to the separate spheres construction of Victorian England, embraced by the growing middle class of late 19th century America. It even bears echoes of French contrasts between the virtuous gentle woman placed on a pedestal and the harlot of the streets, railed against but loved for the independence of her nature. The housewife who managed the domestic economy, provided emotional sustenance, and preserved the morality of society by raising the young and extending the home through charitable activities was championed in the West for subordinating her sphere to that of men "in the interest of national welfare" (Bernard, 1982: 91). We see echoes of these themes in other contributions of this volume, whether it is the suffering songs of Dalit women in rural Andhra Pradesh which address untouchable or lower caste women's structural position in society (Rao in Chapter 5), the persistence of 'homely' as an adjective in matrimonial (Chauhan in Chapter 7), the government justification for violating women's rights in the name of population control (Prasad in Chapter 11), the elite women of Kolkata volunteering in charitable NGOs (Mitra and Van Delinder in Chapter 15), or concerns of women scientists for career and family clashes (Ravikumar in Chapter 17). Channa supplies this kind of fundamental analysis for the 'ideal Indian woman' which undergirds most of the rest of the book.

Mohanty has taken some of the issues raised by Channa further in Chapter 3 of this volume. His contribution lies in a meticulous content analysis of a 'conduct book' in vernacular Oriya, titled, *Gruha Laxmi,* by one Jagabandhu Singh, published in late 1930s or early 1940s, to impress contemporary Oriya women to make themselves aware of the ideal womanhood and orient their behaviour accordingly. Mohanty also cites a few examples of contemporary male writings not really appreciating women's education, along with the female literary genre of the times, airing its reactions to such conduct books attempting to stereotype the role and moral code of conduct of an Oriya wife.

When Jagabandhu Singh was writing his *Gruha Laxmi,* women's schooling in Orissa was considered to be a sort of intrusion of Western values into the living rooms of the orthodox Indians. Singh seems to be apprehensive of higher education that might incite the young Hindu wives to refuse to accept the conventional household ideals. One of the household ideals which Singh obviously refers to is the 'most important' activity of cooking by the Hindu wife, which he fears, might get eroded among the modern educated wives. Singh's advice of abstinence from good food, good dress, cosmetics, and so on by the wives in the absence of their husbands is what Mohanty terms as truly 'the apex of wifely conduct'. So far as social construction of ideal Indian woman is concerned, there is no disagreement whatsoever between the observations of Channa and Mohanty, as both of them indicate the popular rhetoric of idealizing Indian woman within the fold of a Hindu mother and wife, whose identity is always tied closely with the dominant male member of the household – with the father before her marriage, with the husband after marriage, and with her son after she attains motherhood.

Jagabandhu Singh's aphorisms of the ideal Hindu wife and his sacred duties notwithstanding, there have been simultaneous voices of protest by the Oriya literary women of the same period representing alternative rhetoric of female empowerment, to which Mohanty draws our attention. He refers to many issues relating to women's empowerment advocated by the well-known Oriya women writers of that time, including Suprabha Devi, Narmada Kar, Reba Roy, Kuntala Kumari Sabat, Kokila Devi, Sarala Devi and others, encouraging Oriya women to participate in the public space. Mohanty concludes by suggesting that these two mutually antagonistic stands of idealizing Indian woman in the 1930s and 1940s have their "... legacy continue till today and their looming shadow is still felt in many of the educational, literary and cultural institutions of contemporary Orissa; clearly a fact to be noted by those attempting to bring about gender justice and equality among the sexes in the state".

It is now testified beyond doubt that the construction of an ideal Indian (read Hindu) woman is the textual and glorified version of the Indian woman, which is widely different from its myriad folk versions – in the households of peasants, artisans, craftsmen, tribals and other religious groups and sects. An obnoxious trend of levelling of many sociological realities by the guardians of knowledge and power is distinctly visible in constructing an ideal woman in India. Mishra, in Chapter 4 of the volume, points out another case study that corroborates an attempt of oversimplification in characterizing Indian women. And this time, the example is of a tribal woman. In anthropological parlance, Mishra underscores how the tribal woman in India is construed as enjoying a higher status than her Hindu counterpart, just because she contributes to the household economy, and tribal societies still have a customary practice of paying bride price at the time of marriage, however small and symbolic it might be. She examines the gender relations among the Kutia Kondhs of Orissa as reflected in the contexts of cosmology, economy, kinship, ritual and polity to bring to the fore the social relational contexts where hegemonic or other gender beliefs come in to play their roles.

Mishra clearly points out the ambivalence in the expression of gender relations in tribal societies, the Kutia Kandha being not an exception. She alludes to this ambivalence by indicating that despite Kutia Kandhas' cosmological belief of the origin of the tribe from the female deity, Niranthali, and worship of the mother earth in the form of *dharni mata* on many occasions, their women are not allowed to witness, let alone participate, in the much talked about buffalo sacrifice ritual. In a similar vein she indicates how despite their major contribution to family economy, subsistence and the exclusive responsibility of bearing and rearing children, the Kandha women have at best usufruct rights over land and children, while all major decisions relating to agriculture, credit negotiations, liaison with the government officials, etc., are the sole prerogative of the men. Although the institution of bride price that exists even now among the Kandhas is supposed to be one of the indicators of the importance of women's labour, in reality, Mishra observes that decisions regarding marriage, polygyny, and even of undergoing tubectomy are that of their men, suggesting that the analysis of gender relations in a tribal society need to go beyond the conventional public-private, production-reproduction dichotomies to accommodate the dynamics of gender relations. The echo of a need for dehomogenization of the category of 'woman' and to account for the complex combination of economic self-sufficiency with structural dependency in analysing gender relations in tribal societies are conspicuous in Mishra's observations, which endorse both Channa's and Mohanty's views in earlier chapters in the volume.

In the Chapter 5 of this volume, Rao presents the perception of the Dalit women, who were hitherto named as untouchables in India, about men, an oppressive caste hierarchy, and their desire for emancipation through the expressive tradition of singing in their private space, against the conventional portrayal of women by men brought up in a patriarchal society. Rao's discourse explicitly interrogates the projection of ideal Indian women as 'passive' and 'submissive' to the dictates of patriarchal customs and traditions and underlines their outbursts through various folk songs against these customs and traditions, obviously within the confines of their houses and while they work in the agricultural farms. Rao perhaps rightly endorses Challapalli's categorization of Dalit women as 'Dalits within Dalits', as they are doubly disadvantaged by patriarchy as well as gender discrimination.

Rao's analysis of Dalit women's songs clearly drive home the point that despite being a participant in the customs and traditions that regulate Indian rural life, the Dalit women are not inclined to get bulldozed by their diktats. Rao's songs very strongly underscore Dalit women's disapproval of the hierarchical caste system, for the upper caste men also are victims of sensuality and material desire, despite their high caste ideology of abstention from these evils. In some songs, an unfaithful and frolicking husband is rebuked as a deserter and a cobra by his wife, the metaphor used for poison and death. Even the ideal of renunciation vital to Hinduism has been condemned by the Dalit women, in case the husband prefers to renounce the world for religious reasons leaving the unfulfilled sexual desire of the young wife. Some songs metaphorically invite husband's younger brother or other lovers to satisfy the lust of the young lady and enter into extra-marital relations in contradiction to the ideal Hindu practice of strict monogamy. Rao also alludes to the songs that express bitterness in the conjugal family when "(she) feels happy for the death of any member in her conjugal family where there is play of power, authority, restriction, deference and suffering. She desires that her lover should live long. This actually means her longing for love, unconditional affection, friendship and support." Rao contends that sometimes the material conditions rather compel the Dalit women to violate the moral code of conduct to rid themselves of the abject poverty and helplessness. The message Rao intends to give is that Dalit women should not be taken for granted and their covert protest against the oppressive social order should not be underestimated. Although their resistance is yet to be embarrassingly public, their use of symbols of dominators is sufficiently indicative of the disapproval of their status as 'Dalits among Dalits'.

Marriage, Family and Gender

It is an undeniable fact that marriage ensures a distinct status to women in many traditional societies like India. The conceptual difference between a married woman and either a spinster or a widow is purported by differential social and ritual status granted to these categories. Closely linked with marriage in these societies is the age at marriage which is considered to be a key intervening variable in the process of status attainment. Early marriage and shouldering of family responsibilities are intertwined with relative deprivation of educational and gainful employment opportunities, which are pivotal factors in attaining higher status in the society. Besides, early marriage makes the newly-wed couple more vulnerable to share each other's values, concerns and emotions, which are vital for the success of the conjugal life. D. Radha Devi in Chapter 6 of the volume probes deeper into the issue of the age at marriage in India in the light of the recommendations of the National Population Policy, 2000 of India stipulating the age at marriage for women at 20 years, at least not before the age of 18 years, and the ground reality existing in different states and union territories in India. Her data for the study come from the district level Rapid Household Survey on Reproductive and Child Health (RCH) conducted by the Department of Family Welfare, Ministry of Health and Family Welfare, Government of India, launched during 1998-99. From each district, samples of 1,100 households were selected using circular systematic random sampling technique.

The final analysis of the study rather clearly reveals that age at marriage for many women is still below the preferred age of 20 years as underlined in the National Population Policy of 2000. This is despite many legislative measures enacted by the Government of India. The history of such legislation goes back to 1929, when the colonial government enacted the Child Marriage Restraint Act, fixing the minimum age at marriage for the girls at 14 and that of the boys at 18. This Act was amended in 1949 raising the age at marriage for girls to 15. Since these Acts did not yield the desirable result, the Government then passed the Child Marriage Restraint (Amendment) Act, 1978, which increased the minimum age at marriage for girls to 18 years and for boys to 21 years, and significantly prescribed offences under this Act cognizable.

All this stringent legislation notwithstanding, Radha Devi's analysis indicates that almost one out of every ten marriages was conducted before the girl attained at least 15 years. In the states of Bihar, Madhya Pradesh, Rajasthan and West Bengal, child marriages are reported in all the districts. The per cent of districts with at least one child marriage is also fairly high in Andhra Pradesh, Gujarat, Haryana, Karnataka, Maharashtra, Orissa and Uttar Pradesh. Surprisingly there are only 16 districts in the whole country with all reported marriages above 18 years. A total of 137 districts out of 504 districts surveyed had a median age at marriage below 18 years, indicating the slow pace of the Government efforts in raising the age at marriage for girls. It is no wonder that the findings of the survey indicate lower median age at marriage in rural areas of India, particularly among the marginalized SC/ST/OBC populations, among the lower socio-economic groups, and among low literacy groups. This is true in almost all districts of the country. But then why does the practice of lower age at marriage in India continue despite such stringent legislation?

The reasons, Radha Devi alludes to, behind the practice of marriage below the preferred age fixed by the government are many peculiar social and religious practices which still hold their root firmly in the traditional Indian rural society. For example, in many pockets of the country child marriage is still the norm and the parents face social disapproval and disgrace, if the daughter is not married quite early in her childhood. Keeping a daughter of 10 years of age unmarried in some rural societies is considered to demean the prestige of her parents. Rampant illiteracy, more so among women, and strict moral code of caste endogamy are the additive factors that ensure perpetuation of some of these deleterious practices preventing an upward swing of age at marriage for girls in India. The institutions of dowry or marriage payment to the groom by the bride's parents and the status enhancing syndrome of imitating local higher castes that practice child marriage, significantly contribute to lower age at marriage in rural India. Radha Devi notes the daunting reality that two-thirds of the respondents do not identify age 18 as the correct legal minimum age. This is a sad commentary on the awareness of Indian women. She pleads for a holistic approach of raising awareness and improving the economic condition of the women in India, if the National Population Policy, 2000 is to achieve its ultimate goal with respect to the age at marriage.

In most of the sociological and anthropological literature on marriage in India, caste endogamous arranged marriage is cited to play a very significant role due to the much maligned patriarchal structure of Indian society. So far as marriage is concerned, many studies unambiguously assert that caste boundary is the critical threshold beyond which Indian marriages hardly take place. Against this popular yet static approach to Indian marriage, Chauhan argues in Chapter 7 of this volume that although caste endogamy remains important in Indian marriages, the significance of class as a variable in arranging marriages has been increasing. She considers income, education and occupation as the hallmarks of the class phenomenon. She shows that although caste endogamy persists today it is to a lesser degree because of an increasing significance of class. Using an historical method she demonstrates how the Indian marriage has changed and the nature of these changes is gendered, underscoring a more dynamic view of the Indian marriage. Moreover, Chauhan's study, instead of considering dynamism in marriage in the form of just dowry related violence as enunciated by many relatively recent researchers, emphasizes systematic and historical studies placing Indian marriage in a broader economic and political framework of development.

Chauhan's study is based on the content analysis of matrimonial columns in one of the popular English dailies in India, *The Times of India,* in order to demonstrate the changes in marriage with regards to an increasing significance of class and the gendered nature of the process. The study clearly reveals not only an upward trend in the number of matrimonial advertisements that shoot up from 20 to 2,122 during the reference periods of 1950, 1970 and 1990, but also sociologically significant changes in the contents of these advertisements. Chauhan argues that these changes are far from equal for both men and women, thus indicating the 'gendered outcome' of India's post-independence process of modernization. It has benefited men more than women as evidenced by differential rates of literacy and the declining sex ratio. Focusing on caste in marriage, she concludes that although caste ties are gradually declining in general, caste still matters in marriage in India, as the advertisers ask for brides or grooms of the same caste or sub-caste. However, class characteristics are becoming more and more important in arranging marriages for all castes, especially among the men, who are described by the modern attributes of class, viz., education, occupation and income. On the other hand, she observes, women continue to be described by their traditional attributes. Chauhan's penetrating analysis documents that while changes in marriage structure are due to India's ongoing process of modernization, persistence of the priority for caste endogamy in marriage is primarily due to the gender inequality in marriage and society in India.

Gender inequality generally has many manifestations. One such manifestation in a traditionally patriarchal society like India is in the form of domestic violence on women. Many researches indicate that in a patrilocal family, the new bride has to quickly conform to the norms of her husband's family. Violence on women begins as a last resort with the non-conformity or delayed conformity to the family norms, when the 'errant' woman is disciplined by the use of force. Menon and Johnson in Chapter 8 of this volume discuss the widely publicized issue of domestic violence in rural India with the theoretical assumption that in a patriarchal society domestic violence is deployed in the interest of men in controlling the women. But does it mean that the more patriarchal the society, the greater the rate of domestic violence? Menon and Johnson have examined this general assumption with specific hypotheses because of the cultural diversity that India possesses.

Their first hypothesis is based on the regional differences in India. Since the status of women in southern and north-eastern states is relatively higher than the north, they hypothesize less domestic violence in these states compared to North India. The second hypothesis is based on family characteristics and states that violence against women would occur more in joint or non-nuclear families than in nuclear families. Further, if the woman is not a part of the decision-making process in the family, if she suffered abuse in her natal family, if she comes from a lower socio-economic background, and from a religion that does not preach peaceful living like Buddhism and Jainism, then she is more apt to experience domestic violence. Menon and Johnson also have taken into consideration the personal characteristics – if uneducated, unemployed and economically dependent, and possessing an attitude of acceptance of such offence – make them more vulnerable to domestic violence. Menon and Johnson tested their field data with bivariate and multivariate regression models. The study underlines three important characteristics of domestic violence. First, against all expectations, patriarchy does not function as an ideology in all contexts nor necessarily culminates in violence against women. Second, violence is the last resort, when all other tactics have failed to persuade the woman. And third, discourses of love have to be incorporated in understanding domestic violence, because Indian families include dominant as well as subordinate groups living in close proximity bound by familial ties where narratives of love, romance and marriage bind people in relationships of power. Therefore, Menon and Johnson urge us to look deeply into the conditions under which domestic violence takes place rather than assuming that the patriarchal ideology in Indian families as the only necessary evil.

We wonder if the contradiction to their regional hypothesis is in part answered by the persistence of child and early marriage in the north revealed in Chapter 6. Violence may not be required when the bride is still immature and thrust into a new household with different rules and little recourse to opt out or return to natal place. Rather a fatalistic outlook may be more pronounced and inhibit assertiveness in this context. In addition, the rising expectations of the more educated and cared for girls of smaller families in some of the south may set them up for more difficulty curbing their independence in the more mature marriages of the south. Perhaps this reality prevails in relation to the subtleties of patriarchy there.

In contrast to the dominant patriarchal society and ideologies in India, there also exist a number of matrilineal and matriarchal societies widely scattered from the north and north-east of the country to down south. In Chapter 9 Augustine compares two existing matrilineal communities of India; one in the Khasi Hills in North-Eastern India, the Khasis, and the other in Kerala in the south-western corner of the country, the Nairs. Augustine's study strives to provide an empirical and first-hand insight into the present status of the two communities with regard to lineage, inheritance and authority; to examine the factors responsible for sustaining matriliny among the Khasis and for its disappearance from the Nair society; and to examine the differential impact of the modern forces of change on both these communities. The major difference in the family pattern noted by Augustine is that while the Nair family includes lineal as well as collateral kin of the matriarch, the Khasi family restricts itself to the lineals with the principle of ultimogeniture. Further, while the forces of modernization and the less caste defined social hierarchy in Kerala have levelled the rural-urban divide among the Nairs, this distinction is still visible among the Khasis. In rural Meghalaya, the Khasi household is still considered as an asylum for the disabled, old, widows and divorcees, while the Nairs have already given up the joint family system.

Augustine assesses these two matrilineal societies are at two different stages of evolution. While the Nair societies witnessed macro-level change, the Khasis portray only micro-level changes, and she assigns many reasons for this. She is of the opinion that in the Nair society, which is a subsystem of a complex social system of Kerala, the influence of neighbours is more penetrating, thus making them give up their traditional system of *tarawad*. This is not true for the Khasis for they are surrounded by other matrilineal groups. She contends that economic pressure of an emerging cash economy, western education, new administrative system after the kingship lost its hold in Kerala, and changing values seriously weakened the Nair *tarawad* and hastened its disintegration by giving way to nuclear families. Gradually patriliny replaced matriliny among the Nairs. However, she concludes, "Though Nairs of today are legally patrilineal, they are emotionally matrilineal". This is not exactly true for the Khasis, although the trend is clearly visible. Mother's brother is gradually losing his authority as the final arbiter in family affairs due to his new occupation as an employee in the city away from his village. Contrarily, children are seen adopting the family name of the father, if he happens to be an influential person or holding high position in the society. The home of the youngest daughter is no more the shelter for all the matrikin with the kinship responsibilities taking a back seat. Although the shift to patriliny has not yet consolidated among the Khasis, Augustine is visibly apprehensive of its ultimate decline, if the trend continues.

Women, and particularly widows in India, are the victims of social stigmas and the tenets of patriarchy. Social debasement and discrimination of widows is a common phenomenon, which is mainly rooted in traditional values and beliefs. Joseph's observations in Chapter 10 of this volume precisely pinpoint the legal dimensions of widowhood across three major religious faiths in India: Hinduism, Islam and Christianity. She discusses the personal laws in all these religions and place of women and widows in them.

Historically, Joseph contends, wide variations prevailed in personal laws of different religions and between competing sects within religions during the British period due to the latter's policy of non-intervention in social and religious matters of India. There was some improvement in the nineteenth century due to the efforts of social reformers calling for reforms on grounds of humanitarianism and social demands. However, the strengthening of National Movement and personal efforts of Mahatma Gandhi culminated in revising laws, thus removing the legal inferiority of the Indian women and discrimination that affected their lives and personality. The laws relating to widow remarriage, inheritance of the property of the deceased husband, freedom in adoption of an heir, and provisions for maintaining oneself without a state of dependence, etc., have required them to start a new life after the death of the husband. However, Joseph asserts, this excellent social legislation is fraught with problems due to the faith-oriented personal laws that guide the destiny of the widows in India. Her anguish is that even the Government does not question the validity of these personal laws that are detrimental to ensuring self-esteem and higher status to widows in Indian society. For example, while a Hindu widow is free to adopt a child, neither the Muslim nor the Christian widow has this option because of their respective personal laws. Therefore, Josephs urges for a Uniform Non-sexist Civil Code in India, so that the widows can live with dignity irrespective of their faiths. She also pleads for more legal awareness among Indian women through mass media, legal education, voluntary action groups, legal aid agencies, etc., so that the law can help ameliorate the plight of the widows.

This situation with law as the solution for widows in India may want to take a look at the debate about rape law in the America. Some warned that the experience of victims once in the legal system, with all its criteria of evidence and presumed innocence of the perpetrator, often led to another crisis for the victim in having to relive and confront the attacker in order to bring justice. Safeguards through sensitivity training of law enforcement officials and work by advocates have begun to correct this difficulty for such victims. What would it take to find acceptance within one's faith community which feels put upon by the state's authority regarding its traditions and standards? Will a uniform code provide for the cultural awareness change needed to support widows' new rights? Be careful what you wish, for may be the appropriate precautionary note along with urging the extension of widows' rights.

Discourses on human body and its social construction have engaged many scholars in recent times and a feminist perspective on health policies has gradually emerged due to its gendered nature. In Chapter 11 of the volume, Prasad critically looks at these dimensions of the population control or family planning policy in India from a feminist perspective. Since the Indian health situation has parallels with that of other parts of the developing world, she contends, it is important to locate and understand the population debates of India against the global population control discourse. To sum up, she interrogates the politics of population control policies both at the global and national levels.

Prasad initially draws our attention to the lop-sided policies (read as politics) of population control in the West and in the developing countries. She refers to the pro-natal policies of the West vis-à-vis the anti-natal policies in the developing countries; neo-Malthusian mindset in the USA and its fallout on harsh reforms by the developing countries; poor women in these countries as soft targets of medical experiments; forcible use of family control devices by the rural women without appropriate supportive health care system; and socio-cultural variations in the conceptualization of reproductive rights and reproductive health by women in poor countries; etc. She presents a comprehensive history of the Reproductive and Child Health (RCH) policy in India starting with its original conceptualization at the International Conference on Population and Development (ICPD) in 1994 at Cairo, the agenda to which about 179 countries are signatories, including India. But she laments that the spirit of RCH in India has diluted the radical feminist rhetoric considerably and got located in the framework of population control at the cost of other health concerns. What is striking in Prasad's discussion is that the population control policies in India must be looked at from various dimensions, viz., north-south; rural-urban; men-women; rich-poor; Muslim-Hindu; and temporary-permanent contraception. From a gender perspective, she asserts that tradition and cultural stigma place the burden of fertility reduction on Indian women, who are forced to undergo tubectomy without adequate health care facilities in rural pockets. Further, this gender discrimination has also a class dimension, as the poor women are the soft targets of the state population control policies. Even religion is related to the rate of fertility and there is a general perception that Indian Muslims register higher rate of fertility than the Hindus in India. Therefore, Prasad witnesses the predominance of Malthusian perspective everywhere in India, and all political parties are unanimous that population control ought to be given the highest attention, despite their varied ideologies. She presents the example of the current Congress government at the Centre identifying 150 districts as high fertility districts perhaps for intensive population control measures, and the proposal of a two children norm for government functionaries, which go contrary to the spirit of the ICPD agenda on Reproductive and Child Health.

She aptly feels that women in poor countries like India are the most oppressed lot by the state policy of population control and she calls for a paradigm shift from the policy of coercive control of population to improving the socio-economic infrastructure that would benefit the women in poor countries.

Empowerment of the Marginalized

Ideal-typical construction of femininity has most often been ambivalent for it reflects subjective prejudice of the observer. Carrin in Chapter 12 of this volume disagrees with the description by Archer of the Santal erotic beauty, and she believes that the Santal women are the insignia of strong personalities who enjoy life despite all its hardships and their presence in the labour force. She observes that unlike the neighbouring Hindu society, Santal women are valued for their contribution to the family labour and they enjoy more freedom than the Hindu women. They are free to indulge in pre-marital sex, divorce and get remarried without much of a hassle. However, Santal women are at the same time bound by many taboos, particularly in the domain of rituals, although sometimes they are considered to be close to the deities, for which they are feared as well. Carrin corroborates this with the examples of stories that make rounds in Santal hamlets. The forces of patriarchy are visible in many areas, although resentment against this asymmetry is not rare to find. Women among the Santal are denied any share of knowledge and each one of them is considered as a potential witch.

The ambivalence touches its peak when the Santal priest is feminized at the time of his initiation into priesthood. He has to wear a saree and walk with other devotees to sing and beg in the villages. Sacrifice of blood from the body of the priest symbolizes menstrual blood of the women, as offering of anything impure appeases the impure or the malevolent deities. In fact, in order to become a priest, one has to possess both masculine as well as feminine identity. Temporary feminization of the Santal priest notwithstanding, the Santal women sometimes get possessed and become healers, which are not institutionalized in Santal culture, but are located at the periphery of the tribal society. Discrimination of Santal women is evident from the tradition of denying them the ritual knowledge, allowing them to hunt and so on, as a manifestation of the forces of patriarchy. But Carrin questions whether Santal women have tacitly accepted such discrimination and notes that some of them have taken the path of devotion. She recounts the revolutionary role of Santal women in many tribal movements in defending their identity, legitimacy and extricating themselves from the nexus of exploitation.

One of the early steps adopted by the Santal women in fighting the social evil is by participating in Santal insurrection of 1855 and in Tebhaga Movement. Later, under the influence of Christian missionaries and modern education, they actively participated in the missionary campaigns against drinking in tribal areas that invariably affected their daily lives. Subsequently, their role in social reforms movements, such as anti-dowry movement, against deforestation and displacement, etc., is noteworthy. With the spread of modern education in tribal areas, urban and educated Santal women have set many examples by organizing themselves and participating in all walks of life, including politics. Their education, awareness and new dynamic role have offered them a better place in Santal society that compensates the denial of traditional social and ritual knowledge to them which marginalizes them.

In theory, empowerment may have many dimensions. Empowerment of women can be examined at six different levels: individual, family, group, organization, village and community. Similarly, empowerment may be economic, political and social. With many governmental and non-governmental interventions that continue in India for empowering women, Suguna and Sandhya Rani examine their impact on rural women in India in Chapter 13 of this volume. One of the steps in the direction of empowering women is the formation and patronization of many Self-Help Groups (SHGs) in India. This movement has come to India with the realization that to tackle poverty and enable the community to improve its quality of life through social mobilization of poor, especially women, SHGs are the media. The best experiences of organizing SHGs came from the success of the concept of Grameen Bank (Rural Bank) in the neighbouring Bangladesh in the 1970s. The major objectives of the SHGs are to inculcate the habit of saving and banking among the women, to build confidence between women and the bankers, to develop a spirit of collective working, and to involve these groups in various developmental programmes.

In order to assess the role of SHGs in the empowerment of women and capacity building among them, Suguna and Sandhya

Rani have attempted an impact study by selecting an NGO, Royalseema Seva Samithi (RASS), working in the temple town of Tirupati in the State of Andhra Pradesh. Their findings are exemplary in many respects. Since the intervention of the NGO by establishing SHGs for women, it is noticed that 100 per cent of its members have started saving through their respective SHGs. Majority of the members regularly repay their outstanding loans, which is indicative of their earning capacity. The collective action is manifested by frequent meetings of the members, which help in regular interaction, sharing of each other's experiences and evolving strategies to get out of problems, if any. The SHG has given a platform to its women members to expose them to the world outside, to interact with the government officials and to gain confidence in the process. This has culminated in social mobility and helping them to get involved in the decision-making exercises at home as well as outside. Very broadly Suguna and Sandhya Rani underline that SHGs have changed the lives of women in India by providing them opportunities to empower them economically, politically and socially. However, they also point out to the problem of illiteracy, lack of required vocational, managerial and political skills, which women need to be able to reap the full benefit of the SHG movement in India.

Women's empowerment in a traditionally patriarchal society like India has many deterrents. But in a society where women are educated and hence, are aware of their rights, their status is relatively higher than the society with mostly illiterate women, not knowing about their fundamental rights. The State of Kerala with its high rate of literacy has been a model in many respects, including women's empowerment. In Chapter 14 of this volume Shajy and Isac present a comparative picture of women's empowerment in Kerala vis-à-vis India as a whole. Incidentally, Kerala has a high success rate in the implementation of government policies for various public actions in the fields of education, reproductive and child health, adult literacy, to name a few.

While the study strives to compare the situation in Kerala and the whole of India, it specifically aims at examining the status of women in various populations of India existing under a single law; to examine the key variables in determining the status of women; and to categorize people on the basis of the status of their women. In order to achieve these objectives, Shajy and Isac dwelt on three important proxy variables of women's independence: if women require the permission of others to visit friends/relatives, if they are allowed to keep money with them, and if they can visit the market on their own. The source of data for the study is the National Family Health Survey of 1998-99.

The significant difference in socio-economic setting between Kerala and rest of India is the literacy. Similarly, Kerala registers a low rate of fertility and high standard of living index (SLI) compared to the whole of India. With this differential background, the question of freedom of movement of currently married women yielded the expected result. The women in general, and the women of higher age-groups, who are married for longer durations, living in urban areas, and Hindus in particular, have greater mobility in Kerala than in rest of India. In decision-making, women have a greater freedom in smaller households than in larger households both in Kerala and rest of India. Although education is not a significant variable in decision-making in Kerala, it is very significant in rest of India. There is a marginal difference between Kerala and India with respect to keeping money with them, which show an upward trend with higher age, education and household standard of living. There is a religious divide in this respect, as Muslim women have the least freedom to keep money for their personal use. The study reveals that the women in Kerala have a distinct advantage over their counterparts in rest of India with respect to keeping money with them. The trend is not much different for visiting market, though Kerala women enjoy more freedom than other women in the country.

To explain the reasons for greater autonomy of women in Kerala, Shajy and Isac have demonstrated that four variables are significant: the place of residence, exposure to media, education, and age. Therefore, in determining the composite index of the status of women, they have considered four variables, viz., place of residence, exposure to media, women's and their husbands' education. In the final analysis, they contend that the status of women and consequently their empowerment are higher in Kerala than rest of India. This is evident in the freedom to make decisions with regard to movement and money keeping, which impinge on lower rate of fertility. The study concludes with the note that although Kerala and the rest of India are under the same legal and developmental regime, there is much disparity in women's empowerment. The vital need of the hour is to empower the women to take decisions to empower themselves rather than to establish superiority over others.

In common parlance, women's empowerment refers to the poor, oppressed, marginalized and rural women, who need to empower themselves or need to be empowered by others, so that they will be in a position to lead a respectable life and not as a 'second sex'. But there seems to be even the elite, urban-bred, affluent and educated women in the voluntary sector, who use their voluntary roles as an extension of and reinforce their existing social status, class norms, education, upbringing, family values and social networks, thereby constructing their own empowerment with their work. Mitra and Van Delinder bring this out vividly in Chapter 15 of this volume. Through interestingly candid confessions the study records observations from 11 such elite women volunteers working for various voluntary organizations in the city of Kolkata. As they speak about their lives and experiences we see clearly how they have opted for the non-paid jobs for themselves to help the unfortunate women of the city, and in the process, how they secured positions as decision-makers. Mitra and Van Delinder aptly point out how the duties and responsibilities of these women are comparable with those in business or government, but without violating their traditional roles as wives and mothers. These elite women volunteers are as much concerned with empowering their less fortunate counterparts as with empowering themselves through their involvement in voluntary action, particularly when their roles as wives and mothers are no more relevant with their widowed status and/or with adult children. They have rejected the Western definition of feminism as being in conflict with their identities as wives and mothers. Therefore, Mitra and Van Delinder draw our attention to their lived experiences as Indian women volunteers coming from elite backgrounds, they cannot be exactly compared with the women in the West, and hence their empowerment needs different theorization.

Indian Women in Emerging Roles

Although conventionally Indian women are being portrayed as the victims of illiteracy, ignorance and a strong patriarchal ideology, they also have an aspiration to lead a respectable life in the society. Despite all the limitations of being illiterate, not exposed to media, economically and politically marginalized, their zest for establishing themselves in the society has not died down. One such example comes from the women of a little known nomadic snake-charmer community, the *Kela,* of Orissa. Catching snakes from the forests, snake charming in cities and villages, and selling herbal medicines to cure snake bites have been the sole occupation of the *Kela* men. Women of course help them in these pursuits. But at the same time, *Kela* women are skilled in tattooing. The situation has however changed in recent times with the shrinking of forest in Orissa and neighbouring states reducing the snake population considerably and leading to the unavailability of herbal medicines. Tattooing, which was once considered as personal decorations for the rural women, has become out of fashion and is forbidden even in remote rural areas of the state. This has put the *Kela* men and women in severe economic crisis. Mohanty in Chapter 16 of this volume presents the entrepreneurial abilities of the snake-charmer women, both traditionally as well as in the present context. She alludes to their process of socialization which makes the *Kela* women efficient household managers during the long absence of their husbands, good mothers to their children and capable entrepreneurs to contribute to the family economy. Unlike in many other communities, the *Kela* women participate in the decision-making process in their day-to-day activities. They even participate freely in political meetings and have the freedom to express their opinion. Mohanty also notes that in the *Kela* society, barren, widow and divorced women are not discriminated against.

With tattooing becoming unfashionable and snake charming a risky yet unrewarding occupation, the *Kela* women have largely taken over peddling of cosmetics and toiletries along with selling the traditional herbal medicines for snake bites and metal amulets for warding off evil spirits in the country side closer to their settlements. Because they do not possess any land or immovable property, the financial institutions do not lend them any credit support. Therefore, by mortgaging whatever little movable property they have, these women buy cosmetics and toiletries from the city nearby and sell them to their rural women clients with small profit margin. They are conscious of the importance of good rapport in peddling and hence, take no chances in maintaining good relations with their clients. They are vocal, persuasive and skilled in blackmailing the clients emotionally, which make vending a successful enterprise.

They are also skilled in easily establishing bonds of friendship with the client women to maintain a sustained vendor-vendee relationship. Mohanty's observation on *Kela* women is contrary to the ideal-typical social construction of Indian women as submissive and confined to household activities. She finds in them an entrepreneurial spirit of small-scale trading and vending, despite being handicapped by illiteracy and ignorance, and shifting environmental limitations.

Despite the continuance of many traditional values and practices in Indian society that hinder overall empowerment of women, post-independence efforts in education have certainly benefited a section of women in India. Traditionally, the girl children were not encouraged to get formal education, and even if there was some encouragement, it did not exceed the primary level and beyond the age of puberty. This situation has changed for better now with the implementation of the National Policy on Education. With the opening of the market for higher education, now women make their presence felt in the areas of teaching, health care, information technology and other areas of cutting-edge science and technology. In Chapter 17 of this volume, Roopa Ravikumar examines how significant science education is for Indian women and how important it is for them to be employed in a scientific environment. She explores the self-perception of science educated women in Indian society. The women scientists for this study were chosen from two premier research institutions – one a university and the other a renowned research organization – from the state of Tamil Nadu. Altogether a sample of 131 scientists of both sexes from these organizations was interviewed, out of which only 14 were women, constituting a meagre 10.75 per cent of the total sample. Of course, this excluded a large number of women working in other capacities in these research organizations.

In many ways, the findings of this study reveal the general status of Indian women, although the study is confined to the women scientists. For example, those who are unmarried, (two) among them have remained so more due to socio-cultural conditions than by choice. Their age at the time of completing higher studies is considered surpassing the ideal age for marriage. They encounter preferences of an equal or higher educational status of the husband, preference for caste endogamy, belief in horoscope matching of the bride and the groom, locale preference for living together, and the issues of productivity, participation and motherhood, which come in the way of the marriage for the women scientists. The expressions underscore deep cultural stigma attached to lack of marriage. The study clearly reveals the advantage of urban women getting higher science education and employment over their rural counterparts. Similarly, the parental background also has its influence on higher education in science of the women. Educated parents encourage and afford higher education of their daughters, which is not quite so for the less educated parents with limited income. Undoubtedly, many of the women scientists were toppers in their Schools and Colleges and were the recipients of various state supported scholarships. Many scientists regardless of gender are not involved in any social activity due to their professional preoccupations, and most interestingly, there is hardly any time to engage oneself in open political activity, according to the study. This is especially true for women who still face the expectations of more housework despite full-time employment. On the scale of productivity, women scientists are rated higher than the men, because of their publications and attending to other professional activities. Gender discrimination is not experienced by the women scientists in their place of work. Ravikumar also indicates that job satisfaction is very high for the women scientists; they are content with the income and had no qualms about the standard of living.

Some of Ravikumar's final observations on constraints for the women scientists are highly penetrating and call for the need for more research. For example, she comments that although temperamentally women are most suited for scientific pursuits, they are pushed off or suffocated by the rigid and authoritative scientific environment. She also points out the incongruity between a marital life and pursuing a career in science for women scientists. They prefer a transferable job, so that both the spouses can live at one place after marriage. Since Indian women do not like to compromise their roles as mothers and wives due to the gender socialization, they have a preference for teaching for its flexible working hours over the job of a researcher with fixed working hours and strenuous work in laboratories. This has resulted in higher productivity of the single women scientists than the married ones. What are evident from this study are the prevailing social stigmas and cultural bindings that partly discourage the women to take up science education and a career in scientific research.

Many studies in this volume and elsewhere speculate regarding the fact that despite constitutional guarantees and myriad of legislative and administrative measures, gender discrimination exposes its ugly face in all possible spheres of human life in India. Political discrimination on gender lines is one such problem and the theme of Aparna Thomas' paper in Chapter 18 of this volume. She argues that in India political decisions are taken along party lines, and the elected as well as informal political leaders at various levels influence public policies. Therefore, women cannot successfully participate in the decision-making process unless they align themselves with the party and its policies. However, where there is competition between political parties, sometimes women are successful in making their voices heard, while at some other times they are successful when a single party has the majority. Hence, Thomas contends that political parties and elite can both encourage and prevent women's participation in the decision-making process. To demonstrate her contention, she draws empirical data from 3 gram panchayats in Sangli district of the State of Maharashtra from her field study in 2001-02. Incidentally one of these 3 gram panchayats is an all-women panchayat.

Thomas observes that in panchayats with one-party domination, women's voices are heard to some extent, although the caste of the woman members is considered as important. If the members belong to the locally dominant Maratha caste, things go fine; contrarily, if the member comes from a lower caste, viz., potter (locally *kumbhar*), her participation is limited to physical attendance in the meetings at the most. Most of the decisions in the panchayat meetings are in line with the party agenda. But in panchayats without single party domination, however strong they may be, voices of the women representatives are barely heard as the meetings go awry due to factional fights between members of different parties. In the next higher local body, named the panchayat samiti, Thomas observes that most of the decisions are taken by the party and the male members of the samiti, whereas the women members are considered as filling up necessary quotas to ensure the party majority. She alludes to the shoddy deals of both the elected representatives and the government officials for personal benefits. Her observations regarding women's participation in zilla parishad, the next higher political body at the district level, are somewhat different. Although the president of the zilla parishad needs to have the blessings of the state political elites and she has to fall in line with the wishes of the party and its male functionaries, at times the charisma of the women members and women presidents is exemplary and they have carved a political niche for themselves. She contends that party fragmentation becomes an opportunity as well as a constraint for female members at all three levels of panchayati raj in Maharashtra. But it is more beneficial for the women members at the higher level of panchayati raj than at lower levels.

Whatever may be the participation of women in panchayati raj institutions in India, they are severely handicapped by the national political atmosphere and the attitude of the male dominated political parties. The Women's Reservation Bill has been making rounds since the National Democratic Alliance (NDA) was in government till the present rule of the United Progressive Alliance (UPA). Come every session of the Parliament, politicians become active just to draw media attention and rumours go round regarding tabling of the Bill. But eventually nothing emerges till prorogue of the Parliament and the government assurances to place it in the next session. Are our politicians really interested in sharing power with our women? Seculars and fundamentalists alike see to it that the Bill is not passed, which ensures one-third of the Parliament seats for the women in India. Is it for the fear or apprehension of our beloved leaders of losing their hegemonic control over the women?

The Story Behind this Book – Social Scientists Looking at Women

The origin of this book emerged in conversations of the co-editors as one, an anthropologist from Orissa, with higher education in Delhi and teaching in Hyderabad, India, settled into a Fulbright Scholar in Residence appointment at a small liberal arts college in north Texas and found himself next to the other, a sociologist from Indiana, with higher education in North Carolina and previous appointments in upstate New York. They had met briefly over a year before when she heard his presentation about tribal people, which was given to a handful of American faculty attending the first Council on International Educational Exchange seminar to learn more about India at the University of Hyderabad. It was her third trip to India. The SIR programme was his second extensive foreign appointment, having been a Commonwealth Scholar in the United Kingdom, and first time in the United States of America.

As they got acquainted, he started suggesting a joint book project. Both recognized the need for more empirical work on women's lives in India in the academic book market. He saw a potential collection for academic libraries; she desired information in one source that exposed students to recent findings about women in India, from a variety of research methods, involving major social institutions and current issues. They hoped the collaboration would produce a book worthy of reference and classroom assignment.

So a plan emerged. Could they find among their colleagues and associates near and far, research from all major social institutions – family, religion, education, economy and polity? Could they identify studies about women's lives, obstacles, controversies over social practices, and efforts to control their own lives? And if they could, why would these be worthy of a reader's attention?

As social scientists we live in a realm between the humanities and the sciences. This is literally true in our educational administrations – one from a division of social sciences, the other from a school of social sciences at our respective college and university. But is it also figuratively true as we perceive the world around us and seek to better understand it. The culture of a society contains everything we can experience – from ideas and values through social hierarchies to dwellings and physical resources for life and livelihood. We divide it up into narrow disciplinary perspectives at our own peril with consequent lack of complete understanding. But we demand that study be grounded in the reality of daily life. No better topic confronts us with this integrated realization than the last half century's rediscovery of women and gender by the academy. We sought a cross-disciplinary approach to the study of women in India at the turn of the post modern millennium. As we begin the 21st century we wanted to create a resource for social scientists, young and old, to share their recent investigations about women in India and for future social scientists to learn about some of the varieties of empirical evidence and methodologies during their training. We are happy that our contributors include some recently minted PhDs co-authoring with their former professors, as well as colleagues trained in African American Studies, Anthropology, Demography, Economics, Geography, History, Mass Communication, Political Science, Population Studies, Sociology, and Women's Studies. The lone English professor makes a contribution to our understanding of cultural values and social norms in a textual analysis of an advice book which still influences gender dynamics in marriages of Orissa (see Chapter 3). One of the sociologists examines women scientists (see Chapter 17); so we span the area between humanities and science with a foothold in each.

Feminism according to common definitions takes the lives of women seriously, recognizes a system of oppression that has characterized women's position in society, seeks to uncover the origins of that oppression, offers ways to challenge that oppression and promotes equality. Social scientists can make a big contribution to describing that oppression and identifying its correlates. They also address circumstances and organizational strategies that challenge inequalities. They are not just advice-givers or philosophers, they are empiricists, checking their ideas against the reality, moving from theories to observations and back again or growing theory out of the repeated patterns of human behaviour they identify in their studies (Wallace, 1971).

The editors started to take advantage of his contacts in Indian anthropology and sociology and her ten years study of India with increasing interest in women and gender studies along with networks such as Sociologists for Women in Society. What would make this book unique was its emphasis on contemporary social research, recent empirical studies, from many lens and varied methods of data collection and analysis. These studies leave the quantitative versus qualitative debate behind, offering up a host of each for the unique contributions they make to our understanding of women's lives at the micro through the meso and to the macro level of our social existence. What was missing was a book with good coverage of the social world and varied approaches. We are not claiming comprehensiveness so much as providing understanding of many arenas of life with the transparency provided by good social science research processes.

Neither of us as editors perceived a survey type text – those already exist (Khanna and Varghese 1978; Desai and Patel 1985; Desai and Krishnaraj 1987; Bagehi 1995; Tandon 1998a, 1998b; Gupta 2001; Bano 2002; Mishra 2002; Narayan 2002; Jahan 2004; Rao 2004; Srivastav 2004). We do not claim such wide ranging knowledge or expertise. Nor did we imagine being able to write such a book together from opposite sides of the world. More such texts are coming out every month. They tend to sacrifice the discovery of information for the cataloguing of it.

We did not expect to put together the typical reader (Ghadially 1988; Mitra 1997; Ralhan 1995; Jha and Pujari 1996; Upadhyay 1996; Kumar 1999; Ruhuela 1999; Jeyaraj 2001). The focus was more on becoming a forum for the dissemination of recent research. We wanted to collect in one place a variety of empirical studies that focused on women. Nor were we aspiring to encyclopaedic proportions (Shah 1995, 2 volumes; Pruthi and Rani 1994-1997, 15 volumes; Arya 2000, 3 volumes). As we looked at the existing volumes on women in India, they saw offerings which seldom captured the flavour of the research experiences or which pursued a thorough but necessarily limited study. Most books summarized history and research rather than presenting actual studies showing the social research process at work.

Many books on women in India have focused on philosophical debates and contemporary feminist issues (Paola 2004; Chakravarti 2003; Chaudhuri 2004; Ranganayakamma 1999 (translating Hyma); Rao, 2004). While we are aware of the Indian hesitancy to embrace feminism or identify as feminist, this is not a book that will pursue that debate. Whether or not feminism is too Western for compatibility with full understanding and study of women in India is not the issue with these social scientists. We empiricists have a methodology that is embraced more widely and does address the many concerns of feminism without needing to claim an ideology or demand a loyalty oath from contributors. It is the investigative style, collection of evidence, and analysis free from bias that sets the practice off from such sidelining debates as feminist identity.[1] This is not to say our contributors are not passionate or opinionated about women and their contemporary experience in India. Rather that their methods and data allow all to look over their shoulders and perceive how they reach their conclusions. Though some may question the import of science to the subcontinent as if it, too, comes with western gaze, they would be exhibiting a limited historical understanding of the many contributions to science and its advancement which originated in this region of the world. Compared with humanities from Western eyes, science comes to its studies with a little less cultural baggage or impediments. This is not to say that social science is free of bias or not subject to cultural lenses. Certainly our research agendas and our questions are shaped by the values we hold. But social science has more of a chance of escaping the influence of values on conclusions reached with its transparency of method and peer review processes, particularly in cross-disciplinary and international undertakings such as this volume.

Other books have presented one large study with all the limitations of region, time, and content focus of some particular problem or issue (Agnes, 2004; Basu, 2004; Chandra, 2004; Hobson, 1978; Raheja and Gold, 1994; Jacobson and Wadley, 1995; Mehlman and White, 2000 translation of Weinberger-Thomas (1996); Narasimhan, 1999; Ray, 1999; Gulati, 1993; Caplan, 1985). These are interesting for what they contribute to our understanding of important topics related to women in India. Studies of the law (see Chapters 6, 10, and 18) show the efforts to modify social life but they need the reality check of how well the laws are utilized by society and women to improve their lot. It is interesting to note that in Kerala, known for and proud of its fame as a 'development model' (Franke and Chassin, 1989) due to strong social programmes in health and education that raised longevity and literacy much earlier than other parts of India, problems of domestic violence are soaring. Evidence suggests this is not only a matter of wider public understanding of the phenomenon and women's rights with subsequent increases in reporting previously tolerated injustice. There is also a kind of backlash of brutality from men feeling undermined by women's increasing involvement in the world of work and the problems of an economy which cannot provide for so many highly educated people, forcing many to lead distance marriages (Gulati, 1993) while one earns income in the oil rich Gulf States but apart from home and household (personal correspondence from work of SAKHI, Women's Resource Centre).

There is the Srinivas (1996) collection in *Village, Caste, Gender, and Method,* but it spans a career's worth of work of historical importance, with less descriptive sense of the contemporary scene. Given the limitations of any human being, even the most remarkable social scientist is restricted even when endeavouring to provide the most comprehensive of approaches to a topic. We see one volume with many contributors as one strategy for overcoming such human limitation, particularly for a book aimed at the academic audience.

History is certainly an important part of the social sciences, fundamental to all our understanding. Works like Forbes' 1998 *Women in Modern India,* O'Hanlon's 1994 translation and critique of Tarabai Shinde's *A Comparison between Women and Men,* and Walsh's 2004 *Domesticity in Colonial India – What Women Learned When Men*

Gave Their Advice set the ground work for some of this volume's research. But it is the reality of contemporary women's lives that provides the focus of this volume.

Historians have offered much to our understanding of women in India. The British colonial legacy of laws challenging some practices – sati, childhood marriage, dowry – have been traced by many scholars. Social scientists are still measuring the success of changes such as child marriage and pointing to the correlates of its continued practice. Laws and their principles are seldom aligned with actual practices as can be seen in a study of age at marriage across various districts in India (see Chapter 6). What about the governance reforms putting more women and people of different social positions into local governing bodies? Can women make a difference when they gain access to these positions of power? Under what circumstances? How is the social context of implementing such laws promoting or hindering women's participation and influence? Only researchers on the ground can show how effective the law is in reality along with the nuances of social structure that hinder or promote women's contributions (see Chapter 18). The reformers of the first modern century in India who opened up educational institutions and changed expectations for girls and women's engagement in the public realm as well as the household setting would be interested in knowing the level of equality and control that women now exercise. Social scientists comparing highly literate Kerala women with the nation as a whole reveal several realms of women's activity impacted by access to education as well as other cultural factors (see Chapter 14).

We hope you will find these studies as interesting as we have – both in their content and in their methodology. We have enjoyed bringing such a diverse collection together for your perusal. We hope it will inspire much more social science about women in India.

Notes

1. We did not require agreement with statements such as this by Ani DiFranco. "All the decent people, male and female, are feminists. The only people who are not feminists are those who believe that women are inherently inferior or undeserving of the respect and opportunity afforded men. Either you are a feminist or you are a

sexist/misogynist. There is no box marked 'other'." We just asked colleagues, male and female, whose research addressed women in India to submit manuscripts. An independent judge would probably see our contributors as feminists, but many would not so self-identify. As social scientists that is fine with us. We are interested in their data, the methods they used, the questions they asked of it, and the results they presented.

References

Agnes, Flavia (1998), *Law and Gender Inequality* in *Women and Law in India**, Delhi: Oxford University Press. (*three volumes published as one in 2004)

Arya, Dr. Anita (2000), *Indian Women: Education and Empowerment, Volume Two,* New Delhi: Gyan Publishing House.

Bagehi, Jasodhara (1995), *Indian Women (Myth and Reality),* London: Sangam Books.

Bano, Afsar (2002), *Indian Woman: The Changing Face,* New Delhi: Kilaso Books.

Basu, Monmayee (2004), *Hindu Women and Marriage Law* in *Women and Law in India,* Delhi: Oxford University Press. (*three volumes published as one in 2004)

Bernard, Jessie (1982), *The Female World,* New York: The Free Press.

Caplan, Patricia (1985), *Class and Gender in India – Women and Their Organizations in a South Indian City,* London: Social Science Paperbacks – Tavistock Publications.

Chakravarti, Uma (2003), *Gendering Caste – Through a Feminist Lens –* Theorizing feminism series, Kolkata: Stree.

Chandra, Sudhir (1997), *Enslaved Daughters: Colonialism, Law and Women's Rights* in *Women and Law in India**, Delhi: Oxford University Press. (*three volumes published as one in 2004)

Chaudhuri (ed.) (2004), *Feminism in India* – Issues in Contemporary Indian Feminism Series, New Delhi: Women Unlimited, Kali for Women.

Desai, Neera and Maithreyi Krishnaraj (1987), *Women and Society in India,* Delhi: Ajanta Publications.

Desai, Neera and Vibhuti Patel (1985), *Indian Women – Change and Challenge in the International Decade 1975-85,* Mumbai: Popular Prakashan.

Forbes, Geraldine (1998), *Women in Modern India* – The New Cambridge History of India, Vol. IV. 2, New Delhi: Cambridge University Press.

Franke, Richard W and Barbara H. Chassin (1989), *Kerala: Radical Reform as Development in an Indian State,* Oakland, CA: The Institute for Food and Development Policy.

Ghadially, Rehana (ed.) (1988), *Women in Indian Society – A Reader,* New Delhi: Sage Publications.

Gulati, Leela (1993), *In the Absence of Their Men: the Impact of Male Migration on Women,* New Delhi: Sage Publications.

Gupta, N.L. (2001), *Indian Women,* New Delhi: Mohit Publications.

Hobson, Sarah (1978), *Family Web: A Story of India,* Chicago: Academy Chicago Publishers.

Jacobson, Doranne and Susan S. Wadley (1995, 1977), *Women in India – Two Perspectives,* New Delhi: South Asia Publications.

Jahan, Farhat (2004), *Women in India,* New Delhi: Anmol Publications Pvt. Ltd.

Jeyaraj, Nirmala (ed.) (2001), *Women in Society,* Madurai: Lady Doak College.

Jha, Uma Shankar and Premlata Pujari (eds.) (1996), *Indian Women Today – Tradition, Modernity and Challenge,* New Delhi: Kanishka Publishers, Distributors.

Khanna, Girija and Mariamma A. Varghese (1978), *Indian Women Today,* New Delhi: Vikas Publishing House Pvt. Ltd.

Kumar, Indira R. Deepak (ed.) (1999), *Gender and Society in India,* New Delhi: Manak Publications.

Mishra, Saraswathi (2002), *Status of Indian Women,* New Delhi: Gyan Publishing House.

Mitra, Jyoti (ed.) (1997), *Women and Society – Equality and Empowerment,* New Delhi: Kanishka Publishers, Distributors.

Narasimhan, Sakuntala (1999), *Empowering Women – An Alternative Strategy from Rural India,* New Delhi: Sage Publications.

Narayan, Andal (2002), *Women and Indian Society: Options and Constraints,* Jaipur: Rawat Publications.

O'Hanlan, Rosalind (1994), *A Comparison Between Women and Men – Tarabai Shinde and the Critique of Gender Relationships in Colonial India,* Delhi: Oxford University Press.

Paola, Bacchetta (2004), *Gender in the Hindu Nation – RSS Women as Ideologues* – feminist fine print series, New Delhi: Women Unlimited, Kali for Women.

Pruthi, Raj and Bela Rani Sharma (eds.) (1994-1997), *Encyclopedia of Women Society and Culture,* Delhi: Anmol Publications Pvt. Ltd.

Raheja, Gloria Goodwin and Ann Grodzins Gold (1994), *Listen to the Heron's Words – Reimagining Gender and Kinship in North India,* Berkeley: University of California Press.

Rajput, Pam and Hem Lata Swarup (eds.) (1994), *Women and Globalisation – Reflections, Options and Strategies,* New Delhi: Ashish Publishing House.

Ralhan, O.P. (ed.) (1995), *Indian Women Through Ages,* New Delhi: Anmol Publications.

Ranganayakamma (1999), *Housework and Outside Work* (English translated by Hyma), Hyderabad: Sweet Home Publications.

Rao, Anupama (ed.) (2003), *Gender and Caste Issues* in Contemporary India Feminism Series, New Delhi: Women Unlimited, Kali for Women.

Rao, Digumarti Bhaskara and Digumarti Pushpa Latha (eds.) (1999), *Women, Challenges and Advancement,* New Delhi: Discovery Publishing House.

Rao, G. Vijayeswari (2004), *Women and Society,* Delhi: Himalaya Publishing House.

Ray, Raka (1999), *Fields of Protest – Women's Movements in India* – Social Movements, Protest, and Contention Series No. 8, Minneapolis: University of Minnesota Press.

Ruhela, Saryu (ed.) (1999), *Understanding the Indian Women Today: Problems and Challenges,* Delhi: Indian Publishers Distributors.

Shah, Giri Raj (ed.) (1995), *The Encyclopedia of Women's Studies,* New Delhi: Gyan Publishing House.

Srinivas, M.N. (1996), *Village, Caste, Gender and Method,* Delhi: Oxford University Press.

Srivastav, Anita (2004), *Women in India – Problems and Prospects,* Delhi: Indian Publishers Distributors.

Tandon, R.K. (1998a), *State of Women in India,* Delhi: Indian Publishers Distributors.

— (1998b), *Women in Modern India,* Delhi: Indian Publishers Distributors.

Uberoi, Patricia (1994), *Family, Kinship and Marriage in India,* Delhi: Oxford University Press.

Upadhyay, R.K. (ed.) (1996), *Women in 21st Century: Problems and Challenges,* New Delhi: Harnam Publications.

Upadhyay, R.K. and Rajiv Chawla (eds.) (1996), *Women in 21st Century – Problems and Challenges,* New Delhi: Harnam Publications.

Wallace, William (1971), *The Logic of Science in Sociology,* Chicago: Aldine-Atheron.

Weinberger-Thomas, Catherine (1996), *Ashes of Immortality – Widow-Burning in India* translated by Jeffery Mehlman and David Gordon White (2000), Delhi: Oxford University Press.

Part I

Socio-Cultural Context

The first four selections provide analysis of the context of women's lives and a sense of the vast scope within Indian society. Three anthropologists and a scholar of English enlighten us about the cultural values, social norms, and mechanisms of their reinforcement as well as the outlets for challenges to them from women in various corners of society.

We are reminded right away of the interesting cultural mix of expectations on the ideal women in modern India. The approach of Channa is to show the ancient texts in conjunction with the diffusion of the colonial culture, creating crossed signals for women. The inclusion of women writers begins to give this discussion the level of authenticity it has needed in the historian's treatment. The examination of mass media's perpetuation of the 'ideal' in the more popular soap operas of the society link the practices to contemporary life still. Mohanty then takes up the task of reviewing how the social norms perpetuate such expectations for women through analysis of the role of advice books in the continued subordination of women and the privilege granted to the patriarchal perspective. Though this textual analysis might seem out of place in a book of social science studies, it demonstrates the close kinship of content analysis within the humanities and strengthens the contribution by noting the unique social roles depicted in these vehicles of guidance for women's conduct. The social arrangements whereby women leave natal home to join new families at marriage, set them up for such control more readily than other kinship systems. The documentation of such continued use of these modes of passing on tradition helps us see the extent of the reach of patriarchy especially among those with sufficient education to read, the privileged and enlightened upper castes of the society.

Mishra's study then reveals the significance of gender through contradictions in women's lives among the often romanticized tribal peoples. Though not initially focusing on gender in her study of some Kandha practices, she re-examines her data with a gender lens to reveal that despite the importance of women to the economy and fertility as a foundational symbol, women are barred from central ritual practices. She shows how productive a gender perspective can be in returning to existing data and in so doing, invites the reader to reconsider past studies and design future ones without ignoring the obvious and not so obvious inclusions and omissions along such lines. Rao hints further at the possibilities while presenting a cursory analysis of songs sung by Dalit women as a strategy for increasing our critical perspective. The contradictions indicated in this most oppressed group's poking fun at societal hierarchies and moral practices begins to give voice to their structural position's influence in everyday reality. The reported depth of feeling and emotion tied to the singing of such songs helps to verify the relevance of such tools for understanding the lived culture of entire communities and families. The social relationships mocked in such songs provide a new insight on life at the bottom of society and unusual daring on the part of many to question social niceties.

Together the studies of Part I show research that uncovers the roots of contemporary woman's position while revealing many ways that women have helped to create and shape their lot in life. The more unobtrusive approaches which utilize textual records as cultural artifacts to extract new insights about values, norms, and responses of women to their lot in life or general studies retraced with a gendered focus have displayed the evolution of woman's condition as well as the obstacles in her path to freedom and her initiative in questioning the system and challenging the oppressors.

2

The "Ideal Indian Woman"

Social Imagination and Lived Realities

SUBHADRA MITRA CHANNA

There has always been a tension between the richness of diversity of the Indian subcontinent with its many languages, religions and ethnic groups and the monolithic construction of the 'Indian' in which context the term Indian woman or *Bharatiya Nari* is a popular construct of the collective imagination of the public and the print and mass media. The term Indian becomes meaningful and can be understood only in the context of the construction of the Indian Nation, a product of collective response to the colonial experience. However, doubt has often been expressed about the constitution of this collectivity, as to who it really represents and in whose voice it really speaks. Taking one look at the popular image of the Indian woman makes it clear that like the nation the woman is also a product of the elite majority, namely the Hindu, middle class and upper caste. The Devi is a woman with a large *bindi* on her forehead, wearing a *saree* and fair in complexion. She is sexually passive, gentle and self sacrificing, monogamous, looking upon the face of the only one man in her life, her husband, and she is the repository of the honour of the family.

The construction of this image is informed by a complexity of social and historical processes, too complicated to be considered in details, but some of which we shall discuss here. The term Hindu is a difficult construct largely oppositional in character. Thus, to most persons in India all those who are not Muslims or Christians are

Hindus[1]. Even in terms of Indian law, the Buddhists, Jains and Sikhs are hardly considered as non-Hindus. In fact who is opposed to the term Hindu is often a matter of regional experience. My mother-in-law, who belonged to a remote village in north-western Punjab, often asked, who were the Christians? Were they Hindus or Muslims? In a remote Himalayan village in Garhwal, the local Hindus oppose themselves to the Tibetan Buddhists having little idea of what a Muslim means (Channa, 1984), while in the north-eastern region of India the division would be directed more towards the Christians. During the colonial period, the construction of the Hindu was primarily to the exclusion of the Muslims and this remains the predominant concern in the mainstream of Indian heartland. Many scholars have dwelt at length on the construction of the Indian Nation, including Trautmann (1997), Dirks (1997, 2001), Cohn (1996), Chatterjee (1993), etc., to name a few. The major under-pinnings of the works on colonial India have devolved on the construction of caste and gender relations, on the feminization of the conquered, and the imagery of a masculine colonial administration coming to the rescue of the distressed 'nation', symbolized in its women (Tanabe, 1999). Thus both the gendering of the nation as well as gender as a central concern for building up discourses on both colonial rule and nationalism was a reality of colonial times. Scholars like Chatterjee (1993) have sought to reconstruct the women's issues in terms of nationalist sentiments. This paper is however not about the historiography of colonial rule (Channa, 1984), but about the construction of the ideal Indian woman, that actualized into a pan-Indian phenomenon largely because of the unification of identity produced by the colonial rule, or alternatively as a resistance to it. An additional dimension was gender as a matter of contestation of position between high and low castes.

We have little information as to whether the concept of womanhood was at all a matter of discourse in the pre-modern era. Very little exists on record, even in literature, about the lives of ordinary people in India. Most literature of ancient and medieval times was of two types, the oral traditions and the written texts appearing as hand written manuscripts. While the latter were the prerogative of the high castes, the former were largely part of the little tradition of the local people. Both these traditions were highly influenced by the power structure of the society. For example, oral tradition was often carried by the bards who were in the pay roll of royalty. Obviously they would be interested to write about royal personages and praise them. The scribes and Brahmins were also largely state supported.

But during the colonial period, knowledge went public via the print media when the nation started to become literate. In the process a new literati was also constructed although often out of the old. The British went looking for Brahmin *pandits* whom they called as 'professors' but the traditional scribes, the Kayasthas of Bengal and Uttar Pradesh too, took up the opportunity of Western education. But in principle the new systems of knowledge were free to be accessed by any and every one irrespective of caste and gender. A number of women also became literate and as early as the eighteenth century there was a number of literate women in India who began to use the print media to advocate their views to a broader society. The works of these women, mostly of high caste and class, and the issues addressed by them, were pertinent for the elite Hindu women only. The reformist movement taken up by the Indian social reformers too concerned itself with issues of women of upper sections of society and primarily the Hindu women. Thus Chakravorti (1990) writes with reference to the selective construction of identity by the Indian nationalists that "it was clearly a 'Hindu' identity... further ... a specifically Aryan identity ... In Bengal ... (it) led to a simple dichotomization of the population into high castes comprising Aryan and labouring groups comprising un-Aryan". Chakravorti is here referring to the classic work of Bankim Chandra Chatterjee, 'Ananda Math', that is almost a symbol of Hindu nationalism. Trautmann (1997) also makes clear that in the initial period of British rule when they were looking for their long lost kinship with the Indians "... the enthusiasm for India, then, was above all an enthusiasm for Hinduism".

As mentioned before, a number of Indian women became active in this period in the field of education and reform, and journals and writings by women started appearing in the Indian press from the end of the nineteenth century and in the beginning of the twentieth. These were all upper caste Hindu women, like Swarna Kumari Devi of Bengal, Ramabai Ranade, Pandita Rama Bai, Rameshwari Nehru and the foreigner, Annie Besant. The construction of the Indian woman was engendered in the class and caste structure of India that favoured a particular elite point of view.

The colonial period also saw a concerted effort by the British and also by the Indians to reconstruct Indian history. However, the knowledge about India's past that found public expression from largely oral or handwritten origins was in itself a political enterprise. In other words what was translated, written down and considered as true knowledge about the past was both mediated by colonial rule and western patriarchy, and Indian caste rankings. In the construction of knowledge about India, the British were guided by the considerations of the need for a monolithic construction, a construction that would enable their rule with little fuss, what Dirk (1996) has called the 'objectification' of India. Secondly, the world of reality was a world of male intellectualism and elite hegemony. The ideal repository of knowledge was the Brahmin scholar and the reality about the Hindu faith and culture was to be discovered in learned books written in Sanskrit that could be deciphered only by the Brahmin male scholars. In fact, even the local Indian scholars were increasingly marginalized in favour of the European scholars who were well versed in Sanskrit, like Jones, Colebrook and Max Müeller. In her comments on the work of Tarabai Shinde, a nineteenth century Maratha woman, who would qualify as a feminist of the modern times, O'Hanlon (2000) writes, "Here, then we have older brahmanic constructions of feminine nature feeding through directly into colonial print culture, and blending very comfortably with its more Victorian themes". Thus Tarabai was critical of brahmanic and male interpretations of the texts such as the Ramayana as also of the popular Marhatti literature of that time.

Thus when a model of what was Indian was constructed in print and became knowledge accessed by elite, educated Indians, it was definitely not the knowledge of the masses, of women, of tribes, of people on the borders, and of the lower rungs of society.

Thus the ideal Indian woman was the wife of the elite Indian man, the Brahmin *Pandit*, the Kshatriya ruler, or at best, the Vaishya householder. Left out was the woman, who was the labourer, the potter's wife, the washerwoman, the tribal woman and those who were not within the folds of high caste Hindu households. The texts that went into the construction of the ideal woman were the *Dhramashashtras* and the laws of Manu, the Ramayana and the Mahabharata, and not tribal myths and village folklore. Even the interpretations of these texts were of the brahmanical variety and the folk versions were ignored. Anyone familiar with Indian culture would know that in different parts of India various versions of these texts are part of the oral and performing traditions of the local people.[2] Hinduism, as it is practiced in India in different communities and castes, has its own flavour and this makes Hinduism far from the monolithic identity to which it was largely reduced by the western scholars.[3]

The brahmanic versions highlighted only those characters that were in line with the norms of high caste Hindus. Thus overriding the rich variance that is found at the ground level, the postcolonial knowledge served to create stereotypes based upon a definite morality that was a synthesis of values of the western and Indian elite.

Stereotypes about high born women and low born women abound in literature and mythology that is a part of the popular culture, what I will call here as the *devi* (goddess) and *dasi* (servant) polarization. The high born woman is sexually withdrawn and emaciated in her desires, whereas the low born woman is both desirable and often seen as the true subject of love. One may also refer to the amorous relationship of Krishna with Radha, the cowherd woman, which is often depicted as a symbol of eternal and divine love. However, the relationship of Krishna with his queens never attained that status of devotion and love, both physical and spiritual. Thus women assumed two distinct polarities: one of women who were there for men's pleasure and love, and those that were for continuing the patrilineage, women of virtue, who would be ideal mothers to their sons. In the former category came also the courtesans and the *devadasis,* women of knowledge, refinement and culture, and sometimes of power. The polarization in ancient times was not to reduce the category of the public woman to a lowly status. In fact, many of the artistic traditions, including dance forms like Odissi and Bharatnatyam were preserved in temples by the *devadasis*. Moreover as Kersenboom (1991) writes, ".... the *devadasi* is the embodiment of the power *(sakti)* of the goddess and she is also the most auspicious of women", she is dedicated to a divine husband who can never die. Since she can never lose her (double) auspiciousness, she is called 'ever auspicious' (*nityasumangali).* History also reveals that some courtesans held considerable secular power as well. But the powerful courtesan over a period of history became reduced to the '*Angan ki Tulsi*'[4] (the Tulsi or *Ocimum sanctum* plant of the courtyard), the woman shunned by society.

For most of the elite Indians, the physical space of the house was constructed along these ideals. As early as in the times of Vatsayana, during the 1st and 2nd century A.D. we hear of the separation of the house into its inner and outer domains what continued for centuries as the *andar mahal* (inner domain) and *bahar mahal* (outer domain) tradition, found in all elite house architecture up to the colonial period, and even in some parts of rural India (Channa, 1997). This separation again has found many expressions in literature but nowhere as beautifully depicted as in Bimal Mitra's *Sahib, Bibi aur Ghulam,*[5] where the tradition of the husband living a life of pleasure with dancing girls in the *bahar mahal* while wives are condemned to a life of seclusion in the *andar mahal* has been depicted to perfection. The rebellion of the youngest daughter-in-law and her demands to satisfy her desires by living as a true consort with her husband only find a tragic end. Another piece of literature converted to a classic movie is Satyajit Ray's *Ghare Baire*.

Away from the elite print media, the circulation of oral literature, their depiction in the form of *lilas* or plays and performances at the village and community levels had their effect on the minds of the people. Every year people who go to see the performance of the *Ramlila* or take part in the *Pandava lila* of the hills relive the roles of Rama and Sita, and Kaikeyi and Draupadi. No girl in India is ever named as Kaikeyi, because in the Ramayana, her husband King Dasarath had cursed her saying that no father is going to name his daughter after you.[6] One, however, comes across numerous Sita and Savitri and Sulochanas[7] in Indian homes but a Draupadi is also very rare. To the psyche of the Indian men and even women, there exist certain clear role models of an ideal woman derived from these folk models and religious literature. Although alternative models of womanhood like the worship of Draupadi in South India are available, the overriding values were those derived from the mainstream constructed culture of literate scholarship. Thus even the performative aspects of the oral tradition are not immune from culture that is diffused from the top.

However, I do not think any public discourse on women was ever initiated and taken up in any period prior to the colonial period in India. It was only during this time that the question of women became a major issue as the British too had projected the miserable position of Indian women as one of the criteria that justified their rule.

Although most Indians would attribute the *devi* image to be constructed from the traditional past of Hindu India,[8] in reality it was also greatly influenced by the value system of Victorian England and served the patriarchal interests of the elite Hindu men, who having received a very British education were now attempting to resurrect their own women as perfect foil for their nationalist ideals. The Indian Nationalist men claimed superiority on the basis of the moral and spiritual superiority to the West and it was the women who represented this spiritual ideal of the home. However, it was not enough to present the woman as she was then, but she had to be carefully constructed as the ideal woman, the epitome of purity and moral virtues. Towards this end the elite families carefully tutored their women folk, the first step being to separate them from the rustic and the 'lower' women (Sangari and Vaid, 1990). While I can look into my own family, for the 'construction' of the *bhadramahila* in the eighteenth century Bengal, many scholars including Bannerjee (1990) and Borthwick (1984) have talked about it.

The women had also to measure up to the standards of modesty demanded by the western standards. Thus Bengali women who traditionally wore only one *saree* or a single garment were made to wear a petticoat, a chemise and a blouse. As the names indicate these pieces of clothing were all borrowed from the dress of British women at that time. In fact in all parts of India, all these garments were absorbed into the wardrobes of women under their original western names. The aim was to raise the standards of modesty to make the women more compatible with the standards of Victorian modesty and also the gaze of the British who were required to look upon them as virtuous goddesses. The missionaries played active role in this process of re-crafting. The ideals of virtuous motherhood and wifehood were instilled into the upper class women. I went to school in the sixties and remember the values and skills that were preferred in the school curriculum. The major part of the education consisted of learning to knit, sew and keep house, to lay tables, to eat properly at the dining room, hygiene, child care and first aid. In other words, all the qualities that one needed to become the wife of an upper class man in India. Similar things were taught to my grand-mother but by a British instructress at home rather than at school.

Thus Indian women dressed modestly, emblazoned with the marks of superior morality like self-sacrifice, devotion and loyalty that were held up as symbols of the superiority of Hindu culture. At the ground level what it really achieved was a seclusion of the elite woman from her more rustic and underprivileged counterpart – the separation of the *devi* from the *dasi*.

The upper class women were also carefully crafted to become '*memsahibs*' or '*bhadramahilas*' in a way that kept a balance between tradition and modernity that weighed heavily in favour of keeping up the patriarchal rule within the family. Thus women learned about hygiene, baby care, to knit and to sew, and also about personal grooming. But they were not particularly encouraged to step out of the house, to take up paid jobs, to assert their independence apart from their husbands. In this sense they had to be true *ardhanginis* (halves of their husbands), symbolically represented by the wives of the national leaders, Kastur Ba, Kamala Nehru[9] and others. They also had to maintain their sexual purity and upper caste/class women were always expected to be extremely subdued in such matters. The women, who were the objects of respect, were carefully demarked from those who were the objects of lust. This aspect is clearly demonstrated in the literature and mass media of that time. I will give an instance from the nineteenth century Bengali novelist Sarat Chandra Chatterjee's work, *Charitraheen*, in which the character of Satish, a young man of respectable upper class Brahmin family, undergoes pangs of remorse and self-denigration after having caught hold of the end of the servant Savitri's *saree* in a fit of suppressed emotion. The extreme remorse is directed towards the covert content of sexuality in that act, an act for which Satish cannot forgive himself, for he respects Savitri as a decent woman. Savitri works as a domestic servant, but she is not recognized to belong to the class of servants. Here the contradiction between *devi* and *dasi* is very clear. She herself tells Satish repeatedly that he need not bother himself too much with the propriety of his action for she after all is a *dasi*, a servant. But Satish is not ready to accept this for he truly loves her, and since he himself is a gentleman, the object of his veneration cannot possibly be a *dasi* or a woman of a lower class.

This is the root of the ambivalent attitude towards women that is so deep rooted in Indian society. Women in India are certainly seen as objects of respect and of worship, but only some women, not all. The woman who is truly integrated with the patriarchal ideals is the woman who is to be respected.

While men of high status treated their own wives as repositories of virtues, mainly as self-sacrificing subjects, whose only reason for existence was in the person of their husbands, they did not treat them as sexual, for these women were not expected to be physical but transcendental. The objects of sexuality were always the women of lower classes.

This theme has been beautifully depicted in literature and movies. *Ankur*, made by Shyam Benegal, has depicted the theme in which the low caste servant woman is sexually exploited by the landlord, but she has the courage to ultimately stand up for her own rights and to defend her husband, while the high caste born wife of the landlord remains a mute spectator to the drama. *Ankur* also illustrates a very important dimension of marginal womanhood. In spite of being shunned and exploited, she is not a woman without power. She is stronger than her upper class counterpart and may assume a posture of defiance if pushed.

Even anthropological works dealing with lower caste communities and tribes outside the folds of Hinduism have corroborated the relatively greater agency of women of lower castes and classes as compared to women of the upper strata. Also the men and women of the lower castes have their own models of proper behaviour. They resent the stereotypes created by elite men. Thus while men of the upper castes consider the women of the lower castes 'exploitable' and vulnerable, the lower castes have their own version of the 'virtuous' wife satisfying herself with the lower caste servant, again a theme dealt with in several Indian classic writings. The leader of the Dalit movement in India, Shri Jyotiba Phule, had decried the position of high caste Hindu women and had taken the miserable position of the high caste Hindu widow as a sign of degeneration of the caste system. In fact, the two most visible actions taken by Phule for the welfare of society was to open a school for untouchable girls and a home for Brahmin widows in the later part of the nineteenth century. Education of their women was the foremost agenda of the three major Dalit leaders of that time, Phule, Periyar and Ambedkar. In her writings Meenakshi Moon (2003) has written how the Dalit women were always equal partners to their men, and every time a session involving men would take place, the women often had their parallel session. They were also present in large numbers at all the major rallies and demonstrations. Thus from within the Dalit community itself the picture of women was quite opposed to that from the perspectives of the high castes.

But the popular and pervasive model of the lower caste woman certainly opposed her to the high-born woman, and such stereotypes are common in Indian society even today (Channa, 2004). It is especially problematic to fit a modern or westernized woman into the cultural stereotype of the *devi*, a woman who can be respected. It is interesting to note that ever since the Indian man started taking his wife as a companion and a sexual partner, his attitude towards her changed. She no longer was regarded as a *devi*, that position being largely reserved for one's own mother. But even in colonial period the nationalist movement also looked upon the nation as symbolized in the mother image. The working woman especially is yet to come on her own out of the traditional model of the *dasi* into which her role readily leads her. For any woman who worked outside her home was like any woman of the lower castes, and the most important thing was that her body did not have the sanctity of a high-born housewife. In offices and in public buses, in the restaurants and markets, women moving alone out for work, for employment or for doing any kind of work, even if it means buying vegetables, are suspected. She is not easily regarded as a woman of exemplary virtue as she is not confined within the four walls of a home and under the protection of a male. Rampant sexual harassment of women on the streets of Delhi is evidence of this kind of thinking. In fact, even women sometimes attribute such harassment to the 'inappropriate' dress of the working women or so called 'modern' girl. But the fact remains that women irrespective of attire or attitude become a target of harassment by the very fact that they are out of doors without male escort, especially in the northern belt of India.[10]

Even today sentiments of caste and class are interwoven into the behaviour accorded to any woman in India. In a recent issue of *The Times of India* there was a front page photograph of a male computer engineer doing *arti* or worship of an image of Jayalalitha,[11] a political icon of South India, a fair complexioned Brahmin woman considered as goddess (*devi*) by many of her political followers. But the same man would never consider extending the same kind of respect towards his fellow female colleagues and the women he brushes shoulders with in a public place. Working women in India find themselves almost always to be at the receiving end of male disrespect and sexual overtures. Here the low caste labourer working in the fields and the high caste woman, who is a computer engineer, find themselves nearly in the same situation.

The changing society of India is increasingly in a state of dilemma to reconstruct the stereotypes of Indian women, with or without the help of Ekta Kapoor.[12] But what needs to be mentioned here is that even the powerful television media concentrates only on the mainstream culture of India. Nowhere are people on the fringes of Indian society even considered for constructing the television images of ideal or not so ideal men and women. No popular serial or soap ever dwells on Dalits, tribals or on the north-eastern part of India. All stereotypes are Hindu, middle class and virtuous according to textual Hinduism. The television advertisements present an exoticised version of rural India that is far from the reality of poverty and squalor. The fracturing of identity of elite and marginal that was so successfully accomplished in the colonial era is increasingly deepened in the global era as symbols of distinction are getting more and more in the mould of the majority mainstream cultures. The television incidentally is the most popular source of entertainment reaching out to a majority of Indian homes.

Such powerful broadcasting is having the effect of wiping out alternative images and replacing them with stereotypes that are infusing the Indian masses. Just as in the colonial period, the construction of the ideal woman was informed by the Victorian ideals of womanhood, so also in the neo-colonial period, these ideals are formed by the westernized elite and their Right wing counterparts. So, either women are acceptable in the *devi* images of yesteryears or as the modern corporate woman with her hair dyed golden and wearing a smart pant suit. But in the tussle between the modern and traditional, the traditional still holds forte, not because it represents the masses but it represents the elite. The masses in India had always been more modern than the upper castes and classes. When Brahmin widows were shaven and forced to lead a life of asceticism, the untouchable widows could marry again. In the rural areas of Rajasthan a widow continues to wear more or less the same kind of clothes she wore as a married woman. For the women in the north-eastern part of the country, who mostly belong to the tribes, there is no significant change of status of being unmarried, married or a widow. The undue concern with virginity is also not found among all communities and least of all among the relatively marginalized ones.

Even during the colonial times, the Dalit women were emphatic that they already enjoyed the kind of rights that the upper caste women desire, like marrying at a later age, treating the husbands as equal and participating in public affairs. The *dasi* was always more individualistic and self-sufficient than the *devi,* and the latter has always been glorified more for her dependence than her dominance. Even today in the popular soaps on the television the most popular women are still cast in the image of the 'traditional' Indian woman. Most actual traditional women have acquired the symbols of the tradition like the *bindi, sindoor* and *mangalsutra*[13] more from the television than from their grandmothers. In India the worship of woman power has been a part of its very ancient past, dating back to the earliest civilization known in this part of the world. But over periods of time including the contemporary age of globalization, the ideal woman is being reconstructed again and again, not as a person in her own right but only as a foil for the perfect man. Even the most modern woman is created to become a partner to the modern man. A company executive wants his wife to have blond dyed hair and be able to be a perfect companion for his executive parties. But she still does not command respect unless she complements this by being the super mom and ideal daughter-in-law as well. Super women like Tulsi and Pooja Mehta[14] of television soaps are the modern-day icons, but in spite of somewhat different looks the basic principle of being ideal is the same – preserve the ideals of the patriarchal family and sacrifice your own interests for that of the men in your lives.

The real worship of woman power that must have formed the substratum of the Indian civilization based in mother goddess cults of Mohen-jo-daro and Harrappa was soon replaced by its absorption into the patriarchal Aryan culture. Slowly and insidiously the *devi* became a wan image of her powerful self and as pointed out by the famous anthropologist, Mary Douglas – what was dangerous became the polluted. Thus the power of woman was marginalized as pollution. Woman herself became worthy of respect only with reference to the men to whom she was attached. The independent and free thinking women became the *dasi,* the women one enjoyed but did not marry. The self-sacrificing mothers and wives became worthy of respect at the cost of their existence and selfhood. The changes coming about in this image are slow and restricted. It would need a quiet revolution to reinstate the *dasi* on the throne of the *devi,* to recognize the power of womanhood and to admire its potency, to recognize the creative force of the universe as a part of the household and not only as a part of the temple.

Notes

1. The Hindu Marriage Act takes as Hindu, a person who is either born or domiciled in India but does not belong to Judaism, Zorastrianism, Christianity or Islam. Thus most tribes and untouchables, unless converted, are taken as Hindus.
2. See for example Hiltebeitel (1995).
3. See for example, *Hinduism* by V.C. Channa that describes the beliefs, rites and rituals of the Aggarwals of Delhi.
4. The reference here is to a popular Hindi movie of a similar name where the courtesan is referred to as the *Tulsi* plant that is always kept in the courtyard and can never enter the home.
5. This refers to the classic Bengali novel named *Sahib, Bibi aur Gulam* that literally refers to the cards, the King, the Queen and the Knave. The novel is a powerful description of a decaying *zamindar* family of Bengal in the early part of the twentieth century. The youngest daughter-in-law of the household, rebels against having to live a life of seclusion in the *andar mahal* while her husband enjoys with dancing girls in the *bahar mahal.* Her demands to share a sexual life with her husband leads her to become an alcoholic and eventually both husband and wife meet tragic ends while the entire house decays to be replaced by the next generation of educated Indians represented by the erstwhile servant of the house, the knave.
6. The story of King Dasarath and Kaikeyi tells that the king had granted her three boons for saving his life in battle. However, when the eldest son of the king, Rama, from his eldest wife, is to ascend the throne, she asks as one of her boons that her own son Bharat be made king and that Rama be banished into the forests for fourteen years. An enraged Dasarath therefore curses her saying that henceforth no man will name his daughter after Kaikeyi.
7. Sita was the wife of Rama on whose life the epic Ramayana is based. Rama is also considered as the incarnation of the divinity, Vishnu. Sita is considered an ideal wife as she followed her husband into exile and remained loyal to him under all circumstances. Savitri is another mythological figure who married a common man of her

choice although she herself was a princess. She lives a simple life with him and when he dies accidentally, engages the Lord of Death himself in a conversation in which he is made to concede to her the life of her husband. Sulochana was the wife of Indrajeet, the son of Ravana, the king of Lanka. She is the only woman who commits *sati* with her dead husband in the epic poem Ramayana. Incidentally Ravana was a learned Brahmin, Draupadi was the common wife of the five Pandava brothers who are the key characters of the epic poem Mahabharta. She was born of fire and immensely beautiful, but was forced into marrying all five brothers simultaneously. While most Hindus condemn such practice, fraternal polyandry is present among some communities in India. The higher castes in Northern India generally do not consider the Mahabharata fit to be read at home and have an ambiguous attitude towards Draupadi.

8. It is believed that there was a continuity from the Indus Valley Civilization to later cultures and also that the Indus civilization had a strong mother worshipping cult that was mingled with the patriarchal religion of the Vedic Aryans responsible for the *sakti* component of Hinduism (Thapar, 1992).
9. Kastur Ba Gandhi was the wife of Mahatma Gandhi and Kamala Nehru the wife of Jawaharlal Nehru, both of whom joined the Indian nationalist movement along with their husbands.
10. There is a theory of the Inner or Vedic Aryans and the Outer group of the Aryans who had less strong patriarchy than the inner group. Even today it is well recognized that mainstream Indian culture is divided into a heartland Hindu belt characterized by strong control of women and a outer belt where the position of women is more liberal and religion is more broad based and diverse including matriliny and a strong *sakti* cult (Chanda, 1916).
11. Jayalalitha is an interesting example of the *ardhangini* concept. She was the companion of a former and very popular film star and chief minister of Tamil Nadu, M.G. Ramachandran. After his death she catapulted to power as his successor although she was not his legal wife. Today she is both the most powerful political figure in Tamil Nadu as well as regarded as a goddess by the masses.
12. Ekta Kapoor is the daughter of a well known Hindi film star, but is better known for her television serials that have struck a chord with the Indian masses as shown by their immense popularity. She strictly follows a regressive model of a Hindu woman even though all her serials are women oriented.
13. The *bindi* is a red dot on the forehead traditionally made with a red dye called *kumkum* or with the red vermillion powder *sindoor* and

can be worn by both married and unmarried women. The *sindoor* in the parting of a woman's hair depicts her marital status especially in Eastern India. In Western and Southern India the women wear either the *mangalsutra,* a kind of beaded necklace or the *thali,* a kind of pendant in yellow thread round their necks to signify marital status. A widow is recognized by her not wearing even a *bindi* or a black one. But in some parts of India like in the north western region or the north eastern region, and among the tribes and low castes such marks of marital status were not mandatory or even unknown.

14. It is very popular on the television soap to have a woman who is intelligent and smart, capable of professional accomplishment yet conforming to the characters of the *devi* in moral terms, like in her dress and values. Most Indian men aspire for such a wife who would be perfect blend of modernity and tradition to satisfy all their requirements.

References

Bannerjee, Sumanta (1990), Marginalization of Women's Popular Culture in Nineteenth Century Bengal, In Kumkum Sangari and Sudesh Vaid (eds.), *Recasting Women: Essays in India's Colonial History,* 127-179, New Brunswick: Rutgers University Press.

Borthwick, M. (1984), *The Changing Role of Women in Bengal, 1849-1905,* Princeton University Press.

Channa, Subhadra Mitra (1997), Gender and Social Space in a Haryana Village, *Indian Journal of Gender Studies,* 4 (1).

— (1998), Rethinking Anthropological Concept of Tribe, *Eastern Anthropologist,* 51(2).

— (2003), Colonialism, Caste and the Myth of Race: A Historical Perspective on the Interaction of Indian Beliefs and Western Science, In A.K. Kalla and D.K. Bhattacharaya (eds.), *Understanding People of India: Anthropological Insights,* 535-553.

— (2004), Globalization and Modernity in India: A Gendered Critique, *Urban Anthropology,* 33(1), 37-71.

Channa, V.C. (1984), *Hinduism,* New Delhi: National Publishing House.

Chanda, Ramprasad (1916), *The Indo Aryan Races: A Study of the Origins of the Indo-Aryan People and Institutes,* Rajshahi: Varendra Research Society.

Chakravorti, Uma (1990), Whatever Happened to the Vedic 'dasi'? Orientalism, Nationalism and a Script for the Past, In Kumkum

Sangari and Sudesh Vaid (eds.) *Recasting Women: Essays in Colonial History*, 27-87, Rutgers University Press.

Chatterjee, Partha (1993), *The Nation and its Fragments: Colonial and Post-Colonial Histories*, Princeton, New Jersey: Princeton University Press.

Cohn, Bernard S. (1996), *Colonialism and its Forms of Knowledge: The British in India*, Princeton, New Jersey: Princeton University Press.

Dirks, Nicholas B. (1996), Foreword, In Bernard S. Cohen, *Colonialism and its Forms of Knowledge*, ix-xvii, Princeton, New Jersey: Princeton University Press.

— (1997), The Invention of Caste: Civil Society in Colonial India, In H.L. Seneviratne (ed.) *Identity, Consciousness and the Past, Forging of Caste and Community in India and Sri Lanka*, pp. 120-135, Oxford: Oxford University Press.

— (2001), *Castes of Mind: Colonialism and the Making of Modern India*, Princeton, New Jersey: Princeton University Press.

Hiltebeital, Alf (1995), Draupadi Cult Lilas, In William Sax (ed.) *The Gods at Play*, 204-224, New York: Oxford University Press.

Kersenboom, Saskia C. (1991), The Traditional Repertoire of the Tiruttani Temple Dancers, In Julia Leslie (ed) *Roles and Rituals for Hindu Women*, 129-146, Rutherford: Fairleigh Dickinson University Press.

Moon, Minakshi and Urmial Pawar (2003), We Made History Too: Women in the Early Untouchable Liberation Movement, In Aupama Rao (ed.) *Gender and Caste*, 48-56, New Delhi: Kali for Women.

O' Hanlon, Rosalind (2000), *A Comparison Between Women and Men*, New Delhi: Oxford India Paperback.

Sangari, Kumkum and Sudesh Vaid (1990), Recasting Women: An Introduction, In Sangari and Vaid (eds.), *Recasting Women: Essays in Colonial History*, 1-26, Rutgers University Press.

Tanabe, Akio (1999), Transformation of Sakti: Gender and Sexuality in the Festival of Goddess Ramachandi, In Masaku Tanaka and Musashi Tachikawa (eds.), *Living with Sakti: Gender, Sexuality and Religion in South Asia*, 137-169.

Thapar, Romila (1992), *Interpreting Early India*, Delhi: Oxford University Press.

Trautmann, Thomas R. (1997), *Aryans and British India*, Berkeley, University of California Press.

3

Advice to Housewives

'Conduct Book' Tradition in Orissa

SACHIDANANDA MOHANTY

I

Structured in the form of a dialogue between an educated husband who diligently coaches his unlettered wife regarding the ideal wifely conduct, works like *Gruha Laxmi*, the three-volume work by Jagabandhu Singh published during the late 1930s and early 1940s in Orissa were widely circulated and received popular acclaim and sanction. They enjoy a great deal of popularity in parts of rural Orissa even today.

Judged against the backdrop of a widening interest among women in female education and their desire to participate in public space, *Conduct Books* such as those by Singh may be seen as an ambivalent male response at best or an attempt at outright patriarchal control at worst. The conflation between Laxmi, the Hindu goddess of benevolence and prosperity, and the wife who allows herself to be shaped as an 'ideal' woman (read 'self-effacing') by a 'superior' spouse is obvious; it is a frequent and insistent trope that exploits popular mythology and iconography for a largely regressive agenda.

I shall also underline in the essay the prevalent male reservations about western education for woman recurrently voiced in contemporary journals. Finally, I shall invoke the pioneering role of early literary women in Orissa whose writings stand out as an effective contrast to the 'conduct books' like *Gruha Laxmi*. These contributed to consciousness raising among women in the state.

II

A number of features seems to mark the coming of female education into the State of Orissa. Education for girls was initially confined to a few members of the Christian community. In 1871 for the first time a school for Hindu girls was set up at Cuttack in the house of Abhinash Chandra Chattopadhyaya (*Utkal Deepika,* Vol. 6, No. 38, Sep 30, 1871). Even by 1881, the school had registered practically no growth; nor could it catch the public imagination. The number of girls had increased to a mere 25 (*Utkal Deepika,* Vol. 16, No. 44, Nov 5, 1881). Even after the school ran for 10 years at Cuttack city, only four Hindu girls could be enrolled. This fact was much regretted by the then Editor of *Utkal Deepika* who drew attention of parents and urged them to send their girls to the school in larger numbers (*Utkal Deepika,* ibid). Similarly *Utkal Deepika* in its issue of Sep 21, 1871 published a notice by Sri Abhinash Chandra Chattopadhyaya, the Secretary of Cuttack Hindu Girls' School. The announcement is an effective commentary on the state of female education in Orissa:

> A school has been set up in this (Cuttack) city for the education of Hindu girls. Till the construction of a separate building, the instruction will continue to be imparted in my house. The school shall remain open from 10 am to 3 pm. Some may find it hard to send their daughters due to lack of escorts. Please note that a maidservant attached to the school will pick up girls from their respective homes and drop them back after closing hours. Only young girls from respectable families can be admitted. More details can be had by writing to the undersigned.
> - Sri Abhinash Chandra Chattopadhyaya, Secretary, Cuttack Hindu Girls' School.

Both men and women championed female education in Orissa. Many men wrote letters in *Utkal Deepika* in support of the cause. Similarly, writing in another journal *Mukura* a contributor, Ramesh Chandra Mohanty went on to ask in his essay entitled 'Women's education': "Most of the arguments that we offer in the context of *Stree Sikhya* have a single source, namely, fear. We all fear that by the spread of such education, the dominant position of men will go. However, the age of domination is over. It is time for equality now.

Once women are educated, they may not look up to you, but certainly they will treat you as friends. Will that relationship not be more endearing?" (*Stree Sikhya, Mukura,* No 9, Pausa, 1333 Sala, pp. 219-220).

Despite this apparently sympathetic attitude, the approach towards female education remained traditional in many quarters. For instance, presiding over a prize-giving ceremony held on Nov 12, 1871, Commissioner T. E. Ravenshaw declared, "the purpose of female education was not to teach the girls European manners, but to make them good mothers and efficient housewives and enable them to maintain family accounts. He regretted that the Oriyas were in this sense lagging behind the Bengalis". This fact is clearly borne out in the following table:

Year	*Oriyas*	*Bengalis*	*Others*	*Total*
1871	2	10	-	12
1881	2	20	-	22
1884	15	30	-	45

Source: Tabulated from *Utkal Deepika.*

A number of primers were produced for the use of girls of different religious backgrounds. They include *Dialogue Between Mother and Daughter* (Christian Literature, 1869), *Sabitri* (*Girls' Reader,* Dey's Utkal Press, Balasore, 1872), 'Basanta' (a story for women, written originally by Leslie, translated by Reverend J.L. Philips, 1873), *The Duties of Husband and Wife* by Reverend J Philips, 1876, *Balika Patha* (first part) by Baikuntha Nath Dey, 1877 and many others.

Despite these developments, opposition persisted vis-à-vis female education in the State. At times, the voice of a concerned girl gives rise to a cry of despair as we see in the poem of Sushila:

What use is schooling for girls?
Our countrymen ask:
Isn't women's lives meant
for family duties alone?
If learned they shall not go
for sure
to "Kutcheries" for service,
But will roam around

> In unkempt hair....
> - 'A Girl's Cry' by Sushila, a student of Mission Girls' School, Cuttack, *Utkal Deepika*, June 13, 1885. (My translation)

The anxiety of Sushila was not unfounded. A great deal of male reservations was expressed in various columns of newspapers and periodicals. The tendency throughout was to portray female education as an unmitigated source of western waywardness, a gateway for chaos. It was also viewed as destructive of family values and social cohesion. The discourse often came disguised as a humorous account where female bonding was pictured as a dangerous trade union activity. This was a refrain that continued right up to the middle of the last century. Enlightened social legislation in favour of female equality and empowerment was generally viewed with antipathy. For instance, the journal Kumkum published from Bombay (present Mumbai) by Litho Press and edited by a progressive literary couple, Deba and Nuru Mahapatra, featured in its issue No. 6, 1949, a letter entitled 'Only for Men' by Prafulla Kishore Pattnaik, Puri:

> From the pre-historic days, woman has always identified herself as the wife and mother of such and such person. There is always the need of a medium for the sake of her identity. That is a law that distinguished the difference between man and woman. However, a male is always known by his manhood. There is no need to highlight his identity. Because he inhabits the outside world everyone knows him well...

Similarly, Kumkum, No. 7 and 8, June 1950 has a tongue in cheek article entitled 'Nikhila Bharata Patni Sangha' ('All India Wives Association'). There is occasionally a response to such articles in the form of banter. For instance, the article 'Akhila Bharata Swami Samiti' ('All India Husbands' Association') seeks to take sweet revenge on patriarchal pretensions (*Dagara*, 14th year, No. 3, 1950, pp. 5-8).

III

It is in this context that we may now assess the role of Advice for Women Texts. In Bengal for instance, didactic texts such as Gruha Laxmi and Ramanir Kartavya focused on the desirable conduct of women before and after marriage. These attempted moral instructions, especially wifely obedience, through elaborate conversation between a much younger and admiring wife and an older husband, carried out at night. Judith Walsh's well-documented essay 'The Virtuous Wife and Well Ordered Home: The reconceptualisation of Bengali Women and their World' (Judith Walsh, *Mind Body and Society: Life and Mentality in Colonial Bengal'*, Rajat Kumar Ray (ed.), Oxford University Press, Delhi: 1955, pp. 331-63) brilliantly records the 19th century 'advice for women' texts in Bengal. These texts had many parallels in Orissa as well. They enjoyed a wide currency. For instance, the 1946 issue of *Gruha Laxmi*, by the famous Jagabandhu Singh, had gone through an impressive five imprints. In contrast, Sarala Devi's 'Narira Dabi' ('The rights of women'), *Hindustan Granthamala*, Cuttack, 1934, a pioneering text, had a single imprint. The iconography of the cover picture of *Gruha Laxmi* provides an eloquent commentary on the agenda of the author. The cover shows the benevolent Laxmi, the Hindu goddess of wealth and prosperity. Saree-clad she is shown wearing a crown emerging from the placid waters. On her right we see a young elephant, with its trunk raised in an act of salutation. The elephant here symbolizes the ritualistic presence of wisdom and auspiciousness. The presence of swans and flowers add to the overall aesthetic appeal. Goddess Laxmi carries in her two hands lotuses while the other two, pointed downwards, signal an act of benediction.

The picture clearly conflates goddess Laxmi with the ideal housewife. The underlying idea, reiterated at several times inside the text, is to posit her as the source of a desirable wifely conduct. In *Gruha Laxmi* Part III, dated 1940, Singh explains his mission in the following words in the introduction to the book:

> Indian women are generally described as creatures confined to home. We see before our eyes the nature of education for men; female education is decidedly worse.... Education in the schools and colleges is confined to a few. Beyond the textbook and the syllabus, there is very little knowledge available. Girls in our country do not remain in formal institutions of learning beyond the age of 14. Therefore, they should be given such texts whereby they enhance their general knowledge. They must know many things in order to be a good housewife. To fill such a need *Gruha Laxmi* has been composed. (*Gruha Laxmi*, Jagabandhu Singh, Part One, first edition, Cuttack Trading Company, 1940, p. ii). (All translations of passages from *Gruha Laxmi* are by me.)

This note of hope is soon followed by an appropriate and inspiring invocation. The underlying note here is that by the reading of *Gruha Laxmi*, the heroic women of India, the great 'Ramani' of Bharata, would give birth to noble souls. May they fulfil the lofty task expected of them so that a new Bharat would be born again!

In the preface to the volume, dated 1946, the author after duly elevating the lady of the house to spiritual heights of a goddess Laxmi, holds out an appropriate warning:

> It is true that Hindu women so far have not succumbed to the lure of *Alaxmi*. One must ponder, however, whether higher education currently imparted to women would make the continued worshipping of Laxmi possible. The day the Hindu woman refuses to accord respect to the household ideal that will surely be the beginning of *Alaxmi* (Singh, 1946: 3). (Gruha Laxmi, Jagabandhu Singh, Part I, fifth edition, Cuttack Trading Company, 1946, p. iii).

Another fear of Singh is the unwillingness of a newly educated wife to enter into the kitchen. As he asks pointedly: "to relax in bed and read novels is not the duty of the wife. Alas, the modern educated wife, a veritable terror at home, has begun to hate cooking. Cooking is the most important duty among all activities. For without cooking, what shall we eat? And without food how shall we survive?" Singh's exhortations for the ideal wifely conduct soon reaches an apex. For instance, what should an ideal wife do in the absence of her husband? Singh is forthright in his message:

> There should be no make-up when her husband is away. Equally, should she refrain from eating well or dressing well in his absence! She should find no use whatsoever in luxury items at such times. This is the 'Dharma' of all devoted wives, for such women the husband is truly the source of all joy and fulfillment! His joy and sorrow are hers as well (*ibid*, p. viii).

Jagabandhu Singh is clear that his words are not a matter of moral sermons but are meant to be implemented in life, especially by housewives. As he explains in his *Gruha Laxmi* Part II: "Be a well-deserved Aryan woman by performing the right action, and get worshipped in the world. Nothing will be achieved only by the reading of books!...Women who have the noble task of bringing forth children into life must acquire the right kind of knowledge. It is not enough for them to pass only B.A. or M.A. The knowledge that will make them the ideal wife, mother, daughter and the Laxmi of the house, is what must be cherished!" (*Gruha Laxmi*, Jagabandhu Singh, Part II (year not given) pp. 23-24).

There are many such episodes in *Gruha Laxmi* that affirm the value of the right 'education'. For instance, Chapter 3 of *Gruha Laxmi* Part II alludes to the unfortunate suicide of Swarnalata from the neighbouring Bengal. The wife suggests that "perhaps it would have been better for Swarnalata to remain unmarried and safe. She could have studied further, educated girls and made them ideal wives and daughters". The husband has no answer to this and quickly closes the discussion.

At times, the husband offers a number of statements as self-evident aphorisms. Many of these clearly promote patriarchal thinking. For instance, in Chapter 5 of *Gruha Laxmi* Part II, we see the following: "the moon looks beautiful because it is in the midst of planets and stars. The wife looks beautiful in the company of the husband. The king looks beautiful in the presence of the people. However, knowledge looks beautiful everywhere" (p 47). Similarly, "those with nails, horns, and arms are not to be believed. Equally untrustworthy are women and princes" (p. 48).

There are other conversations equally worth noticing from the gender point of view. The following serves as an interesting example:

> "Husband: Ramachandra was born long ago! Today everyone chants his name. He is worshipped as a living God!
>
> Wife: Yes, indeed! I feel a sense of unease however when I think of Sita!
>
> Husband: You might feel bad if you think of this fact alone. But you need to take a larger view of the matter!" (p. 60).

In another sequence, the husband suggests that the songs children sing ought to be meaningful. These, in his opinion, ought to cater to the specific gender needs since boys and girls are meant to carry out different tasks in life. Predictably enough, the song meant for the girl urges upon her to get up early, to be an efficient manager of home and the kitchen, to be a Gruha Laxmi who is a "property of others" and to be a Sita, Damayanti, Laxmi or Saraswati. For only then can Bharat and Utkal wake into a new life!

On the other hand, the male child must leave early for the school; he must concentrate in studies so that he could be a Pandit.

For, is there a greater jewel for a boy, than knowledge? He must get up early without delay, listen to heroic lore and join the generation of the brave! (pp. 78-79).

IV

Thus, it would be seen that the *conduct books* by Jagabandhu Singh create and promote a discourse, which advances a largely male-oriented agenda. It is an interesting response to westernization and female education. In the process, it often takes recourse to intelligent and skillful means for pushing in an ideology of female containment. Many of the rhetorical strategies employed look, on the face of it, innocuous enough. However, presented in the conversational mode between an older male figure with authority and power and a younger spouse 'willing' to learn, the outcome is left little in doubt. It must be remembered that the internalization of the secondary status for the woman/wife takes place at a domestic site, which is probably one of the few private spaces for the young wife. The space contains simultaneously an outlet for carrying out intimate intellectual, emotional and physical/sexual interaction between the spouses. Thereby it becomes a vital site for shaping the 'rightful' female behaviour and wifely conduct.

Significantly enough, while the *conduct books* continued their mission, Oriya literary women around the same time were voicing an alternative rhetoric of female empowerment. For instance, the celebrated *Utkal Sahitya* regularly carried a column by Suprabha Devi called *Nari Prasanga*. Suprabha was the illustrious daughter of Biswanath Kar, the editor of *Utkal Sahitya*. She along with her sister Narmada Kar consistently fought for female education and empowerment. For instance, Volume 30, 1927, issue of the journal carried, (pp. 244-45) among other items, an account about Miss Gertrude Bell, a highly educated woman whose career was held as worthy of emulation. Equally exemplary, according to her, was the exploit of Miss Banu Matwala, a Parsi woman, who had excelled in physical culture and had just returned from Denmark. "We hope," says Suprabha, "that many Indian women will now get trained in the gymnasium to be set up by Miss Matwala. For it is absolutely essential for women to take part in physical culture along with mental education. No longer can a woman afford to be a delicate creature! Today she aspires for freedom and therefore she must build her body and mind. Or else she can never have the boon of full freedom (p. 244).

Similarly, other issues of the journal talk approvingly about 'woman of ancient Greece', 'a conference of Muslim women', 'women in the field of science', 'the military training of American women' as well as 'legislative assembly and the demand of women' (pp. 207-08). The 1928 issue, under the same column (pp. 207-08) offers a flattering portrait of a woman magistrate and a woman barrister. There are also favourable accounts of a Hindu-Muslim marriage and the achievements of women in education. Likewise, 'Nari Prasanga' of 1927 (pp. 550-51) informs the reader about Nari Mangala Samiti of Calcutta, a new woman's periodical from Bengal entitled *Banga Lakshmi* and the report of All-India Women's conference.

In addition, literary women like Reba Ray ('Nirabe,' *Utkal Sahitya,* Chaitra, 1304, Sala, (1897) pp. 51-53), Kuntala Kumari Sabat ('Adhunika Dharma Samasya', *Utkal Sahitya,* 1391, 31/9, 10 Pausa, Magha, 1331 Sala, pp. 391-94), Sailabala Das, 'Janasadharanare Stree Shikya Bistarara Upaya,' ('Ways of spreading Women's education'), *Utkal Sahitya,* No. 2, Jyesta 1323 Sala, pp. 73-80), Bilasini, Kokila Devi, *Utkal Sahitya,* No. 20/5, Bhadra, 1323 Sala, (1915), pp. 231-34), Sarala Devi ('Narira Dabi' ('Rights of Women') Hindustan Granthamala, Cuttack, 1934) and others wrote extensively on women's issues and contributed to a new thinking on the participation of women in public space. Issues like widow re-marriage, women's participation in the national freedom struggle and the trade union movement, etc., were all taken up.

The exact nature of the impact of literary feminism in Orissa is yet to be assessed fully. Similarly, very little attention has been devoted so far by the critics to the relationship between this body of women's writing vis-à-vis the conduct book tradition. Serving mutually antagonistic goals, the two traditions seem to meet rarely, although the two dominant discourses do show an awareness and critique of each other. Of the two, it is unfortunately the advice for women texts that clearly have had the upper hand. Their legacy continues till today and their looming shadow is still felt in many of the educational, literary and cultural institutions of contemporary Orissa; clearly a fact to be noted by those attempting to bring about gender justice and equality among the sexes in the State.

[I gratefully acknowledge help received from the various archives in Orissa, especially the State Archive, Bhubaneswar; the library of Utkal Sahitya Samaj, Cuttack; Visvabharati, Santiniketan; the National library at Kolkata; the personal collections of various writers, especially Brajanath Rath, Balasore. I also thank J.P. Das, New Delhi for his valuable suggestions.]

(An earlier version of this article had appeared earlier in Economic and Political Weekly, Jan 24-30, 2004.)

4

Between the Visible and the Invisible

Gender Relations in a Tribe in India

ARIMA MISHRA

A critical perspective on examining gender relations in tribal areas in the Indian context is missing. This is primarily because gender relation is considered a non-issue since tribal women supposedly have a higher status compared to their non-tribal counterparts. Consequently, studies on tribal women have a tendency towards corroborating the romanticist tradition of Verrier Elwin emphasizing the powerful, courageous, independent image of tribal women in tribal societies. There has been an increasing concern for tribal women's deteriorating economic and social status in the wake of development measures.[1] For instance, studies do highlight the decline in tribal women's status due to development-induced displacement (Fernandes, 2005; Menon, 1992; 1995; Padhi, 1999). These studies discuss about changing economic status of tribal women from economically independent women to mere housewives dependent on their male counterparts, harassment in the hands of non-tribal employers, exposure to many of the non-tribal customs (wife beating, dowry system, etc.) as the direct or indirect costs of displacement. Such discussion on post-displacement status of women does not, however, critically reflect on the gender dynamics at the household level, not merely participation in economic activities but control over resources (land, products of labour), decision-making process, etc., in tribal societies at the pre-displacement stage. There seems to be two sets of assumptions about tribal women. The first is that tribal women essentially have an equal status with their male counterparts (thus higher status compared with non-tribal or more specifically Hindu women). The second, such gender equation suffers a setback either through several development measures and/or through the process of acculturation with Hindu caste women.

These assumptions are informed and influenced, at a theoretical level, by the universality of male dominance and female subordination due to the public-private, production-reproduction dichotomy characteristic of most of the early feminist writings across the globe. Logically, it implies that where such dichotomies are problematic as in tribal societies, gender relations should be equal and that variables like economic factors could account for such gender symmetry. At a more contextual level, these assumptions are also due to the fact that the classical indicators of measuring status of women are influenced by Hindu marriage practices and customs (low age at marriage, bride burning, female infanticide, dowry payment, preference for male children, etc.).[2] Such ethnocentricity blocks academic probing into a wide range of relationships that might exist between men and women in societies of different economic and political complexities.

Tribal women are distinctly visible through their participation in the subsistence economy and the institution of bride price that supposedly guarantee equal or high status to tribal women. What is important is not to contest the high or low status of tribal women but to critically reflect on such mechanical correlates between participation in subsistence economy and sex-related equality or even institution of bride price (absence of dowry) and high status of women. Das (1976) has rightly pointed out the academic fallout of such assumptions and placed the need for examining the conditions under which women exercise control over products of labour and also the social value of their work. While such critical examination has been undertaken in the context of Hindu or even Muslim societies (ibid.), it is conspicuous by its absence in tribal societies. One could also ask here if participation in subsistence economy and bride price are separate indicators independent of the larger context of tribal social organizations. Bride price is not merely a marriage custom, its role in defining and sustaining the overall context of gender division of assets and labour (be it land, children or others) in tribal societies needs to be examined.

This paper in the context of such lacunae in research on tribal women reflects on gender relations among the Kutia Kandhas devoid of any assumptions about either subordination or high status of tribal women. It does not focus on any particular indicator of women's status but seeks to examine gender relations as reflected in interrelated contexts of cosmology, economy, kinship, ritual and polity. In this regard, the social relational contexts where hegemonic or other gender beliefs come in, to play their roles become significant (Ridgeway and Correl, 2004).

This study primarily draws evidence from a tribal village in Kalahandi district of Orissa, India. The area is inhabited by Kutia Kandhas, a section of the Kandha tribe.[3] Other sections of the tribe include the Dongria, Desia, and the Penga.[4] While there are essential similarities among these different sections, they also exhibit a number of differences; hence no generalization can be made of the Kandha tribe as a whole. While the major part of the evidence is drawn from the village Irkuli in Lanjigarh block, I have also drawn upon my observations and interactions with Kandha women from other tribal villages in this block. Irkuli is a small village with 24 households; 17 of these belonging to Kutia Kandhas while 7 are from the distiller caste group of Sundhis. Houses of both these groups are segregated. The Kandha houses are in one locality, rows of houses facing each other while the Sundhi locality is almost half a kilometre away. I have examined in detail the networks among these two groups elsewhere (Mishra, 2005).

Though, I did not set out to study gender in the tribal village when I visited in 1997-1998 for a period of more than six months and later shorter visits between 2000-02, my conventional anthropological orientation (holistic study through ethnography) brought many of these critical aspects of gender relations alive and visible. With scarce written literature on Kutia Kandhas and scarcer writings on reflecting gender (whatever ethnographies exist are silent on gender), the ethnographic inputs from the village were critical for the argument developed in the paper.[5] I was confronted with gender relations as part of the daily mundane affairs. From the day I entered the village as a woman researcher to the day when I left the village to conclude my fieldwork – if notionally, I have witnessed different shades of what could constitute public and private in different contexts among the tribal. I do not wish to argue that gender relations are highly problematic, but to say, that even tribal society offers a critical space to examine gender relations and the existing theoretical approaches are inadequate for such study.

Mother Earth as Creator and Protector

Myths and rituals are not merely interrelated but are important reflections of social structure, feelings and perceptions about social relations. The most important ritual of buffalo sacrifice[6] among Kutia Kandhas paves the way for understanding the Kandha cosmology. Kutia Kandhas claim their origin from a woman in the form of Earth Goddess. "Their main culture hero is a woman or female being whom some Konds call Nirathali, who seems to be a human incarnation of the Earth Goddess" (Paddel, 1995). The popular myth of 'Niranthali-Kapanthali' indicates that the Kandhas are the first human beings on earth. In fact, earth was created for them to live by Niranthali (the Goddess). The sacrifices were initially made which hardened the earth and made it habitable for them to live. The sacrifices thus reinforce this notion of their origin and belongingness to the earth or soil. Almost all the rituals involve sacrifices that serve to establish dialogues with the mother Earth Goddess. Every village has its own sacred space symbolized by stone, pillar or even tree for worshipping Earth Goddess popularly referred to as *Dharni* (earth). These sacred spaces are usually marked either at the entrance or at the far end of the village demarcating a Kandha village from a non-Kandha one and also protecting the Kandhas from outsiders. Buffalo sacrifice also known as *podh puja* (worship of buffalo) or *pausa parba* (December festival) is the single largest ritual that recreates this cosmology. While the symbolic significance of 'buffalo' (that replaced human beings) in the event is not documented anywhere, similar cosmology among the Oglalas could serve as a pointer where the Oglala people equate buffalo with fecundity and nurture (Powers, 1988). The symbolic significance of the sacrifice for highly fertile land and bountiful harvest (and hence the blood of the sacrificed animal is sprinkled on earth) among the Kandhas does point towards a similar meaning. The Kandha priest (*Jani*) while narrating the sequence of events said that through this sacrifice of buffalo "we call our ancestors, gods particularly dharni mata (earth goddess), we tell them we are offering this sacrifice (buffalo) to you, please give us bountiful harvest and make us free from disease".

Quite unfortunately the limited yet significant ethnographies on the Meria/buffalo sacrifice is completely silent on gender (Boal, 1982; Banerjee, 1969; Niggemeyer, 1964). Thus while these studies inform about how the Kandha society is created and recreated drawing boundaries between clans/villages, different sections of Kandhas, Kandhas vs. outsiders (caste groups) thus linking cosmology with social morphology through buffalo sacrifice, the relations between men and women do not find any mention. While all the male and female members in the tribal villages I visited identified themselves with equal intensity with the event of buffalo sacrifice, they also stated that female members were not allowed near the site of the worship/sacrifice. They entertained themselves through singing, dancing, drinking, but from a distance. Anthropologists usually pass off such segregation as a ritual taboo like the routine taboos associated with menstruation, childbirth, pregnancy, etc., which are essentially looked upon as biological. While more research evidence is needed to contextualize such ritual segregation particularly during buffalo sacrifice (which is associated with the very identity of Kandha as earthly people), studies of taboos and pollution related to women in primitive societies show that these are more than biological and linked to the principles of social organization (Douglas, 1966).

Treating ritual pollution or taboo conveniently as a separate indicator independent of other spheres/indicators could be problematic in tribal societies. None of the rituals among the Kandhas belonged to the realm of sacred only; these were economic and social activities as well, because these rituals were linked to the agricultural calendar. Thus the festival of seeds conducted before the sowing period is meant to symbolically offer seeds to the Earth Goddess. It is more of an individual household affair where some amount of rice is taken out and spread in front of the Goddess Earth. A hen, goat (whatever is available with the household) is brought to eat the rice and is subsequently sacrificed. Feast with the sacrifices of hen/goat marks the festival. Sowing is considered inauspicious without this festival. Buffalo sacrifice is conducted usually during or after harvesting season.

The belief in the mother Earth as the creator apart, she is also considered the protector of the Kandhas from the evil supernatural forces. A *bejuni* who is a human representative of the Goddess performs this role. *Bejuni* conforms to Elwin's (1955) description of shamanism among the Soara women. A *bejuni* is beyond the ordinary. The role of *bejuni* is not hereditary; the villagers do not have the prerogative to decide who would be a *bejuni*. A *bejuni* is sent by the Goddess who would come in her dream (usually a young girl) and nominate her. Since that day, she behaves other than the ordinary and the normal. She is considered a spiritual figure. To the villagers, she is a healer, a medicine woman and a counsellor. The belief in evil spirit for explaining deaths, diseases are very strong among the Kandhas. I witnessed an incidence where a family had lost two young members consecutively within a year. This was considered unnatural. Thus the *bejuni* came to the family, talked to them at length, counselled them, promised to identify the spirit and punish. The spirit was identified in a person from a nearby village. Once identified, the person has to accept punishment as decided by the *bejuni* with the consent of the villagers. Such protective role of a woman (even though she is considered as a spiritual figure) exists simultaneously with their ritual segregation.

Behind Lazy Men vs. Hardworking Women

To the outside world of non-tribal residing in tribal areas, tribal women compared to men are considered hardworking. Tribal males are considered lazy, alcoholic and non-enterprising. Though I did not come across any such explicit gendered constructions among the tribal themselves, the tribal women inherently are looked upon as productive assets, those who are expected to provide labour both for domestic and economic activities. It is in the context of these societal expectations, her roles as daughter, wife and mother are situated. Thus her participation in the economic activities (including domestic), the institution of bride price, the custom of polygamy – all confer to this expected role.

The most visible aspect of tribal women is their contribution to the subsistence economy. The principal economic activities in the village is centred around agriculture, both on the hill plots and plain land. The principal crops grown were paddy, ragi (a kind of millet), arhar and local lentils. Every individual household cultivates around 37 decimal of hill plots. In addition, the women develop their small kitchen gardens. All the female members contribute and help their male counterparts in agricultural activities. In fact, the early morning hours bear a deserted look in the village as all the men and women go to the forestland either to engage themselves in the seasonal agricultural related activities or collect firewood. While there are gendered territories in the use of the forest (the males usually going far into the forest, the female members are relatively nearer), female members do not hesitate to stretch further if required for collecting firewood for daily requirements. Women bear the burden of procuring food for daily consumption. This involves, apart from agricultural related activities, digging of roots and tubers, collecting leaves like *kursa* (when eaten suppresses the pangs of hunger) for consumption, particularly during the lean season or hunger months. While all the men and women showed great resilience in migrating outside for any relief-based works, they were keen to work on such government-aided projects in and around the village.

The village had a subsistence-based economy, the household being the unit for production and consumption. While the Sundhi households practice cash cropping (cotton for example), Kandhas are not lured by such commercial agriculture. They prefer cultivation on forest land and plain land for subsistence based crops as they believe many of the lentil varieties when grown on these hill plots taste much better and sweeter than cultivated on plain land. They do however lament the limited output from such land. Agricultural preferences could also be affected by a gradual decline in access to plain land (many of their land have been mortgaged to the Sundhis through informal means) and decline in access to agricultural capital, i.e., improved seeds, bullocks, etc. Many of the Kandh households had outstanding Government loans. As a subsidiary activity, firewood is collected for sale in the nearby market. Men are usually involved in this activity.

On the question of whether such participation in economic activities implies high status, one needs to examine "conditions under which it becomes possible for women to acquire a degree of control over the products of their labour and also the conditions under which their work is socially valued. For an answer to this question, we shall have to examine the relation between men and property" (Das, 1976). Men usually govern access to land among the Kandhas. This is both under the traditional land tenure system (land was controlled by communities and allocated to their members)[7] and the system of individual ownership that emerged through subsequent settlement surveys. Kutia Kandha society is essentially patrilineal, so the inheritance of property is through the male line.

Land is jointly held and rested with the head of the family who is a male member. Since married sons set up independent households, there is informal division of land among the brothers. As per the official record of rights only one female in the village had land right, which she had got after the death of her husband. She is entitled to manage this land as long as she continues to live in the husbands' family. While men have ownership rights, women have user rights to the land and a major part of subsistence production is their responsibility (Mohanty, 1993; Pathy, 1998). Both as unmarried daughters and married women, they exercise users' rights to land in their respective parent's and husband's families.

Women utilize the services of their children for various farming as well as housekeeping tasks. I saw some of the young girls (aged 7-8) staying back in the house to look after their younger siblings while both the parents were away at work. While the women shoulder the major responsibility of procuring food for daily consumption, other domestic activities, bearing and rearing children, men had a prerogative in the decision-making process related to agriculture or even when it came to availing of credit through exchange of non-food items for food. The male Kandha members negotiate with Sundhis in the village or the Dambas (a Scheduled Caste) from the nearby village. I did not see even once any of the Kandha females interacting with the Sundhi females either as part of the normal course of interaction or for such specific negotiations on credit even if most of these credit items involved borrowing of rice, mortgaging jewellery, etc. While the women were aware of the details of these transactions, they expressed their helplessness and lamented that they had fallen prey to such cruel credit transactions. Many older women had lost their *huglas*, the most precious jewellery given to the bride. When enquired, they replied with pain, "we ate selling these". The major agricultural decisions in terms of accessing Government loan, arranging plough, seeds, mortgaging land to the non-tribal were taken mainly by the men. Dube (2001) reflecting on the decision-making process among the tribals in Madhya Pradesh noted that men invariably took the major decisions because "the income of the man is necessary for staple crops, the income of the woman contributes to the cost of salt".

Thus while the Kandha women are expected to contribute productively both in domestic and economic spheres, they have only users' rights to land and also to children. The marriage practice and the institution of bride price sustain such gender division of assets, both land and children, where men have the exclusive rights while women claiming the right to use their husband's land and their husband's children. Such a paradoxical situation of economic self-sufficiency with structural dependence bears striking resemblance with women in African countries (Frank and McNicoll, 1987).

Bride Price and Gender Distribution of Assets

While arranged marriages (village exogamy, tribal endogamy) are the norm, marriage by capture is popular and practically the most common form of marriage. The festival of *Baliyatra*[8] provides a platform for such marriages to take place. In marriage by capture, the boy forcibly takes away the girl and proposes to her on the way. If the girl agrees (disagreement usually implies that the girl would cry), the respective families work out other details, mainly the bride price. If the bride price is amicably settled between the two families, the marriage does get the social sanctity. Nayak (1987) discusses about inter-clan feuds concerning non-payment of bride price. A marriage can never take place if bride price is not settled between the two families. Marriage by capture in principle makes the girl's consent to the marriage mandatory even though within the range of the culturally possible and the prescribed.

The institution of marriage among the Kandhas does not really represent the modern husband-wife conjugal bond but more a contractual relation between two families or even lineages. The bride price usually involves apart from jewellery to the bride, liquor, cash, goat, buffalo, rice and other grains to the bride's families. The economic status of both the bride and bridegroom families ideally should match, because the feast offered to the family of the bridegroom should match with the quantity of the bride price received. The bride price indicates more importantly the rights over the labour of the woman given in marriage. The wife becomes an economic asset to the husband's family; she is expected to provide labour – economic and domestic – to the husbands' family. Married women referred to as 'experienced' in terms of management of household tasks, labour, bearing and rearing children, are more valued than non-married women. Similar practice is noted among other tribal communities (Mann, 1988) as well. The institution of bride price has not remained unchanged though, and it would be fruitful to tap more into the changing aspects of such institution. In one case, the bridegroom's father told me how he had to pay less bride price to accommodate the poor economic status of the bride's family who was already married once.

The Kandhas though not as a norm do practice polygyny, the first wife known as *badli* and the younger as *sanli*. Major part of the childhood for a girl is a preparation for marriage and participation in the wider society. "The girl must prepare to function worthily within her husband's family and to continue his line by bearing and caring for his children" (Boal, 1982:18). Boal also documents the painful tattooing on the upper half of the face when the girls reach ten years of age. When a female child is born, she is made to wear *'khaasu mala'* or a silver chain of coins symbolically representing the significant contribution to her parents and later to her husband's families.

Widow remarriage is common but once remarried, a widow loses any kind of right in the previous husband's families including children. In fact, in some instances, payment has been demanded from the present husbands' families. Elopement is also common among the Kandhas. In some other Kandha villages, I came across a couple of instances of elopement of young mothers. In cases of elopement, the original marriage is annulled and the husband could look for another wife to care for his children, because as stated earlier, tribal women do not have exclusive right over children. They have access to their children or even children's labour so long as they continue to be in the husbands' families. Such unequal distribution of rights over children has often been discussed through metaphor of seed and earth, men providing the seeds and women the field/earth (Dube, 2001).

Fertility confirms a woman's status as a wife, mother, makes secure her continued access to the land and also ensuring that her own family (parents) can keep the bride price. The fertility decisions are made in this context of structural and status dependency. Reproductive decisions are never a women's decision because the institution of marriage serves a larger interest of the husbands' family/lineage than the interests of either the wife or the husband/wife. I witnessed a woman undergoing sterilization in one of the remote hilly Kandha villages. The woman in question happened to be the first wife. The decision to undergo sterilization was not a voluntary one because in any case such modern methods of fertility control are not popular among the tribal. Many other women who had undergone sterilization complained of side effects of such measure (knee pain, weakness, etc.). The families were also to some extent under the 'official' (Government) pressure through the health worker. In these cases, the male members are approached (even though the health worker is a female member and has easy access to females) and are convinced. It is accepted among the tribal (through experience) that with sterilization, women become economically less productive. So in this case, the decision on sterilization was taken only after the husband married again and the second wife came to compensate for the expected loss of labour to the family. While age commands respect among these tribal, the first wife due to her lesser productivity to the domestic and other economic tasks (in the wake of such sterilization measures for instance or any other illness) is treated secondary to the second wife. While more research is required on domestic violence among tribal women, incidence of wife beating was not so uncommon. The day I was leaving the village to come back to Delhi, Dengi Majhi (in her late 20s) urged me to take her with me. She said "Didi, please take me with you. I can go anywhere and work. I do so much of work here at home and my man beats me up at night, usually drunk." Alcoholism or drunkenness behaviour is not a recent phenomenon. Drinking liquor serves many purposes, social, medical and religious among the Kandhas (Das, 1978). Both men and women drink liquor but for women it is usually occasion specific, men take it on a daily routine basis.

Public dealings in the sense of liaison with the Government officials or non-tribal are the prerogative of men. The villagers' association with the State is through the block level Government officers including the medical officers. Women have very limited interaction with the 'Government' as they are considered private faces when it comes to outsiders (be it researchers, Government officers or other one time visitors). Even as a woman researcher, I initially struggled to bridge the distance to interact with women. Yet in such public/private gendered participation, I witnessed one of the tribal women negotiating with the Block Development Officer who had visited the village to include Irkuli in the list of drought affected villages. She was speaking on behalf of the villagers. The village was finally included and relief works were offered to the villagers.

Thus the analysis shows how mere participation in subsistence economy and institution of bride price cannot be looked upon as separate indicators to gauge the status of Kandha women. These need to be contextualized within the essential principle that governs tribal social relations which expects women (as daughter, wife and mother) to provide labour, both domestic and economic. Hence, there is a need to go beyond conventional (influenced by Hindu customs and practices) indicators to examine gender relations in tribal areas. Further, the analysis also shows why gender studies need to look beyond public-private, production-reproduction dichotomies as the basis of universal male dominance and female subordination. The dichotomy in its usual understanding is not merely inadequate in tribal areas but also turns a blind eye to local notions and contexts of public and private. The inadequacy of such dichotomies in cross-cultural research and the need for complex models to understand gender relations and dehomogenization of the category 'woman' is increasingly reflected in recent feminist writings (Mukhopadhyay and Higgins, 1988; Ampofo, Eoku-betts, Njambi and Soirim, 2004). While tribal studies in sociology/anthropology continue to grow, tribal gender relations have not received critical attention. Issues of gender equations, or more popularly issues of tribal women, are considered secondary to more compelling themes on examining tribal customs, rituals, political, economic organizations, tribal development, consequences of tribal-non-tribal interaction, etc. Consequently the few existing studies on tribal women document the decline in social and economic status of tribal women in the context of development measures and interaction with high caste females assuming the high status of tribal women based on visible indicators. The scope of the paper is limited and this is to place the need for more rigorous research on gender in tribal areas in the historical and changing contexts, preferably where tribal women's own voices are heard. We need a theoretical perspective that goes beyond dichotomous stereotypes to accommodate dynamics of gender equations in different cultures and societies, to address paradoxical situation of Kandha women of economic-self sufficiency with structural dependency, with the belief in the role of women as creator and protector and at the same time ritual segregation. Instead of generalizing about tribal women, research should be undertaken to address specificities and complexities among each of the numerous tribes living in different parts of India.

Notes

1. See Singh, Vyas and Mann (eds.) 1988.
2. Indicators for measuring status of women have been varied. It is increasingly been acknowledged by anthropologists that measuring women's status is highly complicated and hence evolving universal determinants for measuring status is a futile task because of its limited applicability cross-culturally (Mukhopadhyay and Higgins 1988).
3. Kandha tribe has been mentioned as Kond, Khond, Kandh elsewhere. I prefer to write Kandha because this is how villagers referred themselves to.
4. See District Gazetteers (Koraput, Kalahandi,) for details on these different sections of the tribe.
5. The colonial ethnographies are of limited help in understanding the tribal Kandhas. These were obsessed with the concern for the need to abolish the infamous human sacrifice and female infanticide (the latter practiced among Kandhas in some parts of Orissa). The political expediency underlying the overemphasis on the irrationality of tribal customs was loud and clear. The latter ethnographies include Banerjee 1969, Niggemeyer 1964, Pathy 1995.
6. Buffalo sacrifice has replaced the earlier *meria* sacrifice where a human being was sacrificed and offered to Earth Goddess. This custom of sacrificing a human being was suppressed during the British rule. For details on this custom, see Niggemeyer 1964, Padel 1995, Boal 1982.
7. Membership in a clan/village ensured inheritable rights over land.
8. *Baliyatra* is a popular festival among the Kandhas particularly in Lanjigarh. This is one festival where the Dongrias and Kutia Kandhas come together. The festival is also celebrated to reinforce the belief in the power of Earth Goddess.

References

Ampofo, A. A., Beoku-bets, J., Njambi, W.N. and Osirim, M. (2004), Women's and Gender Studies in English Speaking Africa: A Review of Research in the Social Sciences, *Gender and Society*, 18(6), 685-714.

Banerjee, Sukumar (1969), *Ethnographic Study of the Kandha*, Calcutta: Anthropological Survey of India.

Boal, Barbara (1982), *The Konds: Human Sacrifice and Religious Change*, Bhubaneswar: Modern Book Depot.

Das, Veena (1976), Indian Women: Work, Power and Status, In B.R. Nanda (ed.), *Indian Women: From Purdah to Modernity*, Delhi: Vikas Publishing House.

Das, Hemant (1978), The Role of Drinking Alcohol in Tribal Societies (In Oriya), *Adivasi*, XVII (1-4), 46-49.

Dube, Leela (2001), *Anthropological Explorations in Gender*, Chap. 3, New Delhi: Sage Publications.

Douglas, M. (1966), *Purity and Danger*, London: Routledge.

Elwin, Verrier (1975), Tribal Women, In Devaki Jain (ed.), *Indian Women*, New Delhi: Publications Division, Ministry of Information and Broadcasting.

— (1955), The Saora Woman as Shaman in *The Religion of an Indian Tribe*, Bombay: Oxford University Press.

Fernandes, Walter (2005), The Impact of Displacement on Tribal Women, In Deepak Behera and Georg Peffer (eds.), *Contemporary Society: Tribal Studies*, Vol. 6, New Delhi: Concept Publishing Company.

Frank, Odile and Geoffrey McNicoll (1987), An Interpretation of Fertility and Populations Policy in Kenya, *Population and Development* Review, 13 (2), 209:214.

Mann, Kamlesh (1996), *Tribal Women: On the Threshold of Twenty-First Century*, New Delhi: M.D. Publications.

Menon, Geeta (1992), Tribal Women: Victims of the Development Process, In Walter Fernandes (ed.), *National Development and Tribal Deprivation*, New Delhi: Indian Social Institute.

— (1995), The Impact of Migration of the Work and Tribal Women's Status, In Loes Schenken-Sandbergen (ed.), *Women and Seasonal Labor Migration*, New Delhi: Sage.

Mishra, Arima (2005), Insiders and Outsiders: Studying Tribal Villages. Paper Presented at the International Conference on Tribal Society in India and Beyond, Sambalpur University, Orissa, November 17-19 2004.

Mohanty, S.C. (1993), Social Position and Property Rights of Kutia Kondh Women, *Adivasi*, XXXIII (2), 16-22.

Mukhopadhyay, Carol C. and Higgins J. Patricia (1988), Anthropological Studies of Women's Status Revisited 1977-87, *Annual Review of Anthropology*, 17: 461-495.

Nayak, P.K. (1987), *Blood, Women and Territory: An Analysis of Clan Feuds among Dongria Kandhas*, New Delhi: Reliance Publishers.

Niggemeyer, Herman (1964), *Kuttia Kond,* Johan Wolfgang Goethe Universitat, Frankfurt-am-main.

Padhy, Itishree (1999), Development, Displacement, Rehabilitation and the Aftermath: An Impact on Tribal Women, In Deepak Behera and Georg Peffer (eds.) *Contemporary Society: Tribal Studies,* Vol. 3, New Delhi: Concept Publishing Company.

Pathy, Jagannath (1995), Colonial Ethnography of the Kandhas: White Men's Burden or Political Expediency, *Economic and Political Weekly,* Jan 28, 221-228.

Pathy, Suguna (1998), Social Production among the Khonds of Orissa, In Deepak Behera and George Pfeffer (eds.), *Contemporary Society: Tribal Studies,* Vol. 2, New Delhi: Concept Publishing Company.

Padel, Felix (1995), *The Sacrifice of Human Being: British Rule and the Konds of Orissa,* Delhi: Oxford University Press.

Powers, Marla N. (1986), *Oglala Women: Myth, Ritual and Reality,* London: University of Chicago Press.

Ridegeway, Cecillia and Correll, Shelley J. (2004), Unpacking the Gender System: A Theoretical Perspective on Gender Beliefs and Social Relations, *Gender and Society,* 18(4).

Senapati, M. (1980), *District Gazetteer, Kalahandi,* Cuttack: Government Press.

Senapati, M. and Sahu, N. (1966), *Gazetteer of India, Koraput,* Cuttack: Government Press.

Sharma, S.P. and A.C. Mittal (1998), *Tribal Women in India,* Vol. 1-3, New Delhi: Radha Publications.

Singh, J.P, Vyas, N.N. and R.S. Mann (eds.) (1988), *Tribal Women and Development,* Jaipur: Rawat Publications.

5

Dalit[1] Women's Voices in Rural Andhra Pradesh, India

N. SUDHAKAR RAO

Expressive tradition has a universal character. Alan Lomax analysing both cantometric ratings and cultural data from 233 cultures across the globe finds that some traits of song performance show a powerful relationship to features of social structure that regulate interaction in all cultures. He says, "... the statistical confirmation is so strong as to indicate that expressive behaviour may be one of the most sensitive and reliable indicators of cultural patterns and social structure" (1968: 4-5). Keeping this statement in view, this paper examines some songs of rural Dalit women in Andhra Pradesh, India in relation to Indian social structure. There have been well documented expressive traditions in South Asia and the songs of Indian women do challenge several presumptions and stereotypical notions about Indian women and the social structure. An attempt is made here to represent the suppressed voices of Dalit women about their predicament. These timeless voices have always been present over the centuries but the indifferent male world pretends to have not ever heard them. The Dalit women are the 'other' here in respect of the researcher's gender that represents the voices. This representation is of his Indian society and culture. Here lies the problem that needs to be addressed before we proceed further to discuss articulation of these feeble voices.

Anthropological discourse on India is as much problematic as the representation of alien culture in anthropological discourse (see Das, 1995). This has come to light prominently from the works of Louis Dumont. In this discourse, Indian anthropologist is seen as an informant imbued in his or her social values and represents 'otherness' of own culture. Further he or she also suffers from the failure to transcend own ideology through an intellectual appropriation of other values according to Dumont (ibid.: 32-33). Dumont claims that the western anthropologist, being an enlightened modern person, is able to transcend from his own ideology and comprehends the values of other cultures intellectually. But Saran refutes this claim and according to him the so-called 'privileged external view' is an interpretation of Indian culture through the categories of the west (Saran, 1962). Srinivas (1996) also dismisses the 'privileged external view' as the 'otherness' spread over the length and breadth of the Indian subcontinent. In Burghart's view Dumont represents Brahmanical view of Hindu society (Burghart, 1990). In this regard Das writes, "In positioning the Brahmin as the only voice, Dumont was in fact participating in the creation of master narrative of Indian society that saw Brahmanic worldviews as somehow representing the whole of Indian Society" (Das, 1995:35). The post-modernist approach appears to offer some solution to the problem of representation of other culture from the 'privileged external view' by treating ethnography as a text (Clifford, 1990), but it does not seem to confront the problem and bestows authority entirely on the native anthropologist. Thus the problem of representation of alien cultures either by the western anthropologists or own culture of native anthropologists remains unresolved. It is my contention that the expressive traditions where actors speak themselves and offer critique of their own society persuade the anthropologist, either native or western, to consider diverse points of view of the social system which structures the lives of the actors. Here interpretation and explanation remains with the actors and the ethnographer provides the context and alludes to the facts referred to by the actors. In this perspective, we may note what Trawick states: "Present-day oral poetry is handled differently. It is incorporated into ethnographic accounts in which the central message is not the poem itself but the report of the ethnographer, his or her findings about the culture from which the poem springs" (Trawick, 1988:194).

The oral tradition of Indian women, though colonists attempt to project Indian women as passive and submissive to the dictates of the male dominated world of customs and traditions, and reformers attempt to silence the contestations of women, ethnography does, in fact, indicate the critique of the traditions and customs even though they actively participate in them (Raheja, 2003). Trawick's "Crying Songs" of Paraiyar women in Tamil Nadu stand out as unique creative genre that sprang up from the culture of exclusion and oppression of the traditions. The source of these songs is unambiguously non-Brahmanical. It is said that each singer makes up her own songs infusing her own experiences, wishes and fears, unique of her own into the songs. These songs represent some grievances that the singer has against some particular person of higher status than herself (Trawick, 1986: 297).

Society and Dalit Women

To some or great extent emotions play their roles in singing songs, and these emotions are essentially social rather than psychological as shown by Lutz and Abu-Lughod. According to them emotional discourses are linked up with two aspects of social relations: sociability and power (Lutz and Abu-Lughod, 1990: 11-14). This observation corroborates the findings of Lomax's global survey as stated earlier. Therefore, it is imperative to examine the social premise of the Dalit women before close attention is paid to the songs of the Dalit women.

The anthropological and sociological construction of Indian society has been diverse from structuralist, ethnosociologist, Marxist and historicist points of view (Singh, 1986: 31-62). I consider only the first one here. Of these four views, Louis Dumont's structuralist view, rooted in tradition, has dominant influence on the understanding of caste system and Indian civilization as well. He finds unity of India through ideology of values; hierarchy in terms of the values of purity and pollution and encompassing of religion. In this perspective, man encompasses woman in a hierarchy where man is superior to woman (Dumont, 1980: 239-242). The caste system that has remained unchanging over the centuries is the basic framework on which Indian society is organized. It hinges on the firmly grounded hierarchy of castes based on the values of purity and pollution. Michael Moffatt (1975) and Dennis McGilvray (1983) also endorse Dumont's views from their empirical studies of untouchable castes in Tamil Nadu and Sri Lanka.

In this structuralists' sight, Dalit (Harijan) are the archetype of pollution in contrast to purity embodied in the Brahmin. Dalits' touch, shadow, breath and even mere presence pollutes the upper castes. Their occupations such as manual labour, scavenging, handling of dead animals, skinning animals, making leather goods, carrying out the cremation of upper castes and so on are considered menial and polluting. Their habits of eating carrion, non-vegetarian foods, drinking liquor and other intoxicants are loathsome to upper castes. Their uncontrolled tongue and behaviour demands the upper castes to keep them far away. The sight of shabby houses, unkept, barely clad men and women do not appeal to the upper castes either. They are apathetically looked down and subjected to several restrictions such as no entry to the temples, not to draw water from the wells of the upper castes, not to use footwear, not to hold an umbrella, not to ride a horse or a bicycle in the streets of the upper castes and so on. This is the polarity between Dalits and others viewed by the structuralists.

The social structure has also been viewed from another important perspective – 'caste', 'class' and 'power' (Beteille, 1965), where inequality forms an important analytic isolate that play very significant role in the structuring of the social system. All these parameters that structure the Indian society favour the upper castes and are intrinsic to caste system. The upper castes control both economic and political life as well of the Dalit. They hold claim on all material sources and the Dalit have been dependent on them for day-to-day survival for ages. They remained as voices of the powerless till recently and have been subjects of all types of exploitation – economic, political and sexual. Any literature on Dalits is replete with exploitation, subjugation, exclusion and commission of atrocities by the upper castes.

Only after independence the amelioration of the situation of Dalits started through various means – legislation and voluntary services – owing to the crusades against discrimination and exploitation initiated by Ambedkar. The integrative approach of Gandhi and several others and protective discriminatory policies of the Government have helped the conditions to improve. Though statutes have abolished untouchability in any form since independence, it still exists in several invisible forms in urban areas and does exist in visible forms in several villages. The conversion of some Dalits to Christianity, Islam and Buddhism has made some impact on their socio-economic life but there is hardly any change in the hierarchical social relationships between higher castes and Dalits particularly in the rural areas. The gap in economic and political fields ever remains considerably between the upper castes and the Dalit.

Like their counterparts Dalits are patriarchal, their women are subjected to men. Women are not decision makers for their castes or communities, and men arrange their marriages. They are expected to be committed and loyal to their husbands. They have to earn wages like their men besides taking care of the children, kitchen and guests. Widowhood does not entitle them for remarriage and their sexuality is controlled under strict surveillance, while men can remarry and flirt around. A Dalit woman poet has succinctly put the predicament of Dalit women as: "Dalit women's issues have less in common with Dalit men's issues than with those of the upper caste women. If there is any soul in this country who is subjected to all kinds of oppression and exploitation, it is the Dalit woman. On one side she is oppressed by the caste system, on the other side she is subjected to gender oppression and class exploitation. She is a Dalit among Dalits" (Challapalli, 1998: WS 21-22). Gopal Guru (1995) argues that the situation of Dalit women is different from that of the non-Dalit women and they have to simultaneously confront the problem of caste as well as patriarchal domination. Therefore, they should talk differently.

The Dalit women who sang songs are from Mala and Madiga castes inhabiting the villages of Thummala Thalupur, Kalichedu and Saidapuram in Gudur Mandalam of Nellore District, Andhra Pradesh. The songs were recorded during 1990-91. These Dalit women singers are wage labourers in the agricultural farms of upper castes. Some also work as labourers in the mica mines operated in these villages from 1950s. Two sub-castes, Harijan and Vetti Mala, constitute the Mala caste. While the traditional occupation associated with the caste system of Vetti Malas is to provide men as cremation attendants for the upper castes, weaving of a coarse cloth for general use by all and a special cloth for ritual purpose for the upper castes is the traditional occupation of the Harijans till recently, which has been given up now. Madiga's traditional occupation that continues till now is to remove the dead cattle such as buffalo, cow and ox, skin the animals and make footwear and leather goods. They are also to play drums on weddings and religious festivals of the village, which is considered a very mean activity. Both the castes are excluded from the main village where the upper caste families live, though they are included in the concept of village as a few of them are employed as village servants and their participation in the village activities is considered necessary.

Songs of Dalit Women

According to native classification, folk songs (*jana padlu*) are of two types – *devuni patalu* and *mamulu patalu*. The former are about praising gods – the devotional songs, and the latter are ordinary songs. These ordinary songs are again contrasted with cinema-*patalu*, film songs, from popular cinemas. *Mamulu* songs include *naretha patalu, nalugu patalu, gobbi patalu* and *jola patalu*. *Naretha patalu* are those sung during transplantation of paddy, ragi (a millet), onion, egg plant, tomato, chillies and the like. These songs are sung less frequently now than a few years before. *Nalugu patalu* are sung at weddings during *nalugu* (a rite). *Gobbi patalu* are actually religious songs sung only during Sankranti festival[2] in praise of gods and goddesses, but songs of this form that cover social themes are also included in this category which are sung at other times. *Jola patalu* are lullaby songs to put children to sleep.

Though these songs are classified according to the occasion or content, they belong to different genres. "Genres consist of regular groupings of thematic, stylistic, and compositional elements" (Hanks, 1987: 670). Following this definition the *nalugu, gobbi* and *jola patalau* are quite distinct in themes, style and composition, and belong to different genres. The *nalugu* songs are sung by the *muthaiduvalu* (married women whose husbands are alive) and these are blessings upon the bride or bridegroom or both, or sometimes upon the pregnant woman during *seemanthaṃ*[3] ceremony while praising gods and goddesses (see for details Rao, 1996: 70-73). However, the Dalit women while retaining the structure and style of the *nalugu* songs sing songs changing the content to make fun of the bride or bridegroom. The singers in this case are those who are in joking relationship with the bride or bridegroom. An example is as follows:

Thella kakara kaya, thalimpu vankaya
Palollo vurindi panasa pandu

Chala chakkani pandu chaliya gumma pandu
Andariki theepainna arati pandu
Jaya jaya mangalam jaya subha mangalam
Aa chanka noka bidda ee chanka noka bidda
Kadupulo bidda kadiladu thunte
Mudu chetla munagaku aaruchetla arataku
Chaladani ma vadina chatti nake
Jaya jaya mangalam jaya subha mangalam

White bitter gourd, fried brinjal (egg plant)
Jack fruit that got soaked in milk
Very beautiful fruit, chaliya pumpkin
Banana is very sweet to everyone
Let there will be victory and prosperity.
Baby on that side of the girdle and on this side as well
Baby inside the stomach is also moving
Drumstick leaves of three trees, banana leaves of six trees
As if not enough my sister-in-law licked the small earthen pot
Let there will be victory and prosperity.

In the above, the last line of the first stanza is repeated in the second stanza, and it is to bless the brother's wife, which appears in several of the *nalugu* songs. In the first stanza the image created is fruit as referent to the bride, in a way a complement, but in the second stanza, there is a wish of having several children, but then there is leg pulling in the last but one line. The sister-in-law is seen as a dissatisfied person despite abundance in the house.

Each of the *gobbi patalu* begins with *gobbiyyalo* and ends up with the same word as refrain as in the following:

Gobbiyyalo amasa purnana adivarana gobbiyyalo
Gobbiyyalo hecchuvai kudinde dudrasi vana gobbiyyalo
Gobbiyyalo ekkipoyi elugonda eduraku mese gobbiyyalo
Gobbiyyalo sagipoyi thageb chaviti neellu gobbiyyalo
Gobbiyyalo thirugochetappudu puliraju vacche gobbiyyalo
Gobbiyyalo emayya pulirajocchinavayya gobbiyyalo

Gobbiyyalo on the Sunday of full new moon day *gobbiyyalo*
.. terrible rain increased …
.. went ahead, climbed the hill fed on leaves..
..moved forward and drank salt water..
..while returning leopard king came across..
..oh leopard king why did you come?..

This is a story transformed as a song using the *gobbi pata* style. In this story, a cow goes to forest for grazing and on her return she encounters a leopard that says he would feast on her. Then the cow prays to the leopard for giving a day's time so that she can go home, suckle her only calf and come back to offer herself to the leopard. Then, the leopard relents to the cow's request, and the cow returns home and suckles the calf. She gives instructions how to lead a good life before coming back to the forest to offer herself to the leopard. Then the leopard refuses to eat the honest and sincere cow that kept her promise. This beautiful story is sung in such a manner using the *gobbi* style that all the listeners remain spellbound and get emotionally charged.

Jola patalu contain the term *lali,* as in the following. These are usually short with two or three stanzas.

Lali lali yanuchu lali patalu padare
Buttalo pandesi balala jola patanu padare
Atha mamalaku kudu bettani kodalunde dekkada
Ukku sthambalakesi viraga deese dakkada
Lali lali yanuchu lali patalu padare

Saying lali sing songs of lali
Rest the baby in the basket and sing jola songs
Where will be daughter-in-law that does not give food to parents-in-law?
There where people are tied at their back to the iron pillars
Saying lali sing songs of lali.

This particular song has a moral that the god of death, Yama, will punish the daughter-in-law that does not treat her parents-in-law properly.

One or a group of individuals sings *naretha* songs. These songs are usually long and differ greatly in theme, style and composition. Women bend and move backward in transplanting the seedlings and while doing so render these songs. When one or two persons sing, one or two other repeat which helps in three ways. The main singer(s) need a respite and also needs time to remember the next line or stanza. Repetition helps the audience to hear once again to understand the contents and also helps committing to memory. It is a learning technique or process; by repeating the songs in the same tune, the novice learns the songs. *Naretha* songs not only help people to bear with the tedium of work, but also they function as an outlet of emotions developed by frustration due to poverty, male domination, sexual harassment and so on. An example is as follows:

Ooru malada chanda ha ha gummadiyyalo
ha ha gummadiyyalo
Guruthugane chinta chettu ha ha gummadiyyalo
Neyyere salenna ha ha gummadiyyalo
Chintha chettuku magga meira ha ha
Gummadiyyalo
Nelakokka pogu neira ha ha gummadiyyalo
Kattu cheruguna rendu ha ha gummadiyyalo
Guvva pillala neiranna ha ha gummadiyyalo

Village is Mala hamlet of Chanda
Tamarind tree is the indicator …
Weaver weaves now…
Set your loom on the tamarind
tree …
Knit a row in a month…
Two at the border …
Brother, knit baby birds…

This is the song of Mala caste people who were traditionally weavers[4] and it is about weaving of a sari. *Gummadiyyalo* is a refrain, which does not have any meaning.

Modes of Singing

There are songs, which do not fall into any of the above categories, but are rendered as per the situation and context. These are often sung while weeding; women sometimes squat or bend during weeding operations and sing these songs. Some songs are rendered during leisure time at home either during day or night as an entertainment and to pass time. These are usually aimed at ridiculing the upper caste in the 'safe space' – private space – that is not accessible to upper castes.

When women are asked to sing songs they were very reluctant and felt shy, this is perhaps natural if a male stranger makes such a request, though not unreasonable. Even if the solicitor is a known male, women generally feel shy. Those who responded positively, first they proposed to sing devotional songs, which put them in a comfortable position as the listeners generally liked to listen to religious songs. Culturally it is that only women of bad reputation sing bawdy songs in public. Then they move on to film songs, particularly the younger singers. Middle-aged married women have sung romantic, suggestive, provocative and vulgar ones with persuasion and encouragement by my assistant in recording them. Folk songs are seemed to be on least priority in a situation such as this.

Women sing lullabies on their own accord without being asked by any one in an effort to quiet a crying babe and they do so loudly that it subdues the cry of the babe. They sing *nalugu* songs with certain demand by the organizers or the participants in order to make the entire occasion interesting and entertaining. The *naretha* songs are sung generally on the request of the co-workers or women sing the songs on their own interest to entertain and amuse the workers by putting down the landlord or men of upper caste women. The *gobbi patalu* follow simple dancing by forming a circle around *gobbi* (goddess represented by a ball of cow dung decorated with flowers, vermilion and turmeric powder) set on the ground in front of the house. The participants of any age move around the *gobbi*, by bending, clapping hands and standing erect and moving clockwise with back and forth movements. It is mandatory to worship *gobbi* goddesses with dance and songs. However, as mentioned above the style of the songs has been adopted for singing at the time of transplantation.

Of the songs collected, numbering more than seventy, some are incomplete because the singer forgot them, and some others are confusing, as they do not make much sense, since no proper meaning and significance can be derived and to whom the songs are addressed. Even the singers could not clearly explain, but laughed off saying that "they are like that". But what is obvious about the songs is that the singer sang very emotionally the songs on recollecting the memories of a dead child, difficulties faced by a woman in the conjugal family, harassment by sister-in-laws or parents-in-law, and desertion by husband and so on. They sang the other songs by distancing themselves with the protagonist without showing much emotion. This distance is more prominent in case of the songs whose theme centred on the violation of norms, moral code and ethics. Even in case of put down songs, where the other person, generally an upper caste person, is ridiculed, and in joking songs at *nalugu* the singers maintained anonymity and distance. In case of songs such as *jola patalu* or the songs that include names and people to be praised, the singers incorporated personal names of the addressee so as to receive his appreciation.

Styles of the Songs

The songs whose theme such as desertion by husband or lover that draw involvement of woman's spirit in it are monologic wherein the addressee, protagonist and singer are clear as in the following song:

> On the edge of the well golden tree
> Boy developed flower garden
> When I went to pluck two flowers
> Small scorpion bit me
> Venkataswamy I cannot forget you!
>
> The tamarind is from Golkonda
> The Valga fish has mouth
> While black pepper is ground near the house
> You are deceived by the smell and left me
> Venkataswamy I cannot forget you!

Here the protagonist laments for desertion of her lover, and here the addressee is apparent, the deserted lover, Venkataswamy. In such songs, the protagonist sometimes blames the woman who has bewitched, along with the man, and at times the song addresses someone to inform the husband the pain and agony of desertion. In the same style there are songs that comment or put down others or express love or passion as in the following:

> Oh my younger brother-in-law, fixing wood on the sides of the wall
> The chip of the wood had hit on my cheek, oh younger brother-in-law
> I am with inexpressible sadness
> If you and I become friends
> We will make ferry boat of flowers and float on it
> Oh my younger brother-in-law if flood comes we will role together.
>
> You do not have your folk, I do not have mine
> On the bank of the river we will build the house
> Oh my younger brother-in-law if flood comes we will role together.

I will fast on Monday and go to god's hill
I got a jewel like child
Oh my younger brother-in-law I forgot to tell the name.

Here, in this song, the protagonist proposes to elope with the husband's younger brother, which is considered immoral.

There are a number of very common type songs, consisting of a dialogue between the lovers, wife and husband, sister and brother, suitor and woman, etc. Sometimes in these songs there is an interlocutor also to fill the gap or to comment or give feedback to the listeners. In case of the song of lovers, one proposes and the other finds certain difficulty as in the following:

Woman: Oh boy raise crop in front of the village, Oh my boyfriend, I will watch it

Man: If I raise crop in front of the village, Oh my girlfriend who will pay the tax?

Woman: If you raise crop in front of the village, I will pay the tax.

Man: If you pay the tax, are you not going to be beaten up by your husband? Oh my girlfriend, are you not going to be beaten up by your husband?

Woman: Can't I sell my chain and pay the tax? Oh my boyfriend raise crop in front of the village.

Man: If you sell your chain and pay the tax, are you not going to be beaten up by your husband?

Woman: If my husband abuses me, Oh my boyfriend, shall I not say that it fell in well?

Man: If you say that it fell in the well, Oh my girlfriend, is he not going to drain the water and search in the mud?

Woman: If he drains the water and searches in the mud, Oh my boyfriend, shall I not say that frog has swallowed it?

Man: If you say that frog has swallowed it, Oh my girlfriend, is he not going to cut open the stomach of the frog?

In the same manner there is a song where the woman says to her lover who proposes to her that if her bangles are broken what reply she should give to her husband and the lover goes on suggesting some reasons. Yet, in some songs, the man proposes and makes promises and tries to lure her with golden ornaments, saris and the like and the woman refuses to accept any of them and sometimes says that he is ugly, immoral and so on. In some cases, the songs are about unfaithful husband, who comes home late and the wife refuses to admit him into the house. In case of sister and brother, there is a demand of sister from her brother for his daughter to be married to her son[5] as a compensation for not inheriting property from their father.

Themes of the Songs

Dalit Women against Caste: A married young Madiga woman sings the following song. The protagonist is a Madiga girl. There is a dialogue between the girl and a Brahmin who falls in love with the girl and involves himself into the most polluting activity of carrying carrion, butchering and eating a dead buffalo calf. The sexual relationship that follows degrades the Brahmin to a state of the lowest caste.

Interlocutor: Handsome Brahmin while praying in the lake
While praying, oh my brother!
A cunning Madiga damsel came that side
Cunning damsel came, oh my brother!
The Madiga damsel liked the Brahmin
Liked the man, oh my brother!

Madiga: "If you want, why don't you come, my Lord?"
Why don't you come my Lord, oh my brother!

Brahmin: "I don't know your village, I don't know you"
I don't know, oh my brother!

Madiga: "Compound wall all around and lime plastering"
Lime plastering, oh my brother!
Near lime plastering, village boundary!
Village boundary, oh my brother!
Near village boundary, the path of Suranna,
Suranna path, oh my brother!"

Brahmin: "I will come and I will come beautiful angel!"
Beautiful angel, oh my brother!"

Madiga: "In the compound of Reddy, a calf died"
Calf died, oh my brother!
Go and bring dragging its leg
Bring dragging, oh my brother!
Cut slowly with small knives
Cut slowly, oh my brother!
Brahmin: "How do I cut, I am a young Brahmin?"
Young Brahmin, oh my brother!
Madiga: "Put your *janjam* (sacred thread) on the peg"
On the peg, oh my brother!
Cut slowly with small knives
Cut widely with big knives
Cut slowly with big knives
Cut slowly, oh my brother!
Cut wide with big knives
Cut widely, oh my brother!
Interlocutor: Cooked delicious food with chilies and salt
Cooked delicious food, oh my brother!
Madiga: "You feed me first and last morsel"
You feed me Sir, oh my brother!
Brahmin: "How do I feed, my beautiful angel"
Beautiful angel, oh my brother!

In a poetic sense, the song is about two polar ends of the society – the Brahmin and the untouchable or Dalit. The pure, vegetarian Brahmin eats the most polluting carrion. However, for the singer, the song does not signify desecration but an attack on Brahmins and the upper castes. The upper castes attribute terrible impurity to the Madigas, but now the latter take symbolic revenge by making the young Brahmin fall in love with a Madiga girl, butcher a dead calf, eat it and have sex with the girl. This also conveys subtle implication that upper castes are not superior beings that have mastered sensuality; they are like any other human beings. In that sense, all humans are the same whether a Brahmin or Madiga.

Dalits refute the charges often made against them by the upper castes that they are lascivious and lack sexual controls or morals. Instead, the Dalit women make those charges against the upper castes.

Man: Open the door my lady, I am drenched in the storm, open the door lady

Woman: I won't open the door, who is the man that has come Lord?

Man: My beautiful lady, I am Ramakrishna who married you, Lady I am Ramakrishna.

Woman: In this night what purpose Ramakrishna has got with me, Lord what work have you got?

Man: My beautiful lady I came for your company, I desired and I have come appreciating you.

Woman: You go in the morning and eat there, you better go to the house of concubines, Lord you go to houses of Kapus[6].

Man: I brought sandalwood paste in a plate and a bunch of flower,

I brought them willingly and in appreciation of you.

Woman: The sandalwood paste and the flowers, you give them to the concubines.

The sandalwood paste and the flowers, you give them to the Kapus.

Man: I will give you ornaments, I will give you saris, I brought them willingly and in appreciation of you.

Woman: The ornaments and saris, you give them to the concubines.

The ornaments and saris, you give them to the concubines.

* * *

Woman: Look Krishna, you tend the cattle, how did you get body pains, Lord, where are the pains?

Man: In the bedroom and on the bed, I got the body pains, my lady, they are the pains of the bed.

Woman: On those golden ears, what are those spots, my Lord what are the spots?

Man: When I was playing a game, I got the turmeric (yellow) powder my lady, I got the turmeric powder.

Woman: On those golden ears, what are those black spots my Lord, what are those black spots?

Man: Oh! Those black spots, my Lady, when I rubbed *kasthuri* flower, the colour got on me.

Woman: You answer appropriately for all, you are learned Lord, you are learned.

This song is about two issues: caste and unfaithful husband. The protagonist asks the husband who he is when he comes home very late on a rainy night. He reveals his identity and attempts to please her, saying that he has brought aromatic paste, scented flowers, saris and ornaments, and she should let him come inside the house. She replies that she does not want them; instead he should give them to his concubines, Kapu (Reddy) women with whom he has spent all day. In the later lines, she suspects him involved in frolicking activities with these women. For the present, it can be noted that the high caste Kapu women are the concubines of a Dalit man.

There are a couple of songs which decry hard agricultural work and exploitation of an agricultural labourer. I present below a song of sexual exploitation by a high caste landlord when a Dalit woman is found at fault or in a helpless situation.

My cunning mother-in-law, *gongura*
Sent me for *gongura*
Sent me for *gongura*
I sneaked into the garden, *gongura*
The Reddy, owner of the garden came in, *gongura*
Snatched my hair, *gongura*
When he grabbed my hair, *gongura*
I didn't know the reason, *gongura*
That fellow said, Shiva, Shiva, *gongura*
That fellow lifted my sari, *gongura*
While he was lifting up the sari, *gongura*
I didn't know why he did so, *gongura*
That fellow said Rama, Rama, *gongura*
While he was untying my blouse, *gongura*
I didn't know why he did so, *gongura*
That fellow said Rama, Rama, *gongura*
That fellow put the spinner and rotated, *gongura*
I did not know the reason why he did so, *gongura*

Gongura is a plant, the leaves of which are consumable; a favourite dish is made out of them along with *dal* (a kind of lentil). The song describes the hypocritical behaviour of a high caste landlord. The landlord appears to be religious person because he always chants the names of the gods like Shiva and Rama, but he rapes a Dalit woman who is found stealing *gongura* in his garden. The woman abuses her mother-in-law for sending her to bring *gongura*. She does not protest because she was committing a crime, and her protest would disclose her theft. In order to cover up the offense she yielded to sexual exploitation; perhaps she thinks that her rape can be kept secret. In any case, the song portrays the hypocrisy and exploitation of the high castes.

Husband – a Snake and a Deserter: Typical of the poetic verse, the songs contain innumerable symbols or codes on a variety of thoughts, categories and items. It is interesting to note that in some songs of the Dalit woman, husband has been symbolized as a cobra, a venomous and deadly poisonous snake. Cobra is an ornament of Lord Shiva, who also keeps venom in his throat, and is the vehicle of Shiva's son, Subramanyam or Murugan. Cobra itself is worshipped as god, Subbarayudu, in Andhra Pradesh. A parallel is drawn between husband and cobra as both are to be worshipped. However, in general usage when cobra becomes a metaphor it carries the negative meaning of poison and death, that means that the husband is like a snake and not a god. Here is a song that describes husband as a cobra.

> I am given to a snake
> Every one got jewel but I got Rayudu, my God!
> Basket maker Medaranna, make a basket
> I will keep the basket on my waist and go on the jungle way
> I will go on the way.
> At the well's bank of golden Venkataiah,
> I will circumambulate the well and salute.
> If I get drowned in the well, what do people think?
> What do the crows, the people, think of me?
> Oh, the sinner parents gave me to a snake.

It is clear from the above that husband is symbolized as a snake. The woman laments for her bad husband and abuses her parents for getting her married to such a man. The snake charmers carry snakes in flat baskets and earn their livelihood by exhibiting them to people. Here, it implies that the husband is taken care of, for he does not provide any economic support and above all he is harmful. She intends to commit suicide by drowning herself in a well, but desists herself from doing so for the fear of public condemnation for her timid act.

The Hindu worldview conceptually divides social life into the roles of householder and *sanyasi* (or ascetic) structurally opposed to each other (Madan, 1982). The former role is concerned with family and material life whereas the ascetic role is concerned with the religious or spiritual life. Though women can become *sanysins*[7], it is difficult for them to leave children. The following song is a critique of the *sanyasi* life of a husband.

> Got up early morning the *sanyasi* fellow and went out
> This fellow pulled down (my life), oh young man!
> If it is said so, how do I feel, oh young man!
> As millet is ground between two houses,
> My fruit like husband is gone,
>
> Won by some one, oh young man!
> In short, short trees, as sticks are picked up, *sanyasi* fellow
> Set his eyes (on me) oh young man!
> Between the two houses, the lintel posts hit, the doorposts hit,
> My head gets pain, feel like dying, oh young man!
>
> Big, big plows, renowned plows, lengthy ropes, oh young man,
> Plow that field, oh young man!

The song basically repudiates the life of a *sanyasi* and also invites a young man to satisfy her sexual needs. The protagonist says that the husband left the house early in the morning never to return ruining her life, being deceived by a *sanyasi*. She invites a young man to plow implying to have sexual relationship with her for her sexual need has not been fulfilled because of desertion by her husband for religious reasons.

Hindu women are expected to be very faithful and loyal to their husbands. But there are a number of songs on the themes of extra-marital relationship with some one or husband's brother. Often it is the woman who initiates this kind of relationship, which is considered unconventional. According to the Hindu sexual moral code a widow is supposed to suppress her sexual desire, but a couple of songs are recorded which describe that widows would be too eager to have clandestine relationships. One of the songs is as follows:

> Go round, go round, oh moon! I am humble,
> Oh! Thief (Lord Krishna), you hide behind the clouds and help this widow
> Oh countless stars, the sisters who lift up and look,
> Oh! Thief (Lord Krishna), you hide behind the clouds and help this widow
> At the well of drinking water, at the garden of flowers,
> You look back again and again (Lord Krishna), help this widow.

The song addresses the moon, which is personified as Lord Krishna. The moon and the night are associated with love affairs and clandestine meeting of the lovers. The relationship of Lord Krishna with women has been interpreted as having both sexual and spiritual meanings for he had many wives. Therefore, the widow pleads with moon, Lord Krishna, to do her the favour of hiding behind the clouds so that in the twilight she meets her lover in the garden of jasmine flowers. We note here that widow is longing to get her sexual desires satisfied which goes against the Hindu moral code.

The above songs convey Dalit woman's concern about caste and spiritual superiority, man's venomous nature, negligence of wife and family, physical domination, desire for forced physical relations in marriage. The women discredit caste or man's domination over her and speak out her sacrificial nature. She desires to enjoy the freedom of a man in marital relations and to possess equal status.

Brother-Sister Relations: Daughters do not inherit property while the sons do so from the father in Hindu society; yet a brother and sister are expected to love each other, show concern for the welfare of each other though they maintain separate and independent houses. More than that in South India, their children do get married and an ideal marriage is a cross-cousin marriage. This type of marriage and South Indian kinship has drawn a lot of interest among the South Asian anthropologists. Here what is to be noted is the mutual claim of brother and sister on each other's children. At times, taking into account economic considerations, they violate the norm by giving away their daughters to some one economically better off instead of brother or sister's son. In the following song, the woman challenges her brother.

Brother: Who are you all in the house? Tell me in detail.

Sister: Brother, I who was born and raised with you.
I am Subhadra, my brother Balabhadra, your sister!
Brother, if I am a male like you, I would have built a house in the lane
I would have built a house in the lane and demanded half of the property,
Brother, give your little daughter to my little son for marriage
Give in marriage my brother.

Brother: My sister, I cannot give my little daughter to your little son in marriage

Sister: Brother, you may give or may not give,
When I die, I will be born as a thorny bush in your house.

A sister comes to her natal home from her conjugal home when her brother is absent. When her brother comes home, he inquires from outside about those in the house. She replies that she is his sister. Since she is a female child of their parents, she did not inherit any property, and therefore, she is poor. Otherwise, she would have got half of the property and built a nice building. Now she demands that his daughter should be given to her son in marriage. The brother refuses her proposal, perhaps for the reasons that she is poor. She gets annoyed at this and threatens or curses that she will take birth as a thorny bush right in his house, which means she will cause innumerable problems to her brother's family. This clearly shows woman's displeasure over discrimination against a girl child in the inheritance of property and authoritative behaviour of the male children.

Conjugal Family of Woman: After marriage a woman gets incorporated into the family of her husband. Ideally, she has to devote herself to her husband, his parents and her children as a faithful wife, pious daughter-in-law and loving mother. People are expected to follow an ideal life, but reality is often different. Umpteen numbers of cases appear every day in newspapers about harassing parents-in-law, unconcerned or hen-pecked husbands and suicides of daughters-in-law. Daughters-in-law in reality are not submissive in every case, they do protest, talk back and ill-treat the conjugal family members. Here is a song that shows woman's bitterness against her conjugal family members in strongest terms.

> My lord, on the way of coming and going, there is mother-in-law's plank
> If parents-in-law die, my lord, my mind feels extremely good,
> If husband's brothers die, my lord, I throw the cart and the bucket there itself,
> If my husband's brother's wife dies, my lord, I wear red sari,
> If my husband's sisters die, my lord, I go from shop to shop,
> If relatives die, my lord, I roll them and put them on the roof,
> If the man who married me dies, my lord, I will sprinkle chilli powder in his eyes
> If my lover lives, my lord, I owe promises to god Venkataramana.

The song clearly says that the woman feels happy for the death of any member in her conjugal family where there is play of power, authority, restriction, deference and suffering. She desires that her lover should live long. This actually means her longing for love, unconditional affection, friendship and support.

Poverty and Social Codes: In several of the songs, the lover is unidentified, but in other songs, he is identified as a high caste person. However, there are quite a few songs where the lover is none other than the husband's younger brother. Since generally a man marries at least one or two years' (sometimes even ten years') younger woman, the man's younger brother would be of the same age as his older brother's wife. In ideal maintenance of social relations, the relationship between sister-in-law and brother-in-law is that of filial and characterized by affective parental relationship. This construction prohibits sexual relationship between the two but there are several songs on this theme. Their relationship is considered immoral. There is another unconventional and considered sinful relationship, between father's younger brother and brother's daughter, which is as follows:

> Woman: *Chinnayana, Chinnayana,* I want to come with you,
>
> Man: Oh my daughter, if you come with me people will blame you,
>
> Woman: At the toddy shop, *chinnayana,* buy me a sari,
>
> Man: I can buy you a sari, Oh my daughter, but people will blame you,
>
> Woman: At the market of Kovuru, *chinnayana,* buy me a new sari,

Man: I can buy you a sari, Oh my daughter, but people will blame you.

The woman proposes to go with her father's younger brother, which implies that she wants to be his wife or mistress. He replies that he is afraid of people's aspersions on her being immoral and sinful. She persuades and requests him to buy a sari at a toddy shop. He says he can buy a sari, but she should not follow him. As this is the basic idea the song continues changing the places and towns like Kovuru, Guduru and so on. First it appears the woman is after the man, but closer examination reveals that she is interested in sari, and because of this, she does not care whether her relationship is within the social code or not. She is extremely impoverished; there is no one to take care of her needs. For a poor woman it does not matter with whom she may live, and she ignores whether the relationship is right or wrong. It overlooks deliberately the social norms and moral codes.

The following is a short song that depicts relationship of a young woman and an old man, and it is a dialogue between friends and the woman.

Friends: Oh broom stalk! How did you stick to him?

Woman: Wait folks, rainy season is ensuing

Friends: The broom stalk is matured, food is prepared
Stir father stir, roll father roll
Oh baldhead, baldhead – woman!
Hay girl! Your husband is good!
(He) went to the town and brought fried lentils.

Woman: My *mama* is good, he brought jasmine flowers

Man: If he sits he can't rise, he can't remove the pot from the hearth

The song is full of metaphors and symbols. The woman is called broom stalk. Binding a few fine and thin stalks of the *cheepuru* bush, a kind of grass, makes the broomstick called *cheepuru*. The inflorescence of the stalk contains numerous seeds; each seed has sharp point and a long tail. They fall off easily, stick to animals, clothes etc., and start pricking. The woman is compared to the stalk as well as the seed. She seems to be thin and easily 'sticks' to people. The friends found that her husband is bald headed old man and therefore, they ask her how did she pursue him to marry. Her reply is that they should keep quiet as rainy days are at hand. The rainy season implies unemployment and starvation because people cannot come out of the houses and work in the rains. They comment, though he is old, he is good man as he brought fried lentils and jasmine flowers from the town. He is old that he cannot move around, which means that he cannot give sexual pleasure. If she goes to earn and if he remains at home he will not be able to cook food also. The woman replies that it does not matter much because he loves her.

There are several songs that depict lax morality and incestuous relations. Such descriptions are hilarious for listeners, but the implications of these songs point to the dependency of women on men and the abject poverty experienced by them. The Dalits are 'excluded' because of their habits from the 'moral' community of upper castes, yet they are expected to adhere to the social rules that other castes follow. Breaking of these social norms signals an escape from frustration and suffering. All Dalits, for that matter, are expected to follow the social moral codes, and a deviation from those codes, knowing the consequences, results sometimes from a compulsion due to circumstances. In the case of Dalits, such compulsions or pressures emerge from poverty. Trawick explains this phenomenon differently; those who are strictly governed by rules tend to deviate in fantasy. She writes, "Still, it is not unreasonable to think that people whose lives are especially damaged by adherence of rules of Indian society might be especially inclined to break rules in fantasy" (Trawick 1990: 248).

This explanation holds true in the cases where songs express longing for a lover or husband's younger brother or any forbidden relationship. But for the songs mentioned above, economic compulsion seems to be primary cause for deviation from the normative social order.

Conclusion

The songs are inadequately interpreted due to space constraints. Nevertheless, the songs convey the points of view held by Dalit women about their society. On the basis of the perceptions of Dalit women regarding caste, doubts arise on the structuralist perspective of caste based on the values of purity and pollution. The voices of Dalit women are loud and clear to send the message of their longing for freedom that man enjoys, speaking about gender equality. They shun discrimination either on the basis of caste or gender. The material basis of the songs is unambiguously social – the deprivation of women from equal treatment either at the level of caste or gender statuses that are linked to the economic factors directly and indirectly. These songs can be taken as a form of resistance against the social system in which Dalit woman are located in the formulations of James Scot's *Everyday Forms of Resistance* (1989). The forms of resistance are indicative of power relations between ideologies, castes and individuals, and these forms involve subjugation. In the process of subjugation, there is freedom for the actors to resist the domination of ideology and of individuals. Though freedom is essential for power to exist according to Foucault (Dreyfus and Rabinow, 1982: 221), it can be neither freely and completely awarded nor completely denied to subordinates. Either situation would be dangerous for power's own existence.

Given the social structural constraints, Dalit women could not openly come out to show their resistance at least in the past, but I believe they have been subverters of the social order. They do show deference to the traditions and customs but cannot remain silent to the unjustified treatment meted to them and therefore, critique the system in passive ways and means. As subverters they used symbols of dominators with different interpretations not really causing any threat to domination. But this use of symbols influences other subordinates to resist the ideological domination of superiors.

Notes

1. The Ex-Untouchable castes today call themselves as Dalits which means, those oppressed. Here the Dalit include both Mala and Madiga castes which predominate in the government's category of Scheduled Castes.
2. It is a festival of harvest, celebrated in January of every year.
3. It is a ritual performed for the pregnant women when the fetus is 24 weeks old.
4. The upper caste Sale are traditional weavers even today. But Mala (Harijan), the Dalit caste, also used to practice weaving as an occupation, which has been given up in this area.
5. This is because of the fact that cross-cousin marriage in the region is a prescriptive form of marriage.

6. Kapu is a land owning farming upper caste and some families of this caste employ Mala or Madiga men as farm servants for a year or certain period of time, which is renewable.
7. Masculine *sanyasi* and feminine *sanyasin*.

References

Beteille, Andre (1965), *Caste, Class and Power: Changing Patterns of Stratification in a Tanjore Village,* Berkeley: University of California Press.

Burghart, Richard (1990), Ethnographers and their local counterparts in India, In R. Fardon (ed.), *Localizing Strategies: Regional Traditions of Ethnographic,* Edinburgh: Scottish Academic Press, 260-78.

Challapalli, Swaroopa Rani (1998), Dalit Women's Writing in Telugu, *Economic and Political Weekly.* XXXIII (17), April 25: WS-21-24.

Clifford, James (1990), Introduction: Partial Truths, In James Clifford and George E. Marcus (eds.), *Writing Culture: The Poetics and Politics of Ethnography,* 1-27, Delhi: Oxford University Press.

McGilvray, Dennis (1983), Paraiyar Drummers of Sri Lanka: Consensus and Constraint in an Untouchable Caste, *American Anthropologist,* 10 (1), 97-115.

Das, Veena (1995), *Critical Events : An Anthropological Perspective on Contemporary India,* Delhi: Oxford University Press.

Dreyfus, H. and Rabinow (1982), *Michael Foucault, Beyond Structuralism and Hermeneutics,* Chicago: University of Chicago Press.

Dumont, Louis (1980), *Homo Hierarchicus,* Chicago: Chicago University Press.

Guru, Gopal (1995), Dalit Women Talk Differently, *Economic and Political Weekly,* XXX (41 and 42), October 14-21, 2548-2550.

Hanks, William (1987), Discourse Genres in a Theory of Practice, *American Ethnologist,* 14 (4), 668-692.

Lomax, Alan (1968), *Folk Song Style and Culture,* New Jersey: Transaction Books.

Lutz, C. and L. Abu-Lughod (1990), *Language and Politics of Emotion,* New York: Cambridge University Press.

Madan, T.N. (1982), *Way of Life-King, Householder, Renouncer: Essays in Honour of Louis Dumont,* New Delhi: Vikas.

Moffatt, Michael (1979), *An Untouchable Community in South India: Structure and Consensus,* Princeton, New Jersey: Princeton University Press.

Raheja, Gloria Goodwin (2003), *Songs, Stories, Lives: Gendered Dialogues and Cultural Critique*, New Delhi: Kali for Women.

Rao, N.S. (1996), Transformative Rituals among Hindu Women in the Telugu Region, *Contributions to Indian Sociology*, 30 (1), 69-88.

Saran, A.K. (1962), Review of Contributions to Indian Sociology's, N.S.IV, *Eastern Anthropologist*, XV, 53-68.

Scott, James (1989), Everyday Forms of Resistance, In Forest D. Colburn (ed.), *Everyday Forms of Peasant* Resistance, New York: M.E. Sharpe Inc.

Singh, Y. (1986), *Indian Sociology: Social Conditioning and Emerging Concerns*, New Delhi: Vistaar Publications.

Srinivas, M.N. (1996), Indian Anthropologists and the Study of Indian Culture, *Economic and Political Weekly*, XXXI (11), March: 656-657.

Trawick, Margret (1986), Internal Iconicity in Paraiyar "Crying Songs", In Stuart H. Blackburn and A.K. Ramanujan (eds.), *Another Harmony*, 294-344, Delhi: Oxford University Press.

— (1988), Spirit and Voices in Tamil Songs, *American Ethnologist*, 15 (2), 193-215.

— (1990), Untouchability and the Fear of Death in a Tamil Song, In Lutz A. Catherine and Lila Abu-Lughod (eds.), *Language and Politics of Emotion*, Cambridge: University of Cambridge Press.

Part II

Marriage and Family

It should come as no surprise that most of our submissions dealt with women in the context of their roles in family life. The studies we find in this section range across the stages of female lives from potential bride to widowhood. They link the lives of girls and women to the future desired. They show that the laws and population policy are strongly linked to the religious communities and patriarchal culture introduced in the first part. The interplay with women's health and girls' education indicate the progress India has made and has yet to make.

Girls are still in the picture of what should be adult roles as D. Radha Devi's major demographic study of age at marriage reveals. The importance of having the big picture and data from across the nation is clearly demonstrated in this household and district level assessment of progress toward the vision proposed in National Population Policy. That vision preferred a marriage pattern of adults, age 21 and over, rather than the many younger brides still common in several northern states. With information from the Rapid Household Survey on Reproductive and Child Health (RCH), Chapter 6 begins with a detailed discussion and graphic displays of how far we have come and how far we have yet to go in freeing women from limited lives which result from too quickly transferring girls to husband's families. At the district level the correlates of development – residential location, caste, literacy, socio-economic status – are intricately linked to opportunities for girls' education prior to marriage and closely tied to the disparity in regional advancement across India. Methodologically, the use of means for household data and median age at marriage for districts show the variety in bride's experiences in India as well as uniformity in some regions with many important development correlations. The classification of age at marriage as child, early, acceptable, and preferred helped present the numeric information in a normative way.

The arranging of marriages has evolved with the dispersal of people in modernizing India. In Chapter 7, Chauhan demonstrates how the use of newspaper matrimonials in the search for prospective brides and grooms reveals the increasing importance of social class characteristics along with traditional caste and suitable personal qualities. Her study recalls some of the earliest analyses of cultural change in the West from the 1960s and 70s which used the historical change in short story fiction from women's magazines to document the changing roles of women in American society (Safilios-Rothschild, 1972, Chapter 2). This unobtrusive measure of social change provides an interesting demonstration of a relatively inexpensive tool for studying this prelude to marriage for women and men. It is instructive, also, to see this kind of method and material used in a gender and development framework. The limitations of focusing on an English daily paper can easily be extended by use of regional papers in different languages. (Editors Note: For our non-Indian readers – 'homely' refers to good domestic skills and interests.)

The darker side of marriage and family is domestic violence and those least likely to be aware of women's rights – rural women – are the victims studied in our third selection. In Chapter 8, Menon and Johnson use data from the National Family and Health Survey (NFHS) but also multivariate analysis to reveal the contribution of various factors to the explanation of an indicator of domestic violence. What is exciting about their study is both the detailed introduction to the information available and how it becomes the indicators to test a variety of hypotheses, but also how many of their reasonable expectations are contradicted by the data. They uncover not monolithic patriarchy but interesting challenges to the contemporary thinking about domestic violence in India. The restriction of the project to rural married women living with their husbands, drops the sample size to 50,000, but also reveals the diversity of women's lives today. Would the hypotheses or findings hold for the urban portion of the NFHS? The answer to that question awaits another research project to replicate and extend their findings. At least they have moved us beyond correlations and trends.

Augustine takes up a very different topic for the family in Chapter 9 – matriliny. Though this form is limited in practice, this study demonstrates the sociological value of studying the deviant pattern to learn more about the normative while revealing the variation. Through a careful introduction to the historically matrilineal Nair society of Kerala in South India and contemporary case studies, she reveals some lingering influences in the familial identity. While this chapter cannot reveal the depth of detail in her forthcoming book, we see the narratives of a few subjects in support of the conclusions and a spreadsheet of key characteristics used to analyse the findings. The other group she explores is the matriliny practicing Khasi of Meghalaya. Again through interviews she outlines the slow transformation of this family system with modern living and immigration to the cities. Still it persists, so marriage and family impacts women's lives differently there. This is a small population, but a distinctive practice from tribal culture. It is the second chapter of the collection to introduce us to the diversity of tribal experience and demonstrates the value of such first hand empirical work in debunking myths and stereotypes.

The last stage of many women's lives is widowhood. Joseph reveals how the laws which deal with this disruptive experience still vary by religious community in India with significant consequences for women's lives. This is particularly true for younger women, not just the elderly, in a culture where child marriage and wider age variation among couples is sanctioned. The framework employed for this comparative study of Hindu, Muslim, and Christian law relevant to widows examines remarriage, possessions and inheritance or property control, adoptions, and guardianship in varying degrees for these religious communities. Chapter 10 also displays the lack of monolithic character within these personal laws given major divisions by schools of practice for all Hindu and Muslim groups. It would help to see a fuller reference to the diversity within Christian communities, but their proportions are more limited in most parts of India. She advocates uniform civil code as a mechanism to bring women more rights and to achieve equality that will help advance the country as a whole.

In the last entry in this section, Prasad returns to this RCH data for a more political analysis of how much population policy affects the lives of women in India today, especially through a focus on reproductive health. The national and international goals (Cairo 1995), which initiated such a massive data collection effort, speak profoundly to the importance of paying attention to women's health and education rather than population control for developing India's future. In examining the southern state of Andhra Pradesh in particular, she provides the kind of analytical focus needed to address policy at the state level as well as the nation. By reviewing the historic positions on population, Chapter 11 bridges the gap between what public officials in India and abroad think regarding policy and what demographic data reveal about disparities in women's health in the implementation of policy.

We come full circle with survey data of household and district level demographic information, content analysis of media, women and household surveys of family life, interviews couched in historical context, comparative analysis of religious community laws, and back to health and development indicators especially for evaluating a state and its policies. Many ways to study women in their family roles.

6

Timing of Marriage in India

Vision and Reality[1]

D. RADHA DEVI

Importance of the Study

Age at marriage is a subject of great practical importance as it is related to both socio-economic antecedents and attainments (Call and Otto, 1977), though its importance is recognized mostly by demographers than scholars of other disciplines. Davis and Blake (1956) treated age at marriage as a prominent variable in the context of reproductive control. McDonald (1981) writes that "in demography age at marriage occupies a predominant place as one of the proximate determinants of fertility and any respectable discussion of fertility trends or determinants refers to the level of age at marriage, at least for women".

Age at marriage is also a key intervening variable in the status attainment process (Bartz and Nye, 1970). This is based on the assumption that, other things remaining constant, late marriage will help to give opportunities for increase in educational attainment and obtain better occupation and better income – all of which are regarded as status indicators. "All these opportunities, which are virtually closed to a girl who marries at 15 or 16, will not only help women understand the value of spacing children and limiting family size later, but also will enable them to play more active roles in family, community, and national development" (Population Reports, 1979). It is also argued that postponement of marriage will make both girls and boys mature mentally and emotionally. A mature couple will have high quality verbal interaction which can affect emotional closeness and sharing of private thoughts, values and concerns – all necessary ingredients for marital adjustments – than a couple that start marriage at an early age (Westoff and Ryder, 1977).

The effect of late marriage on reproduction through shortening the reproductive life span has been recognized even from the time of Thomas Robert Malthus who advocated postponement of marriage as a preventive check to high fertility (Malthus, 1798). Since then many scholars have made known its fertility depressing effect in varying social set-up (Davis and Blake, 1956; Freedman, 1979; Goyal, 1964; Coale, 1965; Agarwala, 1966; Van de Valle, 1972; Coale, 1973; Westoff and Ryder, 1977; Malhotra, 1997). However, reproduction is not the only function of marriage. Marriage heralds the beginning of a new family unit with all the complicated roles and statuses which the members of this unit are expected to play. As such, it is wrong to perceive it only as a reproductive unit, though it is difficult to separate the specific functions of marriage from the broader functions of the family as marriage is an integral part of the institution of the family (McDonald, 1981). In all the societies of the world there are four main functions for a family – reproduction, maintenance, placement and socialization (Davis, 1973), though the stress on each of these functions vary widely from culture to culture. In India, age at marriage is given particular importance in the context of reproduction.

Purpose of this Research

The vision India cherishes is to have the girls married off only after they attain 20 years of age, at least not before 18 years. This is clearly stated as one of the goals set by the National Population Policy, 2000 to be achieved by 2010 (Government of India, 2000). The policy stress is on decentralized planning which calls for information on age at marriage at the micro level not only to prepare the action plan but also to evaluate whether changes are really taking place as desired by the policy at the grass-root level. In this context a study on currently prevailing age at marriage at district[2] level is, indeed, a necessity. Furthermore, such a study is overdue considering the fact that an evaluation of the effect of the Minimum Age at Marriage Act on the behaviour patterns of the people has not yet taken place, even though the Government has been increasing the legal minimum age at marriage from time to time.

Available district level studies on age at marriage are based on small samples and restricted to a few districts (Audinarayana, 1990) or based on estimations obtained from census data (Bhagat, 2002). State level studies based on large scale surveys are also estimations (IIPS and ORC-MACRO, 2000) and conceal a large amount of internal variations. Studies based on actual data on age at marriage of those who got married during a specified time period at the district level for all the districts in the country has not yet been undertaken. It is felt that such a study will portray the real age at marriage situation than any estimations.

The data for the study came from the district level Rapid Household Survey on Reproductive and Child Health (RCH) conducted by the Department of Family Welfare, Ministry of Health and Family Welfare, Government of India launched during 1998-99. From each district, samples of 1,100 households were selected using circular systematic random sampling technique.

The household schedule of this survey has two questions specifically relating to the current age at marriage of girls and boys. The survey was carried out in two phases and the reference period for marriage data was three years prior to the survey. In 1995, there were 506 districts in India and data were collected from 504 (two were omitted because of some problems that prevailed in those districts at the time of survey). On the whole a total of 53,410 marriages of girls of at least ten years were reported from the 529,777 households enumerated in India.

In this study, for easy reference, marriages will be classified into four categories based on completed age at marriage. They are 10-14 years (child marriage), 15-17 years (early marriage), 18-19 years (acceptable marriage) and 20 years and above (preferred marriage). These demarcations of ages are not totally arbitrary. Taking a cue from the generally accepted classification of population below 15 years of age as children, those marriages are classified as child marriage. The legal minimum age at marriage for girls being 18 years, all marriages between age 15 and 17 (both ages inclusive) are taken as early marriage. However, as stated elsewhere in this paper, the Government of India would prefer to have "all marriages of girls to be postponed till they attained 20 years of age, at least not before 18 years". Thus, marriages at age 18 and 19 is taken as 'acceptable marriage' and marriages after the completion of age 20 is considered as 'preferred marriage'. Marriages before 18 years "had profound physical, intellectual and psychological consequences for girls. It also meant premature pregnancy and often lead to a lifetime of domestic and sexual subservience" (French, 2001).

General Situation

India is a vast country marked more by heterogeneity than by homogeneity. The customs and norms vary from state to state; from religion to religion. Cultural variations by caste, place of residence, education and level of wealth are general knowledge. But marriage is an institution, which is common to all and is universal. However, all marriages are not registered. Most of the marriages are solemnized through religious functions.

In many parts of the country, high fertility is still the norm – particularly in places where the son preference is very strong. In the absence of large scale use of contraception, early marriage generally leads to early and repeated pregnancies in quick succession, which is injurious to the health of both mother and child. Recognizing the adverse effect of early marriage and early parenthood on the mental and physical health of the girl and her child, the then Government passed the Child Marriage Restraint Act, 1929 which is an important milestone in the path to increase the age at marriage for girls and boys. This Act fixed the minimum age of marriage for girls to 14 years and for boys to 18 years. Later, the Government of India in its avowed policy of improving the health of women, reducing the fertility level and increasing the status of women, found the legal minimum too low and amended the Act in 1949 raising the minimum age at marriage for girls to 15 years (IIPS, 1995). But the age at marriage remained low and fertility was reluctant to come down. The Government then passed the Child Marriage Restraint (Amendment) Act, 1978 that increased the minimum age at marriage for girls to 18 years and for boys to 21 years and made offences under this Act cognisable.

Despite Government efforts at raising the age at marriage for both girls and boys, there were pressing social, religious and economic factors that reduced the pace with which the age at marriage has been increasing. Of the social variables that affect age at marriage, education stands out as a major one. Since education for girls after marriage is a very rare phenomenon in India, it stands to reason that those who spend more years in school naturally tend to get married late. The relationship between economic aspects and age at marriage has also been studied by many (Driver, 1963; Radha Devi, 1984; Singh and Richard, 1989) which indicates that low age at marriage is more common among the lower income groups or lower occupational groups.

This research deals with districts in this country and the importance given to states is only secondary. However, wherever states are mentioned it should be kept in mind that the three new states (Jharkhand, Uttaranchal, Chhatisgarh) will not be shown separately as they were not formed at the time of data collection. In other words, Jharkhand will be part of Bihar, Uttaranchal will be part of Uttar Pradesh and Chhatisgarh will be part of Madhya Pradesh.

In 2001, of the 32 states and union territories, 6 major states together accounted for 60 per cent of the total population. These states are Uttar Pradesh (17.0%), Bihar (10.7%), Maharashtra (9.4%), Madhya Pradesh (7.9%), West Bengal (7.8%) and Andhra Pradesh (7.4%). This indicates that with respect to any aspect, the situation prevailing in these states will get reflected at the all-India level. These six states can also be grouped into two, with Andhra Pradesh, Maharashtra and West Bengal in one and Bihar, Madhya Pradesh and Uttar Pradesh in the other according to the total fertility rate (TFR). The TFR of the former group varied between 2.5 and 2.8 in 1996 while that of the second group varied between 4.1 and 4.9.

Trend of Age at Marriage in India

The singulate mean age at marriage (SMAM) estimations for girls made using census data is given in Table 6.1. It shows that till 1951 it was below 15 years – quite an unacceptable situation. The increase since then has not been very fast.

Table 6.2 gives the SMAM for girls in the major[3] states from 1971 to 1998-99. The socio-cultural and economic diversity in the country is also reflected in the SMAM. In 1971 in all the 15 major states the SMAM was at least 15 years (the then prevailing legal minimum age at marriage). But it was just about 15 years in Bihar, Madhya Pradesh, Rajasthan and Uttar Pradesh. In these four states, the increase in SMAM during 1971-99 period was relatively high. The least increase was observed in Kerala where the age at marriage for girls was the highest even in 1971 – 21.3 years (a situation of 1.3 years above the envisioned age at marriage of 20 years in 2010 by the New National Population Policy, 2000).

Table 6.1

Singulate mean age at marriage for girls in India

Year	Singulate mean age at marriage	Addition made to age at marriage over the previous decade (years)
1901	13.1	**
1911	13.2	0.1
1921	13.7	0.5
1931	12.7	-1.0
1941	14.7	2.0
1951	15.6	0.9
1961	16.1	0.5
1971	17.2	1.1
1981	18.4	1.2
1991	19.3	0.9
1998-99	19.7	0.4

Source: Agarwala, 1966 and IIPS and ORC Macro, 2000.

Table 6.2

Singulate mean age at marriage for girls in India and major states

Sr. No.	Major States	Singulate Mean Age at Marriage				
		1971	1981	1991	1998-99	Diff. in SMAM 1971-99
1	Andhra Pradesh	16.3	17.3	18.3	18.3	2.0
2	Assam	18.7	Na	Na	21.7	3.0
3	Bihar	15.3	16.6	17.5	18.8	3.5
4	Gujarat	18.5	19.6	19.9	20.2	1.7
5	Haryana	17.7	17.9	18.8	19.8	2.1
6	Karnataka	17.9	19.3	20.1	20.1	2.2
7	Kerala	21.3	22.1	22.2	21.5	0.2
8	Madhya Pradesh	15.0	16.6	17.8	18.9	3.9
9	Maharashtra	17.6	18.8	19.7	19.8	2.2
10	Orissa	17.3	19.1	20.2	21.2	3.9
11	Punjab	20.1	21.1	21.0	22.1	2.0
12	Rajasthan	15.1	16.1	17.5	18.3	3.2
13	Tamil Nadu	19.6	20.3	20.9	20.9	1.3
14	Uttar Pradesh	15.5	16.7	18.0	19.0	3.5
15	West Bengal	18.0	19.3	19.7	19.6	1.6
	India	17.2	18.4	19.3	19.7	2.5

Source: IIPS and ORC Macro, 2000.

Data and Methods

Before actually discussing the findings, Table 6.3 describes the number of households surveyed and the number of marriages reported during the reference period along with the number of districts in each state. As can be seen, the smaller states and Union Territories together account for only 16.9 per cent of districts, 16.5 per cent of surveyed households and 12.9 per cent of total reported marriages. Hence all the tables will not contain the situation of the smaller states and Union Territories, though wherever necessary their situation will be explained in the text.

Table 6.3

Number of districts, households surveyed and number of marriages reported from major states and combined smaller states and Union Territories

Sr. No.	*Names of state*	*No. of districts*	*Households surveyed*		*Reported marriages*	
			Number	*Per cent to total*	*Number*	*Per cent to total*
MAJOR STATES						
1	Andhra Pradesh	23	24,034	4.5	1,610	3.0
2	Assam	22	23,817	4.5	1,734	3.3
3	Bihar	43	46,138	8.7	6,168	11.6
4	Gujarat	19	20,748	3.9	2,349	4.4
5	Haryana	17	17,537	3.3	2,104	3.9
6	Karnataka	20	21,253	4.0	2,450	4.6
7	Kerala	14	14,396	2.7	2,151	4.0
8	Madhya Pradesh	45	46,355	8.7	4,186	7.8
9	Maharashtra	30	32,176	6.1	3,542	6.6
10	Orissa	30	32,214	6.1	2,890	5.4
11	Punjab	17	18,014	3.4	2,282	4.3
12	Rajasthan	30	29,519	5.6	3,214	6.0
13	Tamil Nadu	23	23,850	4.5	2,355	4.4
14	Uttar Pradesh	68	72,262	13.6	7,245	13.6
15	West Bengal	18	19,923	3.8	2,238	4.2
Others(smaller states/union territories)		85	87,541	16.5	6,892	12.9
Total		504	529,777	100.0	53,410	100.0

Source: IIPS, 2001.

The marriage categories used for the analysis with respective marriage age group are provided in Table 6.4 for easy reference.

Table 6.4
Marriage categories

Sr. No.	*Marriage category*	*Age category*
1	Child (CM)	10-14
2	Early (EM)	15-17
3	Acceptable (AM)	18-19
4	Preferred (PM)	20+
	Total	10+

To save time, the rapid household survey of RCH did not include many background characteristics. Hence, the analysis in this study will be carried out only on the basis of limited characteristics, viz., place of residence, caste and economic status. Note that all these variables reflect the socio-economic status of the household in one way or the other. In the absence of data on education for the individual, the district level female literacy rate is considered in this study as an acceptable development variable. The median age will also be calculated and classified on the basis of the above age at marriage categories in this analysis.

Place of residence is either rural or urban. The socio-economic and cultural differences between the rural and urban areas are certain phenomenon in almost all countries of the world even though the rural to urban migration helps to dilute the situation a bit. However, in the major part of India this divide still persists and hence the need to differentiate and examine the prevailing age at marriage situation by place of residence. Generally, observation of traditional values and attitudes are more likely to be found in rural areas than in urban. Besides, in most cases the rural persons are comparatively less literate and less economically well off.

There are too many castes in India to have an individual classification. However, generally castes are grouped into a few categories. There are many castes that are socially and economically backward. With an intention to uplift their situation, the President of India is constitutionally empowered to declare a few castes as scheduled (SC) referring to their listing in Government rosters or schedules. Similarly there are tribes which are more like ethnic groups than castes who also need to be brought to the mainstream of the society. These are all categorized into one group called scheduled tribes (ST). Apart from these two, there are still people who belong to low socio-economic class and are, therefore, categorized into what is called 'Other Backward Class' (OBC). According to the Government policy these three categories are entitled to positive discrimination. All the rest of the castes which include mostly forward castes are usually referred to as 'Other Castes' (OC). In this study the castes will be grouped into two categories, viz., SC, ST and OBC in one group and OC in the other.

Type of house is used as a proxy for economic status. Houses are classified into *Pucca*, Semi-*pucca* and *Kachcha* on the basis of the materials used for construction of houses. Good construction is classified as *pucca* and very bad construction mainly by mud, leaves, tin, etc., are classified as *kachcha*. Semi-*pucca* falls in between *Pucca* and *Kachcha*. *Pucca*, semi-*pucca* and *Kachcha* houses represents high, medium and low economic status respectively.

Female literacy rate (FLR) is also classified as high, medium and low. If the FLR is less than 33.4 per cent, it is taken as low literacy level, between 33.4 and 66.6 is taken as medium literacy level and at least 66.7 per cent is taken as high literacy level.

Generally, for age at marriage analysis, only the average is used. However, here the actual data will also be analysed, to show the details concealed once the average is calculated. It will show the districts where child marriages and early marriages still persist and therefore require special attention from the administrators/policy makers – the main aim of this study.

Table 6.5 gives the background characteristics of the surveyed households in major states. It shows that, of the total selected households 78.9 per cent are from rural areas, 82 per cent belonged to Hindu religion, 61 per cent belonged to SC/ST/OBC and those living in Kachcha (low status) houses formed 39 per cent and those living in Pucca (high status) houses formed 29 per cent. The regional variation in Table 6.5 shows almost the same pattern though with differences in magnitude.

Table 6.5
Selected background characteristics of surveyed households

Sr. No.	States	Residence	Religion		Caste	Type of house	
		Rural	Hindu	Muslim	SC/ST/ OBC	Kachcha	Pucca
1	Andhra Pradesh	73.2	86.4	8.0	71.4	31.6	33.9
2	Assam	88.8	69.6	27.4	44.2	66.1	13.7
3	Bihar	87.9	84.7	13.8	79.3	62.3	16.8
4	Gujarat	66.0	90.1	7.9	57.6	21.6	48.1
5	Haryana	76.0	90.2	4.3	44.9	6.6	42.4
6	Karnataka	69.3	85.4	11.0	54.4	18.8	20.8
7	Kerala	74.6	59.2	21.4	66.2	9.7	56.1
8	Madhya Pradesh	76.5	93.4	4.6	76.5	66.7	17.4
9	Maharashtra	61.8	78.5	11.0	51.4	28.7	29.7
10	Orissa	86.2	95.6	2.0	73.3	70.9	14.6
11	Punjab	72.5	36.1	1.1	45.0	5.6	42.0
12	Rajasthan	77.6	90.0	6.8	53.7	31.8	50.2
13	Tamil Nadu	66.0	89.4	5.1	95.7	25.4	27.8
14	Uttar Pradesh	81.1	82.3	16.9	64.8	38.9	27 .3
15	West Bengal	73.0	74.6	24.2	37.0	60.9	20.5
	Total	78.9	82.1	11.8	60.6	39.0	29.2

Source: IIPS, 2001

Findings – Current Status

Among the total 53,410 marriages reported, 9.1, 26.2, 29.1 and 35.6 per cent respectively are child, early, acceptable and preferred marriages. Most of the total 4,850 child marriages are concentrated in the districts of four major states, viz. Bihar (22.4%), Madhya Pradesh (13.3%), Rajasthan (13.1%), and Uttar Pradesh (21.3%), together accounting for 70.1 per cent. West Bengal also has a fairly high share (6.8%) of the total child marriages. The important point to note here, however, is that almost two-thirds of the total marriages were conducted only after the girl attained legally acceptable age of 18 years with a fairly high per cent of preferred marriages.

Table 6.6

Percentage distribution of marriages by marriage category

Sr. No	State/Union Territories	Short form for states	Marriage category based on reported marriages				Total reported marriages	
			Child	Early	Accept-able	Pre-ferred	Per cent	Num-ber
MAJOR STATES								
1	Andhra Pradesh	AP	7.9	29.1	35.8	27.1	100.0	1610
2	Assam	ASM	4.3	21.9	25.6	48.3	100.0	1734
3	Bihar	BIH	17.6	39.8	25.1	17.5	100.0	6168
4	Gujarat	GUJ	4.9	20.0	31.2	43.9	100.0	2349
5	Haryana	HAR	4.4	25.1	34.9	35.6	100.0	2104
6	Karnataka	KAR	9.8	24.1	26.9	39.2	100.0	2450
7	Kerala	KER	0.0	8.5	23.2	68.3	100.0	2151
8	Madhya Pradesh	MP	15.4	36.2	28.0	20.4	100.0	4186
9	Maharashtra	MAH	6.2	26.0	38.3	29.4	100.0	3542
10	Orissa	ORI	4.4	28.3	24.4	43.0	100.0	2890
11	Punjab	PUN	1.3	9.6	27.6	61.6	100.0	2282
12	Rajasthan	RAJ	19.8	35.2	25.9	19.1	100.0	3214
13	Tamil Nadu	TN	1.3	16.4	28.5	53.8	100.0	2355
14	Uttar Pradesh	UP	14.3	32.9	30.1	22.7	100.0	7245
15	West Bengal	WB	14.8	35.9	23.3	26.0	100.0	2238
SMALLER STATES/UNION TERRITORIES								
16	Andaman & Nicobar	A&N	0.0	9.9	26.4	63.6	100.0	121
17	Arunachal Pradesh	ARP	3.2	28.4	36.5	32.0	100.0	532
18	Chandigarh	CHA	0.0	0.0	16.3	83.7	100.0	43
19	Dadra & Nagar Haveli	D&NH	14.8	35.8	27.2	22.2	100.0	81
20	Daman & Diu	D&D	0.4	16.2	36.3	47.0	100.0	234
21	Delhi	DEL	0.0	6.7	25.2	68.1	100.0	119
22	Goa	GOA	0.6	2.5	6.8	90.1	100.0	161
23	Himachal Pradesh	HP	0.1	3.3	27.7	68.8	100.0	937
24	Jammu & Kashmir	J&K	0.2	2.4	44.1	53.3	100.0	1641
25	Lakshadweep	LAK	0.0	18.2	33.3	48.4	100.0	159
26	Manipur	MAN	1.3	13.1	18.0	67.7	100.0	628
27	Meghalaya	MEG	0.5	1.6	44.9	52.9	100.0	425
28	Mizoram	MIZ	0.0	13.8	32.5	53.7	100.0	203
29	Nagaland	NAG	0.2	23.0	35.9	40.9	100.0	660
30	Pondicherry	PON	0.4	6.6	28.1	64.9	100.0	527
31	Sikkim	SIK	0.6	14.1	28.2	57.1	100.0	170
32	Tripura	TRI	4.4	28.3	25.9	41.4	100.0	251
	Total		9.1	26.2	29.1	35.6	100.0	53410

The state-wise distribution of age at marriage by category is given in Table 6.6. Of the total reported marriages more than 10 per cent of child marriage is observed only in Bihar (17.6%), Madhya Pradesh (15.4%), Rajasthan (19.8%), Uttar Pradesh (14.3%), West Bengal (14.8%) and Dadra and Nagar Haveli (14.8%). Conversely from Kerala, Andaman and Nicobar, Chandigarh, Delhi, Lakshadweep and Mizoram no child marriage is reported.

In Chandigarh no girl got married before attaining the legal minimum age at marriage of 18 years during the reference period. In Goa, Himachal Pradesh, Jammu & Kashmir and Meghalaya less than 5 per cent of the total marriages are found below 18 years of age.

On further analysis at district level, when examining the actual ages at marriage using the mean and median age at marriage, only one district (in Uttar Pradesh) revealed child marriage as the average. The median age at marriage is less than 18 years in Bihar, Madhya Pradesh, Rajasthan and West Bengal (for mean age at marriage replace West Bengal by Uttar Pradesh). The highest median of 24 years is in Goa. Among the major states the highest median age of 21 years is in Kerala, closely followed by Punjab and Tamil Nadu with a median age of 20 years.

Of the major states, Haryana, Kerala, Punjab and Tamil Nadu have no district with a median below 18 years of age and among smaller states and Union Territories all except Dadra & Nagar Haveli and one district in Nagaland fall in this category. However, a median of at least 20 years is found only in Chandigarh, Delhi, Goa, Himachal Pradesh, Jammu and Kashmir, Kerala, Manipur, Meghalaya, Mizoram, Pondicherry, Punjab, Sikkim and Tamil Nadu which together account for one in seven or a mere 15 per cent of the total Indian population.

The per cent of districts with at least a quarter of marriages below 18 years and per cent of districts with median age below 18 years is given in Table 6.7 and it shows that of the major states all except Kerala, Punjab and to a certain extent Tamil Nadu have a sizable per cent of districts with reported marriages falling in this category. But for median age, 72 per cent of the 43 districts in Bihar had a median below 18 years. This is followed by Rajasthan (63.3%), Madhya Pradesh (51.1%), West Bengal (50.0%) and Uttar Pradesh (50.0%), the latter with one below 15.

Table 6.7

Mean and Median Age at Marriage, per cent of Districts with Preferred Marriage and Various Non-Preferred Age at Marriage Measures

Sr. No.	Mean[1]	Median[1]	Preferred Marriage-median age 20+ years (% of districts)	State or Union Territory	Total Number of districts	A quarter or more of the reported marriages falling below 18 years (% of districts)[2]	Median age at marriage below 18 years (% of districts)
				MAJOR STATES			
1	18.2	18.0	8.7	Andhra Pradesh	23	91.3	4.3
2	19.7	19.0	40.9	Assam	22	40.9	4.5
3	16.9	17.0	0.0	Bihar	43	100.0	72.1
4	19.4	19.0	42.1	Gujarat	19	52.6	5.3
5	18.6	18.0	23.5	Haryana	17	70.6	0.0
6	18.9	18.0	30.0	Karnataka	20	60.0	20.0
7	21.7	21.0	92.9	Kerala	14	7.1	0.0
8	17.4	17.1	0.0	Madhya Pradesh	45	95.6	51.1
9	18.7	18.0	10.0	Maharashtra	30	63.3	16.7
10	19.3	19.0	26.7	Orissa	30	70.0	26.7
11	20.4	20.0	94.1	Punjab	17	5.9	0.0
12	17.0	17.0	0.0	Rajasthan	30	100.0	63.3
13	20.2	20.0	65.2	Tamil Nadu	23	30.4	0.0
14	17.5	18.0	7.4	Uttar Pradesh[2]	68	77.9	50.0
15	18.0	17.1	5.6	West Bengal	18	94.4	50.0
				SMALLER STATES/UNION TERRITORIES			
16	20.6	19.0	50.0	Andaman & Nicobar	2	0.0	0.0
17	18.9	18.0	7.7	Arunachal Pradesh	13	76.9	0.0
18	22.7	22.0	100.0	Chandigarh	1	0.0	0.0
19	17.5	17.0	0.0	Dadra & Nagar Haveli	1	100.0	100.0
20	19.7	19.0	0.0	Daman & Diu	2	0.0	0.0

Contd...

Contd...

21	20.7	21.0	100.0	Delhi	1	0.0	0.0
22	23.8	24.0	100.0	Goa	2	0.0	0.0
23	20.9	21.0	100.0	Himachal Pradesh	12	0.0	0.0
24	20.4	20.0	78.6	Jammu & Kashmir	14	7.1	0.0
25	19.9	19.0	0.0	Lakshadweep	1	0.0	0.0
26	23.8	23.0	100.0	Manipur	8	0.0	0.0
27	20.2	20.0	42.9	Meghalaya	7	0.0	0.0
28	21.4	20.0	66.7	Mizoram	3	33.3	0.0
29	19.2	19.0	28.6	Nagaland	7	42.9	14.3
30	21.5	21.0	75.0	Pondicherry	4	0.0	0.0
31	21.2	21.0	75.0	Sikkim	4	0.0	0.0
32	20.3	19.0	33.3	Tripura	3	66.7	0.0
				TOTAL	504	62.9	27.2

Note: 1. Weighted mean and median 2. District Mahrahjganj of Uttar Pradesh is the only district with a median age at marriage falling in the child marriage category, below 15 years (14.5 years)

Earlier marriages below 18 years consists of child marriage and early marriage categories. Though not shown in the Table separately, the situation with respect to these two components is as follows. While in all the major states (except Kerala) child marriages are reported from one district or the other, the same is reported from all the districts in Bihar, Madhya Pradesh, Rajasthan and West Bengal. The per cent of districts with at least one child marriage is also fairly high in Andhra Pradesh, Gujarat, Haryana, Karnataka, Maharashtra, Orissa and Uttar Pradesh. Early marriages are found in almost all the districts with degrees of differences. But 53.5 per cent of the total early marriages are from the districts of Rajasthan (8.1), Madhya Pradesh (10.8) Uttar Pradesh (17.0) and Bihar (17.5) – over half from these four states.

Findings: District-wise Analysis

General situation based on reported marriages

Among the 18,842 marriages (35.2% of the total marriages) conducted before the girl completed 18 years of age, 58 per cent are from Bihar (19%), Madhya Pradesh (12%), Rajasthan (9%) and Uttar

Pradesh (18%), 38 per cent from the remaining major states and 4 per cent from all the smaller states and Union territories.

District-wise, there are 120 districts with no child marriage and these districts are one each in Chandigarh, Delhi, Daman & Due, Goa, Lakshadweep and Andhra Pradesh; two each in Andaman & Nicobar, Haryana, Karnataka and Pondicherry; three each in Gujarat, Manipur, Mizoram, Orissa and Sikkim; five in Meghalaya; six each in Maharashtra, Nagaland and Punjab; seven each in Assam and Uttar Pradesh; eight in Arunachal Pradesh; ten in Tamil Nadu; eleven each in Himachal Pradesh and Jammu and Kashmir; and fourteen in Kerala (see Table 6.8 for names of these districts).

There is no marriage below 18 years in 3.2 per cent of the districts (16 in number) and these districts are from Kerala (6), Tamil Nadu (1), Andaman and Nicobar (1), Chandigarh (1), Himachal Pradesh (1), Jammu & Kashmir (4) and Meghalaya (2). (The names of these districts are given in Table 6.9.)

The relative frequency distribution of districts by marriages below legal minimum age of 18 years based on reported age at marriage is given in Figure 6.1. Seventeen per cent of the districts have only less than 10 per cent of their total marriages below 18 years and another 16 per cent have only 10-20 per cent of the marriages in this category. At the other extreme, 3.4 per cent of the total districts (17 in number) reported more than 70 per cent of marriages falling below legal minimum age at marriage. These districts are from five states – Bihar (2), Madhya Pradesh (3),

Figure 6.1

Percentage distribution of districts by marriages below 18 years of age based on reported marriages

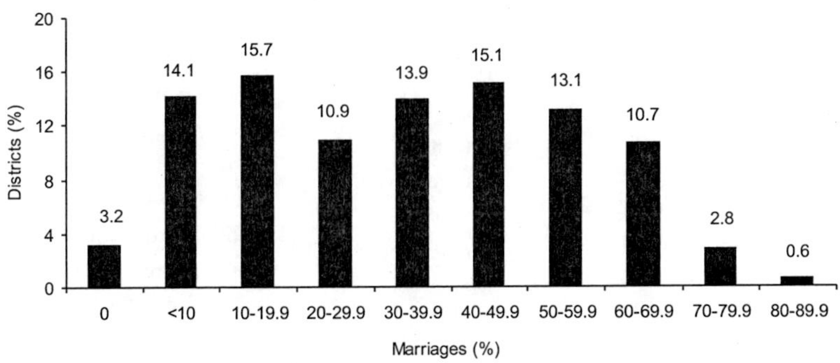

Table 6.8
Districts with no child marriage

Sr. No.	District (State)	Sr. No.	District (State)	Sr. No.	District (State)
1	Aizwal (MIZ)	32	Gurdaspur (PUJ)	64	Meerut (UP)
2	Alappuzha (KER)	33	Hamirpur (HP)	65	Mokokchung (NAG)
3	Almora (UP)	34	Hoshiarpur (PUJ)	66	Mon (NAG)
4	Amravali (MAH)	35	Hyderabad (AP)	67	Namakkal (TN)
5	Amreli (GUJ)	36	Idukki (KER)	68	Nawanshahar (PUJ)
6	Anantnag (J&K)	37	Jammu (J&K)	69	Nicobar (A&N)
7	Andaman (A&N)	38	Jamnagar (GUJ)	70	Nilgiris (TN)
8	Bangalore (KAR)	39	Jharsuguda (ORI)	71	North Cachar Hill (ASM)
9	Baramulla (J&K)	40	Jorhat (ASM)	72	North Sikkim (SIK)
10	Barpeta (ASM)	41	Kangra (HP)	73	Palghat (KER)
11	Bhandara (MAH)	42	Kanniyakumari (TN)	74	Panipat (HAR)
12	Bijnor (UP)	43	Kannur (KER)	75	Papumpare (ARP)
13	Bilaspur (HP)	44	Kanpur Nagar (UP)	76	Pathanamthitta (KER)
14	Bishnupur (MAN)	45	Kapurthala (PUJ)	77	Pauri Garhwal (UP)
15	Budgam (J&K)	46	Karbi Anglong (ASM)	78	Periyar (TN)
16	Chamba (HP)	47	Kasaragod (KER)	79	Phek (NAG)
17	Chandigarh (CHN)	48	Kathua (J&K)	80	Pondicherry
18	Chennai (TN)	49	Kohima (NAG)	81	Poonch (J&K)
19	Chhimtuipui (MIZ)	50	Kollam (KER)	82	Pulawama (J&K)
20	Coimbatore (TN)	51	Kottayam (KER)	83	Raigarh (MAH)
21	Cuttak (ORI)	52	Kozhikode (KER)	84	Rajori (J&K)
22	Dakshina Kannada (KAR)	53	Kullu (HP)	85	Ramanathapuram (TN)
23	Delhi	54	Kupuwada (J&K)	86	Ri Bhoi (MEG)
24	Dhemaji (ASM)	55	Kurukshetra (HAR)	87	Rupnagar (PUJ)
25	Dibrugarh (ASM)	56	Lahul & Spiti (HP)	88	Sambalpur (ORI)
26	Diu (D&D)	57	Lakshadweep	89	Senapati (MAN)
27	Doda (J&K)	58	Lohit (ARP)	90	Shimla (HP)
28	East Garo Hills (MEG)	59	Ludhiana (PUJ)	91	Shivganganagar (TN)
29	East Siang (ARP)	60	Lungeli (MIZ)	92	Sindhudurg (MAH)
30	Ernakulam (KER)	61	Mahe (PON)	93	Sirmaur (HP)
31	Greater Bombay (MAH)	62	Malappuram (KER)	94	Solan (HP)
		63	Mandi (HP)		

Contd...

Sr. No.	*District (State)*	*Sr. No.*	*District (State)*	*Sr. No.*	*District (State)*
95	South Garo Hills (MEG)	104	Thrissur (KER)	114	Wayanad (KER)
96	South Goa (GOA)	105	Tinsukia (ASM)	115	West Garo Hills (MEG)
97	South Sikkim (SIK)	106	Tirap (ARP)	116	West Kameng (ARP)
98	Surendranagar (GUJ)	107	Tuensang (NAG)	117	West Khasi Hills (MEG)
99	Tawang (ARP)	108	Udhampur (J&K)	118	West Siang (ARP)
100	Tehri Garwal (UP)	109	Ukhrul (MAN)	119	West Sikkim (SIK)
101	Thanjavur (TN)	110	Una (HP)	120	Wokha (NAG)
102	Thirunelveli (TN)	111	Upper Siang (ARP)		
103	Thiruvananthapuram (KER)	112	Uttarkashi (UP)		
		113	Wardha (MAH)		

Note: Short form of state names given parenthetically, for full names see Table 6.6

Table 6.9

Districts with no marriage below legal minimum age at marriage of 18 years

Sr. No	*District (state)*	*Sr. No*	*District (state)*
1	Alappuzha (Kerala)	9	Chandigarh (Chandigarh)
2	Ernakulam (Kerala)	10	Lahul & Spiti (Himachal Pradesh)
3	Kollam (Kerala)	11	Doda (Jammu & Kashmir)
4	Kottayam (Kerala)	12	Kathua (Jammu & Kashmir)
5	Pathanamthitta (Kerala)	13	Kupwara (Jammu & Kashmir)
6	Thiruvananthapuram (Ker.)	14	Pulwama (Jammu & Kashmir)
7	Kanniyakumari (TN)	15	East Garo Hills (Meghalaya)
8	Tawang (Arunachal Pradesh)	16	South Garo Hills (Meghalaya)

Rajasthan (4), Uttar Pradesh (6) and West Bengal (2) (and their names are given Table 6.10).

Turning to marriages conducted after attainment of legal minimum age at marriage, there are 374 districts with at least 50 per cent of marriages conducted after the girl attained 18 years of age. Among them, 18 districts have 50-60 per cent of the marriages that could be classified as acceptable (age at the time of marriage being 18 or 19 years). These districts are one each from Arunachal Pradesh (Lohit), Assam (Karbi Aglong), Karnataka (Bangalore Rural) and

Table 6.10

Districts with at least seventy per cent marriages below 18 years of age

Sr. No.	*District (State)*	*Sr. No.*	*District (State)*
1	Nawada (Bihar)	10	Banda (Uttar Pradesh)
2	Patna (Bihar)	11	Basti (Uttar Pradesh)
3	Chattarpur (Madhya Pradesh)	12	Bharaich (Uttar Pradesh)
4	Morena (Madhya Pradesh)	13	Lalitpur (Uttar Pradesh)
5	Shajapur (Madhya Pradesh)	14	Maharajganj (Uttar Pradesh)
6	Bhilwara (Rajasthan)	15	Varanasi (Uttar Pradesh)
7	Bundi (Rajasthan)	16	Murshidabad (West Bengal)
8	Dausa (Rajasthan)	17	Puruliya (West Bengal)
9	Tonk (Rajasthan)		

Nagaland (Mon), two each from Jammu and Kashmir (Rajauri & Udhampur) and Maharashtra (Kolhapur & Satara), three each from Meghalaya (Rai Bhoi, South Garo Hills & West Garo Hills) and Uttar Pradesh (Pauri Garhwal, Rampur & Tehri Garhwal) and four from Madhya Pradesh (Balaghat, Betul, Mandla & Raigarh). Raigarh in Madhya Pradesh and Rajouri in Jammu & Kashmir have 62 per cent and 81 per cent respectively of acceptable marriages.

In 143 districts, at least 50 per cent of marriages were conducted only after the girl attained the preferred age at marriage of at least 20 years. Whereas all the districts in Chandigarh, Delhi, Goa, Himachal Pradesh and Manipur have at least 50 per cent of marriages in the preferred category, there is no district in Bihar, Madhya Pradesh, Rajasthan, Dadra & Nagar Haveli, Daman & Diu and Lakshadweep where preferred marriages reached the 50 per cent mark. Ninety three to ninety four per cent of the districts in Kerala and Punjab, about fourth-fifths of the districts in Jammu and Kashmir, three-fourths of the districts in Pondicherry and Sikkim, two-thirds of the districts in Tamil Nadu and Mizoram also reported preferred marriages of at least 50 per cent of the total marriages.

Median age at marriage

Median age also shows that among the major states there is no district with a median age below 18 years in Haryana, Kerala, Punjab and Tamil Nadu. The names of the 137 districts with a

Figure 6.2

Percentage distribution of the districts with median age at marriage below 18 years of age (N=137)

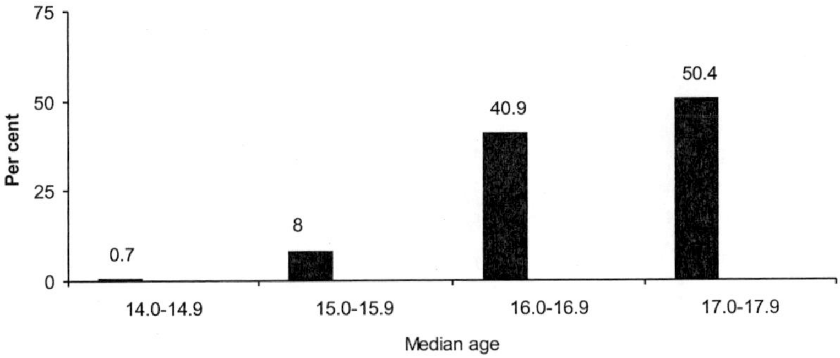

median age at marriage below legal minimum age of 18 years are marked with an asterisk in Table 6.15 and the relative frequency distribution of these districts by median age at marriage is given in Figure 6.2. Additional information relevant to discussion of social characteristics in relation to lower median age at marriage has also been added to Table 6.15 to which the reader may return often in following sections.

It is of some relief to know that half the districts with median age at marriage below 18 years are concentrated in the 17.0 to 17.9 years category, indicating, perhaps, that the day will not be too far when all marriages of girls will be conducted after the girl completed 18 years of age. Considering the singulate mean age at marriage for the country as a whole was only 15.6 years in 1951, this is a great achievement for a vast country like India with all her diverse characteristics.

Almost 90 per cent of these districts with a median of less than 18 years are located in six states: Bihar, Madhya Pradesh, Rajasthan, Orissa, Uttar Pradesh and West Bengal (Figure 6.3).

Of the 85 districts belonging to the smaller states and Union territories, 83 districts have median age at marriage of at least 18 years (the two exceptions are Dadra & Nagar Haveli and Kohima in Nagaland with a median of 17 years). Also it is found that 50 of these districts have a median age at marriage of at least 20.

Figure 6.3

Percentage distribution of districts with age at marriage below 18 years in selected states

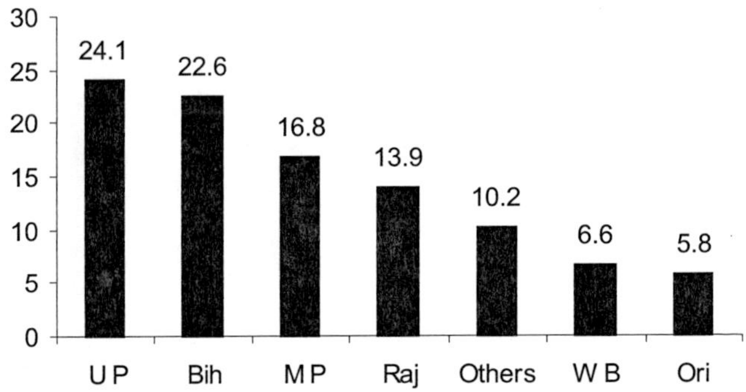

Going by median age at marriage, in Chandigarh, Delhi, Goa, Himachal Pradesh and Manipur, girls marrying after they attain 20 years of age have already became the norm. In Kerala and Punjab also marrying after attainment of at least 20 years have become the norm except in one district each (Malappuram in Kerala and Firozpur in Punjab). However, in the districts of Bihar, Madhya Pradesh, Rajasthan, Dadra and Nagar Haveli, Daman and Diu and Lakshadweep the median age at marriage has not yet reached 20 years in any district.

Age at marriage by characteristics

Since the number of marriages from each district is not sufficiently large for sub-classification into the four categories of age at marriage, only two categories with the legal minimum age at marriage as the cut-off point will be discussed in this section, child/early or acceptable/preferred.

Place of residence

No marriage of girls was reported from the rural areas of six districts and the urban areas of 26 districts during the reference period. The per cent of marriages below legal minimum age at marriage varies in rural areas from zero in 22 districts to 86.6 per cent in Lalitpur (Uttar

Figure 6.4

Percentage distribution of districts by percent share of marriages below 18 years of age in rural and urban areas

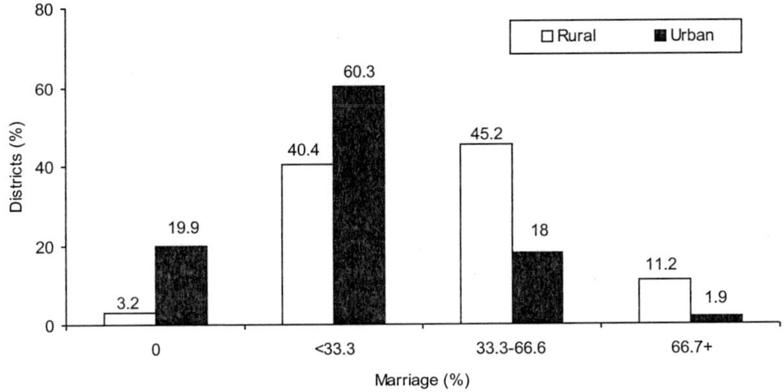

Pradesh) and in urban areas, from zero in 95 districts to 86.7 per cent in Patna (Bihar)[4]. The summary picture is provided in the Figure 6.4.

Whereas 11 per cent of the districts (56 in number) in rural areas have at least two-thirds of the marriages below legal minimum age at marriage, the corresponding percentage in the nine urban areas is only 2 per cent. At the other end, there are just 3 per cent of the districts with no marriage below legally permissible age in rural areas compared to 20 per cent in urban areas. (The names of these districts are given in Table 6.11.)

Median age at marriage by place of residence

The median age at marriage in rural areas varies from 14.0 years in Maharajganj district of Uttar Pradesh to 24 years in Imphal (Manipur), Kottayam (Kerala), and North and South Goa. The corresponding variation observed in urban areas is from 15 years in Nawada, Patna and Rohtas in Bihar to 32 years in West Garo Hills in Meghalaya. The median age for all the marriages reported in rural areas works out to be 18 years and that for urban areas is 20 years – a clear difference of two years by place of residence.

In 30 districts the median age at marriage in the rural areas is found to be higher than that of the urban areas and in another 74 districts there is no difference in the median. However, in all the

Table 6.11

Districts with marriages below 18 years forming at least two-thirds of the total marriages within rural and urban areas

Sr. No.	District (State)	Sr. No.	District (State)
	RURAL	34	Nagaur (RAJ)
1	Ahmedabad (GUJ)	35	Nanded (MAH)
2	Ajmer (RAJ)	36	Nawada (BIH)
3	Ambedkarnagar (UP)	37	Nawrangapura (ORI)
4	Bahraich (UP)	38	Palamu (BIH)
5	Banda (UP)	39	Patna (BIH)
6	Basti (UP)	40	Puruliya (WB)
7	Bhadohi (UP)	41	Rajgarh (MP)
8	Bhilwara (RAJ)	42	Rohtas (BIH)
9	Bhopal (MP)	43	Sagar (MP)
10	Bidar (KAR)	44	Sahibganj (BIH)
11	Bijapur (KAR)	45	Satna (MP)
12	Bikaner (RAJ)	46	Shahdol (MP)
13	Bundi (RAJ)	47	Shajapur (MP)
14	Chattarpur (MP)	48	Shivpuri (MP)
15	Churu (RAJ)	49	Sidhi (MP)
16	Dakshin Dinajpur (WB)	50	Sitapur (UP)
17	Dausa (RAJ)	51	Sonbhadra (UP)
18	Deoghar (BIH)	52	Tikamgarh (MP)
19	Gonda (UP)	53	Tonk (RAJ)
20	Gorakhpur (UP)	54	Udaipur (RAJ)
21	Guna (MP)	55	Varanasi (UP)
22	Hazaribag (BIH)	56	Vidisha (MP)
23	Indore (MP)		URBAN
24	Jhalawar (RAJ)	1	Azamgarh (UP)
25	Jodhpur (RAJ)	2	Godda (BIH)
26	Koraput (ORI)	3	Madhubani (BIH)
27	Kota (RAJ)	4	Murshidabad (WB)
28	Lalitpur (UP)	5	Patna (BIH)
29	Madhepura (BIH)	6	Rohtas (BIH)
30	Maharajganj (UP)	7	Shajapur (MP)
31	Mahoba (UP)	8	Tirap (ARP)
32	Morena (MP)	9	Vaishali (BIH)
33	Murshidabad (WB)		

Note: Short form of state names given parenthetically, for full names see Table 6.6

Figure 6.5

Percentage distribution of districts by marriage category based on median age in rural and urban areas

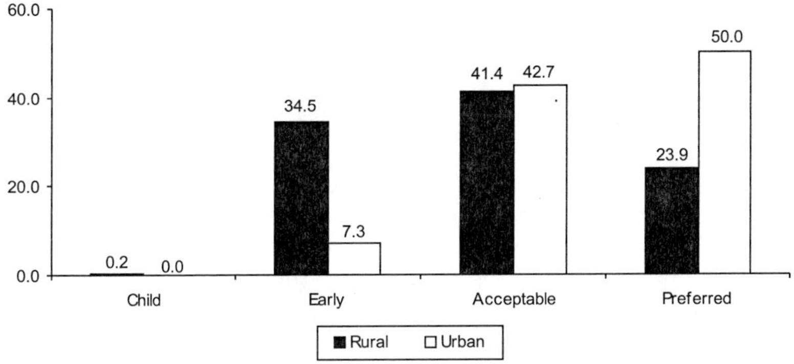

remaining districts reporting marriages, the urban median age at marriage is found to be higher than that of the rural, and in 120 districts the difference is even higher by 2.5 years.

The percentage distribution of districts by marriage category, based on median age, in rural and urban areas is given in Figure 6.5. It is clear from the figure that districts with high early marriages are rural and high preferred marriages are urban, as one would expect.

Figure 6.6

Per cent share of selected states of districts with median age at marriage below 18 years by place of residence

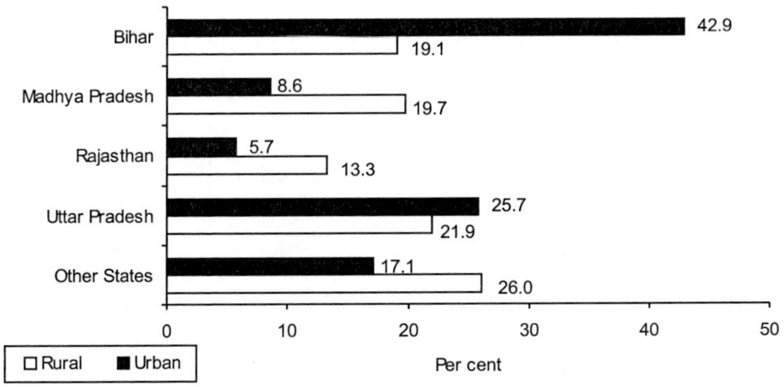

There are 173 rural districts median age at marriage below 18 years and 35 such districts in urban areas. The per cent share of selected states of these districts is shown in Figure 6.6.

The four states (Bihar, Madhya Pradesh, Rajasthan and Uttar Pradesh) together account for 74 per cent of the total number of districts with rural girls marrying below 18 years of age and the corresponding per cent of districts for urban areas is 83. The names of these districts are presented in Table 6.15 and its notes.

Caste

An examination of the age at marriage in each caste group in each district shows that the percentage share of marriages at below legal minimum age at marriage is high among the SC/ST/OBC group than the 'other group' in many districts. In 21 districts no marriage was reported among the castes other than SC/ST/OBC. The variation in the per cent share of marriages below legal minimum age at marriage is from zero in 26 districts to 96 per cent in Lalitpur district in the case of SC/ST/OBC and from zero in 66 districts to 79 per cent in Shajapur (MP)[5] for the 'other caste' group. The summary situation is shown in Figure 6.7.

In seventeen per cent of the districts, the per cent share of marriages below 18 years is at least two-thirds among the SC/ST/OBC group compared to a mere 1 per cent among the OC or

Figure 6.7

Percentage distribution of districts by per cent share of marriages below 18 years of age in each caste group

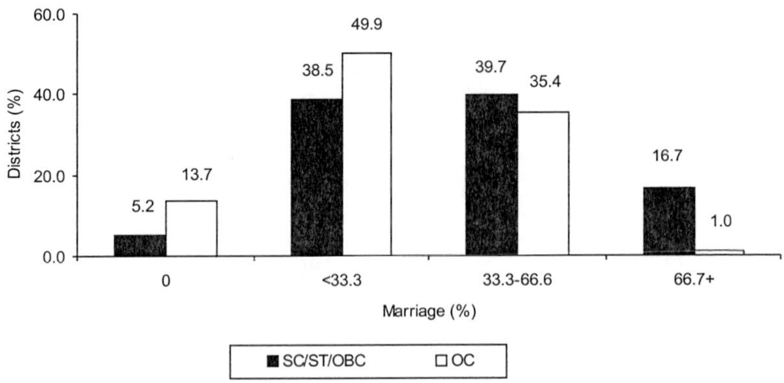

Table 6.12

Districts with marriages below 18 years of age forming at least two-thirds of the total marriages in each caste group

Sr. No.	District (State)	Sr. No.	District (State)	Sr. No.	District (State)
	SC/ST/OBC	31	Godda (BIH)	61	Raichur (KAR)
1	Alwar (RAJ)	32	Gonda (UP)	62	Rajgarh (MP)
2	Ambedkarnagar (UP)	33	Gorakhpur (UP)	63	Rewa (MP)
3	Aurangabad (BIH)	34	Gulbarga (KAR)	64	Rohtas (BIH)
4	Azamgarh (UP)	35	Guna (MP)	65	Sagar (MP)
5	Bahraich (UP)	36	Hazaribag (BIH)	66	Samastipur (BIH)
6	Ballia (UP)	37	Jhalawar (RAJ)	67	Satna (MP)
7	Banda (UP)	38	Jodhpur (RAJ)	68	Shahdol (MP)
8	Barddhaman (WB)	39	Kalahandi (ORI)	69	Shajahanabad (UP)
9	Basti (UP)	40	Khagaria (BIH)	70	Shajapur (MP)
10	Begusarai (BIH)	41	Koraput (ORI)	71	Shivpuri (MP)
11	Belgaum (KAR)	42	Kota (RAJ)	72	Sidhart Nagar (UP)
12	Bhadohi (UP)	43	Lalitpur (UP)	73	Sidhi (MP)
13	Bhilwara (RAJ)	44	Latur (MAH)	74	Sitamarhi (BIH)
14	Bhind (MP)	45	Madhepura (BIH)	75	Sitapur (UP)
15	Bhojpur (BIH)	46	Madhubani (BIH)	76	Sonbhadra (UP)
16	Bidar (KAR)	47	Maharajganj (UP)	77	Sultanpur (UP)
17	Bijapur (KAR)	48	Mahoba (UP)	78	Tikamgarh (MP)
18	Bikaner (RAJ)	49	Mandsaur (MP)	79	Tonk (RAJ)
19	Birbhum (WB)	50	Morena (MP)	80	Udaipur (RAJ)
20	Bundi (RAJ)	51	Murshidabad (WB)	81	Vaishali (BIH)
21	Buxar (BIH)	52	Nagaur (RAJ)	82	Varanasi (UP)
22	Chattarpur (MP)	53	Nanded (MAH)	83	Vidisha (MP)
23	Churu (RAJ)	54	Nawada (BIH)	84	Vishakhapatanam (AP)
24	Darbhanga (BIH)	55	Nawrangapura (ORI)		OTHER CASTES
25	Dausa (RAJ)	56	Palamu (BIH)	1	Dibang Valley (ARP)
26	Deoghar (BIH)	57	Patna (BIH)	2	Dindigul (TN)
27	Dholpur (RAJ)	58	Pilibhit (UP)	3	Murshidabad (WB)
28	Etah (UP)	59	Purba Champaran (BIH)	4	Shajapur (MP)
29	Gaya (BIH)	60	Puruliya (WB)	5	Virudunagar (TN)
30	Ghazipur (UP)				

Note: Short form of state names given parenthetically, for full names see Table 6.6.

other caste group. (The names of these districts are given in Table 6.12.)

Median age at marriage by caste

On the whole, the median age at marriage for all the marriages reported among the SC/ST/OBC group (18 years) is only one year less compared to the median age at marriage for all the marriages reported among the other castes group (19 years). Figure 6.8 gives the percentage distribution of districts by marriage category based on median age, in each caste group, which shows that the per cent of districts with child and early marriages are high for SC/ST/OBC group compared to OC group and the converse is true for preferred marriages.

Figure 6.8

Percentage distribution of districts by marriage category based on median age in each caste group

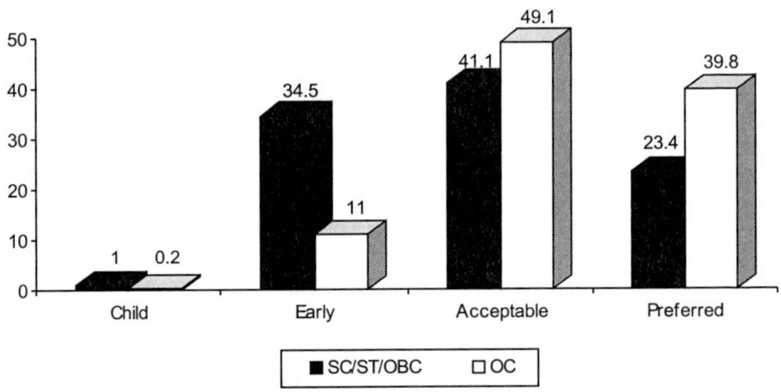

The median age at marriage among the SC/ST/OBC ranged from 14 years in Bahraich, Gonda, Lalitpur, Maharajganj and Sidhartnagar (all from Uttar Pradesh) to 24 years in Imphal (Manipur) and Pulawama (Jammu & Kashmir). Similar variation observed in the other castes group is from 15 years in Shajapur (Madhya Pradesh) and Sonbhadra (Uttar Pradesh)[6] to 25.5 years in Imphal[7]. Median age at marriage of less than 18 years among the SC/ST/OBC group is found in 179 districts and among the other castes group in 54 districts. Among the SC/ST/OBC group three out of every four districts with median age below legal minimum age are from Bihar, Madhya Pradesh, Rajasthan or Uttar Pradesh (Figure

Figure 6.9

Per cent share of selected states of districts with median age at marriage below 18 years by caste

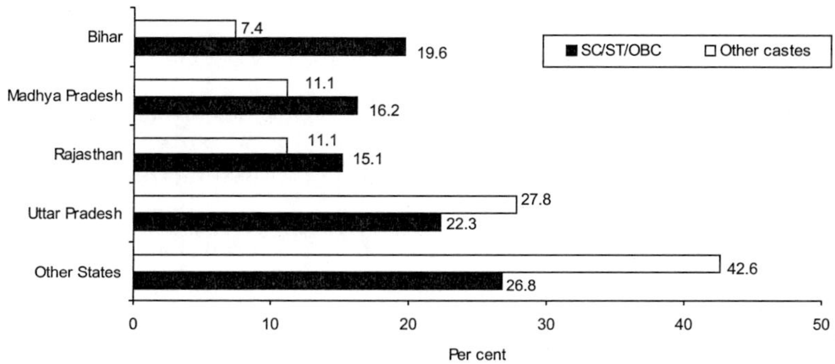

6.9). Similarly among the "other castes" group a large proportion of marriages below legal minimum age (57.4%) are from these states. The names of districts with median age at marriage below legal minimum age at marriage for SC/ST/OBC and 'other caste' groups are part of coding and notes for appended Table 6.15.

Economic status

Economic status as assessed by the type of house they live in shows that there was no marriage conducted during the reference period among the high economic status (HES) group in 14 districts. The corresponding number of districts among the medium economic status (MES) group is 2 and among the low economic status (LES) group is 9.

The proportion of marriages below legal minimum age at marriage is much less among those who are well off than the poor group. The share of such marriages vary from zero in the case of 104 districts to 77.3 per cent in Maharajganj district of Uttar Pradesh[8] among the economically well off persons. The corresponding situation among those who are in the MES category is 40 districts with no such marriages to 96 per cent in Lalitpur (Uttar Pradesh)[9]. Similarly among the LES group, the variation is from zero in the case of 49 districts to 100 per cent in Gandhinagar (Gujarat) and Jhunjhunu (Rajasthan)[10]. The summary situation is given in Figure 6.10.

Table 6.13 (a)

Districts with marriages below 18 years of age forming at least two-thirds of the total marriages among low economic status group

Sr. No.	District (Sate)	Sr. No.	District (Sate)	Sr. No.	District (Sate)
1	Agra (UP)	32	Dausa (RAJ)	63	Kodagu (KAR)
2	Ajmer (RAJ)	33	Deoghar (BIH)	64	Koraput (ORI)
3	Aligarh (UP)	34	Dharwad (KAR)	65	Kota (RAJ)
4	Allahabad (UP)	35	Etah (UP)	66	Lalitpur (UP)
5	Alwar (RAJ)	36	Faizabad (UP)	67	Latur (MAH)
6	Ambedkarnagar (UP)	37	Faridabad (HAR)	68	Madhepura (BIH)
7	Aurangabad (BIH)	38	Faridkot (PUJ)	69	Madhubani (BIH)
8	Azamgarh (UP)	39	Firozabad (UP)	70	Maharajganj (UP)
9	Bahraich (UP)	40	Gandhinagar (GUJ)	71	Mahbubnagar (AP)
10	Ballia (UP)	41	Gaya (BIH)	72	Mahesana (GUJ)
11	Banas Kantha (GUJ)	42	Ghazipur (UP)	73	Mahoba (UP)
12	Banda (UP)	43	Godda (BIH)	74	Mandsaur (MP)
13	Barddhaman (WB)	44	Gonda (UP)	75	Mathura (UP)
14	Basti (UP)	45	Gopalganj (BIH)	76	Morena (MP)
15	Begusarai (BIH)	46	Gorakhpur (UP)	77	Munger (BIH)
16	Belgaum (KAR)	47	Guna (MP)	78	Murshidabad (WB)
17	Bhadohi (UP)	48	Gwalior (MP)	79	Mysore (KAR)
18	Bhagalpur (BIH)	49	Hazaribag (BIH)	80	Nagaur (RAJ)
19	Bhilwara (RAJ)	50	Indore (MP)	81	Nalanda (BIH)
20	Bhiwani (HAR)	51	Jaipur (RAJ)	82	Nanded (MAH)
21	Bhojpur (BIH)	52	Jalaun (UP)	83	Nawada (BIH)
22	Bidar (KAR)	53	Jalgaon (MAH)	84	Nawrangapura (ORI)
23	Bijapur (KAR)	54	Jalna (MAH)	85	Palamu (BIH)
24	Bikaner (RAJ)	55	Jehanabad (BIH)	86	Pali (RAJ)
25	Birbhum (WB)	56	Jhalawar (RAJ)	87	Pashchim Champaran (BIH)
26	Bundi (RAJ)	57	Jhansi (UP)	88	Patna (BIH)
27	Buxar (BIH)	58	Jhunjhunu (RAJ)	89	Pilibhit (UP)
28	Chattarpur (MP)	59	Jodhpur (RAJ)	90	Purba Champaran (BIH)
29	Churu (RAJ)	60	Kaithal (HAR)	91	Puruliya (WB)
30	Dakshin Dinajpur (WB)	61	Kalahandi (ORI)	92	Raichur (KAR)
31	Darbhanga (BIH)	62	Khagaria (BIH)	93	Raipur (MP)

Contd...

Contd...

Sr. No.	*District (Sate)*	*Sr. No.*	*District (Sate)*	*Sr. No.*	*District (Sate)*
94	Rajgarh (MP)	104	Shajahanabad (UP)	114	Tonk (RAJ)
95	Rajsamand (RAJ)	105	Shajapur (MP)	115	Tumkur (KAR)
96	Rangareddy (AP)	106	Shivpuri (MP)	116	Udaipur (RAJ)
97	Ratlam (MP)	107	Sidhart Nagar (UP)	117	Vadodara (GUJ)
98	Rohtas (BIH)	108	Sidhi (MP)	118	Vaishali (BIH)
99	Sagar (MP)	109	Sitamarhi (BIH)	119	Varanasi (UP)
100	Sahibganj (BIH)	110	Sonbhadra (UP)	120	Vidisha (MP)
101	Samastipur (BIH)	111	Sultanpur (UP)	121	Vishakhapatanam (AP)
102	Satna (MP)	112	Theni (TN)		
103	Shahdol (MP)	113	Tikamgarh (MP)		

Note: Short form of state names given parenthetically, for full names see Table 6.6

Table 6.13 (b)

Districts with marriages below 18 years of age forming at least two-thirds of the total marriages among high and medium economic status groups

Sr. No.	*District (State)*	*Sr. No.*	*District (State)*	*Sr. No.*	*District (State)*
	HIGH ES	10	Bhilwara (RAJ)	27	Maldah (WB)
1	East Kameng (ARP)	11	Bikaner (RAJ)	28	Malkangiri (ORI)
2	Maharajganj (UP)	12	Bundi (RAJ)	29	Morena (MP)
3	Murshidabad (WB)	13	Chittorgarh (RAJ)	30	Murshidabad (WB)
4	Patna (BIH)	14	Churu (RAJ)	31	Nagaur (RAJ)
5	Shahdol (MP)	15	Dausa (RAJ)	32	Nawada (BIH)
6	Sultanpur (UP)	16	Dhanbad (BIH)	33	Palamu (BIH)
	MEDIUM	17	Dholpur (RAJ)	34	Rajgarh (MP)
1	Ajmer (RAJ)	18	East Siang (ARP)	35	Rohtas (BIH)
2	Alwar (RAJ)	19	Giridih (BIH)	36	Shajapur (MP)
3	Ambedkarnagar (UP)	20	Gonda (UP)	37	Sonbhadra (UP)
4	Bahraich (UP)	21	Jhalawar (RAJ)	38	Tirap (ARP)
5	Banas Kantha (GUJ)	22	Jhunjhunu (RAJ)	39	Tonk (RAJ)
6	Banda (UP)	23	Kota (RAJ)	40	Udaipur (RAJ)
7	Barddhaman (WB)	24	Lalitpur (UP)	41	Varanasi (UP)
8	Basti (UP)	25	Latur (MAH)		
9	Bhadohi (UP)	26	Maharajganj (UP)		

Note: Short form of state names given parenthetically, for full names see Table 6.6.

Figure 6.10

Distribution of districts by per cent share of marriages below 18 years of age by economic status

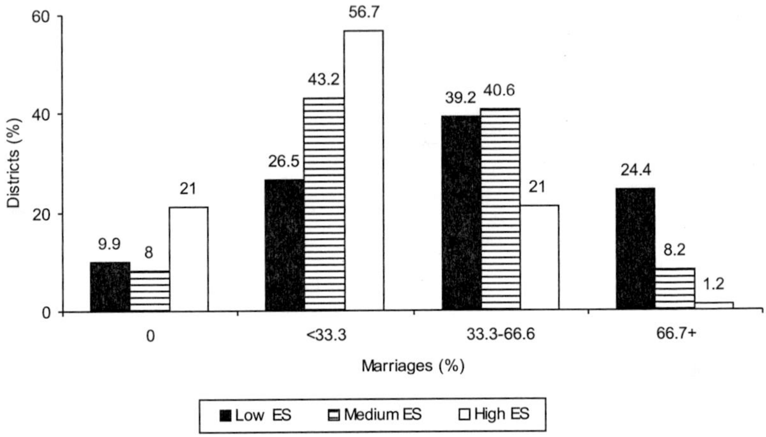

Table 6.14

Districts with marriages below 18 years of age forming at least two-thirds of the total marriages in each category of female literacy rate

Sr. No.	*District (State)*	*Sr. No.*	*District (State)*	*Sr. No.*	*District (State)*
	Low FLR		Medium FLR		Medium FLR
1	Bahraich (UP)	1	Ambedkarnagar (UP)	13	Jhalawar (RAJ)
2	Gonda (UP)	2	Banda (UP)	14	Morena (MP)
3	Lalitpur (UP)	3	Basti (UP)	15	Murshidabad (WB)
4	Maharajganj (UP)	4	Bhadohi (UP)	16	Patna (BIH)
5	Nawada (BIH)	5	Bhilwara (RAJ)	17	Puruliya (WB)
6	Nawrangapura (ORI)	6	Bidar (KAR)	18	Rohtas (BIH)
7	Tonk (RAJ)	7	Bundi (RAJ)	19	Shahdol (MP)
		8	Chattarpur (MP)	20	Shajapur (MP)
		9	Churu (RAJ)	21	Shivpuri (MP)
		10	Dausa (RAJ)	22	Sidhi (MP)
		11	Guna (MP)	23	Tikamgarh (MP)
		12	Hazaribag (BIH)	24	Varanasi (UP)

Note: Short form of state names given parenthetically, for full names see Table 6.6

While there is only one per cent of districts with at least two-thirds of the marriages falling below 18 years among those who are economically well-off, there is 8 per cent among the medium group and 24 per cent among the poor. (The names of these districts are provided in Tables 6.14(a) and 6.14(b) for low and high/medium economic status groups, respectively.)

Median age at marriage by economic status

The median age at marriage among those who are in high economic condition is found to be 19 years as against 18 years for the other two categories. The variation in the median age at marriage in the former group is from 15 years in Patna (Bihar), Maharajganj and Sultanpur (both in Uttar Pradesh) to 27 years in Chandel, Churachandpur and Imphal (all in Manipur)[11]. Among the poor class the lowest median age of 13 years is found in Sidhartnagar (Uttar Pradesh) and a maximum of 26 years is found in Pattanamthitta (Kerala)[12]. Among the medium economic status group the lowest median age of 14 years is found in Bhilwara, Bundi, Kota (all in Rajasthan), Lalitpur and Maharajganj (both in Uttar Pradesh) and the highest median age of 27 years is found in Imphal (Manipur), Sibsagar (Assam) and West Garo Hills (Meghalaya).

The percentage distribution of districts in each economic status category by category of marriage is given in Figure 6.11.

There is no child marriage among those who are in high economic condition and the proportion of early marriage forms only

Figure 6.11

Percentage distribution of districts in each economic status group by marriage category based on median age

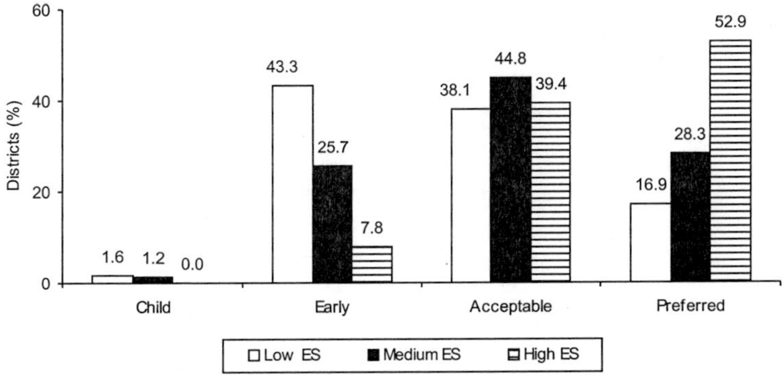

about 8 per cent. This includes two districts each from Arunachal Pradesh, Maharashtra, Nagaland and West Bengal, three each from Andhra Pradesh and Bihar, five from Madhya Pradesh, seven from Rajasthan and 12 from Uttar Pradesh.

The highest per cent of districts with preferred marriages is among the economically better off category (52.9%), and the highest per cent of districts with early marriages is found among the economically poor households (43.3%).

A very negligible proportion of districts reported child marriage with a median age at marriage below 15 years. There are 14 such districts six from the medium economic status group (Bhilwara, Bundi, Kota and Jhalawar from Rajasthan and Lalitpur and Maharajganj from Uttar Pradesh) and eight from the economically poor group (Bahraich, Basti, Gonda, Lalitpur, and Sidhartnagar from Uttar Pradesh, Bhilwara and Jhunjhunu from Rajasthan, and Mysore from Karnataka).

Figure 6.12 gives the per cent share of selected states of the districts with median age below 18 years of age for each economic status category. While the poor households from 223 districts reported below legal minimum median age at marriage the

Figure 6.12

Per cent share of selected states of districts with median age at marriage below 18 years of age by economic status (ES)

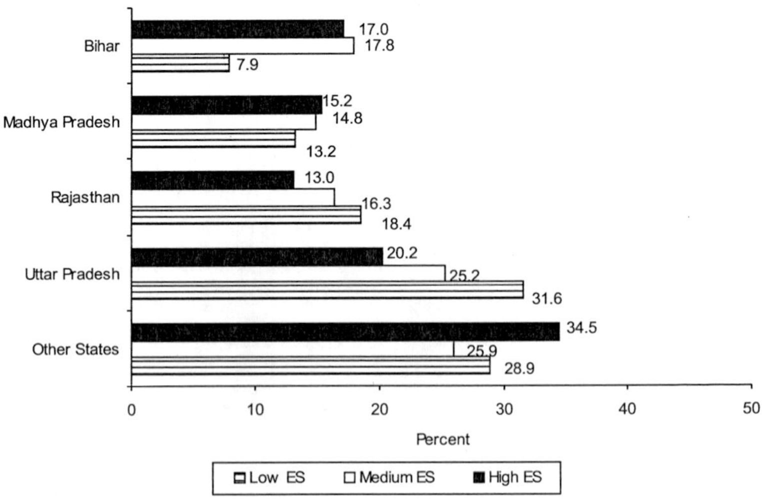

corresponding number of districts for economically better off households is only 38 and that of medium households it is only 135. Bihar, Madhya Pradesh, Rajasthan and Uttar Pradesh together account for at least two-thirds of these districts in all of the economic status categories. The names of these districts are coded in the listing and notes of Table 6.15.

Female literacy rate

In districts with low literacy rate, the variation in the per cent share of marriages below legal minimum age at marriage is from zero in three districts to 83.9 in Lalitpur (Uttar Pradesh). Among districts with medium literacy rate the variation in the per cent of marriages below legal minimum age of 18 years is from zero in the case of five districts to 82.4 per cent in Shajapur (Madhya Pradesh). The corresponding variation for the high literacy rate group is from zero in 8 districts to 50 per cent in Rajnandgaon district of Madhya Pradesh. The percentage distribution of districts by their per cent share of marriages below legal minimum age at marriage is given in a summary form in Figure 6.13.

Figure 6.13

Percentage distribution of districts by per cent share of marriages below 18 years of age in each category of literacy

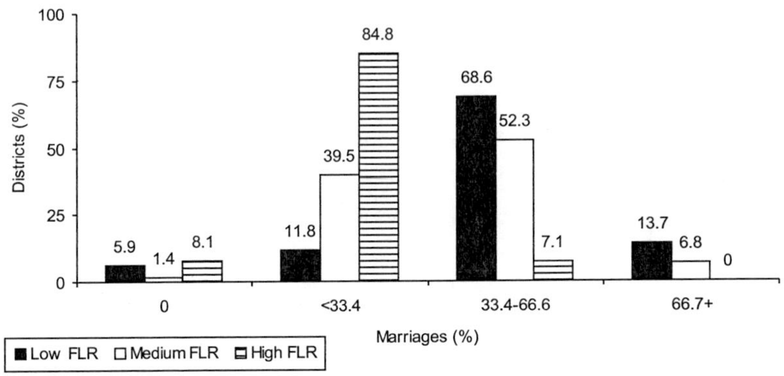

When the literacy level is high, the proportion of child and early marriages is found to be less and vice versa. Most of the districts in the high literacy category have only less than one-third of

Table 6.15

Districts with median age at marriage below 18 years of age – and coded for Place, Caste, Economic Status, and Female Literacy Rates*

Sr. No.	District (state)
	Andhra Pradesh
1	Adilabad (h k)
2	East Godavari (r k)
3	Karimnagar (h)
4	Khammam (u)
5	Kurnool (m)
6	Mahbubnagar (k)
7	Nizamabad (k c)
8	Prakasam (k)
9	Rangareddi (r k)
10	Srikakulam (r h k c)
11*	Vishkhapatanam (r m k y c)
12	Vizianagaram (k)
13	Warangal (r m k c)
	Arunachal Pradesh
14	Dibang Valley (o)
15	East Kameng (h)
16	East Siang (m)
17	Tirap (u m)
18	Upper Siang (h)
	Assam
19	Bongaigaon (m)
20*	Dhubri (r m k y c o)
21	Goalpara (o)
22	Lakhimpur (m)
23	Nagaon (k)
	Bihar
24*	Araria (r k x c)
25*	Aurangabad (u m y c)
26*	Begusarai (r u m k y c)
27*	Bhagalpur (r k y c)
28*	Bhojpur (r k y c)
29*	Buxar (r u m k y c)
30*	Darbhanga (r k x c)
31*	Deoghar (r m k x c)
32	Dhanbad (m k c)
33	Dumka (u m o)
34*	Gaya (r m k y c)
35*	Giridih (r u h m k x c)
36*	Godda (r u k x c o)
37*	Gopalganj (r k x c)
38*	Hazaribagh (r u m k y c)
39*	Jehanabad (r m k y c)
40	Katihar (r k c)
41*	Khagaria (r m k x c)
42	Kishanganj (r m k o)
43*	Madhepura (r u m k x c)
44*	Madhubani (r u k x c)
45*	Munger (r k y c)
46	Muzaffarpur (r k)
47*	Nalanda (r u k y c)
48*	Nawada (r u m k x c)
49*	Palamu (r m k x c)
50	Pashchim Champaran (r m k)
51*	Patna (r u m k y c o)
52*	Purba Champaran (r h m k x c)
53	Purbi Singhbhum (k)
54	Purnia (k c)
55*	Rohtas (r u m k y c)
56*	Saharsa (r k x c)
57*	Sahibganj (r k x c o)
58*	Samastipur (r k x c)
59*	Saran (r m k y c)
60*	Sitamarhi (r u m k x c)
61	Siwan (m k c)
62*	Vaishali (r u m k y c)
	Dadra & Nagar Haveli
63*	Dadra & N H (r m k y c)
	Gujarat
64	Ahmadabad (r m)
65*	Banas Kantha (r m k y c)
66	Gandhinagar (k c)
67	Kheda (k)
68	Mahesana (m k)
69	Surat (k)
70	The Dangs (k)
71	Vadodara (k)
	Haryana
72	Bhiwani (r m k c)
73	Faridabad (k)
74	Hisar (m)
75	Kaithal (k)
76	Mahendragarh (r m k c)
77	Rewari (m)
78	Sirsa (k)
79	Sonipat (k)
80	**Karnataka**
81*	Belgaum (r m k y c)
82	Bellary (r k c)
83*	Bidar (r u m k y c o)
84*	Bijapur (r m k y c o)
85	Dharwad (k c)
86	Gulbarga (r k c)
87	Kodagu (k)
88	Mandya (k)
89	Mysore (r k c)

Contd...

Contd...

Sr. No.	District (state)
90*	Raichur (r m k y c)
91	Tumkur (k)
	Kerala
92	Kasaragod (k)
	Maharashtra
93	Ahmadnagar (c)
94*	Aurangabad (r m k y c)
95*	Beed (r h k y c o)
96	Dhule (k)
97	Gadchiroli (h)
98	Jalgaon (r k)
99*	Jalna (r m k y c o)
100*	Latur (r m k y c o)
101*	Nanded (r m k y c o)
102	Osmanabad (m k)
103	Parbhani (r k c)
104	Pune (k)
105	Solapur (k c)
	Meghalaya
106	East Khasi Hills (o)
107	West Garo Hills (o)
	Madhya Pradesh
108*	Bhind (r h m k y c)
109	Bhopal (r)
110	Bilaspur (k)
111*	Chattarpur (r k y c o)
112*	Damoh (r m k y c)
113	Datia (r m k c)
114*	Dewas (r m k y c)
115*	Dhar (r m k y c o)
116	East Nimar (r k)
117*	Guna (r m k y c)
118	Gwalior (r m k c)
119	Hoshangabad (m)
120	Indore (r k)
121	Jabalpur (r)
122*	Jhabua (r k x c)
123*	Mandsaur (r m k y c)
124*	Morena (r u h m k y c o)
125	Narsimhapur (r k c)
126*	Panna (r h m k y c)
127*	Raipur (r k y c)
128	Raisen (k c)
129*	Rajgarh (r m k y c)
130*	Rajnandgaon (r k z)
131	Ratlam (r k c)
132*	Rewa (r m k y c o)
133*	Sagar (r m k y c)
134*	Satna (r m k y c o)
135	Sehore (r m k c)
136*	Shahdol (r h m k y c)
137*	Shajapur (r u m k y c o)
138*	Shivpuri (r u h m k y c o)
139*	Sidhi (r k y c)
140*	Surguja (r k y c)
141*	Tikamgarh (r h m k y c)
142	Ujjain (r k c)
143*	Vidisha (r k y c)
144	West Nimar (k)
	Nagaland
145*	Kohima (r u h m k y c)
146	Phek (u m)
147	Zunheboto (h)
	Orissa
148*	Bolangir (r m k y c)
149*	Boudh (r k y c)
150	Dhenkanal (c)
151*	Ganjam (r k y c)
152*	Kalahandi (r k x c)
153*	Koraput (r m k x c)
154*	Malkangiri (r m k x c o)
155*	Nawrangapura (r k x c)
156*	Nayagarh (r m k y c)
157	Phulbani (o)
	Punjab
158	Faridkot (k)
159	Firozpur (k)
160	Muktsar (k)
	Rajasthan
161	Ajmer (r m k c)
162*	Alwar (r m k y c)
163*	Banswara (r k x c)
164*	Barmer (r m k y c)
165*	Bharatpur (r h m k y c)
166*	Bhilwara (r h m k y c o)
167*	Bikaner (r h m k y c o)
168*	Bundi (r m k y c)
169	Chittorgarh (r m k c)
170*	Churu (r u h m k y c o)
171*	Dausa (r h m k y c)
172*	Dholpur (r u m k y c)
173	Ganganagar (k c)
174*	Hanumangarh (r m k y c)
175	Jaipur (r m k c)
176*	Jaisalmer (r m k x c)
177	Jalor (k c)
178*	Jhalawar (r m k y c)
179	Jhunjhunu (m k c)
180*	Jodhpur (r m k y c)
181*	Kota (r m k y c)
182*	Nagaur (r h m k y c o)

Contd...

Contd...

Sr. No.	*District (state)*
183*	Pali (r m k y c)
184	Rajsamand (r k c)
185	Sawai Madhopur (r k c)
186	Sikar (k)
187	Sirohi (k)
188*	Tonk (r h m k x c o)
189*	Udaipur (r m k y c o)
	Tamil Nadu
190	Dharmapuri (k)
191	Dindigul (o)
192	Ramanathapuram (o)
193	Salem (k)
194	Theni (k)
195	Virudhunagar (o)
	Tripura
196	South Tripura (c)
	Uttar Pradesh
197	Agra (k)
198	Aligarh (m k c)
199*	Allahabad (r k y c)
200*	Ambedkarnagar (r m k y c o)
201*	Azamgarh (r u m k y c)
202*	Bahraich (r h m k x c o)
203*	Ballia (r h k y c)
204*	Banda (r m k y c o)
205*	Barabanki (r m k y c)
206*	Basti (r m k y c o)
207*	Bhadohi (r u m k y c o)
208*	Budaun(r m k x c o)
209*	Deoria (r m k y c)
210*	Etah (r m k y c)
211	Etawah (k c)
212*	Faizabad (r m k y c o)
213	Farrukhabad (k)
214	Fatehpur (r k)
215*	Firozabad (r m k y c)
216*	Ghazipur (r u m k y c)
217*	Gonda (r u h m k x c o)
218*	Gorakhpur (r h k y c)
219	Hamirpur (r k c)
220	Hathras (r m k c)
221*	Jalaun (r h m k y c o)
222*	Jaunpur (r m k y c)
223	Jhansi (r m k c)
224	Kanpur Dehat (k)
225*	Kheri (r u m k y c)
226*	Lalitpur (r u h m k x c)
227*	Maharajganj (r h m k x c o)
228*	Mahoba (r u m k y c)
229*	Mainpuri (r m k y c)
230	Mathura (m k c)
231*	Mirzapur (r m k y c)
232*	Muzaffarnagar (m c)
233*	Pilibhit (r m k y c)
234*	Pratapgarh (r h m k y c o)
235	Rae Bareli (k)
236*	Shajahanabad (r u m k y c o)
237*	Siddharthnagar (r u h m k x c)
238*	Sitapur (r h m k y c)
239*	Sonbhadra (r m k y c o)
240*	Sultanpur (r h m k y c o)
241	Unnao (k c)
242*	Varanasi (r h m k y c o)
	West Bengal
243*	Bankura (r k y c)
244*	Barddhaman (r m k y c)
245*	Birbhum (r k y c o)
246*	Dakshin Dinajpur (r k y c o)
247	Kolkata (k)
248*	Kooch Bihar (r k y c)
249*	Maldah (r m k y c o)
250*	Murshidabad (r u h m k y c o)
251	Nadia (k)
252	North 24 Parganas (r k c)
253*	Puruliya (r h m k y c o)
254	South 24 Parganas (r k c)
255*	Uttar Dinajpur (r k y c o)

Notes: (i) asterisk indicates districts with median age at marriage below 18 years of age. (ii) Codes used: r = rural u = urban places; c = SC/ST/OBC and o = other caste groups; h = high, m = medium, and k = low economic statuses; and x = low literacy and y = medium literacy and z = high female literacy rates.

the marriages below legal minimum age and there is no district with two-thirds marriage in this category. (For list of districts with at least two-thirds of the marriages below legal age, see Table 6.14.)

Median age at marriage by female literacy rate

On the whole, the median age at marriage for districts with low FLR varies from a minimum of 14.5 in Maharajganj district of Uttar Pradesh to 22 in Anantnag of Jammu and Kashmir. Correspondingly, the lowest median age observed among the districts with medium FLR is 15 years (Basti in Uttar Pradesh, Bundi and Jhalawar in Rajasthan, Patna in Bihar and Shajapur in Madhya Pradesh). In this group, the highest median age of 23 years is found in Pulawama in Jammu and Kashmir. In the highest FLR category the variation is from 17.5 years in Rajnandgaon in Madhya Pradesh to 25 in Imphal (Manipur). There is one year difference in median age at marriage between the low (17 years) and medium (18 years) categories and two years difference between the medium and the high (20 years) FLR categories. The distribution of districts in each literacy rate group by age at marriage category is given in Figure 6.14.

Figure 6.14

Percentage distribution of districts in each literacy rate group by category of marriage based on median age

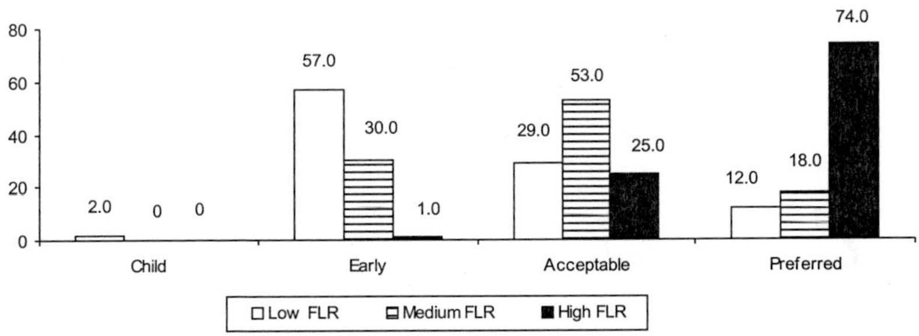

The only district with a median age at marriage below 15 years (Maharajganj) is in the low FLR group. Fifty-seven per cent of the districts in this FLR group had a median age falling in the early marriage category. More than half the districts with medium FLR have acceptable median age at marriage. Preferred age of at least 20 years is found only in 18 per cent of districts in this category. When literacy rate is the highest, all but one per cent of the districts has either acceptable or preferred median age at marriage with 74 per cent falling into the latter category.

Of the 137 districts with a median age at marriage below 18 years listed in Table 6.15, the distribution by FLR group is 30, 106 and 1 respectively for low, medium and high. Seventy-seven per cent of these districts are located in Bihar (22%), Madhya Pradesh (17%), Rajasthan (14%) and Uttar Pradesh (24%) combined. The single district in the high FLR category with a median age at marriage less than 18 years is Rajnandgaon of Madhya Pradesh with a median age of 17.5 years. The per cent share of selected states of the districts with a median below 18 years in the low and median category of FLR group is given in Figure 6.15. The names of all districts for low and medium FLR are incorporated in Table 6.16 and its notes.

Figure 6.15

Per cent share of selected states of districts with median age at marriage below 18 years of age by female literacy rate

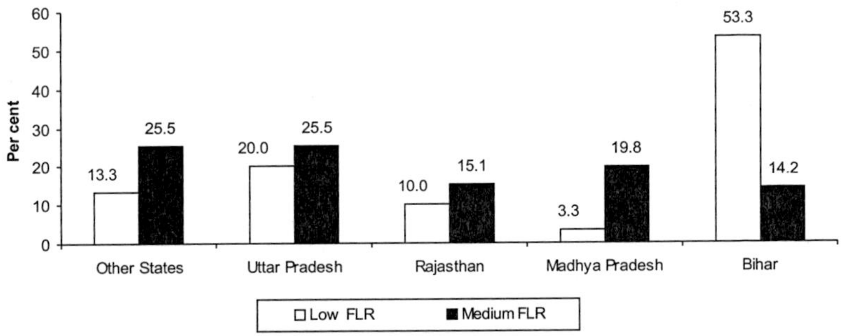

Discussion of Findings

The age at marriage situation as prevailed in late 1990s has been examined in this research with the help of actual reported marriages and the median age at marriage calculated from the reported marriages. The relationship between age at marriage and some socio-economic variables has also been examined. The actual reported marriages had shown that almost one out of every ten marriages was conducted before the girl attained at least 15 years. While in all the major states (except Kerala) child marriages are reported from one district or the other, the same is reported from all the districts in Bihar, Madhya Pradesh, Rajasthan and West Bengal. The per cent of districts with at least one child marriage is also fairly high in Andhra Pradesh, Gujarat, Haryana, Karnataka, Maharashtra, Orissa and Uttar Pradesh. However, when median age at marriage was calculated, a median below 15 was observed only in Maharajganj district of Uttar Pradesh. Table 6.7 makes it abundantly clear that in most of the populous states in the country a sizable proportion of marriages (half or more) were below 18 years.

There were only 16 districts with all reported marriages above 18 years. These districts are Alappuzha, Ernakulam, Kollam, Kottayam, Pathanamthitta, Thiruvananthapuram (all from Kerala), Kanyakumari (Tamil Nadu), Tawang (Arunachal Pradesh) Chandigarh (Chandigarh), Lahul and Spiti (Himachal Pradesh), Doda, Kathua, Kuppuwara, Pulawama (all from Jammu & Kashmir) East Garo Hills and South Garo Hills (both from Meghalaya). A total of 137 districts had a median age at marriage below 18 years and none of these were in Kerala, Haryana, Punjab or Tamil Nadu. (See Table 6.15) Moreover, 77.4 per cent of these districts belonged to Bihar (22.6%), Madhya Pradesh (16.8%), Rajasthan (13.9%) and Uttar Pradesh (24.1%) combined.

Median age at marriage was found to be lower in rural areas, among SC/ST/OBC, among lower socio-economic group and among low female literacy group. This is true in almost all districts. Thus it appears that low level of development has something to do with age at marriage of girls. Also marriage in India, generally, is not just a concern between two individuals but is the establishment of a relationship between two families, the bride and the groom serving as the connecting link. Hence marriages are often arranged by the parents of the girls and boys taking into consideration the family status, economic position, caste, religion, region and the like. There are still areas in this country where the parents believe that the girls should be given in marriage at an early age. Many reasons are given for this in Ancient India, mostly based on religion and social customs. Beliefs like having an unmarried girl of 10 years at home will take the parents to hell; that it will reduce the social prestige of the parents; that it reflects the low status and lack of affluence of the family, etc. are some such reasons (For a detailed version see Reddy, 1998). Widespread illiteracy adds to these myths. Further, marriage restrictions based on the endogenous character of different caste groups reduced the field of selection for a partner and hence the parents usually take the first opportunity to get their girls married and at an early age. With the passing of time early marriage became a norm and deviation from it was seen as a matter of social disapproval and even social disgrace. As in any other social aspect, the low caste people in their eagerness to imitate the higher caste people married the girls even in infancy (Reddy, 1998). Another important factor that plays a major role in the timing of marriage now in India is dowry – an octopus that is spreading its tentacles across the society, squeezing it mercilessly irrespective of caste, creed or class.[13] Though illegal, social convention has strengthened its practice to the point of endangering the very lives of girls and young women as other researchers can attest.

Thus, age at marriage in India is not a simple problem which can find a simple solution. Yet the Government is trying to raise the age through legislation. In this context it is important to know whether a sizable majority of the people of this country know that there is a legal minimum age at marriage for girls and that it is 18 years. This knowledge among the ever married women in the 13-49 age group has been collected by the National Family Health Survey (IIPS, 1995) and it has found that two-thirds of the respondents could not identify age 18 as the correct legal minimum age at marriage for girls. In a male dominant society like India, perhaps the knowledge of the women may not be as important as that of men. But no survey has been undertaken to find this out. If the actual age at marriage is any indication, this knowledge is not widespread.

Thus, raising the age at marriage calls for a holistic approach which will be directly related to overall development of the country. It is also pertinent to spread the knowledge of the provisions of the Age at Marriage Act through all types of mass media, if the Government is serious about achieving its envisioned age at marriage of 20 years for girls. In addition, this research suggests that programmes which improve the economic status of women's households and literacy of women, especially in the four states of Bihar, Madhya Pradesh, Uttar Pradesh and Rajasthan, certainly should receive attention if the government wants to succeed in raising age at marriage.

Notes

1. This is a revised version of the paper accepted for presentation at the PAA meeting of 2003 held in Minneapolis during May.
2. The smallest administrative unit.
3. States having a total population of at least 10 million in 1991 census.
4. The single marriage at age 17 in Godda, two marriages at age 16 in Madhubani (Bihar) and one marriage at 16 in Tirap (Arunachal Pradesh) are not considered.
5. The single marriage at the age of 14 years in district Dibang Valley (Arunachal Pradesh) is not considered.
6. The single marriage at age 15 reported from Faridkot district of Punjab and the single marriage at age 16 reported from Kaithal district of Haryana are not considered.
7. The single marriage at age 29 reported in the district The Nilgiris of Tamil Nadu is not considered.
8. The single marriage at age 16 reported from East Kameng district of Arunachal Pradesh is not considered.
9. The single marriage at age 16 reported from Tirap district of Arunachal Pradesh is not considered.
10. Same as note 5.
11. The single marriage each at age 27 in Mokokchung (Nagaland) and Tamenglong (Manipur) are not considered.
12. The single marriage at the age of 29 years in North Goa is not considered.
13. Dowry or *Dahej* is the payment in cash or/and kind by the bride's family to the bridegroom's family along with the giving away of the bride, called *Kanyadaan* in India. *Kanyadanam* is an important part of Hindu marital rites. *Kanya* means daughter, and *daan* means gift. Dowry, which initially started as some kind of pocket money to the groom among the affluent has spread like wild fire among all and sundry. Now besides money, material goods like car, apartments, refrigerator, music system, utensils of all variety, etc., are also finding its place in the dowry basket and not only for the groom but also for the groom's family members! The practice of dowry is prohibited by law through the Dowry Prohibition Act of 1961. However, the practice is still continuing with increased vigour in all the regions of the country irrespective of caste or class to such an extent that the parents of a girl will start worrying about dowry from the time of her birth. Arguably, earlier the marriage, lesser the dowry.

References

Agarwala, S.N. (1966), "Raising the Age at Marriage for Women – A Means to Lower the Birth Rate", *Economic and Political Weekly,* December 24.

Audinarayana, N. (1990), *Socio-cultural Dimensions of Marriage in Rural India,* New Delhi: Mittal Publications.

Bartz, K.W. and F.I. Nye (1970), "Early Marriage: A Propositional Formulation," *Journal of Marriage and the Family,* 32:258-268.

Bhagat, R.B. (2002), *Early Marriages in India: A Socio-geographical Study,* New Delhi: Rajat Publications.

Call, V.R.A. and L.B. Otto (1977), "Age at marriage as a mobility contingency: estimates for the Nye-Berardo Model", *Journal of Marriage and the Family,* 39:67-79.

Coale, Ansley, J. (1965), "Factors Associated with the Development of Low Fertility: An Historic Summary, Proceedings of the United Nations World Population Conference, Belgrade, Vol. 2, pp. 205-209.

— (1973), *The Demographic Transition,* International Population Conference, Liege, Vol.I, pp.53-72, Leige: IUSSP.

Davis, Kingsley and Judith Blake (1956), "Social Structure and Fertility: An Analytic Framework", *Economic Development and Cultural Change,* 4: 211-235, April.

Davis, Kingsley (1973), *Human Society,* New York: The Macmillan Company.

Driver (1963), *Education, manpower and development in South and Southeast Asia,* New York: Praeger Publishers.

Freedman, Ronald (1979), "Theories of Fertility decline: A Reappraisal", in P.M. Hauser, (ed.) *World Population and Development,* Syracuse, New York, Syracuse University Press.

French, Joan (2001), Quoted in UNICEF calls for global campaign to end child marriages, 9-3-2001.

Government of India, 2000, *National Population Policy 2000,* New Delhi.

Goyal, R.P. (1964), "Birth rate can be reduced by a third by late marriage," *Yojana,* August, 30.

IIPS (International Institute for Population Sciences) (1995), *National Family Health Survey (MCH and Family Planning), India, 1992-93.* Mumbai: IIPS.

IIPS and ORC Macro (2000), *National Family Health Survey (NFHS-2), 1998-99: India,* Mumbai: IIPS.

IIPS (2001), *Reproductive and Child Health Project, Rapid Household Survey (Phase I & II), India, 1998-1999,* Mumbai: IIPS.

Malhotra, Anju (1997), "Gender and the Timing of Marriage: Rural-Urban Differences in Java", *Journal of Marriage and the Family,* Vol. 59, pp. 434-450.

Malthus, Thomas Robert (1798), *An Essay on the Principle of Population,* Sixth Edition, London: John Murray, 1826.

McDonald, Peter, F. (1981), "Social Change and Age at Marriage", *Proceedings of the International Population Conference,* Manila.

Population Reports (1979), *Age at Marriage and Fertility,* Series M, Number 4, Special Topic Monograph, Population Information Program, Baltimore: The Johns Hopkins University.

Radha Devi (1984), "Age at marriage of working and non-working women in Trivandrum district", *Bulletin of Gandhigram Institute of Rural Health and Family Welfare Trust,* 19 (3): 5-14.

Reddy, Krishna (1998), *Marriage, Population and Society: Demographic Perspective of a Social Institution,* New Delhi: Kanishka Publishers, Distributors.

Singh, R.P. and J. Richard (1989), "Socio-Economic and Demographic Correlates of Age at Marriage, *Demography India,* Vol. 18, 183-190.

Van de Valle, Etienne (1972), "Marriage and Marital Fertility" in D.V. Glass and Roger Revelle (eds.) *Population and Social Change,* Edward Arnold.

Westoff, Charles, F. and Norman B. Ryder (1977), *The Contraceptive Revolution,* Princeton: Princeton University Press.

7

"Seeking a Suitable Match"

Economic Development, Gender, and Matrimonial Advertisements in India

RICHA CHAUHAN

Caste endogamous[1] arranged marriages are the most notable aspect of Indian marriage structure. This has been pointed out by many studies (see, Kolenda, 2003; Srinivas, 2002; Derne, 1995; Uberoi, 1994). Marriage is typically "allowed only within one's own local caste group or an allied caste of relatively similar status" (Milner, 1994:60). Arranged marriages, particularly, caste endogamous marriages, continue to be the norm in India even today.

In a recent survey of Indians in the age group 20-35, 81 per cent had an arranged marriage (Jain, 1996: 78). In another survey more than half (56%) of those surveyed showed their support for marrying someone of the same caste[2] while about a third (31%) disagreed either strongly or somewhat with the notion of "marrying someone of the same caste" (Ghose and Jahagirdar, 1998: 69). Thus, caste endogamous arranged marriages remain the most salient part of marriage structure in India.

However, this emphasis on caste endogamy in Indian marriages erroneously minimizes the significance of class – income, education and occupation – as a factor in the marriage structure. The continued emphasis of caste endogamy gives us a static view of the marriage structure in India. I argue that although caste endogamy remains important in Indian marriages, the significance of class as a variable in arranging marriages has been increasing. In this study I will show that although caste endogamy persists today it is to a weaker degree because of an increasing significance of class. Using an historical method I demonstrate that the Indian marriage has changed and the nature of these changes is gendered. Such an approach, I argue, highlights a more dynamic view of the Indian marriage.

Theoretical Context

Marriage in India has traditionally been very closely related to the caste hierarchy and caste endogamy has remained a critical point in arranging marriages. Many studies that examine Indian marriages do so in the context of describing the caste hierarchy. Some researchers even argue that the caste endogamy essentially defines the caste structure (Milner, 1994: 143; Srinivas, 1989; Klass, 1980). For instance, Klass uses the term 'marriage circle' to denote sub caste. Each caste is divided into sub-castes, and it is a sub-caste of an individual that is his/her unit of social interaction. In every village, or every region, as Klass notes, "every household is normally a constituent member of such a marriage circle" (1980:98) thus demonstrating the close connection between sub-castes and the endogamous principle in Indian marriages. Today, with modernization, although "substantial number of people are no longer morally outraged by the idea of inter-caste marriage... marriage across caste lines, when the castes have widely differing statuses, would still be regarded as 'deviant' (Narayan, 1993: 160).

Prior studies on Indian marriages and the family life examine these institutions mostly as an extension of the caste structure itself. Consequently it gives us a static view of both, the Indian marriage structure and also the caste structure. There are recent studies that look at the changes in the Indian marriage; however, they focus mostly on one of its aspects – dowry related violence within Indian marriages (see, e.g., Rudd, 2001; Vindhya, 2000; Kapadia, 1995). Systematic and historical studies that place Indian marriage in a broader economic and political framework in society have been lacking. Here, I try to redress this deficiency.

As Judith Stacey points out, "as a social, not natural entity, the family unit will always be situated in the broader social, economic, and political context of its period" (1983:12). Thus it is important to place marriage and family not only in the broader context of political economy, but also to historicize it. Such a view of marriage better illuminates changes in marriage. Also, such an approach highlights the relationship between social institutions and the nature of the development process in a non-Western society like India.

I use a gender and development framework to examine these changes in Indian marriages because it provides us with a "new lens...a gendered one" (Blumberg, 1995:10). The focus in "gender and development is not women *per se* but on gender relations, i.e., the relations between women and men in a variety of settings. Many of these are ... relations a person is involved in on the basis of their position in a network of kinship and affinity" (Young, 1997: 51). Such an approach focuses on the "fit between family, household or the domestic life and the organization of both political and economic spheres" (Young, 1997: 52). Thus, using a gender and development approach to examine Indian marriage helps us bring to light how some of its aspects have changed while others are maintained within the context of modernization in India.

The most important change in Indian political economy since its independence in 1947 has been an increase in the significance of class relative to caste in determining an individual's status in the society (Kapadia, 2002; Srinivas, 1996; Beteille, 1996). Although caste remains important, the rigidity of caste structure has weakened in many respects in modern India. For example, the rigidity of occupations by caste and the 'pollution-purity' aspect as highlighted by Dumont (1970) has declined (Srinivas, 1989; Mayer, 1996; Beteille, 1996). Although divisions remain, members of all castes interact with one another in more proximity than ever before, especially in urban areas.

The rising significance of class has occurred in part due to an increase in access to education and non-manual occupations for the bottom rungs of the caste hierarchy – the untouchables – referred to now as the scheduled castes. Education and access to non-manual occupations were historically denied to these groups within the traditional caste hierarchy. An increase in access to education and non-manual occupations has been a result of political policies such as reservations policy (affirmative action) for the Scheduled castes and overall economic development (Mendelsohn and Vicziany, 1998). Thus the traditional caste structure has changed significantly with regards to the aspects of pollution, rigidity of occupations and the overall dominance of the upper castes.

While the significance of caste has declined in determining the status of individuals in society, the significance of class has increased in this respect. I will show that these changes in the economic stratification have also extended to the sphere of marriage, but the nature of this change is gendered.

Method

I examine the changes in the Indian marriage structure by undertaking a content analysis of the matrimonial advertisements (classifieds) in a leading Indian daily newspaper, *The Times of India*. *The Times of India* is considered a major newspaper[3] in India and has a nation wide circulation. I examined a purposive sample of 262 editions of the newspaper at three different points in history: 1950, 1970 and 1990. Within each of these time periods I examined daily editions of four months – March, June, September, and December. The matrimonial classifieds in the year 1950 and 1970 (March, June, September, and December) appeared daily. However, the matrimonial classifieds by 1990 had begun appearing weekly (every Sunday); thus I examined the matrimonial advertisements appearing every Sunday in March, June, September and December of 1990[4].

Both the spread of various months as well as the years of the advertisements are chosen mostly as a means of comparison in this case study. Such different points of comparison, especially within a case study, help us verify the strength of our explanation – the changing caste/class relationship.

The Indian Constitution was adopted in 1950, making caste discrimination illegal. Thus we can consider this year as a beginning of a political challenge to the traditional caste hierarchy and a good starting point in an historical study such this. A comparison with classifieds in 1970 and further in 1990 demonstrates the extent of these changes in the caste structure. By examining the caste/class dynamics over these two time periods we can obtain a picture of how caste is changing in the arena of marriage.

The matrimonial classifieds were studied to demonstrate the changes in marriage with regards to an increasing significance of class and the gendered nature of the process. I will show how class as denoted by education, income, and occupation has become more important in arranging marriages. The advertisements have been analysed qualitatively.

This study focuses on the marriage patterns among Hindus in India since the factor of caste is strongest in this group. Moreover, the study is largely confined to the middle and upper-middle classes that would be the dominant sections of the population using an English language daily. My examination of an English language daily limits the sample to a certain group in the society – educated, English speaking, middle classes. Future research with regional dailies – both English language and/or local, regional languages could be undertaken to further pursue the arguments presented here.

Data

Classifieds in 1950

A total of 122 editions of *The Times of India* were analysed in the year 1950 that covered the months of March, June, September, and December. In this period matrimonial advertisements appeared under the general section of the classifieds in the paper. The total number of matrimonial ads in each of these months in 1950 is shown in Table 7.1.

Table 7.1

Matrimonials in 1950 by each quarter

Month	*Number of matrimonials*
March	20
June	31
Sept	26
Dec	43

A typical classified in 1950 read as follows:

"Wanted a Tamil [South Indian linguistic group and State] Sartha [subcaste] bridegroom of about 25 [age] in good business or service [salaried job] for a fair, beautiful girl of 19 of same sect enrolled in B.Sc. [Bachelor of Sciences]" (*The Times of India*, March 28, 1950: 2).

"Wanted for handsome Nair (Kayastha) [subcaste; caste respectively] officer, 30, pay 600... really pretty bride, Govt officer's daughter, any Province, language, but real beauty" (*The Times of India*, June 2, 1950: 2).

"Really beautiful, tall, slim and educated match (24-27) [age] for a Punjabee Khatri [region; subcaste] bachelor govt officer (35) drawing over Rs 800" (*The Times of India*, December 4, 1950: 2)

In all of the classifieds that appear in this period, what is notable is that women are described in very specific terms of their physical appearance, personality, and household skills, such as 'sweet tempered', 'fair', 'beautiful', 'artistic', 'expert in household and needlework', while men are described in general traits of their caste and age. At this point in time we do not observe the detailed class attributes of their occupation or education which suggests that class considerations are not dominant in comparison to caste.

The sample that was examined for this period (March, June, September, and December) matrimonial classifieds remain low in number compared to the rest of the classifieds. Typically the matrimonials do not even cover one full column at this point in time; they are less than half of one column out of the total of five or six columns of general classifieds. The low number of classifieds suggests that placing an advertisement for marriage was not a common and acceptable means of arranging a marriage. Furthermore we note that references to subcastes are prominent in the form of groom from the same sect or 'Tamil Sartha' or 'Gaud Saraswat' indicating that endogamous unit of caste remains significant in this time period.

Advertisements in 1970

By 1970, India had achieved some important milestones in its political economy, though widespread poverty remained. For example, on the one hand, by 1970 India gained self-sufficiency in food production (Keay, 2000: 524) but on the other, one of the main slogans for a national election in 1971 used by Mrs. Indira Gandhi was 'Garibi Hataao' (Out with Poverty) (ibid.: 523). Within this context, the reservations policy in India continues to bring about changes in the traditional caste structure.

These changes can be seen particularly with reference to the literacy rates among the scheduled castes. The literacy rate among Scheduled Castes increased from 10.27 per cent in the 1961 census to 14.67 per cent in the 1971 census, although it lagged behind the literacy rate for general population (Mendelsohn and Vicziany, 1998: 141).[5] Thus, the traditional caste hierarchy continues to change.

With regard to the matrimonials during this period a total of 122 editions of *The Times of India* were examined covering the months of March, June, September, and December in the year 1970. Like the classifieds in 1950, the matrimonial advertisements in 1970 still appear in the general classifieds section of the newspaper. However, we can see that the number of classifieds has increased compared to 1950. The number of advertisements in various months during 1970 is shown in Table 7.2 below.

Table 7.2

Matrimonials in 1970 by each quarter

Month	*Number of matrimonials*
March	210
June	121
Sept	72
Dec	104

In this time period, we observe that the class attributes of men have become more prominent and are sometimes emphasized more than their physical appearance or personality traits. Women, however, continue to be described in terms of their physical appearance and domestic personality. For example, an advertisement in March 1970 read:

> "Handsome South Indian Brahmin boy, 29, engineer, 167 cms [height] drawing above four figure [salary] proceeding to USA shortly, seeks fair, beautiful, healthy, accomplished graduate bride having well connected parents domiciled preferably in Bombay/Bangalore/Madras" (*The Times of India,* March 19, 1970:2).

Another classified also emphasized the class attributes of the groom.

> "Wanted a beautiful educated homely bride for a Kayastha, [subcaste] 24, [age] mechanical engineer with bright prospects serving in a reputed firm in Bombay salary Rs 1400 per month. Father University professor" (*The Times of India,* September 17, 1970: 2).

The advertisements placed by parents of young women seeking grooms also emphasize their daughter's physical appearance and 'pleasing personality' and they too demand specific class attributes in prospective grooms. The following classifieds illustrate these qualities:

> "Correspondence with horoscopes invited from Tamil Smartha Brahmin [region/linguistic ethnic group, subcaste, caste] parents/boys under 30 employed decently public/private sector for girl 24, tall, slim, fair, post graduate science well-up in home management, father senior Central Government officer retired" (*The Times of India*, June 25, 1970: 2).

> "Wanted: highly educated well-placed boy around 28-30 for MA [Master's degree] domesticated girl age 25 from Arora family" (*The Times of India*, June 28, 1970: 2).

However, there are two noticeable changes in the classifieds that appear in this time period. One, there is an increase in the number of classifieds that appear in the newspaper. Secondly, in those classifieds where families seek a prospective bride for their sons, we now see instances of families who invite correspondence from employed women. However, contrary to men, these employed women have to also demonstrate qualities of a 'good traditional daughter-in-law'. For example:

> "A Suitable Agarwal [subcaste] match between 29-33 for well connected, highly educated Ph.D. girl, well versed in household work" (*The Times of India*, December 23, 1970: 2).

Even an advertisement placed by a woman's family for a woman with professional accomplishments reads:

> "matrimonial correspondence invited from Sindhi boys for pretty, young, graduate girl of 23, working in foreign mission, accomplished in music and other homely [domestic] activities" (*The Times of India*, June 7, 1970: 2).

Women continued to be described in terms such as 'well versed in domestic chores', 'domesticated', or 'accomplished in homely activities'.

Thus we begin to see the gendered nature of changes in the matrimonial advertisements where women's traits continue to be described in terms of 'traditional' gender traits and men are increasingly described in 'modern' terms of their class attributes – high incomes, prestigious occupations, association with foreign countries and their educational attainments.

Advertisements in 1990

The matrimonial advertisements in 1990 continue to demonstrate significant changes. First, the advertisements have started to appear weekly, in every Sunday edition. Further, there is an enormous increase in the numbers of advertisements being placed in the newspaper. I looked at a total of 18 editions of *The Times of India* in 1990 covering the months of, March, June, September, and December. The number of matrimonial advertisements has jumped from hundreds to thousands and instead of appearing in the general classifieds section of the newspaper, now they appear in a separate matrimonial classifieds section.

In this period the advertisements typically span more than one full page of the newspaper. For example, in the June 3, 1990 edition, the matrimonial ads appeared on two pages. One full page, consisted of nine columns of matrimonials with an average of 25 advertisements per column, while the second page consisted of approximately 4 columns with an average of 25 advertisements in the column thus giving us approximately 325 advertisements for that edition (*The Times of India,* June 3, 1990, p.2; 4).

The advertisements are also better organized now – there are separate sections of 'Wanted Brides' and 'Wanted Grooms'. Within each of these sections, the classifieds are organized alphabetically. These changes could easily be attributed to editorial decisions. When comparing the three decades, we can see the seasonal/ monthly variations as well as the changes over the decades. Figure 7.1 demonstrates the dramatic changes in the matrimonial advertisements comparing 1950, 1970, and 1990.

As the modernization process of India continues in the nineties, caste structure remains significant in society. In particular, caste has become an important political identity (Keay, 2000: 533). At the same time the social rigidity of caste continues to decline.

The modern challenges to the traditional caste hierarchy continue with expansion of opportunities to the Scheduled Castes via reservations policy and overall economic growth. The literacy rate among the scheduled castes, for instance, increased from 21.3 per cent in 1981 to 37.4 per cent in 1991 (Mendelsohn and Vicziany, 1998: 141). Thus the traditional caste hierarchy continues to weaken,

Figure 7.1

Comparisons of The Matrimonial Ads in The Times Of India 1950-1990 (quarterly)

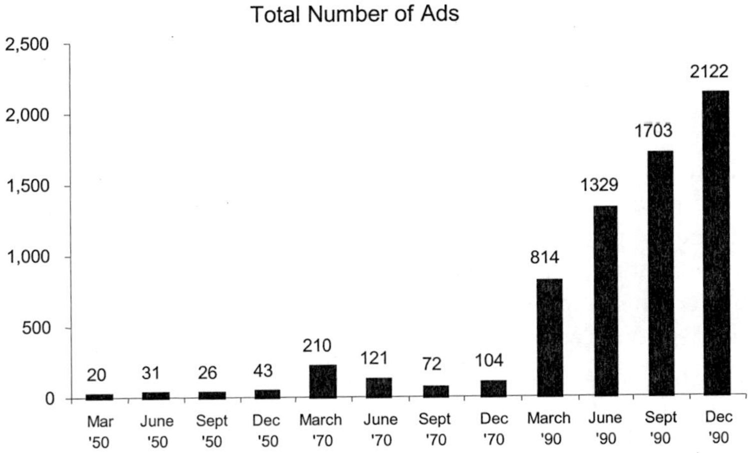

and despite an increased politicization of caste we continue to observe a weakening of the significance of caste identity in other social arenas including, marriage. These changes are reflected in the matrimonial advertisements by the nineties.

Matrimonial classifieds in this time period have started including advertisements that show a loosening of caste endogamous requirements for marriage. We see phrases such as, 'caste no bar' or 'no bars' or 'no dowry, caste bar' that represent a trend towards broadening of the caste endogamy for seeking matrimony as illustrated in the following classifieds:

> "Alliance invited for U.P. Kayastha boy [region/subcaste] age 24 height 183 cms, final year Medical settled in Belgium from fair, tall, educated girls, caste no bar" (*The Times of India*, December 9, 1990: 18).

> "168/28/4500 [salary] handsome MBBS Maratha seeks [bride] fair Doctor/Computer/Engineer/Chartered Accountant. No bars" (*The Times of India*, December 9, 1990).

> "Alliance invited by Bombay based Doctor M.D. Rs. 4000 Maharashtriyan Maratha [regional/linguistic group; subcaste] girl 28/260 beautiful slim from Doctor, Engineer, or any other

> highly qualified. Caste no bar" (*The Times of India*, March 11, 1990: 4)

We begin to see two important changes in the matrimonial advertisements during this period. First, we see a weakening of caste endogamy in matrimonial classifieds. Secondly, the dramatic increase in the number of ads being placed suggests that it is becoming an acceptable and common way of arranging marriages. Despite these changes the overall gender disparities remain and they are reflected in the advertisements.

Families continue to emphasize the traditional gender attributes of physical appearance, pleasing personality, and competence in running a household in their daughters, even employed and educated ones while seeking very 'modern' attributes in the grooms. Classifieds such as below illustrate these comparisons:

> "Alliance invited for Punjabi Arora [region/linguistic ethnic group; subcaste] girl 22 years/160 centimeters, convent educated [likely to be fluent in English, a desirable trait] graduate, homely, beautiful, sharp features [facial] from business family. Only status family need apply" (*The Times of India*, Mumbai, March 11, 1990: 4).

> "Match for North Indian Brahmbhatt Brahmin girl, 19/156 cms, graduate, good looking, homely. Father in government service" (*The Times of India, Mumbai*, March 11, 1990: 4).

> "29/177 USA qualified Computer Engineer Brahmin, handsome, fair intelligent, dynamic, starting own computer industry. Seeks extremely beautiful, fair, slim, intelligent bride" (*The Times of India, Mumbai*, December 1990:18).

Also, for the most part, classifieds posted by men or families seeking brides have a longer list of attributes they are looking for in the bride to be. In contrast, advertisements seeking grooms seem to have only a minimum of requirements of a groom to be – that he be of a certain age and be employed. Many advertisements posted by women's families seeking grooms also emphasize the employment status of the male guardians in the family – such as father or brother's status – demonstrating the dependent status of women in the family. This is rare among classifieds placed by men's families.

Advertisements post-1995

An examination of matrimonial classifieds in *The Times of India* today reveals that there have been very significant changes in as far as the way they are organized. I could not determine an exact date when these changes started, but it appears that 1995 onwards the classifieds in the newspaper started to be divided into highly specialized categories based on religion, occupations, and linguistic regions.

There were on an average 28 categories of matrimonial advertisements placed by both men's and women's families in the editions that I analysed (*The Times of India*, June 4, 1995; January 10, 1999:8-10; September 12, 2004). Advertisements placed by men and women's families are now divided on the basis of caste affiliations such as Brahmin, Kayastha, Jat, Khatri, Agarwal, Gujarati Patidar and so on; religious affiliations such as Muslims, Christians, Sikhs; linguistic or regional affiliations such as Oriya, Bengali, Malayali, Telugu, Punjabi, even emigrant status such as those residing in the US, Australia or UK.

The organization by various categories seems to be an editorial decision because other newspapers do not necessarily have that format. For example, another major daily *The Hindu*, published from Chennai had different categories based on language groups and also fewer advertisements. The categories by *The Times of India* could also be a function of the number of advertisements received by the newspaper.

Nevertheless, the post-1995 advertisements continue to support the argument that the traditional caste endogamy is weakening for considerations of marriage. In particular, the category titled, 'cosmopolitans' is a good evidence of this point. In this category endogamous caste associations are not critical and those who advertise (both men and women's families) emphasize their 'cosmopolitan' status by stating 'caste no bar' as part of their classifieds. This was a trend that we saw had begun to appear at a smaller scale in the classifieds in 1990. By late nineties, this has become an established category and a typical classified in the cosmopolitan category read:

> "Seeking beautiful, very fair, tall, medical graduate girl for very handsome Agarwal boy 27/182 [age and height]. Caste no bar" (*The Times of India*, January 17, 1999: 7).

> The factor of endogamous subcaste units has become less critical in the classifieds in this time period. As Beteille points out, "ambiguity over what constitutes the unit of endogamy has almost certainly become more pervasive now" (1996: 164).

Another very significant change that appears in the classifieds during this period is the category of classifieds placed by the scheduled castes. This would have been very unusual in the earlier classifieds. All of the classifieds placed by the scheduled caste families are for sons and daughters who are educated and employed in white collar occupations. The following is a good example of this category of classifieds:

> "Invited: match for a Ramdasia Scheduled Caste boy, 27/5'10"; Class I civil engineer; from tall, fair, beautiful well-educated girl" (*The Times of India,* January 10, 1999: 9).

> "Dhobi [the lower caste of a washerman] Boy, B.E.[Bachelor in Engineering] 29/160, Government job, Rupees 10K wants vegetarian, religious girl" (*The Times of India,* Sept 12, 2004: 7).

Thus we see that caste endogamy is weakening along with concurrent indications of an increasing significance of class in arranging marriages in India today. This is further exemplified in the variety of the occupational categories in the classifieds. Now, in addition to caste, religious, and regional categories there are a number of classifieds placed on the basis of specific occupations such as, doctors, engineers, MBA [business school graduates], and accountants and so on. These categories are used by both women and men's families in order to ease the matching of the corresponding occupation or educational attainment.

Finally, we also see a category titled, 'Working Girls' representing employed women. This is clearly an indication that the employed status of women is becoming common among the middle classes who advertise in the newspapers. However, the fact that there is such a separate category implies that employed status of women is still seen as deviant as compared to that of men. Despite the employed status of women, such advertisements continue to describe women in traditional aspects of their physical appearance and personality, in addition to their employment status. For example:

> "Alliance invited from Chartered Accountants/MBA/Professional boy from good family for 22/160 Charter Accountant

girl, very fair, slim, beautiful, pleasing personality, sharp features" (*The Times of India*, January 17, 1999:4)

Another classified reads:

"Wanted: Administrative services, professionals, suitable match for graceful, poised, fair, slim, beautiful girl, 5'2", 24 years, finance MBA. Belongs to a reputed family" (*The Times of India*, January 17, 1999: 14).

Thus we see that although women's employment status is becoming an added factor to attract well placed grooms, it does not offset the traditional gender traits of pleasing personality, or physical appearance. The salaries of employed women are not advertised as a central attraction in the marriage unlike men's salaries which are advertised very prominently. In fact, in the ads placed by men's families, the prospective groom is rarely described as having 'pleasing personality' or beyond the basic minimum of physical attributes of height and age.

Discussion

This study of matrimonial advertisements in India found that with modernization, as economic stratification in society has changed in terms of caste and class, so have these factors in the sphere of marriage. With an increase in the significance of class over caste as a determinant of an individual's status in society we also see an acknowledgement of these considerations in the arena of marriage. The rigidity as far as which sub-castes constitute an endogamous group has shown signs of abating for considerations of marriage.

However, we see that this process of change in the marriage structure has gendered outcomes just as there are gendered outcomes of the overall development process in developing countries (Young 1997; Blumberg 1995). Thus, modernization has benefited men more than women as can be seen by the continuing gender inequality. For instance, one of the class attributes – the literacy rates – among men and women remains unequal in India. While the literacy rate for men in India has increased from 27.6 to 75.3 per cent during 1951-2001, the literacy rates for women lagged at 8.8 per cent in 1951 and 53.7 per cent in 2001 (Observer Research Foundation, 1992: 63, censusindia.net). Furthermore gender inequality in the form of declining sex ratio in India has been well documented (Krishnaji, 2000; Das Gupta and Shuzhuo, 1999; Sen, 1990). Sex ratio in India has continued to decline from 946 women per 1,000 men in 1951 to 929 women in 1991 (Bose, 1991: 50) although it increased to 933 by 2001 census (censusindia.net/results).

When we look at the lower castes, a similar pattern emerges where men have gained more from modernization than women. For example, the literacy rate of scheduled caste women – 24 per cent in 1991 – lagged behind the overall scheduled caste literacy rate – 37.4 per cent in 1991 – (Mendelsohn and Vicziany, 1998: 35, 141) By the 2001 census although there are gains made by both men and women, disparities persist[6]. By 2001 census, 11.5 per cent of Scheduled caste male literates in India have finished matriculation/secondary level of education, while 8.5 per cent of scheduled caste females have done so[7] (censusindia.net). Thus in the context of changing ranking systems, men of all castes, including the scheduled castes, have gained more than women. Men are described more prominently in terms of their class attributes which are more prestigious in a changing structure of the ranking systems.

This study shows that when we link broader macro-social changes with the changes in the marriage structure we see that marriage in India has not remained static. It has changed, but continues to retain some of its traditional elements. With regards to caste in marriage, we see caste moving in two directions: On the one hand, there is evidence that caste still matters as indicated by the advertisements asking for similar caste grooms or brides. On the other hand, there are indications that caste is not as important anymore in marriage as denoted by the various considerations that compete with caste now and also the extension of traditional upper caste norms among the scheduled castes such as the classifieds placed by them. In particular, we see that class considerations are becoming important in arranging marriages for all castes.

The weakening of caste ties is also demonstrated by growing usage of matrimonial classifieds as a means to arrange marriages. Although the advertisements are placed by the parents of the son or daughter, the importance of other kin ties in arranging marriages has declined which traditionally played an important role. This is clearly indicated by an increase in the number of advertisements in the last two decades.

Conclusion

In this study of matrimonial advertisements in India I show that the Indian marriage structure is changing as well as persistent. By placing the marriage structure within the framework of gender and development we can see the dynamic relationship between gender and the political economy. With modernization, economic stratification has changed in all areas of society including marriage. However, the benefits of these changes are accrued more to men than women as seen by the modern attributes that are attached more to men than women. Men are increasingly described in modern attributes of class – education and occupation, while women continue to be described in the traditional attributes of personality traits.

This historical analysis of Indian marriage demonstrates that changes in the marriage structure result from modernization, while the persistence of the traditional aspect of marriage – caste endogamy – is an outcome of the gender inequality in marriage and overall society. Both of these aspects of marriage can be explained by the gendered nature of the modernization process and also the gendered nature of the social institutions of caste and marriage.

Notes

1. Traditionally the caste structure has been divided into four *varnas* or castes: Brahmins (priests and teachers), Kshatriyas (warriors and rulers), Vaishyas (merchants), and Shudras (manual labour). The Untouchables (those engaged in 'polluting' occupations), now referred to as the Scheduled Castes, have traditionally been considered outside of the caste hierarchy. Each caste comprises of many *jatis* or sub-castes which are the reality for most Hindus and the rules regarding marriages and other social associations are governed by one's *jati,* which are numerous.
2. In this survey, 13 per cent neither agreed nor disagreed with the notion that they will marry someone of the same caste (Ghose and Jahagirdar, 1998: 69).
3. *The Times of India* was launched in 1838 and today has a daily circulation of more than a million copies (www.etgmr.com).
4. The shift of matrimonials from daily to Sunday editions in 1990 may have been an editorial decision; a cursory look at an earlier edition of *The Times of India,* March 1980, showed that by this time the classifieds were being published on Sundays.

5. The literacy rate for the general population rose from 24.02 per cent to 29.45 per cent between the 1961 and the 1971 censuses (ibid.).
6. In 2001 census, 27.9 per cent of Scheduled Caste males and 29.8 per cent of females had primary level education. The comparable national rates were 24.8 per cent among males and 28.2 per cent among females (censusindia.net).
7. The comparable national rates were 15.2 per cent among males and 12.5 per cent among females (censusindia.net).

References

Beteille, Andre (1996), Caste in Contemporary India, In C.J. Fuller (ed.), *Caste Today*, Delhi: Oxford University Press.

Blumberg, Ruth. L. (1995), Introduction: Engendering Wealth and Well Being in an Era of Economic Transformation, In R.L. Blumberg, et al. (eds.), *Engendering Wealth and Well Being*, CO: Westview Press.

Bose, Ashish (1991), *Demographic Diversity of India,* Delhi: B.R. Publishing Corporation.

Census of India: www.censusindia.net/results/C_series.

Das Gupta, Monica and Li Shuzhou (1999), Gender Bias in China, South Korea and India 1920-1990: Effects of War, Famine, and Fertility Decline, *Development and Change,* 30 (3), Special Issue on Gendered Poverty and Wellbeing.

Derne, Steve (1995), *Culture in Action: Family Life, Emotion, and Male Dominance in Banaras, India,* Albany: State University of New York Press.

Dumont, Louis (1970), *Homo Hierarchicus: The Caste System and Its Implications,* Delhi: Vikas.

Ghose, S. and A. Jahagirdar (1998), Cool in Kaliyug, *Outlook,* December 14, 1998: 60-70.

Government of India (1992), *Eighth Five-Year Plan, 1992-97,* Vol. II, Sectoral Programmes of Development, New Delhi: The Planning Commission.

— (1993), *Census of India 1991, Series-1 Paper 1 of 1993,* Union Primary Census Abstracts for Scheduled castes and Scheduled Tribes, New Delhi: Registrar General and Census Commissioner.

Jain, N. (1996), A Search for Intimacy, *India Today,* December 31, 1996: 78-85.

Kapadia, Karin (2002), Translocal Modernities and Transformations of Gender and Caste, In Karin Kapadia (ed.), *The Violence of Development,* London: Zed Books.

— (1995), *Siva and Her Sisters: Gender, Caste, and Class in Rural South India,* Boulder, CO: Westview Press.

Keay, John (2000), *India: A History,* New York: Grove Press.

Klass, N. (1980). *The Emergence of the South Asian Social System,* Philadelphia: Institute for the Studies of Human Issues.

Kolenda, Pauline (2003), *Caste, Marriage and Inequality: Essays on North and South India,* Jaipur: Rawat.

Krishnaji, N. (2000), Trends in Sex Ratio: A Review I Tribute to Asok Mitra, *Economic and Political Weekly* 35 (14): 1161-63.

Mayer, A.C. (1996), Caste in an Indian Village: Change and Continuity, 1954-1992, In C.J. Fuller (ed.), *Caste Today,* Delhi: Oxford University Press.

Mendelsohn, Oliver and Marika Vicziany (1998), *The Untouchables: Subordination, Poverty and the State in Modern India,* Cambridge, UK: Cambridge University Press.

Milner, M. Jr. (1994), *Status and Sacredness: A General Theory of Status Relations and an Analysis of Indian Culture,* NY: Oxford University Press.

Narayan, Uma (1993), Paying the Price of Change: Women, Modernization, and Arranged Marriages in India, In M. Turshen and R. Holcomb (eds.) *Women's Lives and Public Policy,* CT: Greenwood Press.

Observer Research Foundation (1992) *India 1992,* New Delhi.

Rudd, Jane (2001), Dowry Murder: An Example of Violence Against Women, *Women's Studies International Forum* (24) 5: 513-22.

Sen, Amartya (1990), More Than 100 Million Women are Missing, *New York Review of Books,* 20 December: 61-66.

Srinivas, M.N. (2002), *Collected Essays,* New Delhi: Oxford University Press.

— (1996), Introduction, In Srinivas (ed.), *Caste: Its Twentieth Century Avatar,* New Delhi: Viking.

— (1989), *The Cohesive Role of Sanskritization and Other Essays,* Delhi: Oxford University Press.

Stacey, Judith (1983), *Patriarchy and Socialist Revolution in* China, Berkeley: University of California Press.

The Times of India (Mumbai), March 28, 1950; June 2, 1950; December 4, 1950.

— (Delhi), March 19, 1970; June 7, 1970; June 25, 1970; June 28, 1970; Sept 17, 1970; December 23, 1970.

— (Mumbai), June 3, 1990; March 11, 1990; December 9, 1990; June 4, 1995.

— (New Delhi), January 10, 1999; January 17, 1999.

— (New Delhi), September 12, 2004.

Uberoi, Patricia (1994), Introduction, In Patricia Uberoi (ed.), *Family, Kinship and Marriage in India,* New Delhi: Oxford University Press.

Vindhya, U. (2000), Dowry Deaths in Andhra Pradesh, India, *Violence Against Women* (6) 10: 1085-1108.

Young, Kate (1997), Gender and Development, In Nalini Visvanathan, et al. (eds.), *The Women, Gender and Development Reader*, London: Zed Books.

8

Patriarchy and Paternalism in Intimate Partner Violence

A Study of Domestic Violence in Rural India

NIVEDITHA MENON AND MICHAEL P. JOHNSON

Violence against women is a social phenomenon that crosses age, culture, and national boundaries. In all societies, women have been subjected to cultural and familial institutions that result in physical, sexual, and psychological harm. These acts of violence have worked to subjugate women and have contributed greatly to the gender inequality that is prevalent all over the world. In India, this violence takes the form of rape, sexual harassment, female infanticide, widow burning, dowry deaths, and domestic violence. The focus of this chapter will be on domestic violence in India.

As with family violence in Western societies, violence within the Indian home has long been considered a 'private matter'. Beginning in the 1970s with a focus on the problem of dowry deaths, the Indian women's movement has brought attention to the wider problem of domestic violence, redefining dowry deaths and other violence against women as a product of unequal relationships between men and women in India (Pande, 2000; Omvedt, 1990). Many women's organizations were formed to examine the problem of domestic violence at the local and national level. The movement not only gave rise to new laws specifically to address dowry and domestic violence (Bloch and Rao, 1997), but also sparked an explosion of research in this area by social scientists, social workers, and policy makers (Daga, et al., 1998; Datar, 1996; Jaiswal, 2000). Official estimates from the Ministry of Law, Justice and Company Affairs speculate that over 60 per cent of urban households experience domestic violence (defined by the Indian legal system as physical or mental torture), out of which five per cent report the matter to the police and prosecute the perpetrator of the abuse (Jaising, 2001). As for domestic violence more narrowly defined in terms of physical assaults, a number of studies suggest that the rate of domestic violence in households ranges from 33 per cent to 66 per cent (Magar, 2001; Mitra, 1999; Rao, et al., 2000; Bhatti, 1990; Visaria, 1999; Poonacha and Pandey, 1999, Martin, et al., 1999).

The diversity of India's population (Katzenstein, 1989) has led researchers and activists to broaden their focus to a more contextualized view wherein the effects of the intersection of caste, religion, and class on the prevalence and form of violence could be recognized (Vindhya, 2000; Abraham, 1995). This broader view has mainly focused on patriarchy as the primary lens through which domestic violence is addressed (Mies, 1980). Many researchers see prevalence of domestic violence as a manifestation of patriarchal values in the family (Krishnaraj, 1989; Vindhya, 2000; Visaria, 1999; Ganesh, 1989, Moore, 1994) and as "an instrument of power used by…men to keep…women in their place" (Ray, 1999). Therefore, regional differences and associated cultural differences preclude a 'universalist' approach, requiring researchers and activists alike to examine patriarchy as it is manifested in every class, caste, language and regional category.

Central to this discussion of the relationship between patriarchy and the use of violence against women is the site of such violence – the home. Women's position in Indian society has been partly shaped by the ideology of the Indian family. Although the family is theoretically a sanctuary for women, it also has the potential of acting as a prison with a restrictive code of conduct (Abraham, 1995). The hierarchy of relationships that typically characterize a patriarchal home "develops along age and gender lines" (D'Cruz and Bharat, 2001), so that young women entering a patriarchal household are vulnerable to acts of violence from their marital family. In fact, research indicates that if the new member of the household is unable to adjust to the household, violent means are sometimes used to elicit obedience from her (Mukhopadhyay, 1998; Ghadially and Kumar, 1988). Also, when a woman does not succumb to traditional socialization and does not conform to traditional gender roles, she is more likely to be beaten by her family (Goode and Tambiah, 1973). These acts of violence also tend to be socially accepted (Agnes, 1990; Srinivasan, 1998). Although violence against women is generally frowned upon, there is a cultural acceptance of men disciplining or taming their women, so that "when a man cannot tame his wife in any other way, he uses force" (Agnes, 1990). Bhatti (1990) also reports that most of the respondents in his study agreed that men beat women because they have to be controlled and kept in their place. Therefore, feminist theories of heterosexual intimate partner violence are rooted in the assumption that such violence, or at least some such violence (Johnson, 1995), is deployed in the service of men's interest in controlling 'their' women (Johnson, 1995; Kurz, 1989; Pence and Paymar, 1993).

Armed with this feminist theoretical understanding of the relationship between patriarchal attitudes and violence against women, we set out to investigate the more general argument that social contexts that are more patriarchal will produce more intimate partner violence against women. Support for this seemingly straightforward extension of feminist theories of intimate partner violence is surprisingly limited. Early work in the United States by Yllö and Straus (1983) found a curvilinear relationship between a state-level index of the status of women and state rates of assaults against wives. In a more global study, however, Levinson (1989) found positive relationships between a number of measures of gender inequality and wife beating for the cultural groups documented in the Human Relations Area Files. As you will see, our investigation of intimate partner violence in contemporary India has led us to revise that hypothesis and to frame our interpretation of the data in terms of Jackman's (1994) work on paternalism. We will present this extension of feminist theories of intimate partner violence following the presentation of our original hypotheses and the data that led us to revise them.

Hypotheses

Region

While the pervasiveness of domestic violence goes unquestioned, the extent of the violence and the manifestation of the violence are different for different regions (Miller, 1999). The research on regions has usually concentrated on the north-south cultural dichotomy

(Miller, 1999). While this comparison is useful, it does not recognize the diversity among areas within the north or the south. Thus, we examined differences among various regions and hypothesized that because the north-eastern and southern parts of India have documented high-status for women (Miller, 1999; Srinivasan, 1998), they would report a lower incidence of violence compared to the northern regions.

Family Characteristics

Non-nuclear family structure

One of the more common forms of the patriarchal family form in India is the joint family, in which married couples move into the husband's family household, and the wife comes under the patriarchal control of the head of the household, typically a senior male member of the family. We hypothesized that because of the 'traditional' nature of the joint family system, a woman is more susceptible to abuse from joint family members (Fernandez, 1997; D'Cruz and Bharat, 2001). Because the dataset that we used for this study (Demographic Health Survey, 1999) provides limited opportunity for constructing the complex relationships that represent joint family systems, we had to be satisfied with indirect indicators of the 'jointness' of respondents' families. So while we hypothesized that there would be more violence against women in traditional joint families than in nuclear families, the categories of comparison are in fact non-nuclear (which would be predominantly joint) and nuclear.

Joint decision-making

We also hypothesized that if a woman has autonomy in the household, she is less likely to be beaten by her husband (Visaria, 1999). In other words, we expected that if there are other members in the household who make decisions for the woman, be it her husband or other family members, she will be more likely to be abused.

Natal family violence

Apart from these factors, we also examined the woman's history of abuse. Because marriages are usually endogamous in India, women are very likely to transfer to households similar to their own (Das, 1975; Madan, 1975; D'Cruz and Bharat, 2001). If the ideology of the threat of violence was present in her natal family, it is likely that the belief systems of the marital family would be similar. Thus, if the woman experienced physical assault in her natal home, chances would be higher that she would experience physical assault from her husband.

Socio-economic status

Research in India has documented that women from lower socio-economic status experience more physical violence than women from higher socio-economic status (Bhatti, 1990; Visaria, 1999). While non-physical forms of abuse are prevalent in higher socio-economic categories, reports of physical assault are substantially higher in the lower classes. So we hypothesized that reports of physical violence will be less likely for families with higher socio-economic status.

Religion

The variability reflected in a region may be related to variations in religious affiliation. Because there is a politically charged religious propaganda that suggests that some groups might be more violent than others, we chose not to hypothesize too broadly about effects of particular religions on domestic violence. In India the effects of religion are also complicated by the fact that because the states are divided on linguistic bases, religious groups are likely to adhere to some extent to the cultural norms of the region, rather than the general norms of their religion (Ray, 1999). The only specific prediction that we were willing to make was that there would be a lower prevalence of violence amongst religions that advocate peaceful ways of living, i.e., Buddhism and Jainism.

Personal Characteristics

Education

One of the major predictors of domestic violence is education. The risk of being beaten is substantially reduced if the woman is educated. Many policy recommendations therefore concentrate on the education of women as a key factor in reducing violence (Ray 1999). Thus, we proposed that women will report a lower incidence of violence if they are highly educated.

Labour force participation and financial independence

Labour force participation and financial independence are important factors. Because working women typically contribute to the family income, it is hypothesized that the self-reliance of these women will lower the chances of abuse (Levinson, 1989; Mencher, 1989; Arora, 1999). Therefore, the chances of experiencing abuse from their husband are reduced for women who are engaged in the work force. However, in many parts of the country, women engaged in the labour force are likely to give their entire income to their families. Thus, work force participation might not automatically make them financially independent. To gauge the effect of financial independence of women on the experience of domestic violence, we have included the variable in the study. We proposed that women's financial independence, apart from their labour force participation, will lower the incidence of violence (Mencher, 1989).

Attitudes towards domestic violence

There is considerable variability in women's own attitudes towards domestic violence. Some women believe that there are conditions under which a husband is justified in beating his wife. They do not consider such 'punishment' to be violent (ICRW, 1998). Therefore, we predicted that attitudes endorsing the use of violence will be reflected in higher incidence of spousal violence. The more positive a woman's attitudes towards domestic violence, the greater the likelihood that she will experience abuse from her husband.

Methods

Sample

The dataset used in this study is the Demographic Health Survey conducted in India in 1999, otherwise known as the National Family Health Survey (NFHS-1999). The main objective of this survey was to obtain state-level and national-level information on various aspects of health such as fertility, family planning, nutrition of women and children, and quality of health and family welfare services. NFHS-2 is a nationally representative household survey, covering over 99 per cent of India's population living in all 26 states. The overall target sample size of the survey was approximately 90,000 ever-married women between the ages of 15 to 49.

Because of the complexity and diversity involved in the examination of domestic violence in India, we narrowed the focus of this study to rural women. We further narrowed the sample to women who were currently residing with their husbands, to ensure that the absence of the husband in the household did not compromise the rates of domestic violence reported by women. Thus, the sub-sample for this study consists of married rural women who are living in the same residence as their husbands. These two specifications reduced the size of the sample to approximately fifty thousand women.

Questionnaires

The NFHS-2 survey used three questionnaires – the Household Questionnaire, the Woman's Questionnaire and the Village Questionnaire. Only the first two are used in this study. The Household Questionnaire collected information from the head of the household and in the absence of the head of the household, from any other member of the family, on various characteristics of the health of all its members, such as the presence of asthma, tuberculosis, malaria, etc. It also collected information on characteristics of the household such as number of members living in the household, religion of the family, ownership of property or house and other information. The responses to the household questions established household members' eligibility for the Women's Questionnaire.

All women in the household aged 15 through 49 who were currently married, formerly married, or widowed were interviewed using the Women's Questionnaire. Eligible women from the households were asked about age, marital status, education, and employment status. The majority of the questions in the survey were focused on the reproductive behaviour of the women, addressing issues of use of contraception, sources of family planning, reproductive health, and knowledge of AIDS. As women's reproductive health is closely related to their physical well-being, women were also asked about their experience of domestic violence in the household and their attitudes towards violence.

Measures

Dependent Variable: Husband Violence

A series of two questions assessed intimate partner violence. The first whether the woman has experienced violence from anyone:

— Since you have completed 15 years of age, have you ever been beaten or mistreated physically by any person?

If the respondent answers in the affirmative, she is prompted by the next question:

— Who has beaten or mistreated you physically?

Interviewers were instructed to record all the persons the respondent disclosed. The answers to these questions can include members of the natal family, marital family, and also strangers. We coded women who were beaten by no one or only someone other than their husband as 0 and those beaten by their husbands as 1.

Independent Variables

Region. The Women's Questionnaire begins with questions regarding the place of residence of the respondent, including the state in which the respondent resides. We have collapsed the 25 states into six broad regions as follows:

North (Delhi, Haryana, Himachal Pradesh, Jammu and Kashmir, Punjab, Rajasthan)

Central (Madhya Pradesh, Uttar Pradesh)

East (Bihar, Orissa, West Bengal)

Northeast (Arunachal Pradesh, Assam, Manipur, Meghalaya, Mizoram, Nagaland, Sikkim)

West (Goa, Gujarat, Maharashtra)

South (Andhra Pradesh, Karnataka, Kerala, Tamil Nadu).

We were guided by the Census of India and NFHS-2 to use these categories, which tap into the cultural, social, historical, and physical proximity of the states within each regional category.

Family Characteristics

Non-nuclear family structure: In the Household Questionnaire, there are a series of questions that inquire about the number of persons living in the household; their individual relationship to the head of the household; and the age, place of residence, literacy levels and marital status of each member of the family. The researchers working with the raw data manipulated this information into a variable that describes the household structure of the family, focusing only on adults. The categories are as follows.

— No adults
— One adult
— Two adults, opposite sex

— Two adults, same sex
— Three+ related adults
— Unrelated adults.

Because this study examines only women who are currently residing with their husbands, only two categories of this variable were relevant, 'two adults, opposite sex' and 'three+ related adults,' corresponding to nuclear and non-nuclear families, respectively. According to this variable construction, a nuclear family is defined as a family structure that consists of the husband, wife and perhaps some children. A non-nuclear family consists of a husband, wife and other adults, which could include their adult children or other adults, any of whom may have families of their own living within the same household and extended family members of the head of the household.

To measure women's autonomy in the household, the NFHS-2 requests information about women's participation in making household decisions. The question in the original survey was formulated as follows:

— Who makes the following decision in your household?
— What items to cook
— Obtaining healthcare for yourself
— Purchasing jewelry or other major household items
— Your going and staying with parents or siblings
— The answer choices were:
— Respondent
— Husband
— Jointly with husband
— Others in household
— Jointly with others in the household

Another question that related to autonomy was about freedom of movement. The respondent was asked if she needed permission to visit relatives or go to the market.

The complications of creating a scale out of these items led to our final decision to choose one 'best' item to tap autonomy. Because the owner of jewelry in an Indian household is identifiable, we hypothesized that the possession and purchase of jewelry gives women ownership and a modicum of control over that resource (Jacobson, as cited in Leonard, 1979). Jewelry is a piece of property that women can claim rights to and the decision-making process for purchasing such a valuable resource is indicative of women's position and autonomy in the household (Leonard, 1979).

Socio-economic status of the household: We used the presence of basic amenities and possession of commodities in lieu of income levels. In the Household Questionnaire, inquires were made by interviewers about consumer goods that the household possesses. The question is worded as follows:

Does the household own any of the following:

— A mattress
— A pressure cooker
— A moped, scooter or motorcycle, etc.

The Household Questionnaire also asks about the use of amenities by the household. For example, the households were asked about the type of fuel that they used for cooking. The question is worded as follows.

— What type of fuel does your household mainly use for cooking?
— Wood
— Crop residues
— Dung Cakes
— Coal/Coke/Lignite
— Bio-Gas, etc.

The choices given are an indicator of the standard of living of the household. For example, households that use wood for fuel are less likely to be wealthy compared to households that have access to electricity. Similar questions such as source of drinking water and type of toilet facility are also included in the original questionnaire as an indication of socio-economic status.

After reliability tests were performed using all the indicators of socio-economic status, we identified the following final set of 15: the use of electricity, radio, television, bicycle, motor cycle, mattress, cot/bed, table, clock/watch, pressure cooker, sewing machine, water pump, source of drinking water, type of toilet facility and main cooking fuel. We dichotomized the responses to indicate the presence and absence of consumer goods and amenities, and created a scale of socio-economic status by taking the sum of the dichotomized variables. The range of the scale is thus 0 to 15, the lower numbers indicating lower socio-economic status (alpha = .82).

Natal family violence: As mentioned before, women who reported they were beaten after the age of 15 were asked the identity of the perpetrator. We constructed a scale of natal family violence by taking the sum of the dichotomous responses for each of the following relationships: mother, father, stepfather, stepmother, brother, or sister of the respondent. Thus, the potential range of the scale is from 0 to 6. The actual range of the scale is from 0 to 3. The lowest value, 0 indicates that no member of the natal family had abused the respondent and the highest value 3, indicates that three types of natal family members had beaten the respondent since the age of 15.

Personal Characteristics

Education

Education of the respondent is measured by various questions in the questionnaire. Respondents were asked if they ever attended school, what was the highest grade they completed in school, and whether they could read or write. Researchers handling the raw data combined the answers to all the education questions into a number of simpler formats for easier investigation. Out of the many choices, we used the following variable for its ability to capture the variation in the sample. The categories are:

— Higher Secondary complete or more (equivalent to completing senior high school in the United States)
— High School complete (equivalent to completing sophomore year of high school in United States)
— Middle School complete (equivalent to finishing 8th grade in United States)
— Primary School complete (equivalent to finishing 5th grade in United States)
— Literate, < Primary school complete
— Illiterate

Labour force participation

In the Women's Questionnaire, the working status of the respondent was addressed in a variety of questions and although analyses of all of these factors may be useful in assessing the impact of labour force participation on the experience of violence, for the sake of brevity and simplicity, we analysed only one critical aspect of working status. Women were asked whether they worked for family or outsiders. The question was worded as follows:

— Do you do the work for your family's farm or business, for someone else, or are you self-employed?
— Family farm/Business
— Someone else
— Self-employed.

This aspect of women's work was chosen for two reasons. It gave an indication as to the autonomy of women's work, and also of the physical mobility of the women and interaction with the outside world. For example, women working for someone else were more likely to work outside the vicinity of their households, whereas women working on a family farm were more likely to interact only with family members. Also, women who worked for someone else or were self-employed were mostly paid in cash whereas those who worked on the family farm/business were not paid at all.

Financial independence

Financial independence of women is usually tied to their working status. However, in a patriarchal household, this relationship is not inevitable. Women might be working full time, but not be in control of their own money. So, we used a question that gauged the financial independence of all women, working and non-working:

Are you allowed to have some money set aside that you can use as you wish?

Women were asked to respond in a yes/no format. One of the possible problems of using this question is that it does not give us any indication whether the woman controls the use of this financial resource for herself or for her family. It is quite possible that a woman's husband gives her some money for household expenditures about which she has enough discretion to respond affirmatively to the question. This use of money does not constitute financial independence on the part of the woman. However, given the lack of alternatives, and also the fact that this question was asked of both working and non-working women, we decided to include it in the analyses.

Attitudes towards domestic violence

In order to gauge the extent to which the respondent justified domestic violence, the NFHS-2 included the following:

Sometimes a wife can do things that bother her husband. Please tell me if you think a husband is justified in beating his wife in each of the following situations:

— If he suspects her of being unfaithful
— If her natal family does not give expected money, jewelry or other items
— If she shows disrespect for her in-laws
— If she goes out without telling him
— If she neglects the house or children
— If she doesn't cook food

The women were asked to agree or disagree with each statement and were also given the option of marking "I don't know" as an answer choice. We dichotomized the separate variables such that agreement would imply a more permissive attitude towards domestic violence. We summed all the responses and constructed a scale that varied from 0 to 6 (alpha = .81). Low values indicate that women endorsed fewer statements, and higher values indicate that women endorsed more statements justifying domestic violence.

Results

All hypotheses were tested in bivariate and multivariate logistic regression models. The data are summarized in Table 8.1.

Table 8.1

Zero-order and multivariate relationships of independent variables with husband violence

	Zero-Order Relationship			*Multi-variate Relationship*		
Predictor	*B*	*SE B*	e^B	*B*	*SE B*	e^B
Region						
North	-	-	-	-	-	-
Central	.73	.04	2.07**	.56	.04	1.75**
East	.82	.04	2.27**	.79	.05	2.20**
North-East	-.05	.05	.96	-.04	.06	.96
West	.13	.05	1.13	.01	.06	1.01
South	.86	.04	2.36**	.69	.05	1.99**
Family Characteristics						
Religion						
Hindu	-	-	-	-	-	-
Muslim	.14	.04	1.15**	.20	.04	1.22**
Christian	-.61	.06	.54**	-.43	.07	.65**

Contd...

Contd...

Sikh	-.48	.09	.62**	.60	.10	1.83**
Buddhist/Neo Buddhist	-1.20	.17	.30**	-.60	.18	.55*
Jain	-1.27	.52	.28	-.54	.53	.59
Others	-.01	.10	.99	.23	.12	1.26
Family Structure						
Nuclear	-	-	-	-	-	-
Non-Nuclear	-.37	.02	.69**	-.20	.03	.82**
Socio Economic Status	-.14	.00	.87**	-.04	.01	.97**
Women's Autonomy						
Respondent	-	-	-	-	-	-
Husband	-.17	.05	.85**	-.23	.05	.80**
Jointly with Husband	-.48	.05	.62**	-.36	.05	.70**
Others in the Household	-.71	.06	.49**	-.58	.06	.56**
Jointly with Others	-.10	.06	.37**	-.59	.07	.55**
Natal Family Violence	.55	.04	1.73**	.61	.04	1.83**
Personal Characteristics:						
Illiterate	-	-	-	-	-	-
< Primary School Complete	.37	.05	.69**	-.17	.05	.84**
Primary School Complete	-.57	.04	.57**	-.27	.04	.76**
Middle School Complete	-.90	.06	.41**	-.45	.06	.64**
High School Complete	-1.20	.08	.28**	-.80	.08	.45**
Higher Secondary School Complete	-1.88	.14	.15**	-1.32	.14	.27**
Labour Force Participation						
Non-Working	-	-	-	-	-	-
For Family Member	.36	.01	1.44**	.28	.03	1.33**
For Someone Else	.83	.03	2.29**	.51	.03	1.67**
Self Employed	.51	.05	1.66**	.38	.06	1.47**
Financial Independence	-.09	.02	.91**	.02	.03	1.02
Attitudes towards D.V.	.17	.01	1.19**	.14	.01	1.15**
Constant				-1.65	.07	.19

Note: e^B = *Exponentiated B.* *p <.01. **p < .001. *The dependent variable is Hit by Husband.*

Region

The results in Table 8.1 indicate that there is significant variability with respect to region, but that it was not in line with our hypothesis that the rates of husband violence would be lower in the southern and northeastern regions than in the northern regions. In fact, the odds of being beaten by one's husband in the 'liberal' south were twice the odds of being beaten in the north (2.36), and the odds in the north-east were quite similar to those in the north.

Family Characteristics

Non-nuclear family structure

At the zero order, the odds of being beaten are actually less for women living in a non-nuclear setting than for those living in a nuclear household (odds ratio = .69). Although the effect is reduced somewhat by controls (.82) it remains significant (see Table 8.1).

Joint decision-making

When we examined decision-making with respect to purchasing jewelry as an indicator of patriarchal structure, we found that compared to respondents in families in which women made the decision themselves, those who lived in families in which the decision involved people other than their husbands had lower odds of being beaten. The odds-ratio for women who reported that these other individuals (apart from the husband) made the decision by themselves was .49; it was .37 for those who reported that 'others' made the decision jointly with the respondent (see Table 8.1). Looking across the categories of decision-making, we see that there is a systematic reduction of odds when decision-making is made by persons other than the respondent. Once again, these patterns are opposite to those that we predicted, and they hold up even after controlling for the other variables in the model.

Religion

At the zero order, the effects of household religion on the odds that a woman will be beaten by her husband are significant (see Table 8.1). Compared to Hindus, the odds of being beaten are slightly, but significantly higher if the woman is Muslim (1.15). Women from all other religions seem to fare better than both Hindu and Muslim women. As predicted, Buddhist and Jain households are the least likely to contain husband violence.

Socio-economic status

At the zero order, for every unit increase in the possession of basic amenities or commodities, the odds of being beaten by one's husband are reduced by a factor of .87, and although the effect is reduced by controlling for the other variables in the model (.97), it remains significant.

Natal family violence

At the zero order, natal family violence does have a strong relationship with likelihood of being beaten by one's husband. For each additional type of natal family member who had beaten the respondent, the odds of being beaten by one's husband increases by a factor of1.73 (see Table 8.1). The effect is basically unchanged by controls.

Personal Characteristics

Education

As predicted, the zero-order relationship between education and husband violence is negative. The odds of being beaten decline regularly with each increase in the level of education until the odds of being beaten for women who have completed higher secondary or more are only about one-seventh (.14) those of illiterate women. These effects remain essentially the same in the multivariate model.

Labour force participation

The zero-order relationship between labour force participation and domestic violence reveals that the odds of being beaten are greater for women who work, especially so for women who work for someone outside the family (see Table 8.1).

Financial independence

At the zero order, the results indicate that the odds that women who were allowed to have money set aside would be beaten are less than those of women who do not have that independence (odds ratio of .91).

Respondent's attitudes towards domestic violence

At the zero order, we see that each unit increase in the acceptance of justifications for violence increases the odds of being beaten by one's partner by a factor of 1.19.

Discussion and Conclusions

Many of our most central findings, specifically those most relevant to our hypotheses about the effects of patriarchal contexts on the likelihood of intimate partner violence, were not only contrary to our expectations; they were in the opposite direction. We found that intimate partner violence was less likely in the 'conservative' north than it was in the 'liberal' south. We found that the likelihood of domestic violence was less in non-nuclear (joint) families than in nuclear families. We found that women were less likely to be victimized by violence if they were not in control of decision-making of the household, especially if that control was shared with someone other than their husband. We found that women were less likely to be beaten if they are not employed, and that the risk of being beaten is especially high for women who work for someone other than family. All of these anomalous findings, taken together, suggest that our seemingly straightforward application of feminist theory is inadequate as an explanation of variations in rates of domestic violence.

Although feminists have generally argued that family violence is about patriarchal power and that men use violence in the family in order to maintain control over 'their' women, less attention has been given to the argument that violence is likely in most cases to be the control tactic of last resort. We would argue that patriarchal control of women, especially within families, is virtually the prototypical case of 'paternalism,' defined as "a system under which an authority treats those under its control in a fatherly way especially in regulating their conduct and supplying their needs" (Webster's 1972).

Mary Jackman's *The Velvet Glove* (1994) provides an extensive analysis of the role of paternalism in the maintenance of long-term, institutionalized inequalities. She argues that in any such relationship, it is in the interests of the dominant group to control without the use of "force [which] only structures the game in combative terms, making resistance the readiest response" (p. 9). Thus, "the abiding quest is to preserve an amicable relationship with subordinates and thus to preempt or subvert conflict" (p. 11). The argument for violence as a control tactic only of last resort is not new and, as citizens of two countries that are former colonies of the British Empire, we cannot resist presenting Edmund Burke's eloquent 1775 statement on this matter in his "On conciliation with the colonies" (as cited in Jackman, 1994: 62-63):

> First, Sir, permit me to observe that the use of force alone is but *temporary*. It may subdue for a moment, but it does not remove the necessity of subduing again; and a nation is not governed, which is perpetually to be conquered.
>
> My next objection is its *uncertainty*. Terror is not always the effect of force, and an armament is not a victory. If you do not succeed, you are without resource; for, conciliation failing, force remains, but, force failing, no further hope of reconciliation is left. Power and authority are sometimes bought by kindness, but they can never be begged as alms by an impoverished and defeated violence.
>
> A further objection to force is, that you *impair the object* by your very endeavors to preserve it. The thing you fought for is not the thing which you recover, but depreciated, sunk, wasted, and consumed in the contest.

We would add that in the case of domestic relations of inequality husbands in most cases feel genuine affection (if not love) for their wives and want very much for that affection to be reciprocated.

Love is also, however, a powerful ideological force. As Jackman (1994) puts it, "by making love the very instrument of coercion, dominant-group members swathe the unequal exchange with subordinates in the warmth of personal affection even as they hem in subordinates' options with a taut thread" (82). When affection and love become the basis of a relationship between individuals in a family, the power relationships tend to be masked by a discourse of love that rarely addresses power dynamics, and violence can even be seen as symbolic of that love, as in a jealous rage. One of the primary reasons that paternalism is so invisible is because family relations are imbued with a rhetoric of love and harmony, affection and obligation.

This is not to discount that individuals feel genuine love, but merely to acknowledge that these bonds also contain power relationships within them, rendering family relationships into bonds of love, companionship, power, and authority. While researchers have tended to confound "violence with malice and the desire to control women with a hatred of women" (Jackman, 1999:

300), the systems of patriarchy and paternalism are in fact a more "complex set of values that include an exalted respect for the stability and privacy of the nuclear family unit...and the earnest belief that spousal love both permits and heals impulsive violence" (Jackman, 1999: 301). Although modes of resistance to authority, structure, and social control do exist within the family, the preferred strategy used by dominant members to deal with resistance is one of 'gentle' persuasion backed by patriarchal ideology, rather than active force. Therefore, while paternalism may have the appearance (or even the reality) of benevolence, it is still an ideology that serves to dominate and control subordinates, generally without the use of force.

The fact that force is generally not used does not imply that it is never a part of the discourse of paternalism, which is often couched in such a way that that the threat of violence is subtle but present. For example, the patriarchal ideology does not preclude the use of violence among family members in the Indian context. In fact, corporal punishment for children is still considered a valid and useful form of discipline. Therefore, it is not outside the purview of the ideology of patriarchy to use violence in certain circumstances. The threat lurks quietly in the background until "under extreme duress, [it] is moved to a more conspicuous position" (Jackman, 1994: 59). The payoff for using force in a relationship is to demonstrate unequivocally the power relationships between individuals (ibid.: 62), but it arises only after persuasion has failed, in circumstances in which individuals do not accept the gendered scripts of a society or culture.

In addition, compliance with the dominant group ideology is often rewarded with social and material favours and 'reasonable' advances (ibid.: 78). This 'conditional' love tends to be based on an idealization of a subordinate subject. For example, the definitions of the ideal 'woman,' 'wife,' and 'mother' are well-defined by role, function, and appearance and are often used to objectify women and place them in subordinate roles. The idealizations also enable dominant groups to 'reward' women who try to achieve these ideals – "with love, affection and praise" (ibid.: 79) – and punish women who reject them, through direct and indirect means. Women thus are moved to "subject their bodies to physical confinement or mutilation to gain acceptance, or better yet, win social admiration" (ibid., 1999: 309). Especially in a family setting, this system of reward and punishment can be an extremely effective force. In addition, even men who repeatedly physical means to control their wives are also violating these structured and systematic forms of social control, often prompting condemnation on the part of other members of the society, or even from their own family members (Jackman, 1999). Applying these arguments to the case at hand, it would follow that when family power is heavily concentrated along patriarchal lines, the likelihood of using violence will be reduced because the structure effectively imposes cultural, social, and physical restrictions on family members. In such situations, because control over women is already well established, the use of violence is redundant.

In the joint family system, where mechanisms of control not only take the form of specific and rigid role expectations, but also encompass monitoring of behaviour by multiple family members, women's lives are controlled to quite a degree by the institutional structure of the family system. Violence in this case is unnecessary. On the other hand, nuclear families, especially in this age of increased labour force participation of women, have very unclear role expectations and poor systems of structural control. In a nuclear family structure, unencumbered by additional members, women can use their limited authority to challenge and work around social roles and expectations, without the structural control of the joint family (Ray, 1999). In such situations, violence may be used as a 'necessary' means to control and subjugate the women (Singh, 1999). In fact, Mahajan (1990) reports that one of the main reasons that men give for their wife battery is the assertion of their authority. When women acquire any measure of independence, via decision-making powers, labour force participation or from the structure of the nuclear family, they are more likely to be victims of violence from their partners.

Thus, we have to debunk the idea of "...conflict as the exclusive symptom of exploitative relations consensus as the indelible sign of function integration" (Jackman, 1994: 2), especially in social relations where dominant and subordinate groups have to live in close proximity and in family relations, where the narratives of love, romance, and marriage bind people in relationships of power. Open hostilities in these cases are not feasible. In family relationships bound by love and duty, control and power cannot be openly contested. This implies that patriarchy as an ideology does not always function in the same way in different contexts. In joint family systems where there is a systematic structure of power hierarchies and familial and spousal duties attached to each member of the family, resistance to power and control is much less likely to be resolved through violent means. In a nuclear family, however, where women are partly independent of structured roles, it is likely that violence is used as an effective means to control the mobility and freedom of women. Thus, the ideologies of patriarchy do not function in a unilateral manner; they encompass a broad range of principles, rules, and structures, the application of which are diverse and often times, contradictory.

In conclusion, three important characteristics of domestic violence emerge from the results of this study. First, patriarchy does not necessarily lead to the use of violence. Second, violence may be used primarily as a means of last resort, after all other control tactics have failed. Third, discourses of love have to be incorporated into our understanding of violence within the family. Summarily, it is not enough to understand that a patriarchal family system occasionally endorses acts of violence, or that violence is a man taking control rather than a man out of control. A deeper understanding of the conditions under which violence is used by patriarchal families to control recalcitrant women will enable us to more fully comprehend the complex ways in which patriarchy and paternalism control women's lives.

References

Abraham, M. (1995), Ethnicity, Gender, and Marital Violence: South Asian Women's Organizations in the United States, *Gender and Society*, 9(4): 450-468.

Agnes, F. (1990), Wife Beating: Changes in Social Structure Crucial to Combat the Problem, In S. Sushma (ed.), *Violence Against Women*, 57-70, Jaipur: Arihant Publishers.

— (1993), The Anti-Rape Campaign, In C. Datar (ed.), *The Struggle Against Violence*, 99-150, Calcutta, Street.

Anonymous (1992), Legal Aid Handbook I: Domestic Violence, *Kali for Women*, Gayatri Offset Press.

Arora, B. (1999), Indian Women, Work and Participation, In J.M.S. Verma (ed.) *Gender Justice in India*, Rohtak: Spellbound Publications.

Bhatti, R.S. (1990), Socio-cultural Dynamics of Wife Battery, In S. Sood (ed.), *Violence Against Women*, 45-56, Jaipur: Arihant Publishers.

Bloch, F. and V. Rao (1997) *Terror as a Bargaining Instrument: A Case-Study of Dowry Violence in Rural India,* Providence, Rhode Island, Brown University.

Daga, A.S., S.J. Jejeebhoy, et al. (1998), *Domestic Violence Against Women: An Investigation of Hospital Casualty Records, Mumbai.* Preventing violence, caring for survivors: Role of health professions and services in violence, Mumbai: Research Centre of Anusandhan Trust.

Das, V. (1975), Marriage among the Hindus, In D. Jain (ed.), *Indian Women,* New Delhi: Ministry of Information and Broadcasting, Govt. of India.

Datar, C. (1993), The Women's Movement in Maharashtra, In C. Datar (ed.), *The Struggle Against Violence,* 1-50, Kolkata: Street.

D'Cruz, P. and S. Bharat (2001), Beyond Joint and Nuclear: The Indian Family Revisited, *Journal of Comparative Family Studies,* 32(2): 167-194.

Fernandez, M. (1997), Domestic Violence by Extended Family Members in India: Interplay of Gender and Generation, *Journal of Interpersonal Violence,* 12(3): 433-455.

Ganesh, K. (1989), Seclusion of Women and the Structure of Caste, In Leela Dube (ed.), *Gender and the Household Domain: Social and Cultural Dimensions,* 75-98, New Delhi: Sage Publications.

Ghadially, R. and P. Kumar (1988), Bride Burning: The Psycho-social Dynamics of Dowry Deaths, In R. Ghadially (ed.), *Women in Indian Society: A Reader,* New Delhi: Sage Publications.

Goode, J. and S.J. Tambiah (1973), *Bride Wealth and Dowry,* Cambridge: Cambridge University Press.

ICRW (1998), A presentation of a number of studies addressing various aspects of violence against women; focus on India, *International Center for Research on Women,* Washington, DC: 1-8.

Jackman, M.R. (1994), *The Velvet Glove: Paternalism and Conflict in Gender, Class, and Race Relations,* California: University of California Press.

— (1999), Gender, Violence, and Harassment, In J.S. Chafetz (ed.), *Handbook of the Sociology of Gender,* 275-317, New York, Kluwer Academic.

Jaising, I. (2001), *Law of Domestic Violence,* Delhi, Universal Law Publishing.

Jaiswal, S. (2000), Health Records and Domestic Violence in Thane District, Maharashtra, *Domestic Violence in India: A Summary Report of*

Four Record Studies, 6-14, Washington, DC: International Centre for Research for Women.

Johnson, M.P. (1995), Patriarchal Terrorism and Common Couple Violence: Two Forms of Violence Against Women in U.S. Families, *Journal of Marriage and Family*, 57, 283-294.

Johnson, P. and Jennifer Johnson (2001), "The Oppression of Women in India", *Violence Against Women* 7(9): 1051-1068.

Katzenstein, M.F. (1989), Organizing Against Violence: Strategies of the Indian Women's Movement, *Pacific Affairs*, 62(1): 53-71.

Krishnaraj, M. (1989), Introduction, *Gender and the Household Domain: Social and Cultural Dimension.* M.K.K. Chanana, New Delhi: Sage Publication, 4: 1-30.

Kurz, D. (1989), Social Science Perspectives on Wife Abuse: Current Debates and Future Directions, *Gender and Society*, 3(4): 489-505.

Leonard, K. (1979), Women in India: Some Recent Perspectives, *Pacific Affairs*, 52(1): 95-107.

Levinson, D. (1989), *Family Violence in a Cross-Cultural Perspective*, Newbury Park, CA: Sage Publications.

Madan, T.N. (1975), Structural Implications of Marriage in North India: Wife Givers and Wife Takers Among Pandits of Kashmir, *Contributions to Indian Sociology* (N.S.), 9.

Madhurima (1996), *Violence against Women: Dynamics of Conjugal Relations*, New Delhi: Gyan Publishing House.

Magar, V. (2001), Resisting Domestic Violence and Caste Inequality: All-Women Courts in India, In F.W.T.K.M. Blee (ed.), *Feminism and Antiracism: International Struggles for Justice*, 37-58, New York: New York University Press.

Mahajan, A. (1990), Investigators of Wife Battering, In S. Sood (ed.), *Violence Against Women*, 1-10, Jaipur: Arihant Publishers.

Martin, S.L.T., A.O., Maitra K. and Marinshaw, R. (1999), Domestic Violence in Northern India, *American Journal of Epidemiology*, 150(4): 417-426.

Mencher, J.P. (1989), Women Agricultural Labourers and Land Owners in Kerala and Tamil Nadu: Some Questions About Gender and Autonomy in the Household, In Leela Dube (ed.), *Gender and the Household Domain: Social and Cultural Dimensions*, 117-144, New Delhi: Sage Publications.

Mies, M. (1980), *Indian Women and Patriarchy*, New Delhi: Concept Publishing Company.

Miller, B.D. (1999), Wife Beating in India: Variations on a Theme, In J.K.B. Dorothy Ayers Counts, and Jacquelyn C. Campbell (eds.), *To*

Have and to Hit, 203-215, Urbana and Chicago: University of Illinois Press.

Mitra, N. (1999), Best Practices among Responses to Domestic Violence in Maharashtra and Madhya Pradesh, *In Domestic Violence in India: A Summary Report of Three Studies*, 18-27, Washington, DC: International Centre for Research on Women.

Moore, E.P. (1994), Law's Patriarchy in India, In Hirsch (ed.), *Contested Series: Law, Hegemony and Resistance*, 89-117, New York: Routledge.

Mukhopadhyay, S. (1998), *In the Name of Justice: Women and Law in Society*, New Delhi: Munshiram Manoharlal Ltd.

NFHS-2 (1998-1999), *India-National Family Health Survey*, Maryland: ORC Macro.

Omvedt, G. (1990), *Violence Against Women: New Movements and New Theories in India*, New Delhi: Pauls Press.

Pande, R. (2000), From Anti-arrack to Total Prohibition: the Women's Movement in Andhra Pradesh, India, *Gender, Technology and Development*, 4(1): 131-144.

Pence, E. and M. Paymar (1993), *Education Groups for Men Who Batter: The Duluth Model*, New York: Springer.

Poonacha, V. and D. Pandey (1999), Responses to Domestic Violence in Karnataka and Gujarat, In *Domestic Violence in India: Summary Report of Three Studies*, 28-41, Washington, DC: International Centre for Research on Women.

Rao, S., I.S., et al. (2000), Domestic Violence: A Study of Organizational Data, In *Domestic Violence in India: A Summary Report of Four Records Studies*, 15-24, Washington, DC: International Centre for Research on Women.

Rao, V. (1998), Wife abuse, its causes and its impact on intra-household resource allocation in rural Karnataka: A "participatory" econometric analysis, In R.M.S. Marithreyi Krishnaraj, Abusaleh Shariff (eds.), *Gender, Population and Development*, 94-121, Delhi: Oxford University Press.

Ray, R. (1999), *Fields of Protest: Women's Movement in India*, Minneapolis: University of Minnesota Press.

Shiva, M. (1999), Violence against Women, *Health for the Millions*, 25(1): 36-38.

Srinivasan, P. (1998), Explanations of Domestic Violence in India and the United States: A Comparative Analysis, *Center for the Study of Crime, Delinquency and Corrections*, Carbondale: Southern Illinois University, 149.

Vindhya, U. (2000), Dowry deaths in Andhra Pradesh, India: Response of the criminal justice system, *Violence Against Women,* 6(10): 1085-1108.

Visaria, L. (1999), Violence Against Women in India: Evidence from Rural Gujarat, In *Domestic Violence in India: A Summary Report of Three Studies,* 9-17, Washington, DC: International Centre for Research on Women.

Waters, A.B. (1999), Domestic Dangers: Approaches to Women's Suicide in Contemporary Maharashtra, India, *Violence Against Women,* 5(5): 525-547.

Websters' Seventh New Collegiate Dictionary (1972), Springfield, MA: G. and C. Merriam.

Yllo, K. (1983), Sexual Equality and Violence against Wives in American States, *Journal of Comparative Family Studies,* 14(1): 67-86.

9

Two Images of Matriliny

The Khasi and the Nair

CELINE AUGUSTINE

The scientific study of family and kinship systems is only a century old, but in that brief period it has engendered more controversy and a greater variety of theoretical formulations than have most aspects of human society. Intensive fieldwork methods developed during the early twentieth century produced a new body of detailed information on kinship, marriage and the family. We can look forward to a continued flow of empirical data on kinship and family and a continuing dialogue between studies utilizing analytic variables and statistical methods on the one hand, and intensive studies of a more limited range but concerned with kinship and family organizations as wholes, on the other.

The similarities and differences in marriage and family organizations cross-culturally have led to several theories based on both speculation and empiricism. Bachofen, McLennan, Tylor and Morgan all had their views on various practices of marriage and types of family forms existing in human societies. India's many religious communities, castes and tribes in different cultural regions present an extraordinary variety of family systems and the patterns of kinship found in our country cover almost the entire gamut of known kinship systems.

Empirical studies contributing to the understanding of kinship and family in India are of varied kinds. Some valuable information are found in the general works on the tribes and castes of various regions, and in individual studies of particular tribes, castes and villages attempting total coverage of their cultures and social system. Their coverage includes descriptive accounts and analytical descriptions; simple comparisons and analysis based on local, regional and national comparative data; and conceptual clarifications and meaningful discussions of methodological problem. Well-thought-out studies of the family in tribal groups can provide us with meaningful comparative data that would help us understanding the family structure in other communities as well as in Indian society in general. The family influences the whole life of society in innumerable ways and its changes reverberate through the whole social structure. There is no doubt that the spread of knowledge and projection of new images and attitudes through the mass media of communication have influenced both the institution of the family and the strength of kin orientation.

This study is an attempt to examine and analyse the two existing matrilineal communities of India; one in the Khasi Hills in North–Eastern India, the Khasis, and the other in Kerala, the South-Western corner of the country, the Nairs. On a casual visit to the Khasi villages I was stunned by the freedom enjoyed by these women. For the first time in my life I came across a world where I found women to be absolutely free. She is not dictated by anybody. She is responsible to herself and her kin and family. Nobody would ask her who her father is or who her husband is, before they get to know the person, unlike in a patriarchal set-up, where she has to demonstrate her identity as the daughter or the wife of so and so to the world. My interest in observing certain common features in Nair and Khasi societies prompted me to undertake this study.

There have not been enough evidences to establish a direct connection about the matrilineal origin of the communities under study. The worldwide distribution of matrilineal civilizations and their location in the extreme south-west and north-east of India have been discussed in a series of writings by Ehrenfels. In his work on the comparative study of matrilineal civilizations in India, he mentions some connection between these two cultures. His thesis 'mother-right' indicates a pre-Aryan connection between the Indus civilization and the South Indian type of culture. He feels that the centrifugal direction of the mother-right culture was originated by the Indus civilization and that the NAY (Nair) people appears to have created the ancient matriarchal civilizations in the

Mediterranean Basin, oriental Africa, the Near East and especially Southern Arabia. He suggests that the inter-connection of the Kerala group with the North-East has been contemplated as a possibility before.[1] After comparing the patrilineal and matrilineal groups in India he reveals that there is a palpable difference in the economic position, personal freedom of movement and decision, marking a line between (a) the matrilineal South and North-East Indian women on the one side as compared to North Indian ones on the other, and (b) between the matrilineally determined 'lower' and the more outspokenly patriarchal 'higher' classes respectively in the South.[2]

It is interesting to notice the grip of the female in these societies in tracing descent, inheritance of property, role in decision-making, etc., which is envied by their counterparts all over the world. The Nairs who were enjoying comfortable dominance for about 700 years because of the patronage of the upper castes, in the rigid caste-structure of Kerala society, were to experience a crisis in the second half of the nineteenth century which led to its gradual disintegration. The Khasi society, on the other hand, which is still strong in its matrilineal culture has reached the point of time where the need is felt for a serious introspection and revaluation of its institutions, laws and long cherished customs. Though matriliny was the rule among the Nairs of Kerala for a very long time, due to various socio-politico-economic reasons it crumbled here paving way to patrilineal system. Still the remnants of matriliny are very much alive among them. For the Khasis, on the other hand, matriliny is the rule from time immemorial and even today, in spite of the fact that the Khasi society also is familiar with modernization and new technological advancements.

Conceptual Issues

Marriage and Family

Kinship begins with the family. In one sense, the whole society begins with the family because a society is a living entity that must continually be replenished. In all human societies provision must be made for biological and social reproduction, if the society is to continue. Mating and procreation provide for the continuity of the biological species while socialization relates it to the equally important continuity of social structure and cultural pattern. Biological parenthood, of course, is possible outside the marriage and is hardly unusual, but no society permits promiscuous parenthood. Thus, by making marriage a condition for the creation of families, that is, by insisting that parenthood be preceded by marriage, human societies provide for their own perpetuation.

G.P. Murdock after studying 250 societies attributes four functions fundamental to human social life – the sexual, the economic, the reproductive and the educational. Without provision for the first and the third, society would become extinct; for the second, life itself would cease; for the fourth, culture would come to an end.[3] The existence of elementary family creates three special kinds of social relationships; the relation between parent and child, that between children of the same parents (siblings), and that between husband and wife as parents of the same child or children. A person is born or adopted into a family in which he or she is son or daughter and brother or sister.

Bachofen states that in the beginning, humanity lived in a state of sexual promiscuity, which excludes all certainty as regards paternity; that lineage, therefore, could be reckoned only through the female line. He uses the term 'hetaerism' for this stage. Consequently, women who, as mothers, were the only definitely ascertainable parents of the younger generations, and were treated with a high degree of consideration and respect which, according to Bachofen's conception, was enhanced due to the complete rule of women (gyneacocracy). That the transition to monogamy, where the woman belongs exclusively to one man, implied the violation of a primeval religious injunction (that is, in actual fact, the violation of the ancient traditional right of other men to the same woman), a violation which had to be atoned for or the toleration of which had to be purchased by surrendering the woman for a limited period of time.[4]

On the basis of the interpretation of kinship terms as survivals of previous marriage forms, Morgan contended that marriage was evolved from promiscuity through a series of progressive stages to monogamy and that descent through the maternal line had preceded that through paternal line, the former passing to the latter when property relations were established and paternity was no longer doubtful. Briffault suggested that where agriculture had persisted, which from the beginning had been the province of women, the matriarchal civilization had been the rule. It enhanced the position of women not only as the owners and heiresses of the land but also through their traditional association with agricultural magic and religion.[5]

Readings on the beginning of society reveal that women had a highly respected position among all savages and all barbarians of the lower and middle stages and partly even of the upper stage. The social status of the lady of civilization surrounded by sham homage and estranged from all real work is socially infinitely lower than that of the hard-working woman of barbarism, who was regarded among her people as a real lady. The women were the great power among clans. Bachofen blames women for the transition from group marriage to temporary or permanent marriage to pairing marriage with a hope for getting the right to chastity, which subsequently led them to the introduction of strict monogamy, for women only. The overthrow of mother-right was the world-historic defeat of the female sex. The man seized the reins in the house also, the woman was degraded, enthralled, the slave of the man's lust, a mere instrument for breeding children. The first effect of the sole rule of the men was the emergence of the 'patriarchal family'.[6]

Kinship

A clear understanding of the descent and lineage patterns becomes difficult without a proper knowledge of the kinship structure. Kinship terms like father, mother, son, daughter, brother, sister, etc., are expressions of ideas actually in force concerning nearness or collateralness, and equality and inequality of blood relationship. The original ties of kinship are invariably individual but later on develop, multiply and become largely communal, so that, at the end the individual finds himself at the centre of a complex system of multiple ties – a member of several groups: the family, the local group, the clan, and the tribe. Thus kinship, even in its origin, is a cultural rather than a biological fact. This becomes from the outset deeply modified by such elements as maternal or paternal counting of kinship, matrilocal or patrilocal residence, the relative position of husband and wife in a community, etc.

Sociologically, kinship is a compound and complex network of ties, so every native nomenclature consists of several layers or systems of kinship designations. Kinship system presents to us a complex set of norms, or usages, of patterns of behaviour between kindred. For Radcliffe-Brown a kinship system is a network of social relations, which constitutes part of that total network of social relations, which he calls the 'social structure'. The rights and duties of relatives to one another and the social usages that they observe in their social contacts are parts of the system.[7]

Descent

In the discussion of the origin and evolution of kinship organizations, we are concerned not only with their forms but also with the rules of descent, which regulate their membership. The main issues connected with descent are twofold: (1) the priority of male or otherwise of female descent, and (2) the cause of the transition from one form of descent to another. Two persons who are 'kin' are related to one another in two ways: either one is descended from the other, or both of them are descended from a common ancestor. 'Kinship' is simply a relation between the 'kin', i.e., persons related by real putative or fictive consanguinity. Thus a child is equally kin to father's and mother's kin. It is to be remembered that 'descent' refers to the social relationship of parents and children, not to the physical relation. Kinship is based on 'descent', and what first determines the character of a kinship system is the way in which descent is recognized and reckoned. To define the kin of a given person his descent is traced back to a certain number of generations, to his four grandparents, his eight great grandparents, or still further all descendants of his recognized ancestors, through both females and males, who are his cognates.

Lineage

The members of any descent group will be related to one another through both male and female links. The matrilineal/patrilineal type of system is usually called unilineal, using only one 'line' in tracing kinship for some purposes. The members of a group are related to each other by common descent; they will be descended from a common ancestor or ancestress in either the male line (patrilineally) or the female line (matrilineally) or through links of both the sexes (cognatically). Such a group, which has perhaps a name, property or ritual or some activity in common, is a descent group, a group formed on the basis of descent from a common ancestor.[8] Where the actual relationship between members in such a group can be demonstrated, and is not simply assumed, the group is called 'lineage'. As is generally understood, a lineage is a corporate unilineal descent group of which the members can establish demonstrable genealogical relationships to each other.

When a son succeeds his father he may attain a status very similar to that of his father, but a daughter cannot do so to the same extent. Where the rights and duties derived through the father preponderate in social importance over those derived through the mother we have what it is usually called a patrilineal system. The matrilineal system emphasizes and maintains a close bond between brother and sister at the expense of the bond between husband and wife. In an extreme patrilineal society the bond between husband and wife is strengthened at the expense of the bond between brother and sister. Extreme patrilineal systems are comparatively rare and extreme matrilineal systems perhaps even rarer.

The major difference between the two family patterns cluster round the fact that the patrilineal family concentrates power in one authority – the father, whilst the matrilineal family brings into prominence (a) the authority of the bodily weaker family members such as mother and sister, and (b) the distribution of authority between three important family members, i.e., mother, maternal uncle and father.[9] In the latter, the father is generally of great importance in the psychological sphere of matrilineal families, even though his position is based more on affection than on legal responsibilities towards or institutionalized rights over his children.

Some Selected Studies

The works of Thomas Trautman, Meyer Fortes, Robin Fox, Radcliffe-Brown, Engels, Christine Oppong, Schneider, Iravati Karve and Leela Dube are significant in this area. Similarly among the studies pertaining to Khasi and Nair matriliny the works of Gurdon, Keith Cantlie, R.T. Rymbai, J.N. Chowdhury, Tiplut Nongbri, I.M. Syiem, Kathleen Gough, Sreedhara Menon, Jeffrey Robins, Puthenkalam, Samuel Mateer and Mannathu Padmanabhan are of great use.

The worldwide distribution of matrilineal societies and their location in the extreme south-west and north-east of India have been discussed in a series of writings by Ehrenfels. He attempts to analyse the two types of societies and shows the difference between the two structures. The patrilineal family concentrates power in one authority – the father, while the basic structure of the matrilineal family pattern is that of plural authority, and that both the Nair 'tarawad' and the Khasi 'Kur' rest on three basic faces of authority: mother, maternal uncle and father.[10]

In her study Chie Nakane joins Ehrenfels in pointing out that in matrilineal systems the ownership of property and the authority over the property never rests in one person as in the case of father/husband of the patrilineal systems and the succession of these two offices follows the female line (mother-daughter) and male line (mother's brother's son) respectively. She presumes that this duality of office-holding individuals within the succession rule is the intrinsic cause of complications and variations in matrilineal systems.

Christine Oppong in her work documents the kind of changes taking place in urban African family life with particular reference to the conflicts associated with change in matrilineal kinship systems and the effects of education, migration and urban residence upon domestic life.[11] Nongbri feels that the major contradiction that arises in the Khasi society like in any other matrilineal system is from the disjunction between the line of descent and inheritance on the one hand and the structure of authority and control on the other.[12]

Kathleen Gough after her extensive work on the Nair matrilineals and many other matrilineal societies in different parts of the world comes to the conclusion that the increasing productivity does strengthen the matrilineal descent group and weaken the marriage ties.[13] However, she suggests, when economic changes occur which permit men to enter individual positions of access to livelihood or to accumulate personal property as a source of livelihood, the disintegration of matrilineal groups and the emergence of the elementary family as the key unit in a bilateral system evolves.

Jeffrey Robin's work deals with the breakdown of the Kerala matrilineal social system due to the impact of cash economy, western style education, improved communication and a British inspired system of law on the complex social structure of an Indian Princely States.[14]

Theoretical Background

Descent theorists are concerned with groups, a theoretical interest that is derived from the British tradition of functionalism, which dominated the anthropological thinking in Britain and most of the Commonwealth from the 1920s to the 1950s. Functionalists such as

Radcliffe-Brown saw societies as being made up of component parts – institutions (like marriage, chieftainship, or the stock market) and systems (like kinship, politics or economics). Descent theorists take a functionalist view in their appraisal of the significance of group structure. In descent theory the mechanisms of recruitment to groups, and the social functions such groups perform, are the primary foci of the study.

The followers of the functional school insist on specialized analysis and comparison of existing systems and institutions like matriliny, matrilocal marriage and residence, etc., without bothering whether these may be regarded as vestiges of the earlier presence of mother-right. Their conclusion is that empirically patrilineal and matrilineal descent groups have important structural differences since specific males (as husband, father, etc.) hold formal authority over the patrilineal group, while under matriliny other males (as brothers, mother's brothers, etc.) have such authority.

The analysis of the family from a functional perspective involves three main questions. First, what are the functions of the family? It is assumed that society has certain functional prerequisites or basic needs that must be met if it is to survive and operate efficiently. The family is examined in terms of the degrees with which it meets these functional prerequisites. A second and related question asks, "What are the functional relationship between the family and other parts of the social system?" It is assumed that there must be a certain degree of integration and harmony between parts of the social system if society is going to function efficiently. The third question is concerned with the function performed by an institution or a part of the society for the individual. In the case of the family this question considers the function of the family for its individual members.

Merton[15] defined and explained the term 'function' to which he also added the concept of 'dysfunction', which implies the elements of strain, stress and tension on the structural level, providing an analytical approach to the study of dynamics and change. Durkheim believed that not only a given society displayed a degree of 'solidarity' but quite the opposite a degree of 'anomie'. Functional inconsistency exists whenever two aspects of the social system produce a conflict, which can only be resolved by some change in the system itself. No social system ever attains to a perfect consistency, and it is for this reason that every system is consistently undergoing change. Parsons assumes that social structure is made up of institutions, institutions of roles, and roles of mutual expectations. Parsons[16] assumes that it must meet the prerequisites of latent pattern maintenance, integration, goal attainment and adaptation.

Levy has brought the formulations of both Merton and Parsons together with unusual compactness. He uses the concept 'functional requisite' which he defines as a generalized condition necessary for the maintenance of the unit with which it is associated. A 'structural requisite' is defined as a pattern of action necessary for the continued existence of the unit with which it is associated. A 'functional prerequisite' is conceived as a function that must preexist if a given unit in its setting is to come into being. A 'structural prerequisite' is conceived as a structure that must pre-exist if a given unit is to come into existence in its setting.[17]

However, the functional approach alone is not sufficient to explain the two societies and the changes that have taken place or are taking place in them. Functionalism conceives family as a welfare system with a homogeneous structure forcing adaptability on the members to bring about stability and order in the system. Very often stability is equated with gender inequality. Hence, it fails to conceive the conflict and resilience in the systems. One approach alone is not sufficient to explain most of the sociological phenomena. The disintegration theory would be appropriate to explain the changes that take place in these societies.

The disintegration theory states that with the changes in the forms of production and of wealth, characterized by cash crop farming and wage work, there is a tendency, first, to narrow the generation depth and span of effective matrilineage, and second, to strengthen the elementary family as a significant economic residential and socializing unit. Gradually, the matrilineal groups break down, especially for purposes of inheritance, into small uterine sibling groups and their immediate descendants through females. A transitional picture of initial decay of the larger unilineal groupings followed by conflicts within it due to the increasing demand for autonomy within the elementary unit is observed.

Fortes believe that the conflict between conjugal and paternal ties on the one hand and matrilineal ties on the other have been much aggravated by missionary and modern economic influence.[18] Gough feels that the root cause of modern kinship change in these societies appears rather to be the gradual incorporation of the society into a unitary market system, which is based on fuel technology of an industrial nation. These conquered societies entered the market system of these industrial nations as a result of three main pressures; the industrial nations search for raw materials or semi-processed materials, their search for markets for their own manufactured goods, and their need to gather cash taxes to support new administrative institutions. In the changing situation, if, however, personal accumulation of wealth and new profit making enterprises are involved, leading to a change in the structure of production, then a new set of economic relationships would be evolved which would be partly instrumental in the process of kinship change.

The Present Approach

Though the structure and variance are not inherent in any social system, a particular social structure remains stable or accurate only for a particular period of time, i.e., as long as the functional prerequisites or needs of the social system are sufficiently met. In the wake of the strong forces of change, if certain institutions in the social system fail to fulfil their duties to the whole, i.e., the family, they are bound to be replaced by new institutions or units. The intensity or the speed with which they get substituted and the levels of replacement of the units in the family system, are significant for the sustenance or the decay of the system.

The main principles of matrilineal culture in both the societies were clan endogamy, clan authority theoretically in the hands of the mother, authority of the mother's brother, matrilocal marriage or visits of the husband to his wife and succession of dignities from the mother's brother to the sister's son, etc. However, the scholar portrays the 'brother-sister relationship' as the nucleus of matriliny and the three factors; matrilineal descent, female inheritance and the authority exercised by the mother's brother, as its core elements. The descent or lineage gives identity to its members while the 'inheritance' gives power and recognition to the females and the 'authority' gives the power for absolute control to the maternal uncle. These core elements are the 'functional prerequisites' for any matrilineal system as they were indispensable for the continued functioning of matriliny in the two communities. However, under the wake of strong currents of modernization, education, mass media, urbanization, westernization, and the influence of Christianity, both the societies have been affected, though they had differential influences on the two communities. In the course of the historic evolution of the community, if any of these elements become an obstacle to its progress, then, we assume that it becomes dysfunctional, which means, the system has to look for new functional alternatives thereby adapting itself to the changed situations calling for a change in the structural prerequisites also.

Socio-Cultural Background of the Study Communities

It would be difficult to understand the intricacies of the structure and the changes these societies are going through without understanding them properly and adequately. Hence, a brief account of their social system is given below.

Who is a Khasi?

Meghalaya, "the abode of clouds", is the homeland of three of India's ancient hill communities, the Khasis, Garos and Jaintias; all matrilineal. The Khasi people occupy a unique position both from ethnic and linguistic points of view among the congeries of the tribes inhabiting the mountainous terrain of India's northeast. Dance, music and sports reflect their way of life. The non-controversial definition of a Khasi is that a Khasi is a person born of a Khasi mother, irrespective of the fact whether the father is a Khasi or a non-Khasi. The Khasi Lineage Bill 1997 defines a Khasi as one whose parents are/were both Khasis and whose clan name is taken from the mother. The Bill further states that to be a Khasi the person will have to know the Khasi language unless prevented from knowing it by circumstances beyond his control like living outside the area. He must also observe and be governed by the Khasi matrilineal system, Khasi law of inheritance and succession and the Khasi laws of consanguinity and kinship.[19]

One cannot conceptualize the Khasi matriliny without a proper understanding of its kinship structure. The society is divided into a number of clans or *Kur* on the basis of matrilineal principle, which traces their origin from a common ancestress. The *Kur* or clan is split into a number of *jait* or sub-clans which again leads to its branching off into smaller units known as *Kpoh*. The *Kpoh* or lineage claims its origin from a common great grandmother. It is divided into a number of family units called the *Iing*, which keeps the ancestral property and performs religious ceremonies.[20]

Each *Iing* has a common *Iing Seng* (house of organization) or *Iing Khadduh* (house of the youngest daughter) where the rituals of the *Iing* are carried out.[21] The core of the *Iing* consists of two persons, one holding authority, the *U Kni*, and the other owning property, the *Khadduh*. The rule of succession is strictly matrilineal. The spouses or any member who is not a member of the *Iing Seng* are not allowed to take part in these ceremonies. The authority goes from mother's brother to sister's son while the property is handed down from mother to daughter.

The rule amongst the Khasis is that the youngest daughter inherits the bulk of the family property and she 'holds' the religion, *ka bat ia ka niam*. The other daughters also can inherit a portion of the ancestral property if the family has sufficient means. The youngest daughter's *(Ka Khadduh)* house is called *ka iing seng* and it is here that members of the family assemble for family ceremonies. The members have a right to be fed and looked after in case of any disaster. All sisters have a right to occupy a portion of the family land as co-parceners and *Ka Khadduh* cannot deprive them of this right. In many cases the *Khadduh* becomes burdened with the responsibility of providing for more members when she has not enough means. Even when no property is inherited, the responsibility of caring and providing for the old parents and other matrikin still falls on her, which is not shared by other sisters

The maternal males are motivated to protect their sister's offspring as their own. In fact, their activity in reproduction consists of giving seed (*bet symbai*) to another matrilineal group (*Kur*). The high position of *u kni* (maternal uncle) depends upon his role as one that performed the religion of the house and knew the various implications of the rites and ceremonies. Khasis consider the procreation of the child as the chief end of marriage. A Khasi's reproductive functions would be incomplete without having a female child. She will be the future bearer of seed for her matrilineal group. The child is the heir of its mother, whoever may be its father. Hence, the question of illegitimacy for children does not arise among the Khasis.

In contrast to *Iing*, which is an exclusive matrilineal group, the household includes the 'affines' as well. The basic residential unit comprises the mother, her husband and their children. If there is a married daughter in the house then the daughter's husband too would be a member of it. As far as the residence of women is concerned, the Khasi keeps to the strict rule; women belonging to different descent groups never live together. The rule among the Khasi is that a woman, if she is not the heiress, will branch off after her marriage and though she herself will continue as member of her mother's *Iing,* the third generation from her will form an independent *Iing*.

The Nair Social System

The Nair community constitutes the third and the last of the honoured castes of Kerala who formed the chief militia in Cochin, Malabar and Travancore states. They were, in fact, the magnets of the rulers in Kerala, which they managed through their educational qualifications and patronage of Dewans. They held or controlled most of the land in many of the villages. Though they were not ritually as pure as the higher castes, they had a fairly high ritual status, which gave them the great advantages over low caste men and non-Hindus. The Nairs of Kerala are different from other castes mainly because they trace their descent in the female line and they had a marriage system in which they are allowed to have several husbands simultaneously with strict rules of hypergamy. Inheritance through females necessarily binds to foster the visiting husband system, which is similar among the Minangkabaus of Sumatra.

The Tarawad

The matrilineal system of the Nairs is more popularly known as *Marumakkathayam.* The word *marumakkathayam* must have been coined because of the special relationship that exists between the uncle (mother's brother) and his nephews and nieces. The *tarawad* or *marumakkathayam* joint family consists in theory of all persons who can trace their descent in the female line from a single ancestress. In its simplest form, it is one, which consists of a mother and her children living together with their maternal uncle, that is, the mother's brother, as *karanavan,* or the senior male member of the family. In its complex form it consists of a mother and all her children, both male and female, all her descendants by her daughters, all her brothers and sisters and the descendants on the sisters' side, which means all the relatives of the woman on the female side, however distant their relationship, live together in the same block of buildings, have a common table, enjoy all her property and share it after her death in common with one another. In short, it consists of a woman, her brothers and sisters, her own and her sisters' descendants.

Each member of a *tarawad* acquires an interest in the *tarawad* properties by reason of his or her birth alone and when any member dies, the interests of that member devolves upon the other members of the *tarawad*.[22] The notion of *tarawad* is that the entire family is its owner; it is impartible, except by common consent, and inalienable permanently, except by the consent of all the members, and that each individual member is entitled to be maintained. Under this system, individuals are assigned to their mothers' lineage or clan and not to their father's. The name of the father is very often unknown to a Nair child.

Karanavan

In theory, *tarawad* had been described as the realm in which women ruled, but in practice it was ruled by the matriarch, the *Karanavan*. He acts as the manager and virtual head of the *tarawad* (lineage) property. The senior male member of the *tarawad*, by right of birth, becomes the *karanavan*, on whom the headship of the *tarawad*, the right of management of its affairs and possession of properties thereof, are vested by law. The spirit of the law governing these *tarawads* is that while the joint property belongs to the females, their natural incapacity for family government has made the eldest male member the life trustee of joint estate. The *Karanavan* of a *tarawad* has two capacities, the temporal and the spiritual. In the former he is the manager of the family properties, maintains the junior member, and acts as a mouthpiece of the *tarawad*. In the latter he presides at the family ceremonies and performs all the religious duties, which are incumbent on the *tarawad*

Who is a Nair?

One can understand the Nair matriliny only in the background of the marriage system of the two dominant castes in Kerala – the Nambuthiri [23] and the Nair. In the social hierarchy of Kerala, the Nambuthiris occupied the topmost position. They enjoyed very high social status and exercised tremendous influence over the people in religious, social and economic spheres and were conservative in their habits. The Nambuthiri Brahmins have a patrilineal and patriarchal joint family (*illam*) in which a man, his wife, his children, his sons' wives and children live. In the Nambuthiri patrilineal extended family, only the eldest son was permitted to marry within his caste with Vedic rites, and to get children for his family. The younger sons were prohibited honourable marriages with persons of their own caste, and were forced to contract connubial relations with the women of matrilineal Kshatriya and Nair castes. The offspring thus born cannot be a Nambuthiri, but can only be a Kshatriya or a Nair. Thus the Nair was the child of a Kshatriya male and a Nair female, or a Nambuthiri male and a Nair female.[24]

Sambandham

The marriage system prevalent among the Nairs was called the *Sambandham*. It was a state of concubinage to which the woman entered on her own choice and she was at liberty to change as and when she pleased. The *Karanavans* of the families arranged it. *Sambandham* was dissoluble at will and often it happened so, due either to the misunderstandings and incompatibility of the partners or the dislike for the *karanavans*.[25] The wife and husband do not rely on each other for economic support and their financial interests were separate. In all possible respects attempts were made to reduce the intensity of marital ties for the sake of the unity of the *tarawad*. The marriage bond being reduced to its barest essentials the affinity that it created between the 'kin' and the married couple was feeble in the extreme.

By 1847, this society, which had survived fundamentally unchanged for 700 years, got affected by various socio-economic-political factors. As a result of the colonialism and the shift of administration from the traditional to the modern, the Nairs lost their grip, which they managed through their female connection with the rulers. The British inspired system of education and the legislations regulating marriage and property, led to the decline and disintegration of Nair *tarawads*. The Nairs started experiencing a crisis in their matrilineal system, which ultimately led to its disintegration.

Objectives of the Study

This study focuses on the kinship systems, the lineage practices as well as the inheritance and authority patterns of the Khasi and Nair societies. Given under this broader frame the specific objectives of the study are:

- to study historically and examine the present status of the two communities with regard to lineage, inheritance and authority;
- to examine the factors responsible for sustaining matriliny among the Khasis and for its disappearance from the Nair society; and
- to examine the differential impact of the modern forces of change on both these communities.

Methodology

I adopted the case study method, which included intense interviews and personal observations. Fifteen families each were selected from both the communities out of which ten each are documented in the work. By forcing different perspectives on the same phenomenon the researcher has qualitatively portrayed divergent images that might emerge from each perspective. Because the single case study is treated as cluster of heterogeneous units of analysis the term 'case cluster' also is used to designate the method.[26]

The study is comprehensive in nature, which includes data keeping in view of the generational depth of a few families. Oscar Lewis' method of studying 'Five Families' of Mexico is adopted here, in which he has introduced a method of seeing individuals as they present themselves within families, which were also carefully placed within specific milieus.[27]

I was already familiar with the elevated position of Nair women in their families and communities since I hail from the same area, although from a different community. In the course of an informal visit to a Khasi village, I was fascinated by the family system and the status enjoyed by these women. My great appreciation for the freedom enjoyed by women from these communities prompted me to conduct a study on the family and social life of these people.

Besides primary data, which were collected through case study method, the secondary data were collected from published observations and studies, which included books, journals, government reports, gazettes, census reports, legal documents as well as other relevant publications. The intention has been to provide sufficient references to put this study into a general framework. Comparative materials on matrilineal kinship systems offered by leading scholars on the subject were examined which explain the social, political, economic and educational changes as well as the Christian and

British influences, the role of the various reform movements, the legal measures, etc., all playing together at a particular phase in Kerala history revealing how it affected the matrilineal matrix of the communities. But their differential influence on both the societies was significant. From this, the factors, which were responsible for the decline of matriliny in Kerala and its sustenance in Khasi society, could be evolved.

In the second stage of the study, meetings and discussions with experts, intellectuals, academicians and social workers were conducted in these societies. I was fortunate in getting good friends in the Khasi land who could give me lots of information and good education about the Khasi. So I could interact with them very closely. As I am from Kerala and ours is a heterogeneous society consisting of people from different religious and caste backgrounds, I grew up seeing the Nair customs and practices. Hence, understanding the Nair community and its structure and functioning were never a problem for me. My friends in the Khasi land used to take me around, explain their history, beliefs, celebrations, festivals, family systems, etc. I used to attend their social functions, weddings, important festivals (*Nonkrem* dance), funerals, etc. We used to go to the remote villages with splendid orchards of oranges and pears to see and interact with the Khasi folk in their original setting. It is here one sees the real empowered women who fight against nature to earn the livelihood and bring up their families. No doubt, these women carry with them a sense of fulfilment and pride which you cannot find among the womenfolk elsewhere.

For the case study I selected cases falling in the age group of 30-60 keeping in mind to accommodate rural-urban, employed-unemployed and rich-poor variables also. A few families with three generations were also selected from both the communities in order to watch the changes over generations. Random visits to the families were done over a period of two years. In the beginning the Khasis were not co-operative; they were rather reluctant to open up and give frank responses. But after frequent visits and establishing rapport with them, they became very friendly and started even sharing some of their problems with me. Still many of their explanations did not tally with reality. In such instances my personal observations were of great use. I also used to interact with their husbands to get their views and feelings on many issues. For the analysis, each case was scrutinized individually from various dimensions and the findings of all the cases were codified together. The secondary data, which included published materials as well as the opinions of the experts, were of great help in finding explanations for some of the findings.

Cases, Analysis and Discussion

This chapter comes from an extensive research work soon to be published in book form. Space limitations prohibit elaborate details here. The cases are summarized in the form of some tables so that reference to them allows the reader some comparative perspective.

Though the two systems appear to be the same, the study shows significant differences in their family patterns. The Nair household comprises of the mother, all her children and descendants on the female line while the spouses are excluded. It perpetuates and keeps expanding on the vertical as well as collateral lines. The Khasi household, on the other hand, consists of the woman, her husband, and the husband and children of the youngest daughter. It perpetuates on a vertical line with the youngest daughter holding the household while all the other daughters get segmented off gradually. After the disintegration of the *tarawad* system, the educated Nairs moved largely to the cities hunting for jobs and setting up nuclear families. Due to modernization, increased transportation facilities and the availability of good educational and health centres all over the state, there is not much difference between the rural and urban folk in Kerala. Still a large proportion of Nairs are concentrated in the cities due to the easy accessibility to job centres. However, majority of the Khasis still live in villages. There is a marked difference between the lifestyles of the rural and urban Khasis. The elite Khasis live in and around the township while the non-elites live mostly in the rural areas where, the living conditions are most deplorable without proper sanitary, health and educational facilities.

Family Pattern

Today there is no hard and fast rule among the Nairs regarding their family pattern because of the changes that have taken place. The general practice is that in Trivandrum area, among the upper class Nairs, the girl at her marriage usually inherits a house to which the couple moves after marriage, while among the middle and lower income groups the couple stays along with the girl's family, as in case 11, or in a portion of the family house as in case 13. There are instances where the lonely mother comes and stays with the daughter in her son-in-law's house and the mother staying with her son and daughter-in-law in the son's house or the daughter-in-law staying in the husband's ancestral home (case number 18). In case number 19 the woman stays alone with servants as both her sons are working outside and staying with their wives and children. But it is significant to note that none of the cases have shown the magnanimity of accommodating a sick, handicapped, widowed or divorced brother, sister, uncle or aunt as it used to be in the earlier days. Also it is important to note that in all these cases the parents or the widowed mothers have their own assets or income to compensate for their expenses in the children's houses.

Unlike the Nairs, the Khasis still follow the joint family system, especially in the rural areas. Majority of the Khasi population belong to the lower class and they live in villages. These joint families act as an asylum for the disabled, old, widowed or divorced. Their family system is such that the elder daughters move out from the maternal home when they get one or two children and put up their independent houses with their husbands and children, while the youngest continues to stay with the parents and inherit the ancestral home. But among the Christian Khasis and town dwellers, we see an increasing trend towards nuclear families.

The size of the Khasi household is much larger when compared with the Nair household. Regarding the number of children we observe a decline among Nairs, while among the Khasis, it is still very high. Most of the Nair families have one or a maximum of two children. But the Khasi families still have many children as in cases 2 and 8 where they have 13 and 12 members respectively. The average size of the Nair household as per the sample is 4.2 while that of the Khasi is 7.

Education and Occupation

The academic and professional achievement of Khasi in general is much less compared to that of the Nair. This may be due to the fact that education was a major asset in Kerala for many generations, while for the Khasi, it is not much old. But the elite Khasis are highly educated and they used to send their children outside for higher education. Case number 4 shows that the woman, who is 73, was educated in the United Kingdom. Due to the differences in the educational opportunities between the two communities, there is significant difference between them with regard to the employment and occupational activities.

The Khasi sample shows that majority of the women from the lower groups and villages are still engaged in small business or farming activity which generates just enough income for the running of the family. In the first generation we find most of the women engaged in agriculture, business or even breweries. In case Nos. 2 and 8, the old village women run beetle nut shops assisted by their husbands or sons-in-law. In case 3 the lady does farming in her orchard mostly by herself. But the Khasi women from the urban areas take up paid jobs. They tend to depend increasingly on their husbands' income as well.

When we analyse the occupational pattern of the Nairs we observe stratification on the basis of income and class to which they belong and also on the basis of the generations. The first generation Nair women were mostly full time homemakers except the ones from economically lower brackets. The men were the breadwinners and it was undignified for them to send women for outside work. In the second generation also we observe that the upper class women in spite of being highly educated were not allowed to take up jobs, while the middle class and low class women take up jobs. In the third generation, i.e., the present one, no matter what their classes or qualifications are, the girls are aggressively active in their professions. This trend is observed among the elite Khasis also.

Inheritance and Income

The inheritance pattern of Khasis is that the youngest daughter inherits bulk of the assets while the other daughters and sons practically get nothing to inherit. In the rich families the other children get a house or a piece of land. In any case when a new *iing* (household) is formed it takes the name of the female. The maintenance and running of the family is woman's responsibility as the inheritance goes on the female line. In poor families women get very little or no financial support at all from their husbands as majority of men in this category are either drug or alcohol addicts. The children belong to the *Kur* of their mothers and hence the sons' children cannot inherit from their father's *Kur*. But they can inherit the father's earnings since a man's earnings after marriage normally goes to his wife and children.

In the case of Nairs, traditionally the *tarawad* properties belonged to all the members of the joint family. With the disintegration of the joint family today, all the members of the family inherit equal share. Hence both the husband and wife get an equal share on their ancestral properties. Thus the *tarawad* system has died out paving way to the nuclear family system. This nuclear set-up is absolutely self-centred and the members do not have the heart to waste their money or time on kin feelings and kin obligations.

As Table 9.1 reveals the per capita income of the Nair families is higher compared to their Khasi counterparts. The Nair families are smaller in size and higher in earning capacity. One significant observation is that those who are rich among the Khasis are quite rich, richer than their Nair counterparts of the same category while those who are poor are miserably poor, poorer than Nairs of identical situation. The upper class Khasi families have their income from businesses connected with coal, limestone, etc., while the middle class depends mainly on some clerical or teaching jobs. The situation of the lower class families, which live in rural areas, is most pathetic with no education, very little availability of jobs, population explosion, lack of enterprising nature, etc.

Lineage

The lineage and the descent for the Khasi continue in the female line. They have prescribed certain norms for its continuation. Generally the youngest daughter inherits the ancestral house with all its responsibilities, privileges and obligations. Along with the ancestral house, the clothes and ornaments also go to the *Khadduh*. But there is no hard and fast rule that the ancestral house should go to the youngest always. In case number 4, the ancestral house was given to the 3rd daughter of the family as the youngest could not stay in the ancestral house fulfilling the *Kur* obligations. In case 4, the *Khadduh,* who is the heiress of an elite family, did not conceive any child. In order to continue the lineage she adopted the children of a deceased sister of hers and installed her niece as the *Khadduh* and the nephew as the *Kni* for the whole family. There are also instances when women did not have female descendants merging with their maternal *Kur*. In case 2, which is a very poor family with a large family and limited income, the ego expects her daughterless widowed, unemployed sister to join them as soon as her nephew marries and goes off to the wife's house. She already has a divorcee

Table 9.1

Case Information for Twenty Women from Meghalaya and Kerala Matrilineal Groups

Case	Age	Religion/Caste	Marital Status and Family Type	Resides	Education	Employment	Family Size	Monthly Income Per Capita
1	44	Indigenous/Khasi	Divorced, extended	Urban	Educated	Employed	8	Rs. 3371
2	38	Indigenous/Khasi	Married, joint	Rural	Literate	Housewife	13	Rs. 231
3	54	Christian /Khasi	Married, joint*	Rural	Illiterate	Self-employed	4	Rs. 500
4	73	Indigenous/Khasi	Widowed, joint	Urban	Well-Educated in United Kingdom	Family Business and Plantation	5	Rs. 80,000
5	60	Indigenous/Khasi	Married, nuclear	Urban	Graduate	Retired from University	4	Rs. 7,125
6	66	Christian/Khasi	Married, nuclear	Urban	Educated	Housewife	5	Rs. 30,000
7	35	Christian/Khasi	Married, nuclear	Rural	Illiterate	Maidservant	8	Rs. 275
8	60	Indigenous/Khasi	Divorced, joint	Rural	Illiterate	Small business	12	Rs. 560
9	45	Christian/Khasi	Married, extended	Urban	Secondary school	Housewife	7	Rs. 171
10	45	Hindu/Punjabi	Married Khasi, nuclear	Urban	Educated	Social worker	4	Rs. 1250
11	76	Hindu/Nair	Widowed, extended	Urban	Illiterate	Maidservant	5	Rs. 160
12	50	Hindu/Nair	Married, extended	Urban	Post graduate	Bank officer	4	Rs. 10,500
13	53	Hindu/Nair	Married 2, extended	Urban	Literate	Self-employed	3	Rs. 250
14	46	Hindu/Nair	Married, extended	Rural	Post graduate	Employed	4	Rs. 5125
15	47	Hindu/Nair	Married, nuclear	Rural	Literate	Self-employed	4	Rs. 312

Contd...

Contd...

16	40	Hindu/Nair	Married, nuclear	Rural	Primary	Self-employed	4	Rs. 225
17	49	Hindu/Nair	Married, extended/ patrilineal	Urban	Graduate	Unemployed	5	Rs. 3000
18	50	Hindu/Nair	Married, extended/ patrilineal	Rural	Graduate	Housewife	5	Rs. 6200
19	75	Hindu/Nair	Widowed, patrilineal	Rural	Matriculate	Unemployed	1	Rs. 75,000
20	31	Hindu/Nair	Married, extended/ temporary	Urban	Post graduate	Employed	7	Rs. 14,288

* Though married, husband is absent, woman lives with daughters, takes support of her brother and married sons live in wives' houses.

Table 9.2

Lineage, Decision-making and Inheritance

Case	*Age*	*Community*	*Lineage*	*Decision-making*	*Inheritance from - amount*
1	44	Khasi	matrilineal	ego	Mother, the house bought by father for mother - moderate
2	38	Khasi	matrilineal	ego's mother	House and a piece of land from the mother - very poor
3	54	Khasi	matrilineal	ego	Father. He bought land for children after loosing mother and before he left to new wife's residence - poor
4	74	Khasi	matrilineal	ego	Mother - very rich, plantations, coal mines, buildings
5	60	Khasi	matrilineal	ego	Acquired by both husband and wife - moderate
6	66	Khasi	matrilineal	husband, minister in government	Mother - very rich, plantation, coal business, buildings
7	35	Khasi	matrilineal	husband	Mother - very poor, both work
8	60	Khasi	matrilineal	ego, divorcee	No inheritance, self-acquired house - very poor
9	45	Khasi	matrilineal	ego	Mother, but does not look after the mother - moderate
10	45	Punjabi/Khasi	new lineage	both together	Husband's mother - moderate
11	76	Nair	bilineal	son in-law	Husband (who acquired the house) - poor
12	50	Nair	matrilineal	ego	Both lines - moderate, both are bank officers
13	53	Nair	matrilineal	ego, husband drunkard	Mother - very poor
14	46	Nair	patrilineal	husband and wife together	Both sides - moderate, both working
15	47	Nair	matrilineal	ego	Mother - very poor, both work
16	40	Nair	patrilineal	husband	No inheritance, spouse acquired house - very poor, husband handicapped
17	49	Nair	patrilineal	husband	Both sides, wife and husband's house - moderate
18	50	Nair	patrilineal	husband	Both sides, mother-in-law's house - moderate
19	75	Nair	patrilineal	husband (though now deceased)	Husband - very rich, Kshatriya, plantation, buildings
20	31	Nair	patrilineal	husband (though away at sea often)	Both sides - moderate

brother staying with her who also does not have a stable job or income

On the contrary, the lineage and family looses its importance among the Nairs today. Cases 11 and 13 do not even bother to know their *tarawad* (family) names. They said that their ancestors came to Trivandrum long back and from then onwards they use only the house numbers for identification. Most of the families in the towns now use only their house numbers unlike in the earlier days when the family names were the main index of one's status in the society. When asked whether they continued the lineage rituals, majority said that from their parents' time onwards they have stopped doing it. Five of the first generation women said that they occasionally go to their family temples and entrust money to the *Poojaris* (priests) for conducting *poojas* (rituals) for the *Kuladevatas* (family Goddesses), because they are afraid, if they displease these deities, it can bring curses (wrath) to the family. Though some of the respondents still follow the religious rituals, some others mostly of the second generation, considered these rituals superstitious and abstained from them. This reveals that the family name and lineage is gradually loosing its importance among Nairs.

The study shows a very significant factor that majority of the Nair parents preferred to live with their daughters than daughters-in-law. A large proportion of the parents said that they will have equal partition among the children but will keep the house for the daughter, while a minority said that they would give it to their sons. Increasingly children take the surnames of their fathers but there is a tendency among some parents to give surnames to the children that conceal both the father's and mother's identities.

On the whole we can say that the Nairs today are more self-oriented while the Khasis are still kinship oriented. Among the urban Khasis we see an increasing number of nuclear families emerging. The influence of Christianity and modernization in this regard is significant.

Decision-Making

There is no society that is absolutely patriarchal where the power and authority are fully with the males, nor can we envisage a society where the power and control are absolutely with the females. It is only a legal overemphasis on one side of kinship followed very often by a strong emotional feeling. We come across matriarchs in patriarchal societies as well as patriarchs in matriarchal societies. The lineage practices and the authority structure of any society are determined not only by the cultural matrix of that society, but by individual variations as well.

The major aspects of decision-making considered for the study were: decisions regarding disposal or purchase of property or house, decisions regarding the sale or purchase of gold or any costly kitchenware, decisions regarding future and education of children, decisions regarding marriage of children, decisions regarding the choice of occupation for members, etc.

The study reveals that among the Nairs, the heads of families are the husbands or in their absence, the sons. The first generation women said that in their times the husbands were the heads of the families and all the major decisions of the family were taken by them only. But they also mentioned that during their parents' and grand parents' time decisions were taken by the *tarawads.* Majority of the second-generation women who are educated and earning said that the major decisions were taken by their husbands in consultation with them. Choice of occupation is left to the freedom of the children though they are guided toward certain professions.

A significant change is noticed here in the attitude of the first generation women towards decision-making. In this category women suddenly started leaving all the decisions of the family for their husbands. Also they mentioned that during their parents' time decisions were taken by the *tarawads*. This change in decision-making toward patriliny indicates the disintegration of the *tarawads*.

Most of the urban Khasi women said that their husbands were the heads of the families though in reality they themselves were the heads. Majority of the rural women admitted that they or their mothers were the heads. All the cases said that the major decisions regarding the purchase or sale of property, decisions regarding *Kur* matters, etc. were taken by the woman of the house (the mother or *Khadduh*) in consultation with the *Kur* members. Majority said that the decisions regarding the future and education of children were jointly decided by the woman and her husband. Decision regarding the choice of occupation, all of them said, was the concern of the individual member. Similarly, when asked about the choice of the spouses and the fixing up of marriages for children, all the cases said, it was absolutely left to the person concerned. Arranged marriages are very rare among Khasis.

Analysis

After analysing the two societies we understand that these two are at different stages of evolution. Macro-level changes have taken place in the Nair society leading to its disintegration owing to the impact of modernization, education and a marginal effect of Christian influence. Though the same factors had reached the Khasi Hills also, their impact on the society was minimal and it could bring about only micro-level changes.

The major reason for the differential influence of the above mentioned factors on these societies could be the heterogeneous nature of the Kerala society and the homogeneous nature of the Khasi society. The Nair community is only a sub-system in the whole social system of the Kerala, while the Khasis and the Jaintias, the two matrilineal communities inhabiting the Khasi Hills, form the whole social system. The Nairs in Kerala live side by side with other patriarchal communities like the Nambuthiris, Christians, and Muslims, etc., who have had their influences on this community. The Nairs did not have the required strength to resist the various forces of social change that acted on them simultaneously. Besides, the movements started by various caste groups, the new education system sponsored by the European missionaries, the communist movement and the impact of mass media together hit the social system to undermine the supremacy of the Nairs.

A significant factor that led to the disintegration of matriliny in Kerala was the weakening of the landholdings by the Nairs. On the change over to cash economy large areas of land were transferred to Christians and other enterprising communities. The Nairs could no longer maintain the Nair *tarawads* with their meagre income that came from limited land holdings. They had no option but to partition the *tarawads* as they found it economically unviable.

Indeed, the economic pressures, the new administration, the changing values and the rigorous new value system, which were the concomitant of the new resources, seriously weakened the Nair matrilineal joint family and hastened its disintegration. The core elements of matriliny, the lineage, the avuncular authority and the female inheritance were more suited to a time when the landed property was concentrated in the hands of the Nairs, Nambuthiris and Kshatriyas. But it was proved to be ill suited to the changing situation when most of its elements became dysfunctional and the brother-sister bond, which was the nucleus of matriliny started fading away.

During the second half of the nineteenth century various socio-political and economic factors were thrown upon the Kerala society resulting from the impact of a cash economy, western-style education, improved communication and a British inspired system of law on the complex social structure of an Indian princely state. By 1847 the Nairs who were enjoying comfortable dominance were to experience a crisis in their matrilineal system, which was to contribute vitally to the decline of their power.

By this time the British consolidated their rule over Indian subcontinent and they exerted their influence even on the native state of Travancore. With this the kingship lost much of its glory. The administration got modernized and the new administration required qualified hands from the government regulated schools which found the Nairs unfit for the new jobs. The period between 1910 and1920 saw the emergence of various caste movements and demonstrations against the supremacy and dominance of the higher castes. A high density of population, high rate of literacy, high rate of unemployment and poverty, and a shattered social system led to the formation of Communist movement in Kerala. Around this time many urban centres emerged attracting a large number of educated youth for job opportunities in the towns. The qualified Nair youth started migrating to these urban centres in large numbers leaving their joint families behind and creating nuclear families near their job places. In the changed situation women started leaning on their husbands for additional expenses and luxuries.

The various acts and legislations regulating marriage and enabling the woman and children to inherit their husbands/fathers was a serious set back for the kinship relationships in the matrilineal joint family. Similarly various land reform acts which were passed at different stages relating to the partition of *tarawad* properties and the abolition of absentee landlordism, tenancy provision, land ceiling, etc., deeply affected the matrilineal system. This along with other factors of modernization created turmoil in the Nair community that necessitated a change in the whole social system.

Thus in the last half of the nineteenth century a society which had survived fundamentally unchanged for 700 years came unhinged. A movement from ascribed to achieved status began, a movement from the interdependence of castes to the competition of individuals, from traditional authority to modern bureaucracy.

The new functional alternatives called for was partition of the *tarawad* property based on an equal share principle. Similarly, the avuncular authority was substituted by paternal authority and tracing of lineage on female line by the male line. The *tarawads* disintegrated giving rise to nuclear families. The brother sister relationship which was the nucleus of the *marumakkattayam tarawads* got replaced by the husband-wife bond which becomes the nucleus of the new set-up. Thus came a shift from matriliny to patriliny. Though the new system is patrilineal one cannot attribute an absolute allocation of lineage, authority and inheritance to the male line.

The Khasi society has reached the point of time where the need is felt for a serious introspection and re-evaluation of institutions, laws and cherished customs, and their relevance in the present day context. The Khasi has come a long way from the traditional way of living and the subsequent agricultural practices to that of the modern urbanized living. Modernization and all that goes with it like education, industrialization, urbanization, literacy, communication, transportation, etc. have played a key role in changing the ways of thinking and acting of this so far isolated community. The impact of globalization is fast acting on this society. The advent of Christianity and the forces of modernization and globalization in Khasi society have undoubtedly weakened the matrilineal system and have played a vital role in the process of cultural revivalism.

The new class of professionals, bureaucrats and technocrats which is the offshoot of modern education resulted in making a large number of Khasi men and women hold responsible and competent jobs. This new sense of independence is in constant conflict with clan solidarity as cohesion of the clan, which primarily centred on land, has naturally disintegrated. The shift of occupation from agriculture to salaried jobs resulted in a migration from villages to towns. This new development has not left the Khasi matriliny unscathed but led to a pull between avuncular and paternal authority. Traditionally, the maternal uncle had a major say in his clan affairs. He used to be the final arbiter in matters concerning the sale of property, the engagement and marriage of his nephews and nieces and settling of family disputes. In the changed situation the spatial distance between his ancestral house and his place of work becomes widened leading to a widening of social distance between the two; hence resulting in a conflict of loyalties.

Today the role of the *Kni* is symbolic, he is now informed of family happenings but he does not make decisions. Thus the importance given to the mother's brother is fading into the background and the father gradually advances to the forefront of the conjugal home.

An important source of contradiction in Khasi matriliny is the intense role conflict that the system generates for men. The matrilineal culture generates a conflict between the husband and the wife's brothers. The Khasi makes a sharp distinction between kin and affines; kin loyalties are emphasized at the cost of affinal ties. Khasi kinship imposes a dual loyalty upon a man. Though he is considered an outsider to his wife's clan and lineage he is expected to fulfil his responsibilities as a husband and father and also to provide for his wife's family when he stays with them. At the same time as a son he owes religious and jural obligations to his mother and sister. Thus men are torn between the responsibilities towards their natal home on the one hand and their wife and children on the other.

The role of the father in Khasi society as in other matrilineal societies is ambiguous because traditionally the Khasi see the maternal uncle as the figure of authority. The pull between the avuncular and paternal authority has led to a new trend in Khasi kinship structure. This is the emergence of the mother figure as a dominant personality. The close bond, which exists between mother and child in Khasi kinship leads to the establishment of maternal authority. The economic dependence of the woman upon the husband, which is a consequence of globalization and modernization, is the first step towards breaking down of traditional matriliny

The strain generated by role conflict affects Khasi women more intensely. A woman cannot be fully sure that her husband has more loyalty towards her and her children than to his sister and her children. Besides, the women feel that their rights and privileges in society turn out to be more burdensome duties and responsibilities. They experience a disjunction between the line of descent and inheritance on the one hand and the structure of authority and control on the other, especially in the traditional families. While the youngest daughter has numerous familial and kinship obligations because she inherits the family property, she does not possess authority commensurate with her duties and responsibilities.

Today *Khadduhs* are becoming increasingly self-oriented forgetting kinship responsibilities. It is ironical that in Khasi Hills there is a newly opened SOS Children's Village catering to the neglected/abandoned children. This type of a situation was unheard of in the Khasi land as the *iing seng* (the house of the *khadduh*) was the house for all the needy.

It is observed that an increasing number of Khasis are taking the surnames of their fathers, especially if the father is a popular man or a person holding a high position in the society. Some add the surnames of both the father and the mother to their names.

Another serious problem that affects the Khasi society today is the frustration among the men, especially the youth, because of the dwindling of the power of the maternal uncle in his natal home and disproportionate recognition and respect he receives in his conjugal family. Men become disillusioned and many are taken to drinks, drugs and other antisocial activities.

In this turmoil the merits and demerits of matrilineal system in the Khasi society is hotly debated. Even while there is a strong opposition to any change from the present matrilineal to a patrilineal system, there are a growing number of people, even women, favouring the shift to patriliny.

The functional prerequisites which necessitated the survival and continuance of Khasi matriliny were the three core elements – lineage, inheritance and authority. Though the Khasi society is undergoing a phase of transition due to the inroads made by education, mass media and other cultural forces it has not succeeded in abandoning the matrilineal structure of the society. The study reveals that the same functional prerequisites are not necessarily indispensable for the continuance of the social system. Similarly the Nair society, though it has shifted from matriliny to patriliny, still is left with the remnants of matriliny as remarked by a prominent Nair leader, "Though Nairs of today are legally patrilineal, they are emotionally matrilineal".

Notes

1. Ehrenfels, V. (1953) The Comparative Study of Matrilineal Civilizations in India, *Journal*, University of Guwahati, IV.
2. Ibid.

3. Murdock, George Peter (1971) The Nuclear Family, In Nelson Graburn (ed.) *Readings in Kinship and Social Structure*, New York: Harper and Row Publishers.
4. Bachofen (1931) In F. Engels, *The Origin of the Family, Private Property and the State*, Moscow: Progress Publishers.
5. Bhattacharya, N.N. (n.d.) A Stock of Studies on the Matrilineal Societies of Eastern India, Dept of Ancient Indian History and Culture, Calcutta, (Mimeographed).
6. Bachofen op. cit.
7. Radcliffe-Brown, A.R. (1952) *Structure and Functions in Primitive Society*, London: Routledge and Kegan Paul.
8. Fox, Robin (1967) *Kinship and Marriage*, Harmondsworth: Penguin.
9. Ehrenfels, V. (1953) Comparative Study of Matrilineal Civilizations in India, *Journal*, University of Guwahati, IV.
10. Ibid.
11. Oppong, Christine (1974) *Marriage Among a Matrilineal Elite*, Cambridge: University Press.
12. Nongbri, Tiplut (1988) Gender and the Khasi Family Structure: Some Implications of the Meghalaya Succession of Self Acquired Act 1984, *Sociological Bulletin*, 37.
13. Gough, Kathleen (1972) Nair Central Kerala, In David Schneider and Kathleen Gough (eds.), *Matrilineal Kinship*, Allahabad: A.H. Wheeler and Co. Private Limited.
14. Jeffrey Robin (1996) The Decline of Nair Tarawads, In N. Jayaram and Satish Saberwal (eds.), *Social Conflict*, Delhi: Oxford University Press.
15. Merton, Robert K. (1972) *Social Theory and Social Structure*, New Delhi: Amerind Publishing Co.
16. Parsons, Talcott (1951) *The Social System*, Glencoe, Ill: The Free Press.
17. Martindale, Don op. cit.
18. The Modern Disintegration of Matrilineal Descent Groups, In David Schneider and Kathleen Gough (eds.), *Matrilineal Kinship*, Allahabad: A.H. Wheeler, 1972.
19. The Khasi Hills Autonomous District Council, *Khasi Social Customs of Lineage Bill*, 1997, Shillong.
20. Pakyntein, Valentina (1996) The Khasi Clan; Changing Religion and its Effect, In J.S. Bhandari (ed.), *Kinship and Family in North-East India*, Vol. II, New Delhi: Cosmo Publications.
21. Gurdon, P.R.T. (1975) *The Khasis*, New Delhi: Cosmo Publications.

22. Variar, Sreedhara (1969) *Marumakkathayam and Allied Systems of Law*, Cochin.
23. In Kerala the following social hierarchy based on dominance and sub-ordinance of caste groups were followed; Nambuthiris, Kshatriyas, Vaishyas, Shudras and untouchables.
24. Karve, Iravati (1965) *Kinship Organization in India.*, Asian Publishing House.
25. Fawcet, F. (1990) *Nayars of Malabur*, New Delhi: Asian Educational Services.
26. Lewis, Oscar (1959) *Five Families*, New York: Basic Book.
27. Ibid.

10

Widowhood and the Law in India

A Sociological Analysis

RAMOLA B. JOSEPH

The general advancement facilitated by modern technology has aroused a new awareness in mankind about the subordination of women and their problems. Subordination of women can be traced back to various reasons: first, the various forms of social and psychological control which have existed to keep women in their 'place'. The physical strength and alleged dominance of men has been an important instrument of controlling women's freedom of action. The traditional image of the male as the 'protector' owes a great deal to the notion that women cannot defend themselves and men, therefore, must take charge of their lives physically. The same notion of male strength has historically been responsible for restricting jobs involving heavy labour to men. This is the main reason why women historically have accepted the dominance of men in their lives.

The second reason is the economic control that has kept women in their place. The root of women's subjection has been their economic dependence on men. As long as women were denied the opportunity to earn their own living, there could not be equality between sexes.

Third, the psychological message given to women that they should be happy with their place has proved most effective instrument of social control. The qualities that receive the most praise were those traditionally associated with being a 'lady', not an assertive individual ready to face the world.

Finally, another unique reason has been the internal pressure of women on each other. From generation to generation mothers teach daughters to please men, providing instructions which prepare the new generation to assume the roles of mothers and housewives. Over the centuries women themselves have been the most ardent traditionalists.

Thus, subordination of women has been caused by physical, economic, psychological and internal pressure reasons. The situation becomes much more miserable when taking into consideration the plight of widows. In a way, this is the sociological dimension of the issue because it can be said that the degree of emancipation enjoyed by widows is the measure of its general cultural advance.

The death of a family member affects not only the individuals in the family but also the family unit collectively. The precise difficulties the family faces and the manners in which they cope with them depend on particular circumstances. Nevertheless, a few generalizations can be made with respect to the kinds of problems that frequently develop.

There are, of course, a number of factors determining this disruptive potential of death, including:

- ***Who dies***: In modern societies death is largely confined to the old and hence the death of a child is more emotionally devastating for those of the parent generation than the death of those of the grandparent and great-grandparent generations. In the case of the death of an only child, there is also the death of parental roles and an increased likelihood of divorce. In the patriarchal families of the past, the death of a father was also the event that allowed other families to enter into this family, as children went in their own ways.
- ***The contribution of the deceased to family solidarity***: As families become more mobile both geographically and socially, it is the grandparent generation that provides the key familial bond. It is at their homes that family members reunite during the holidays; it is their increasing need for assistance that becomes the basis of renewed bonds between siblings who previously had "gone their own ways". With parental death, however, these ties between aunts, uncles, and cousins can be severed – particularly if there were battles over inheritance.

- ***How family members die and patterns of familial assistance in their dying process***: Some deaths, like suicide, can be highly stigmatizing for family members. Inequalities in care, such as when the burden of nursing a dying mother falls on the shoulder of just one child and other children shirk their responsibilities; it can trigger hostilities toward non-contributory siblings.

Parental Death

Next to the death of spouse and offspring, the death of one's parents often produce the greatest degree of grief. With the death of the last parent, one not only is 'orphaned' but typically enters the status of the family elder. One also becomes next generation 'up to bat' with the Grim Reaper, as Ralph Keyes, author of *Fathers on Sons*, observes:

> I think when you lose your parents, it's like that line of defense is gone. You're at the rear of a formation of soldiers being shot at and the first two rows collapse... I remember when my mom died a minister said to me that you feel vulnerable in a way you didn't when your parents were still alive. You have to step forward and say, "I'm ready to assume responsibility in the world".

For the family as a whole, one obvious effect is the disruption of normal activities. This in turn may lead the surviving family members' to gain greater resolve to face their loss collectively. On the other hand, it may lead to fragmentation similar to that, which follows a divorce. Indeed, divorce and death often have similar effects on children. Removal of an authority figure may lead them to take on greater responsibilities in the family, and greater independence, or it may lead to family conflicts and a lack of family solidarity. It may also break the remaining ties between brothers and sisters who live apart.

Bereavement has a profound and more individual effect, too, on the surviving spouse. This might be enhanced if the couple were married for most of their lives and particularly if they shared their last years together in isolation from their children. Studies in the United States have shown that, in general, a husband who survives the death of his wife has greater difficulty in coping than a wife who survives the death of her husband. Not only does a surviving husband have to cope with emotional loss but he also has to take on tasks such as cleaning and cooking – which in many modern societies are still usually done by the wife. On the other hand, some sociologists have argued the reverse, that a surviving wife has greater difficulty, owing in part to the larger number of women who live to an advanced age and the resulting greater difficulty they have in finding a new husband.

Widowhood

Examination of the marital status of those who are 65 and above in the combined 1973-94 NORC General Social Surveys shows that the chances of women being widowed are three times that of men (56% to18%). Sally Cline, the author of the famous book, *Lifting the Taboo: Women, Death and Dying,* observes:

> The Old English *"widewe"* originated in the Indo-European root *"widh"* meaning to be empty or separated. The Sanskrit *"vidh"* means destitute or lacking. Joseph T. Shipley in the *Dictionary of Word Origins* points out that "since marriage has made two of one, a widow is a woman that has been emptied of her." Other writers confirm this notion: "She was a widow, that strange feminine entity who had once been endowed with a dual personality and was now only half of what she had been." (p. 147) These meanings are not similarly affixed to widowers.

To be first widowed in one's friendship structure can be highly stigmatizing as one is perhaps perceived to be a threat to couple relationships. Often their identities were so totally dependent upon that of their spouses that when death did occur these females lost a significant portion of their very self-concept. On the other hand, as age discrepancies between husbands and wives were greater in the past than in the present, many husbands may have prepared their wives to be widows. These are the generations of women who were generally too old to be affected by the feminist movement of recent decades. For more recent generations of women, however, things may be different as women may be more likely to have anticipatory socialization for widowhood because of previous divorces and because a greater portion of their identities are derived from their activities in the work world.

In societies, such as in India, widows are given distinctly inferior social status to married women and have a much harder time than widows in the West. In most parts of India, widows are not permitted to wear brightly coloured clothes or to look after their appearance, attendance at certain rituals, notably weddings, is forbidden to them. Indeed, it has been suggested that the practice of 'suttee' (immolation of the widow), formerly practiced in India was in part encouraged by the extreme hardships that widows faced in medieval Hindu society. Even in modern India, widows are isolated from the mainstream of social life. They are not permitted to attend any public function, and if at all they manage to make their appearance, they have to face severe criticism and contempt. They are often insinuated for showing utter disregard for tradition. In some of the villages in India, death of the husband is seen as a curse or wrath of God and hence they are totally isolated from the community. Consequently, these poor women, who are often uneducated and unemployed, have to live the lives of either beggars or are debauched by the anti-social elements of society. The plight of widows is sometimes so lamentable that they often resort to take the easy way out – 'suicide'. The attitude towards the widows is never questioned, and if at all someone ventures, she is confronted with obfuscating rigmarole regarding traditional values, beliefs and customs.

The relentless efforts of social reformers have been fruitful to some extent, at least in creating some sympathy towards the crying stance of widows. However, they often fail to accomplish something of enduring nature, though their endeavours remain extremely laudable. At this juncture, the imminent and logical way to alleviate the hardships of widows is that which is backed up by the nation and its constitution, namely, the **LAWS.**

However, India being a country with religious heterogeneity could not produce a legal support which is all encompassing in nature. As the religious statuses of women are diversified, the laws had to be formulated in accordance with the scenario of each religious community. This situation has lead to the construction of personal laws for each religious community and its denominations.

Personal Laws in India

'Family Law' in India is the law governing the formation of the family and the rights and obligations arising out of family relationship. The law applicable in such matters is the 'personal law' of the persons concerned. This has to be determined with reference to the religion which the individuals concerned profess. The law relating to marriage, divorce, adoption, guardianship, devolution and disposition of family property, maintenance, succession and inheritance are the areas generally covered by 'personal law'.

Therefore, such laws differ from person to person according to his/her religion. Even among persons belonging to the same religion, there may be differences according to the various 'schools of thought' or the 'sects' or sub-sects to which the people belong. On matters covered by personal laws, there may not be any 'lex loci'.

Matters relating to the family and those incidentals to such relationship are governed mainly by the personal laws like Hindu law, Muslim law and Christian law. Though similarities exist, there is considerable difference between these personal laws, because the sources from which these laws are taken are different. Hence, the status of widows within these three communities is also different.

Hindu Law

The Hindu system of law is based on the concept of dharma. It represents the privileges, duties and obligations of a Hindu, his standard of conduct as a member of the community and as a member of a particular stage of life or 'Ashrama'. Dharma refers to that which has to be done to secure visible and invisible good. Dharma has been defined as "what is followed by those learned in Vedas and what is approved by the conscience of the virtuous who are exempt from hatred and inordinate affection". Each and every custom and traditional practice of a Hindu is governed by the concept of Dharma.

Sources of Hindu Law

Traditional or Classical Sources

1. *Sruti* (Veda): *'Sruti'* means 'that which is heard'. The reference is to what was heard from God by the sages. References to secular law in the *Vedas* are mingled with ethical and religious matters. Eighteen *Upanishads* are also taken as a part of *Sruti.*
2. *Smriti*: It means 'that which is remembered'. *Smriti* give the basic source of Hindu law. They are referred to as the *Dharmasastras* constituting the foundation of law. The ancient sages are the authors of *Dharmasastras*. *'Manu Smriti'* is a complete code giving a reservoir of law. The precepts contained in the *Smriti*s were subjected to various interpretations, which in turn, gave rise to commentaries called *Nibandhas* or Digests.
3. *Achara* or Usage: Even the Supreme Court has regarded custom as a source of law.
4. Justice, Equity and Good Conscience: In the absence of any provision in the *Smriti* or in the event of conflict between

Smritis, principles of justice, equity and good conscience could be applied.

Modern Sources

1. *Shastric* Laws: Principles of *Mitakshra, Dayabhaga* and commentaries are authoritatively ascertained.
2. Custom or Usage: In the Hindu system of law "clear proof of custom or usage will outweigh the written text of law".
3. Legislations: Written laws provided by the legislature.
4. Judicial Precedents: In the absence of statutory provisions and custom, rules of traditional Hindu law as derived from the commentaries and digests have to be followed.

Schools of Hindu Law

The Hindu law as administered today in India is only a *Vyavahara* law of the *Smritis* or Hindu *Dharmasastras* modified by customs and statutes and interpreted by judicial decisions. The interpretations given by various commentaries to the basic doctrines of *Dharmasastras* resulted in the establishment of different schools of law. There is considerable diversity in the doctrines followed in different parts of the country. Strictly speaking, there are only two different schools, namely, *Mitakshra* and *Dayabhaga*. The Mitakshra is followed throughout India except Bengal, where Dayabhaga is reckoned as of superior authority.

Differences between Mitakshra and Dayabhaga

1. The term '*Sapinda*' has been interpreted differently. While kinship is followed on consanguinity or blood relationship or propinquity under *Mitakshra*, under the *Dayabhaga*, it is the principle of religious efficacy or spiritual benefit. The Hindu Succession Act (1956) has done away with such a distinction.
2. *Mitakshra* has established the birthright of the son over the ancestral property held by the father and this entitled the son to claim partition of the property during the father's lifetime. *Dayabhaga* does not recognize such rights.
3. *Mitakshra* recognizes the right of the son to control and challenge unauthorised alienation of ancestral property by father. The son has no such right under *Dayabhaga*.
4. In a *Mitakshra* coparcenery, no one has got a defined or ascertained share in the property. There is both unity of title and

unity of possession in the entire joint family properties. Upon the death of a coparcener his interest passes by survivorship to other coparceners. Under the Dayabhaga, on the death of the father, his son takes the father's property in quasi-severalty whereby each brother is free to alienate his share.

5. A woman cannot be a member of a *Mitakshra* coparcenery. *Dayabhaga* recognizes the right of a widow to succeed to her husband and to enforce partition against the husband's brothers on her own account, even in an undivided family, if he dies without a lineal male descendant. The Hindu Succession Act (1956) alters the law and ranks the widow, daughter and mother among class I heirs.

Thus, we find that significant differences exist between the two schools of thought within the Hindu community itself.

Widow's Power to Remarry

The rules under the *Dharmasastras* are not uniform. Early marriages were common among girls; even those who were below ten years in age were given in marriage. Moreover, widows were not permitted to remarry. So, there were a large number of very young widows. And naturally this created a lot of social problems. Hence, in 1929, the Child Marriage Restraint Act was passed. The law which made a landmark in the lives of widows was the Hindu Marriage Act, 1955. This law has made the marriage of a widow permissible and smoothed the conditions of widows very much, bringing them into the mainstream of society.

Widow's Power to Adopt

Hindu Maintenance and Adaptation Act, 1956 has given widows the liberty to adopt a son or daughter under certain conditions. Since 1956, a female Hindu has the capacity to take a son or daughter in adoption if:

(a) She is of sound mind.
(b) She is not a minor.
(c) She is not married.

If married, a woman can adopt if her marriage has been dissolved or her husband is dead, or has completely and finally renounced the world, or has ceased to be a Hindu or has been declared by a court of competent jurisdiction to be of unsound mind.

If the adoption is of a son, the mother by whom the adoption is made must not have a Hindu son, son's son or son's son's son living at the time of adoption. This may be by blood relationship or by adoption. If the adoption is of a daughter, the mother by whom the adoption is made must not have a daughter or son's daughter living at the time of adoption. The power of the female under the Act rests with the widow. The right provided in favour of a woman to make an adoption and that too of a boy and a girl and even both has fundamentally changed the concept of adoption in Hindu law. When a female is adopting and the person adopted is a male, the adoptive mother must be at least 21 years older than the person to be adopted.

Under the old law, a woman was not entitled to make an adoption in her own right. Similarly, girls were not adopted. But in the case of widows, the right of adoption was subject to differences of opinion depending upon the different interpretations given to the text of Vasishta – "nor let a woman give or take a son in adoption without the consent of her lord". This portrays the subordinate status of women in those times. However, in some places like Benares, the widow could adopt if she was properly authorized by the husband while he was alive. If there was no prohibition against adoption, a widow could adopt according to the interpretation in Western India. In the Madras School, the want of husband's consent could be supplied by his *Sapindas*. "When a Hindu dies leaving a widow and a son and that son dies leaving a natural born or adopted son, or leaving no son but his own widow to continue the line by means of adoption, the power of the former widow is extinguished and can never afterwards be revived". Thus, the principles which existed for three quarters of a century were reaffirmed by Mahajan C.J. who summed up the propositions thus:

(1) The interposition of a grandson or the son's widow, competent to continue the line by adoption brings the mother's power of adoption to an end.
(2) The power to adopt does not depend upon any question of vesting or divesting of property.
(3) A mother's authority to adopt is not extinguished by the mere fact that her son had attained ceremonial competence.
(4) The true rule is that when a son dies before attaining full legal competence and does not leave either a widow or a son or an adopted son, then the power of the mother which was in abeyance during his lifetime revives, but the moment he hands over the torch to another, the mother can no longer take it.

A widow on her remarriage loses her capacity to give in adoption her son by the former husband under the old law which is also changed under the provisions of the Act. The Supreme Court held that when a Hindu widow adopts a son he becomes affiliated to the deceased husband of the widow so that the deceased husband would be deemed to be the father of the adopted son. In that case, the adopted son was held to be a preferential heir to the properties of the deceased father in the capacity of a nearest reversionary.

Doctrine of Relation Back

Regarding the rights over properties, a huge number of cases came up before the courts in India and also the Privy Council because of the fictions attached to a widow's power of adoption. In many cases, the widows adopted long after the demise of their husbands. Though effected by the widow, an adoption was, in fact, made for and on behalf of the deceased husband and by the fiction the adopted boy would be deemed to have been in existence at the time of the death of the widow's husband. Further consequences were to follow as if the deceased had left behind a male issue. This principle known as the "doctrine of relation back" posed a number of problems about the divesting of rights over the property vested in others. Regarding adoptions after the commencement of the Act, the provisions make it clear that the effect of adoption is only prospective in operation.

Formerly, though the widow was entitled to be the nearest heir of a sonless person, she was given only a limited estate. Hence, as a consequence of the power of adoption exercised by her the estate with her would vest with the adopted son.

J. Krishna Iyer has laid down the following propositions:

(1) A widow's adoption cannot be stultified by an anterior partition of the joint family and the adopted son can claim a share as if he were begotten and alive when the adoptive father breathed his last.

(2) Nevertheless, the factum of partition is not wiped out by the lateral adoption.

(3) Any disposition testamentary or *inter vivos* lawfully made antecedent to the adoption is immune to challenge by the adopted son.

(4) Lawful alienation, in this context, means not necessarily for a family necessity but alienation made competently in accordance with law.

(5) A widow's power of alienation is limited and if – and only if – the conditions set up by the Hindu law are fulfilled will the alienation bind a subsequently adopted son.

(6) Once partitioned validly, the share of a member of a *Mitakshra* Hindu family in which his own issue have no right by birth can be transferred by him at his will and such transfer, be they by will, gift or sale bind the adopted son who comes later on the scene.

The old concepts of adoption by the widow on behalf of the deceased husband, the doctrine of relation back, diverting of properties already vested etc. even today show their shadow in some of the decisions dealing with adoptions after the commencement of the Act. This is inconsistent with the general features of the new Act and the equality of status on the basis of sex provided for by the new legislation.

The Supreme Court held that a person adopted by a Hindu widow after the coming into force of the Hindu Adoptions and Maintenance Act, 1956, can claim a share in the property which had devolved on a sole surviving coparcener on the death of the husband of the widow who took him to adoption. Where a widower or bachelor adopts a child, any wife whom he subsequently marries shall be deemed to be the stepmother of the adopted child.

Minority and Guardianship

Guardianship is the relationship existing between an infant or a ward or some person who has the right to control him, and ensure his maintenance, education and welfare. The law relating to minority and guardianship of Hindus is now contained in the Hindu Minority and Guardianship Act, 1956. A Hindu widow who is entitled to act as a natural guardian of her legitimate children may by will, appoint a guardian for any of them in respect of the minor's person or separate property or for both. Any appointment made by the husband will be of no effect on the face of the appointment made by the widow. This is an important implication from sociological point of view because it increases the power of the widow in society or gives her a social recognition.

Maintenance of Widowed Daughter-in-law

Section 19 of the Act makes provisions for the maintenance of a widowed daughter-in-law. The conditions are:

(1) She should be unable to maintain herself out of her own earnings and property.
(2) If she has no property, she should be able to get maintenance from the estate of her husband, father or mother, son or daughter.
(3) The father-in-law has no obligation if he is not possessed of co-parcenery property.
(4) The father-in-law has no obligation if he is not possessed of coparcenery property out of which the daughter-in-law has not obtained a share.

So also the obligation will cease on the remarriage of the daughter-in-law.

By implication, the alternations specified in Section 19 (1) are, when she is in a position to maintain her from:

(1) Her own earnings of property
(2) The estate of her deceased husband
(3) The estate of her parents
(4) Living son or daughter
(5) The estate of her son or daughter

Property

Mitakshra Joint Family

Under the *Mitakshra* System, a joint Hindu family consists of all the male lineal descendants of a common male ancestor and includes their mothers, wives or widows and unmarried daughters. Possession of property under *Mitakshra* Law is not an essential prerequisite for the construction of a joint family. When the family owns property, it may have the features of restrictive and joint ownership. When there is only a sole surviving male member or even when such a person has also died leaving behind his widow there is the possibility of adoption and then continuing with the family.

Women are not coparceners and are not entitled to acquire any right over joint family property by virtue of birth. Some enactments like the 1937 Act granted the widow of a coparcener the right to take the share of the husband for the lifetime after whose death such share would devolve on surviving coparceners. But the Hindu Succession Act of 1956 (S.14) has converted such life interest into absolute interest. The Class I heirs include widows also.

Under Hindu law, the manager of a joint family is called *Karta*. Normally, the father will be the *Karta* or manager. Where the father is not alive and the family consists of brothers, the elder brother can act as manager. A junior member may act as *Karta* with the consent of the other coparcener when a senior member gives up his right of management. The Supreme Court pointed out that as a woman is not a coparcener she cannot be a *Karta* even though she inherited a fractional share in the coparcenery property under S.6 of the Hindu Succession Act.

Dayabhaga Joint Family

The distinguishing features of the *Dayabhaga* on comparison with *Mitakshra* coparcenery are:

(1) The sons have no right of ownership in the wealth of the living parents, but in the estate of both when deceased.
(2) The father has unlimited power of alienation.
(3) During the lifetime of father the sons have no right to claim partition.
(4) There is no coparcener during the father's life time.
(5) Coparceners take definite share.
(6) Women may also be coparceners.
(7) Survivorship is not applicable.

The female sharers include the wife, widowed mother and widowed grandmother.

Succession

Unchaste behaviour of a widow will cause a bar for inheritance under *Mitakshra*. In *Dayabhaga* unchaste behaviour of any woman will be a disqualification irrespective of the nature of relationship with the last male holder.

Section 24 of the Hindu Succession Act, 1956 provides for disqualifying certain widows from inheriting as widows. The Hindu Widows Remarriage Act, 1856 contains a provision whereby a widow forfeited the property inherited from her husband on her remarriage unless a custom to the contrary was proved. Section 24 covers the following widows who may come in as heir of the intestate:

(i) Widow of a predeceased son
(ii) Widow of a predeceased son of a predeceased son
(iii) Widow of a brother.

They will not be entitled to succeed to the property of the intestate as such widow. If the widow has got the inheritance before the remarriage it would become the absolute property of the widow.

Stridhana literally means woman's peculium (private property), that is, property where she has absolute ownership. Section 14 of the Hindu Succession Act (1956) is of a declaratory nature and confers full ownership to any property possessed by a female Hindu. The source from which the property obtained is unnatural.

A widow or other limited heirs have no general power of alienation of the property inherited by her from the deceased owner. However, there are exceptional circumstances in which there can be a valid alienation. They are for (1) religious or charitable purposes and (2) legal necessity. But a widow is not competent to alienate any portion of the husband's property for her sole spiritual benefit. A Hindu widow is entitled to make a valid alienation of property for a legal necessity.

Surrender is the voluntary self-effacement of the rights over the husband's property held by the widow in favour of the reversioner's. It is a renunciation of rights accelerating the reversionary succession. It must be bona fide surrender not a device to divide the estate with the reversionary, and it must be made in unreserved and absolute terms.

By analysing all the above laws, we find that legislation has definitely helped to enhance the status of Hindu widows. When compared to ancient times, they are getting more liberty, rights and privileges, which have helped them to come to the forefront in Society and strive for more achievements.

Muslim Law

Muslim personal law is founded on the divine revelations embodied in the *Quran*. Muslims are divided into two sects, namely, the *Sunnis* and *Shias*. The *Sunnis* are divided into four sub-sects, namely, the *Hanifis, Malikis, Shafeis* and *Hambalis*. The *Shias* are divided into three sub sects, the *Ismalias, Ithraasharias* and *Zaidiars*.

The majority of the *Sunnis* in India are followers of the *Hasnifi* School named after Imam Abu Hanifa. The important texts of Muslim law are *Hedaya, Fatawa, Alamgiri, Sharaya ul-Islam* and *Al Sirajuyyali*. The primary sources of Muslim law are the *Quran, Sunna* or traditions, *Ijma* and *Qiyas*.

Dower or Mehr

Just like Hindu widows, Muslim widows have also the right to remarry. In this context, Dower or *Mehr* is one of the most important institutions of Muslim family law relating to marriage. It is an obligation imposed upon the husband as a mark of respect for his wife. The main object of dower is to offer protection to the wife against the arbitrary powers of the husband in exercising the right of divorce. One important right of a widow to enforce payment of dower is the right to retain possession of the husband's properties until her dower is paid. Essentially, the possession must have been obtained lawfully. It must be without any force or fraud. The right of retention of the widow will pass to her heirs on her death. The widow is entitled to satisfy the amount due to her out of the income arising out of the property retained. She is entitled to have possession until the claim is satisfied. If there is excess, she has the liability to account for such excess. One essential condition is that the widow should be in possession of the properties at the time of the death of the husband. The period of limitation will not run against the widow as long as the widow is in lawful possession of the husband's property. The right of retention will be lost when the widow's possession is gone, that is, where a Muslim widow came into possession of her husband's property, lawfully without force or fraud, and still claimed dower debt, her right of retention of the property existed till it was discharged and could be exercised by her heirs after her death.

Tabina

Adoption (*Tabina*) has no recognition in Muslim law. The Muslim law confers no right in favour of an adopted son or daughter. According to *Quran,* one who is another person's son does not become his natural son merely by virtue of a declaration.

Minority and Guardianship

Under *Sunni* law, it is the mother who is entitled to custody of children during their tender years. In the case of girls, this right to custody will extend till they attain the age of puberty, that is, fifteen years of age. In the case of boys, the mother will have the right for custody till the age of seven. The right will continue with the mother even after divorce. The mother is deemed to be disqualified to have the custody of the child in the following cases:

- When a divorcee or widow having custody of the child, she marries another.
- When she is found to lead an immoral life, or is of bad character, or is otherwise found guilty of such conduct which is against the interest of the child.

Under *Shia* law, the mother has the right to have the custody of her children during the first two years. Then the father will have the custody of the son and the mother will have the custody of the daughter till the seventh year.

When considering both *Sunni* and *Shia* law, we can say that it puts the widow in an inferior position. In Sunni law, we even find that the mother loses the custody of the child if she marries another. Hence, the widow is prompted to play stereotyped roles with limited rights.

Nafaqa

A widowed or divorced daughter is also entitled to claim maintenance (*Nafaqa*) from the father if she is not able to maintain herself. This is a major advantage as far as widows are considered, especially, those who are not economically independent. Hence, *Nafaqa* helps Muslim women to maintain themselves as well as their children, if any.

Property

Women are given absolute rights over property. If a Muslim dies, leaving behind a son and a daughter, both are entitled to inheritance. In the share allotted to the daughter, she has absolute rights. The same rule applies to a widow or a mother.

Among the pagan Arabs before Islam, inheritance rights were confined exclusively to the male relatives. The *Quran* abolished all these unjust customs and gave all the female relatives inheritance shares:

> From what is left by parents and those nearest related there is a share for men and a share for women, whether the property be small or large – a determinate share (*Quran* 4:7).

Muslim mothers, wives, daughters, and sisters had received inheritance rights thirteen hundred years before Europe recognized that these rights even existed. The division of inheritance is a vast subject with an enormous amount of details (*Quran* 4:7, 11, 12, 176). The general rule is that the female share is half the males except the cases in which the mother receives equal share to that of the father. This general rule if taken in isolation from other legislations concerning men and women may seem unfair. In order to understand the rationale behind this rule, one must take into account the fact that the financial obligations of men in Islam far exceed those of women. A bridegroom must provide his bride with a marriage gift. This gift becomes her exclusive property and remains so even if she is later divorced. The bride is under no obligation to present any gifts to her groom. Moreover, the Muslim husband is charged with the maintenance of his wife and children. The wife, on the other hand, is not obliged to help him in this regard. Her property and earnings are for her use alone except what she may voluntarily offer her husband. Besides, one has to realize that Islam vehemently advocates family life. It strongly encourages youth to get married, discourages divorce, and does not regard celibacy as a virtue. Therefore, in a truly Islamic society, family life is the norm and single life is the rare exception. That is, almost all marriage-aged women and men are married in an Islamic society. In the light of these facts, one would appreciate that Muslim men, in general, have greater financial burdens than Muslim women and thus inheritance rules are meant to offset this imbalance so that the society lives free of all gender or class wars. After a simple comparison between the financial rights and duties of Muslim women, one British Muslim woman has concluded that Islam has treated women not only fairly but generously.

When analysing the Muslim law, we find that the Muslim widows have a strong legal background but what is lacking is an awareness regarding these laws. Muslim women are still very conservative and very often they are not conscious of their rights and privileges. So in spite of the laws, they have to remain in an inferior position in society.

Christian Law

The Christian widows have also the right to remarry. Regarding succession, the relevant provisions of the Indian Succession Act, 1925, are to be followed by intestate succession among Christians. The result is that daughters are to be treated equally with sons in respect of intestate succession. Under the Travancore Christian Succession Act, 1902, a daughter was entitled to 1/4th of the value of the share of sons or Rs 5,000 whichever is less. If 'Streedhanam' was promised by the intestate even this right would not be available to the daughter. The widow was entitled only to a life interest in the property of the intestate which was terminable on death or remarriage. Under the Indian Succession Act, a widow is entitled to 1/3rd share in the property of the intestate, the remaining 2/3rd will go in favour of the lineal descendants. If there is no lineal descendant but has left persons who are kindred to him, the widow takes one half and the kindred will take the other half. If there are no kindred, the widow will take the whole (Champapilly, 1997).

One of the most important differences between the Quran and the Bible is their attitude towards female inheritance of the property of a deceased relative. The Biblical attitude has been succinctly described by Rabbi Epstein:

> The continuous and unbroken tradition since the Biblical days gives the female members of the household, wife and daughters, no right of succession to the family estate. In the more primitive scheme of succession, the female members of the family were considered part of the estate and as remote from the legal personality of an heir as the slave. Whereas by Mosaic enactment the daughters were admitted to succession in the event of no male issue remained, the wife was not recognized as heir even in such conditions.

Why were the female members of the family considered part of the family estate? Rabbi Epstein has the answer: "They are owned – before marriage, by the father; after marriage, by the husband."

The Biblical rules of inheritance are outlined in Numbers 27:1-11. A wife is given no share in her husband's estate, while he is her first heir, even before her sons. A daughter can inherit only if no male heirs exist. A mother is not an heir at all while the father is. Widows and daughters, in case male children remained, were at the mercy of the male heirs for provision. That is why widows and orphan girls were among the most destitute members of the Jewish society.

Christianity has followed suit for long time. Both the ecclesiastical and civil laws of Christendom barred daughters from sharing with their brothers, the father's patrimony. Besides, wives were deprived of any inheritance rights. These iniquitous laws survived till late in the last century.

Christian Parents can now Adopt

In a bold and definitive judgment, Justice F.I. Rebelo of the Bombay High Court held that high courts do indeed have the powers under Article 225 (in matters of protection of minors and children) to give children and minors up for adoption, even if there are no legislations for adoption in some personal laws. In fact, a child's right to be adopted, the High Court has held, flows from Article 21 of the constitution that guarantees life and liberty to every individual. And since the Christian Religion does not bar any Christian couple from adopting (the Christian Adoption and Maintenance Act, 1955, supported by the Catholic bishops and the Maharashtra Adoption Act, 1995 are pending with the legislatures) the court has held that the absence of a legislation cannot stop guardians from seeking adoption.

Sociological Significance

In *Lifting the Taboo: Women, Death and Dying*, Sally Cline observes how the stigma of being a widow derives from status typically occupied by females. About 85 per cent of wives outlive their husbands. In couple-oriented patriarchal societies, the widow is one often viewed as being unavailable, uninteresting and being either sexually uninviting or a predator. The social debasement of widows stem mainly from traditional values and beliefs.

Studies of widows have located the common themes of financial stress, feelings of aloneness, loss of friends and social isolation and problems with other family members. Children, for instance, may deny their widowed mother opportunities for substitute intimate relationships, demanding a nun-like status out of respect for their deceased father. Never again do they see the widow as a human being with humane attributes.

During the British period, the general policy of non-intervention in social and religious matters perpetuated multiple systems thereby preventing normal adjustment to socio-economic changes, which led to stagnation and hardening of differences between the various religious communities and even within the sub-sections of the communities. The nineteenth century social reformers attempted some marginal adjustments arising from humanitarian considerations and social demands. With the strengthening of National Movement and the efforts of Mahatma Gandhi, a demand grew for bringing major changes in law, for removing the legal inferiority of women and for ending the discrimination against them in matters which affected their lives and personality. Reform of Hindu Law was thus initiated even before Independence although, but because of conservative resistance, it could only be given effect to during the 1950s in a piecemeal fashion.

In such a pitiable plight, widows find that legislation provides an orientation to set things right in their life. We find that laws provide them the right to freely choose a partner again and enter into marriage. With the inheritance laws, widows can do away with the aspect of poverty which usually haunts them after the death of her husband. Moreover, adoption opportunities provided by law can make their lonely life more appealing. The laws help the widows to gain status and establish their human rights. They help in eradicating discrimination in the provision of shelter, facilitating land and property rights for women, making adoptions and also maintaining oneself after the death of the partner. Legislation helps widows to start a new social life and to become active again. It helps them to face new challenges and to take up new role, to enter new commitments, and to enjoy new experiences

Social legislation, though progressive and revolutionary in nature, does not help many Indian women, especially widows, who are bound by personal laws. In its attempt to maintain secular society and freedom of religion, the government does not question the validity of personal laws even though they are detrimental to enhancing the status of widows. The personal laws of the three communities differ in various aspects. For example, any Hindu can adopt a son or daughter by virtue of their personal law. However, in the case of a Muslim or Christian widow this is not possible because Muslim personal law does not give any recognition to adoption nor does the Christian community. What emerges after the analyses of personal laws is a diversity of laws for the different communities that is unhealthy for a democracy's advancement. There should be a single code for all. Secularism cannot be carried on by recognizing such a variety of laws on the same subject. This has specially affected the status of Indian women, for the welfare measures fall short of arousing the communal sentiments.

The disparity between the personal laws should be eradicated. There should be a uniform civil code which will help widows in all communities to face their new challenges in a more active way. Moreover, it will help the promotion and protection of the rights of women in society. In an unbiased manner the uniform civil code should be able to eliminate all forms of coercion and discrimination against widows in different communities. The women's organizations of today are demanding a uniform, non-sexist civil code, which would be helpful to all Indian women, irrespective of religion, caste or community. It should also be able to acknowledge that widows, too, play a key role in social development, and as such, their social status should be enhanced, with attention to the rights, capabilities and responsibilities.

India definitely has come a long way from the time when child marriage was common and widow remarriage was prohibited. Life was hard if a woman succeeded from escaping the funeral pyre of her deceased husband, where she was expected to be burnt alive. But the majority of widows do not have an easy access to justice and only a few have the resources to obtain legal redress. In addition, being ignorant and carrying the perceptions of 'widow's status', women, themselves, are affected by numerous traditional practices often based on superstitious taboos, religious beliefs and misinterpreted religious tenets which make even laws ineffective in supporting their personal development. A vigorous programme of legal awareness must be mounted and dispensed through formal and informal schooling, workers' education schemes, adult education programmes, mass media, voluntary social action groups and legal aid agencies. Laws relating to widows should be able to strengthen their footing in areas like health, education, employment, housing and social security. They should also be able to create an adequate environment for the full and harmonious development of widows. Can legal aid provide the strategy and the means for structural and attitudinal changes for delivery of equal justice? The answer lays not so much on the law and its procedures but on the men and women who invoke the law, interpret it, administer and adjudicate it.

The good news is that more and more women are becoming aware of the changing social milieu that torpedoes the traditional stigma concerning widowhood, and welcomes a tomorrow which treats them as responsible, credit-worthy citizens. There are many widowed women who have proven that they can start over, succeed and beat the odds. Being a widow is not the end of the world, but it definitely calls for a new beginning.

Key Terms

lex loci: This is law applicable to all the people within a territory, e.g., Shariat law.

Dharmasastras: In Sanskrit it means 'righteousness science'. It is the ancient body of jurisprudence that is still fundamentally the family law of India and is in force, subject to legislative modification in India.

Mitakshra and Dayabhaga: Two important Vedic schools which contain rules of conduct and rites inspired by Hindu sacred texts.

Vyavahara law: The law based on custom or usage in Hindu tradition.

Sapinda: Refers to the bowl of rice offered to the ancestors which symbolizes the propitiatory rites for ancestors. Sapinda means people belonging to the same pinda and performing the rites oriented to the same ancestors.

Coparcenery: It refers to joint ownership or joint heirship of property.

Quasi-severalty: Legal right of exclusive possession without a joint interest in any other person.

Vasishta: An ancient Hindu Seer.

Inter vivo: Transaction between two living persons.

Karta: It refers to the eldest male member in a joint family who looks after all the family matters including those concerned with property.

Widows: By the Hindu Women's Right to Property Act 1937, a widow became entitled to the same share of a son and to succeed along with the son. The widow of a predeceased son also became entitled to inheritance.

Intestate: The person who has made no valid will before his death.

Peculium: An absolute ownership over professional earnings and other acquisitions.

Reversioner: The heirs of the last full owner would be entitled to succeed to the estate of the limited owner on the death of the latter.

Sunni: Member of one of the two major branches of Islam, the branch that consists of the majority of that religious adherent. Sunnite Muslims consider their sect as the mainstream and traditionalist branch of Islam, as distinguished from the minority sect, the Shiites.

Shia: The Shia are the only important surviving sect in Islam. They owe their origin to the hostility between Ali (the fourth caliph and son-in-law of the prophet) and the Umayyad dynasty (661-750). Thus, Shia refers to the branch of Islam comprising sects believing in Ali and the Imams as the only rightful successors of Mohammad and in the concealment and messianic return of the last recognized Imam.

Imam Abu Hanifa: Muslim jurist and theologian whose systematization of Islamic legal doctrine was acknowledged as one of the four canonical schools of Islamic law.

Quran: The book composed of sacred writings accepted by Muslims as revelations made to Muhammad by Allah through the angel Gabriel.

Sunna: The body of Islamic custom and practice based on Muhammad's words and deeds.

Lyma: Arabic, meaning 'agreeing upon' or consensus. It is the universal infallible agreement of the Muslim community, especially of Muslim scholars on any Islamic principle at any time.

Qiyas: It is the analogical reasoning as applied to the deduction of juridical principles from the Quran and the Sunna.

Dower or Mehr: It is a gift of money or property by a man to or for his bride.

Streedhanam: It is the money, goods or estate that a woman brings to her husband in marriage.

References

Champapilly, Sebastian (1997), *Christian Law of Succession in India,* Cochin: Southern Law Publishers.

Emannuel, Todd (1985), *The Explanation of Ideology: Family Structures and Social System,* France.

Mehta, Rama (1987), *Socio-legal Status of Women in India,* New Delhi: Mittal Publications.

Nair, Krishnan M. (1998), *Family Law 1,* The Academy of Legal Publications, Thiruvananthapuram.

Nair, Krishnan M. (1999), *Family Law 2,* The Academy of Legal Publications, Thiruvananthapuram

The Indian Express, Oct 28, 1999.

Pruthi, Raj Kumar et al. (eds.) (2001), *Women in Law and Politics,* Jaipur: Mangal Deep Publications.

Todd, Emannuel (1999), The Explanation of Ideology: Family Structures & Social System.

http://expressindia.com/ie/daily/19991028/ige28059.html.

http://www.trinity.edu/~mkeral/fam-div.html.

http://islamcity.com/mosque/w_islam/inhrt.htm.

www.mahalibrary.com.

11

"A Small Family is a Happy Family"

The Politics of Population Control in India

SHEELA PRASAD

Recent debates in the history of modern medicine are critical of the hegemonic role that western medicine has played across the world and the inherent sexism that it symbolizes. Lesley Doyal argues, "... sexism is often more overt and apparent in medicine than elsewhere" (Doyal, 1979: 237). Feminist scholars over the last few decades have been increasingly addressing both these issues through their interrogation of modern medicine. Their insights have provided much of the grounding for the discourses on the social construction of medicine.

Contextualizing Women's Health

Modern medicine is foregrounded/premised on the biomedical model which assumes that the determinants of health and illness are largely biological and have little to do with the socio-economic environment. This model subscribes to the mechanistic worldview that looks at the human body as a sum of its parts similar to a machine. It is within this framework that the female body has been understood and medical practice generally structured in modern medicine. Feminist scholars have been engaged in commenting on the tensions within such an approach, particularly the bias against women.

Women's bodies have been represented as 'weaker', 'lesser', 'inferior' as they are measured against male standards and are found different. This difference gets translated as inferior and these views get expressed in the medical texts, become practices and get legitimized. It is women's role in the reproduction that has always got medical attention and most medical texts speak of the 'natural' role of women to reproduce and emphasize aspects of health related to motherhood. The reproductive anatomy of women became a special field of study – gynaecology – and the uterus and ovaries were seen as the dominant control organs for women. This gendering of the body as male/female resulted in a persistent bias of doctors towards women's reproductive health and the perpetuation of a stereotyped image of women's motherhood roles and health needs. It meant that infertility is often treated much more sympathetically than an unwanted pregnancy; the demand for an abortion by a married woman generates greater reluctance than that by an unmarried woman; many problems of women are seen as psychosomatic and not physiological; and contraception is largely seen as the responsibility of women.

Focus of this Paper

It is this engagement of women with the health care system that this paper attempts to critically review. Women's health experiences in India raise certain questions about the construction of medical knowledge and the inadequacy of the medical/health system to articulate their specific needs. It is important to critique these 'accepted' medical practices as health policies are framed around them. The population control or family planning policy in India, the focus of this paper, offers a site for critical inquiry from a feminist perspective. The history of family planning (FP) in India is discussed to tease out the major strands of tension and shifts in policy over the last few decades. The Indian health situation has parallels with that of other parts of the developing world. It is, therefore, important to locate and understand the population debates of India against the global population control discourse.

Global Politics of Population Control

Population control has a long global history – the fear of 'overpopulation' goes back to the middle ages. The present population control programmes draw their legitimacy largely from Thomas Malthus. In his famous essay "An Essay on Population" (1798), Malthus linked population growth with food production and predicted that while the former would grow in geometric progression, the latter would grow only in arithmetic progression. Malthus' anxiety, against the background of the French Revolution, provided the foundations for a strong population control movement. Since the early 20th century, fertility control debates dominated any discussion on poverty, development and environment. Population control was seen as a cure for poverty, communism and the environmental crisis.

In the 1920s, Eugenic concerns took over the Malthusian arguments with Margaret Sanger of the USA declaring, "… more children from the fit, less from the unfit – that is the chief issue of birth control" (quoted in Lupton, 2003: 150). Darwin's thesis in which favourable variations tend to be preserved and unfavourable ones destroyed was extended to people – whites and non-whites. The decrease in population of whites in the USA between 1800 and 1900 provided the Eugenists with a rationale for pushing such a biased birth control policy. This saw the emergence of population control policies that were targeted at the poor in the developed world and later at women in the developing world.

The politics of population control is well documented (Mass, 1976; Gordon, 1978; Doyal, 1979; Hartman, 1992; Prasad and Nair, 1994; Karkal, 1995). This section presents an overview of the history of population control policies and the major shifts that have occurred since 1950. The Eugenics movement saw an attempt to control fertility of some sections of women in the West. With this the beginning of population control emerged which was quite different from birth control. While safer birth control was a demand that came from the women's movement and the right of individual women to take control over their bodies, population control pushed policies that aimed at controlling the fertility of certain sections of women. The state, international funding agencies and NGOs all began to pressurize women in direct and indirect ways to limit family size. This led to the growth of a population lobby that owed allegiance to the ideas of Malthus and believed that the major problem facing the world was rapid population growth of the developing world. The USA was the most vocal advocate of this view from the 1960s, with both the US government and private organizations such as the Rockfeller Foundation, International Planned Parent Foundation (IPPF), Ford Foundation, and later Population Council, all actively involved in supporting population control campaigns in the developing world (Doyal, 1979: 280).

The revolution in China and Cuba brought the threat perception of communism into population policy. It became important to limit the population of the poor countries in order to keep the revolution away. An outcome of this kind of thinking in the USA was the steep rise in investment funds to the developing countries, particularly Latin America. Aid came with certain conditions or strings attached that saw population control policies being pushed in a big way in these countries. Since 1965, USA has contributed more to foreign population control programmes than all other countries combined. The main recipients of US funds for population control are India, Pakistan, Bangladesh, Mexico, Brazil and Indonesia (Karkal, 1993).

In the 1960s and 70s the introduction of the Green Revolution in the developing world was linked to population control programmes – the perception being that food shortages were due to exploding population growth in these countries. India's food crisis in the mid-1960s and the need for urgently importing food grains from the USA is one such example. Along with US food aid to India came funds and the urge for a commitment from the Indian government to frame strong policies to limit family size. The most recent justification for controlling population growth in the developing world is the environmental crisis – 'overpopulation' is now identified as the major cause of environmental degradation. The large numbers of poor in these countries are seen as responsible for burdening the environment and hence the slogan, 'poverty pollutes'. The contribution of resource intensive development models, the environmental costs of large projects, the over consumption lifestyles that these models have encouraged are often ignored and only the poor, who are usually the victims of a degraded environment, blamed. In environmental terms, over consumption in the west is equally, if not more, polluting than the large numbers of poor in the developing world. But while limiting fertility in the latter is a major global concern, reducing consumption levels in the west is never addressed seriously. One can argue that if families in the developing world should have only one or two children, then families in the developing world should also have only one car, one air-conditioner, one refrigerator, no guns, etc., to reduce per capita waste generation. As Betsy Hartman argues, "... left out of the picture are the real culprits: capitalist exploitation of both people and nature, obscene income and consumption disparities, inappropriate technologies and hyper militarization" (Hartman, 2004). Today, added to this list is the spread of AIDS which is also linked to rapid population growth, especially in the context of the African counties.

The International Conference on Population and Development (ICPD) at Cairo in 1994 attempted to shift this focus from coercive population control to a more gender sensitive reproductive health policy. This platform provided a space for women's groups both from the developed and developing world who voiced their protests and concerns against demographic targeting of poor women. The ICPD agenda, to which about 179 countries are signatories, talks of empowering women in education, health and economic opportunities along with a focus on provision of reproductive health services. The agenda on reproductive health emerged from the discourse on reproductive rights that came from feminist movements in the west

Reproductive Rights and Reproductive Health

The discussion on Reproductive Rights (RR) emerged from the women's movement engaged with control over the body and sexuality. Reproductive rights recognize the basic right of all the couples and individuals to decide freely and responsibly the number, spacing and timing of their children, the right to have information and make decisions, and the right to attain the highest standard of sexual and reproductive health. The Reproductive Rights discourses grew out of the experiences and needs of western women and were received with mixed feelings. The Vatican, some Islamic countries and the Protestant fundamentalists while saw these rights as undermining the family and the community, the radical feminists argued that these rights may represent population control indirectly for poor women. A larger constituency of global funding agencies, international NGOs, governments and many women's groups saw reproductive rights as necessary for empowering women (Rao, 2004:1). It was the women's groups who were responsible for placing the Reproductive Rights agenda centre stage at the ICPD at Cairo in 1994.

It is from the reproductive rights debate at Cairo that the concept of reproductive health emerged. Reproductive rights see women as subjects and not objects of population policies and hence the shift to the Reproductive and Child Health (RCH) policy that got formalized at Cairo with World Bank support. Reproductive health is defined as a state of complete physical, mental and social well being and not merely the absence of disease or infirmity, in all matters relating to the reproductive system and to its functions and processes (Lingam, 1998). This definition of reproductive health broadens the scope of meaning to include not just physiological factors but social contexts and includes safe motherhood, contraceptive choice, child survival, control of STDs and AIDS, and awareness building. Today the term reproductive health is found as the central agenda in all policies aimed at women's health and population control. The implication of the Cairo revolution while progressive had different meanings for women in the west and in India, especially, poor women, which will be discussed in a later section.

To summarize some major points that emerge from the discussion on global politics of population control are presented below:

- While there are strong pressures for imposing anti-natal policies on poor women in the West and the developing world, white women in the West are encouraged to have more children through pro-natal policies of the State.
- The neo-Malthusian mindset is much more powerful in the USA than in Europe as evident from funding programmes and official policy agendas. Very little money flows from Europe for population control programmes in the developing world.
- This obsessive engagement with a neo-Malthusian ideology makes it easier for the US to 'blame victims' and drag its feet on joining any global protocol on environment where it would be forced to bring in some harsh reforms for its own citizens.
- Poor women in the developing world continue to be soft targets for the testing of new contraceptives, including long acting hormonal contraceptives that have proven side effects on women, especially those already in poor health.
- While it is generally recognized that the health service delivery is poor in the developing world, especially in rural areas, the contraceptives that are pushed on poor women demand high levels of skill, are provider dependent and require higher levels of technological support from the health care system and are more expensive.

- Fertility rates or demographic transition happened in the West with better health care, nutrition and public health and without any population policy.
- Reproductive rights and reproductive health have very different meanings for women across varied socio-economic contexts.

Reproductive Health in the Indian Context

India was among the 179 signatories to the Cairo resolution which marked a shift in the way population, development and reproductive health were conceptualized. It meant a break from demographically driven population policies in India and many parts of the developing world, it brought in questions of gender relations and it broadened the scope of the policies by drawing attention to developmental factors.

The RCH programme in India was launched in post-Cairo conference period in 1997. It was preceded by the Maternal and Child Health programme of the 1970s and the Child Survival and Safe Motherhood programme of 1992 (Ramasubban and Jejeebhoy, 2000). The RCH programme attempted a reorientation of the Family Planning programme by encouraging smaller families through helping clients meet their own health and family planning goals. The aim was to move away from the earlier target incentive approach, focus on decentralized participating planning and provide quality services. At a more conceptual level, the RCH programme claimed to be gender sensitive and talked the language of the women's movement in terms of endorsing 'choice', 'control', 'empowerment', 'rights' and 'decision-making'. The RCH policy drawn on the principles of ICPD continues to be located in the framework of population control, which dilutes some of the radical feminist rhetoric that RCH has co-opted from the women's movement.

A recent study (Kumar, 2002) argues that in the RCH programme the interventions by the state are bounded by its understanding of women's roles within society and development. The author concludes that in the RCH women are constructed largely as mothers; the role of women in supporting development efforts is recognized; the policy interprets gender quality in terms of increasing male responsibility in the RCH programme; and the policy promotes a conception of gender that is abstracted from embodied woman and generalized as an individual who is the member of a community. While the RCH has the potential to improve women's access to better reproductive health care, in terms of empowering women to question and change gender relations it may not achieve much in its present format.

At the level of interventions, the RCH has initiated the following policy measures. The programme takes a life cycle approach to women's health providing services from childhood to adulthood. This includes addressing the health of the girl child from birth to old age with an adolescent awareness programme for young girls also envisaged. The latter focuses on issues related to sexuality, menstrual hygiene, contraception, safe sex, pregnancies and infections. The RCH services are limited to not just family planning and maternal health but extend to treatment of reproductive tract infections, STDs and AIDS. The programme envisages greater decentralization with more participation between the Auxiallary Nurse Midwives (ANM), women and the panchayats. Male involvement in family planning is encouraged through awareness and counselling. To achieve these objectives, the RCH policy has proposed that select Primary Health Centres (PHC) work for 24 hours, while others would be better equipped to handle deliveries, abortions and contraceptive services. The appointment of a gynaecologist in every PHC is under consideration, while posting a lady doctor in most PHCs is now being implemented. The RCH sees a close partnership between the public and private sector – private gynaecologists and anaesthetists can be called upon to work for the PHC on a payment basis. As a long term policy this private/public initiative may have adverse implications for public health care.

The reproductive health agenda has broadened the services available to women of all age groups and diffused the strident population control approach. It attempts to empower women through awareness generation and addresses the reproductive health needs of women and girls. While the RCH is certainly an improvement over the population control approach, yet in the Indian context, it is still seen as voicing population control concerns and pushing for limiting women's fertility as its main agenda. Since the ICPD in 1994, several states have drafted their own population policies (Andhra Pradesh, Maharashtra, Rajasthan, Madhya Pradesh) that see fertility reduction as a primary objective. This is in contrast to the earlier policy where States followed a common national population policy. Further, in these and other States, incentives and disincentives for achieving family planning targets are also encouraged, which goes against the spirit of the ICPD. While the RCH was conceptualized as empowering women, in practice, it still clings to the population control mindset and has not been able to disassociate itself from it. The following section will discuss some evidences of this with examples from India.

Implications of the RCH Policy – Experiences from India

A reading of women's health indicators across the States in India would be useful in providing insights into gender based disparities in India. Further, an analysis of women's health status brings out the excessive focus on family planning at the cost of other health concerns. Table 11.1 presents various demographic and health indicators for the various states of India. A glance at the Table 11.1 clearly brings out the interstate variations in health status across the country. At a macro level, there is a marked north-south divide with the southern states and Maharashtra reporting a better profile on most indicators than north, east and north-east India. Within the south, one finds that A.P. presents the worst profile on health variables compared to the other southern states. The Couple Protection Rate (CPR) is highest in Punjab, Karnataka, AP and Gujarat while it is lowest in the north-east. This indicator reflects the strong family planning approach advocated in the former states as part of RCH policy.

Masculinization of the Sex Ratio

Most of India has an adverse sex ratio with the country average being 933 women per 1,000 men in 2001 (Table 11.1). The only major State which has more women than men is Kerala with 1,058 women. It is interesting to note that some of India's richest states have the worst sex ratio in 2001 – Haryana 861, Punjab 874, Gujarat 921 and Maharashtra 922. The four southern states have a better sex ratio than the rest of India. This adverse sex ratio which is characteristic of South Asia indicates the low social and health status of women in this region. The strong son/male child preference in India works against the girl child and the female foetus. The advancement of scientific technologies has meant availability of the amniocentesis test or the test to determine abnormalities in the foetus, but this test today, in many parts of north and west India is being used to

Table 11.1

India – Demographic and Health Profile, 2001

S. No.	Stateor Union Territory	Census of population (in 000s) 2001	Annual Exponential Growth Rate (%) 1991-2001	Literacy Rate % Female, 7 years & above in 2001	Sex Ratio - females per 1000 males - 2001	IMR (Infant Mortality Rate)2001[1]	TFR[2] 1999	Mean age at effective marriage (females) 1999	CPR[3] (in %) 31st March 2000 (Prov.) By All Means
	INDIA	1,027,015	1.93	54.28	933	66	3.2	19.6	46.2
I.	**Major States**								
1	Andhra Pradesh	75,728	1.30	51.17	978	66	2.4	18.1	52.8
2	Assam	26,638	1.73	56.03	932	73	3.2	20.4	15.2
3	Bihar	85,879	2.50	33.57	921	62	4.5	18.9	21.2
4	Chattisgarh	20,796	1.66	52.40	990	76			
5	Gujarat	50,597	2.03	58.60	921	60	3.0	20.1	52.8
6	Haryana	21,083	2.47	56.31	861	65	3.2	19.3	49.4
7	Jharkhand	26,909	2.09	39.38	941	62			
8	Karnataka	52,734	1.59	57.45	964	58	2.5	19.7	56.3
9	Kerala	31,839	0.90	87.86	1058	11	1.8	22.1	39.6
10	Madhya Pradesh	60,385	2.18	50.28	920	86	3.9	18.8	45.9
11	Maharashtra	96,752	2.04	67.51	922	45	2.5	19.3	49.3
12	Orissa	36,707	1.48	50.97	972	90	2.7	19.8	37.6

Contd...

Contd...

13	Punjab	24,289	1.80	63.55	874	51	2.5	21.0	65.5
14	Rajasthan	56,473	2.49	44.34	922	79	4.2	19.3	36.1
15	Tamil Nadu	62,111	1.06	64.55	986	49	2.0	21.1	50.4
16	Uttar Pradesh	1,66,053	2.30	42.98	898	82	4.7	20.1	38.0
17	West Bengal	80,221	1.64	60.22	934	51	2.4	19.6	32.2
II	**Smaller States**								
1	Arunachal Pradesh	1,091	2.33	44.24	901	39	2.8	NA	14.0
2	Delhi	13,783	3.81	75.00	821	29	1.6	NA	27.0
3	Goa	1,344	1.39	75.51	960	19	1.0	NA	23.9
4	Himachal Pr	6,077	1.62	68.08	970	54	2.4	20.8	46.9
5	J & K	10,070	2.55	41.82	900	48	NA	NA	14.4
6	Manipur	2,389	2.63	59.70	978	20	2.4	NA	17.8
7	Meghalaya	2,306	2.62	60.41	975	56	4.0	NA	4.7
	Mizoram	891	2.56	86.13	938	19	NA	NA	34.3
9	Nagaland	1,989	4.97	61.92	909	NA	1.5	NA	8.2
10	Sikkim	540	2.85	61.46	875	42	2.5	NA	21.5
11	Tripura	3,191	1.46	65.41	950	39	3.9	NA	23.4
12	Uttaranchal	8,480	1.76	60.26	964	48			
III	**Union Territories**								
1	A&N Islands	356	2.39	75.29	846	18	1.9	NA	38.4

Contd...

Contd...

2	Chandigarh	901	3.39	76.65	773	24	2.1	NA	33.5
3	D&N Haveli	220	4.65	42.99	811	58	3.5	NA	27.5
4	Daman & Diu	158	4.42	70.37	709	40	2.5	NA	29.3
5	Lakshadweep	61	1.59	81.56	947	33	2.8	NA	7.2
6	Pondicherry	974	1.87	74.13	1001	22	1.8	NA	58.4

Source: Dept. of Family Welfare (2001), Family Welfare Programme in India, Govt. of India, p. 260.

Note: 1. Infant mortality rates for smaller states and Union Territories are for the period 1999-2001.
2. Total Fertility Rates (TFR) for smaller States and UTs are three year moving average, 1996-98.
3. Couple Protection Rate (CPR) is provisional and like TFR and Mean age at effective marriage, unavailable for states created in 2001.

determine the sex of the foetus. A growing trend now observed in both urban and rural India is the use of this test find out the sex of the foetus and then to be pressured to have an abortion if the foetus is female.

This becomes evident if we compare 0-5 years sex ratios or child sex ratios (CSR) across states and over time (Census of India 2001). The number of girls below 5 years as compared to boys in the same age group has been declining since 1961. Between 1991 and 2001 the CSR in urban India has declined from 935 to 903 and in rural India from 948 to 934. Most states report a decline in CSR between 1991 and 2001 except Sikkim, Tripura, Kerala and Mizoram. The most worrying decline is found in Punjab (793), Haryana (820), Gujarat (879) and H.P. (897).

While this masculinisation of the sex ratio is happening over the last few decades, it has sharpened in the last decade with the help from developments in modern technology. Female infanticide and the now more common, female foeticide, is taking place in higher numbers in the prosperous regions, urban areas and among educated couples particularly in north and west India. Unethical medical practices by doctors in urban centres and now in rural areas, has allowed female foeticide to take on alarming proportions. A very strong son preference and the financial burden of dowry in getting girl children married, are two major factors that explain this trend. Added to this, the population control programme has succeeded in pushing the small family size as the ideal among the richer and urban sections of society. As a result, if couples are limiting family size to two children they would like to ensure that at least one of them is male. Societal expectations of a son and the pressures of the state to have only two children force pregnant women to negotiate a thin balance that finally rejects the female foetus.

Data on CSR suggests a link between affluence, smaller family size, gender bias, unethical medical services and female foeticide. The aggressive promotion of population control programmes, and now RCH, has seen a reduction in family size, but this has come at the cost of the girl child. Among the poor, the practice of female foeticide though present is low. Demographic transition that is accompanied by the lowering of fertility rates has in the case of India come at a price. In Indian society, motherhood especially as the mother of a son, gives women a higher status within the family.

Unless the RCH approach moves beyond fertility control to address questions of gender equality, the future years may witness a further masculinisation of the sex ratio in India.

Fertility Decline in Andhra Pradesh: A Model to Follow?

That the obsessive engagement with fertility control in the RCH continues in spite of its progressive language can be observed by a review of the population growth rate decline in A.P. In 2001, AP's Total Fertility Rate (TFR) was 2.39 and the population growth fell from 2.14 in 1981-91 to 1.36 in 1991-2001. This decline in decadal population growth in 2001 was the sharpest among all the States of India (Figure 11.1). The target of replacement level fertility is calculated as a TFR of 2.1 and it is estimated that urban A.P. reached this figure in 1996. The sharp fall in TFR in A.P. between 1991-2001 is largely attributed to its successful family welfare programme of which RCH is an integral part. In demographic and more specifically fertility control discussions in India, the decline in population growth in A.P. is held up as a success story. In fact, in the corridors

Figure 11.1

States Recording Decline in Population Growth Rates Between 1981-91 and 1991-2001

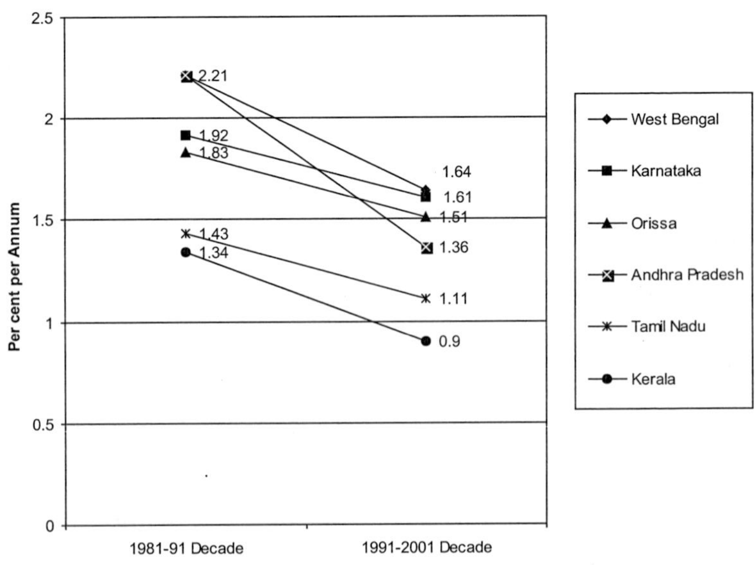

of the Ministry of Health and Family Welfare at New Delhi, there are debates on how to use the A.P. model to bring down fertility rate in the northern states (Bihar, Madhya Pradesh, Rajasthan, Uttar Pradesh) which are seen as the "problem states of high fertility". Does A.P. provide the right model for these other states to emulate? Has A.P. achieved demographic transition in the way that the concept is usually understood?

An analysis of the demographic dynamics of A.P. provides some disturbing insights. While A.P.'s fertility rate is approaching replacement level, this is not accompanied by much improvement on other demographic and social development indicators. The mean age at marriage for females in A.P. is 15.1 much below the legal age at marriage for girls of 18 years – the average for India is 16.4. A.P. has the lowest age at marriage for girls among the four southern states and this trend has not changed during the last decade. Low age at marriage means early start of child bearing and the median age of women at first birth in A.P. is 18.1 years. About one fourth of women in the age group 15-19 years are either mothers or pregnant with their first child. This age at first pregnancy is also lowest in A.P. from among the southern states. A large proportion of these young women are pregnant within the first year of marriage (Balasubramanian, 2005).

The use of temporary methods of contraception is very negligible – less than 1 per cent. The general pattern observed is that most women have the desired number of children in the first few years of marriage and then opt for a permanent method of contraception, namely sterilization or tubectomy (female sterilization). In A.P. female sterilization accounts for 60.2 per cent of the total contraceptive methods used, male sterilization is 2.2 per cent, spacing method 0.8 per cent, while 36.8 per cent women are not using any method (Figure 11.2). If one compares the pattern of contraceptive use by age of women it is noted that in the 15-19 age group only 6.5 per cent of women use any contraceptive, but by age group 25-29 about 70 per cent of married women report use of contraception, majority of them opting for a permanent method of sterilization (Figure 11.3). The contraceptive use pattern by parity suggests that only 13.6 per cent women in A.P. use a contraceptive after the first parity, while about 82 per cent use contraception after their second parity (Balasubramanian, 2005). The median age at sterilization of married women in A.P. at 24.5 years is the lowest in the country.

Figure 11.2
What contraceptive methods are married women in Andhra Pradesh currently using?

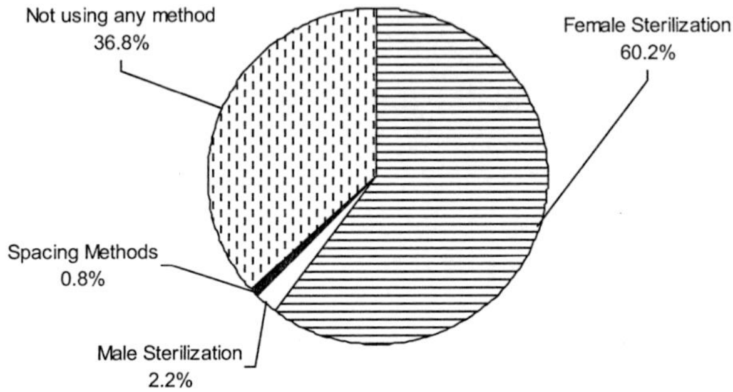

Source: Eligible Couples Survey

Figure 11.3
Contraceptive Use by Age

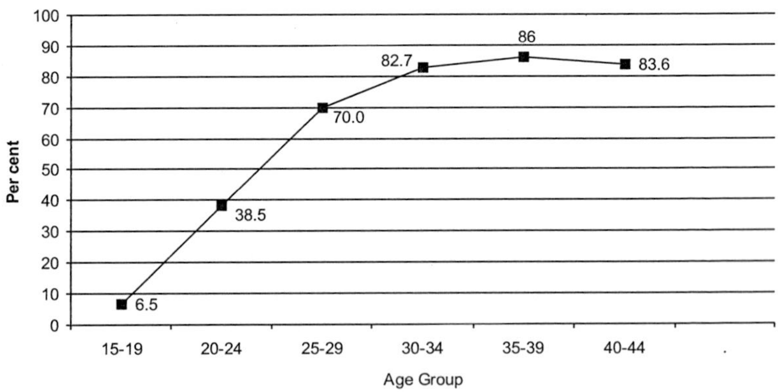

Source: 2003 Survey

This suggests that the age at stopping child birth or the reproductive span of women in A.P. is short at around 9.8 years. This figure is one of the lowest reproductive spans in the country and about 60 per cent of the births in A.P. are concentrated among women less than 25 years of age. The implications of this shortened reproductive span on women's health have not been addressed by RCH. The aggressive RCH programme in A.P. has made sterilization possible for a large numbers of women, both urban and rural, but has not seriously thought through what the compression of reproductive cycle can do to women, both physiologically and psychologically. There are reports that menopause starts early for women with this kind of reproductive history. Linked to this is the growing rate of hysterectomies reported from some parts of A.P.

With a well performing RCH in place, it would be expected that A.P. would have higher number of deliveries in institutions. But this is not so, as A.P. has only about 40 per cent of its deliveries in institutions. This compares very poorly with the other southern states where far more institutional deliveries take place. It is surprising that while tubectomies done in A.P. are the highest among the southern states, the same health facilities are not mobilized for institutional deliveries. The couple protection rate in A.P. is also high (52.8%) compared to Kerala and Tamil Nadu. The maternal mortality rate and infant mortality rate are again high in A.P. compared to the southern states (Figure 11.4). The point I am

Figure 11.4

Infant Mortality Rate for Selected States of India, 2002

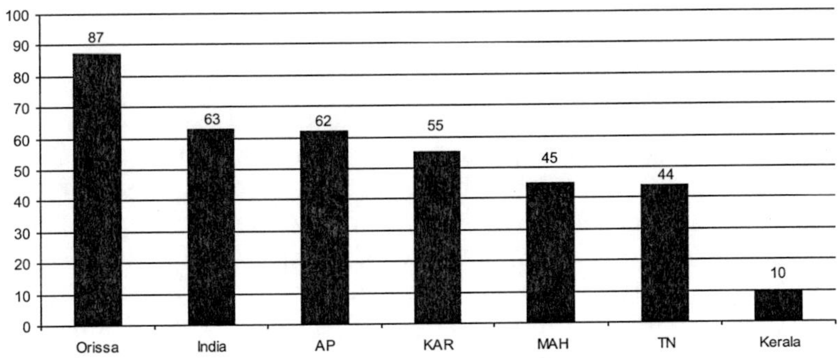

Source: SRS

attempting to make is that in A.P. it appears as if the health services are geared and summoned to deliver largely for population control services. This Malthusian bias in health is found even in the RCH policy where we notice that the emphasis is again on fertility control.

The decline in fertility is also not associated with a rise in female literacy as A.P.'s literacy rate at 51.17 per cent is below the national average of 54.28 per cent and much lower than that of the other southern states. The Human Development Index for A.P. for 1981 and 2001 shows that the rank of the state has slipped between this period and is below the national average. The state was ranked 9th in 1981 and in 2001 its rank was 10th (Balasubramanian, 2005). This demographic mapping forces us to locate discussion on the fertility decline of A.P. against the backdrop of an aggressive population control policy of the State. For the State controlling population was accorded high priority, while other social variables were seen as marginal. (See Table 11.2)

Table 11.2

Socio-Economic Indicators

Indicator	*Andhra Pradesh*	*India*
Per cent literate (age 71)	61	65
Per cent female literate (age 71)	50	54
Median age at marriage for females	15.1	16.4
Per cent of women age 20-24 married by age 18	56	50
Infant mortality rate	62	63
Per cent urban	27	28
Human Development Index	0.416	0.472

Source: Balasubramanian, K. (2005)

Recent reports from A.P. talk about incentives, awards, disincentives, targets, and camps for family planning even after 1996 and the post Cairo phase of RCH. Districts that achieved sterilization targets were awarded ranks and awards while poorly performing districts were pulled up. This kind of an approach resulted in the mobilization of the entire Government health machinery towards achieving family planning goals at the cost of neglecting other health needs. Under the guise of promoting RCH and indulging in the double speak language of empowerment of women, A.P. state aggressively pushed a target driven policy to bring down its fertility rate and now claims to have achieved demographic transition. A.P. is now held up as a model state in the country that has achieved rapid fertility decline.

It is interesting to map the path of how the 'model' states of fertility decline have changed over the last few decades in the country. Till 1980s Kerala was India's 'model' state with a social development profile comparable to many western countries in both education and health indicators. The Kerala model of social development was much discussed and written about and possibilities to replicate this model elsewhere were debated. It needs to be mentioned here that the Kerala model had a socio-political history that was based on a more equitable pattern of gender relations than the rest of India. In a haste to bring down fertility this model was not an ideal one as it involved improving more structural indicators, besides education and health. In 1980s, the State of Tamil Nadu attempted to emulate the Kerala model of demographic transition, but largely focused on improving maternal and child health. By the 1991 Census, Tamil Nadu had been able to sharply bring down its population growth rate while its performance on female literacy, infant mortality and other health indicators were not as well matched. In the 1990s the 'model state' to emulate for reducing population growth rate became Tamil Nadu as it had achieved a sharp decline in fertility in just a decade. For a liberalizing A.P. in the 1990s in a hurry to reduce fertility, the model state to follow was not Kerala, but Tamil Nadu. The Kerala model made many demands from the state that necessitated long term structural changes in the system.

The success story of Tamil Nadu was an easier option to explore for A.P. that had put fertility control as a top priority in its Vision 2020 document. In 2001, the census results revealed that A.P. had reported the sharpest decline in fertility rate between 1991 and 2001. A new 'model' was in place for the Malthusian lobby. Since then it is the achievement of A.P. that is discussed and sought to be replicated in the "high birth rate" problem states of North and Central India. It is important to recall that fertility decline in Tamil Nadu was accompanied by improvements in other social indicators, though not as much as it should have been. In the case of A.P. we observe that the state's claims about its demographic transition are based on just the decline in population growth rate, while other demographic variables remain unchanged. Such a model of success for replication is disturbing as it legitimizes pushing a very aggressive population control policy to achieve decline in fertility rates. The A.P. model of fertility decline has come about in spite of a continuing very low age at marriage, low female literacy, high infant mortality, high morbidity of women and low institutional deliveries. For the Indian Government the A.P. model is an easier option to push (as compared to Kerala and Tamil Nadu) in the other high fertility states, as these are the states with lowest social development indicators and hence more difficult to address. A.P. has proved to these other states that fertility decline can be possible without much effort to improve/change other social parameters. In a world with a Malthusian dominated mindset the A.P. model is seen as a success story.

Concluding Comments

That a politics of fertility control exists in India in general, and A.P. in particular, is obvious from this discussion paper. In the context of India, the population control policies have various dimensions/ dichotomies that need to be explored and understood: north-south; rural-urban; men-women; rich-poor; Muslim-Hindu; and temporary-permanent contraception. The southern states are ahead in their demographic transition but each of these four states has had a very different approach and history towards achieving fertility decline. The northern states are seen as the demographic problem states and today it is here where most of India's Malthusian efforts and funds are focused. It is ironical that rural India which is largely illiterate bears the brunt of permanent sterilization – in 1980-81 of the total sterilizations 68.3 per cent were in rural areas, in 1990-91 this figure was 68 per cent, while in 2000-01 it rose to 72.3 per cent. In the case of IUD insertions the share of rural India is much higher: in 1990-91 it was 79.4 per cent and it increased to 81.3 per cent in 1999-00 (FWP in India Yearbook 2001: 179-180). It does appear surprising that while health facilities are poorer and more difficult to access in rural areas, the contraceptives methods that require higher levels of health services and skills, are the contraceptive choices that are offered to rural women and men.

Women shoulder most of the burden of fertility reduction as the percentage of female sterilization or tubectomies to total sterilization has risen from 78.6 per cent in 1980-81 to 97.1 per cent in 2000-01. To this figure if we add the use of temporary contraceptive methods like IUDs, abortion and oral pills, the share of women in adopting contraception further increases. Women as targets for contraception often mean that poor and rural women, who are already in poor health, suffer the side effects of these contraceptives and have very limited access to basic health care in times of need. Male responsibility in contraception is low and is a more difficult issue for the states to address. It is much easier for the states to coerce women into contraception for two reasons: first, for the state, women are a more passive constituency, and second, the contraceptive methods for women are more long acting and can be controlled as they are provider dependent. The gender dimension also includes within it a class dimension. Poor women and men are the soft targets of the state population control policies as they use government health care facilities more than others. It is easier for the state to use arm twisting tactics on the poor to get them to use contraception. Incentives for those who get sterilized in the form of cash or kind or easier access to a Government scheme are some of the measures used to get the poor to agree to use contraception.

The predominance of the Malthusian perspective has had another fallout on the fragile social fabric of India. Demographic rates, particularly those related to fertility, are given much more importance and coverage than other socio-economic variables. The comparison of fertility rates across religions provides a 'fertile ground' for breeding misconceptions about the 'other'. Many Indians would like to believe that there is a Hindu rate of population growth and a Muslim one, with the latter being much higher than the former. In a multi-religious society like India where religious identity linked perceptions can be used to build public opinion, the obsessive engagement with fertility control keeps fertility rates as a burning issue in mainstream debates. This helps to fuel resentment against the Muslims who are seen as having a large number of children and 'multiplying rapidly' as compared to the Hindus and other religious groups whose growth rates are falling. The close link between religion and fertility behaviour among Muslims is a matter of national debate due to the Malthusian fear of high population growth. The 2001 Census of India report on religion when released in September 2004 generated intense controversy with academics, media and the Government all pitching in with analysis, clarifications and accusations. This paper, while not going into the details of this analysis, would like to argue that much of this finger pointing at the Muslims is due to the fact that fertility control is seen to be such a desirable national objective that those groups whose fertility rates do not decrease as desired or targeted are seen as being against national interest and looked upon with suspicion.

The strong control that the Malthusian view has on the Indian state can be gauged from the fact that while the earlier Government of the right wing Bharatiya Janata Party (B.J.P.) had its own reasons for its aggressive population policy (that saw the Muslims as not practicing contraception), the new Congress Government too subscribes to a similar opinion. There are reports (*The Hindu* 26.09.2004) that the present ruling Government has plans for a targeted population control programme in 150 high fertility districts across the country. These 150 districts have been identified out of a total of 209 districts that are labelled as high fertility districts. Such a policy, while claiming not to be coercive, goes against the spirit of the ICPD. The new Government is also attempting to push a two-child norm for Government functionaries, a bill that was first adopted by the state of Haryana and is under consideration in Maharashtra, Himachal Pradesh, A.P. and Madhya Pradesh. The consequences of this kind of legislation will be an increase in sex selection tests and female foeticide. Population control policy makes strange bedfellows – political parties which disagree on most other issues, agree on this. Population growth is so strongly imprinted in popular consciousness that it cuts across political affiliations and parties.

This review interrogates the politics of population control policies at both the global and national levels. The popular Government slogan that "a small family is a happy family" that has seen attempts to push this as a universal norm cutting across class, caste, religion is extremely problematic. Women, especially poor women, who are at the receiving end of such policies, are subject to new kinds of oppression by the State as a result. While Indian women have not just been passive receivers and have negotiated this oppressive system in some ways, it has sometimes come at the cost of their health. The RCH approach has certainly broadened better health possibilities for women but it too is still structured within the framework of fertility control. This primacy that is given to reduction in fertility in the RCH limits its empowering potential and burdens women with the guilt of 'overpopulation'. Unless there is a paradigm shift in thinking, from perceiving population control as the solution to all the problems of India, to viewing improvements in various other socio-economic variables as necessary, women in India and other parts of the developing world will continue to be the 'targets' of the 'war on population'.

References

Balasubramanian, K. (2005), Demographic Dynamics in A.P., Paper Presented in Expert Group Meeting on "Determinants and Consequences of Demographic Transition in AP", Academy for Nursing Studies, Hyderabad. April 16th.

Doyal, L. (1979), *The Political Economy of Health,* London: Pluto Press.

Gordon, L. (1997), *Woman's Body, Woman's Right: Birth Control in America,* New York: Penguin Books.

Hartman, B. (1992), Population Control and the New World Order, Paper Presented at UNICED, Rio de Janeiro, June 6th.

— (1999), Cross-Dressing Malthus, www.zmag.org, Sept. 23rd.

Karkal, M. (1993) Population Control: International Politics, Paper Presented at Workshop on "Population Control Policies and Women in the Third World", Hyderabad, January 28th-29th.

— (ed.) (1995), Our Lives and Our Health, The Coordination Unit, World Conference on Women, New Delhi.

Kumar, R. (2002), Gender in RCH Policy, *Economic and Political Weekly,* August 10, 3369-3377.

Lingam, L. (ed.) (1998), *Understanding Women's Health Issues,* New Delhi: Kali for Women.

Lupton, D. (2003), *Medicine as Culture,* New Delhi: Sage.

Mass, B. (1976), *Population Target: The Political Economy of Population in Latin America,* Ontario: Charters.

Prasad, S. and Nair, S. (1994), Conflicts over Populations: A Gender Perspective, In R. Melkote (ed.), *Indian Ocean: Issues for Peace,* 145-163, New Delhi: Manohar.

Ramasubban, R. and Jejeebhoy, S.J. (eds.) (2000), *Women's Reproductive Health in India,* Jaipur: Rawat Publications.

Rao, M. (ed.) (2004), *The Unheard Scream: Reproductive Health and Women's Lives in India,* Zubaan: New Delhi.

Part III

Empowerment of the Marginalized

In this part we move to the second most common theme for studies by social scientists studying women in India – their empowerment. We find a variety of methodologies as well as a vast range of subjects studied. The researchers come from three continents, too.

No consideration of empowerment would fail to mention the Adivasis and Subalterns. First Carrin enlightens us with an exploration of the Santal women. This case study of the largest tribal group in India considers legends and cultural sanctions toward women as witches, a means of control not unlike that of Salem in 17th century America. However, the Santal women make use of the fear of witches and organize parallel councils to secure some status. Through many examples Carrin challenges a strictly subordinate or powerless interpretation of the Santal women. Especially potent are her descriptions of their involvement in social movements since the 19th century.

In the next selection, Suguna and Rani provide an overview of the strategies and initiatives of self-help groups (SHGs), a common vehicle for women's empowerment. Their thorough review of past development efforts and the emergence of the SHG movement sets the stage for a brief analysis of those in Andhra Pradesh, a southern state which is home to almost half the SHGs in India. The brief descriptive survey shows how many small scale groups operate and how much these vehicles succeed for the poor women who predominate as members of most of the groups. This is the kind of story that needs wider sharing. Would that their sample was larger or replicated in other parts of India to demonstrate the status of these efforts elsewhere. It was good to see the local study of half the SHGs, five in all, and random sample of 50 women from them to assess the utilization of this vehicle of empowerment. More discussion of translation issues working with such populations would help other researchers, too.

Shajy and Isac employ demographic survey data to compare the State of Kerala, known for better development indicators, with India as a whole regarding some measures of women's independence. While it would be better to compare Kerala with the rest of India excluding Kerala, they proceed in contrasting these two populations on general indicators of development. Their significant results from this comparison are all the more revealing in the contrasts found. They examine the extent of women's freedom in relation to many factors – demographic divisions of place of residence, ethnicity, age, marital duration, children ever born and household size; cultural distinctions of religion and exposure to media; and social differences of education (both spouses) and standard of living. After reviewing the literature regarding women's empowerment, they detail how these factors affect women's ability to operate without permission to visit relatives and friends, go to the market or set aside funds for personal spending. Through both bivariate associations and multivariate logit regressions they document the significance of all these factors for women in India as a whole, and for some factors still related to restrictions on women in Kerala. In a final step they complete the contrast with a set of composite risk groups by place of residence, exposure to media and levels of literacy for both spouses while controlling for the impact of age, caste, religion, number of children ever born, household members, and standard of living. This reveals striking contrasts for women in India, but fewer for Kerala women whose general literacy and exposure are far greater. It is an interesting example of secondary data analysis which succeeds in revealing some of the complexity of women's position and the elements which make for greater independence in their living.

In a final entry of this part Mitra and Van Delinder reveal an interesting twist in their study of how elite women discover their own empowerment through volunteer work with oppressed women in Kolkata. This qualitative study of eleven upper class women volunteering in the subordinate (non-political) NGOs of that north-eastern city provides substantial content for the understanding volunteerism in India and in relation to that of western cultures. These women vary in age and family status and found mixed support for their work. Their commentary on 'feminism' echoes much of the discourse of contemporary writers – some embracing the concept with their own qualifications, others dismissing it as in outright contradiction to the centrality of family life for these women and most of Indian society. Through in-depth interviews the researchers have managed to sort out the development of these work careers for these women personally and in the wider context of their families' initiation or growing support through appreciation of the public recognition of their contributions through involvement in the NGOs. Many identify their work as a natural extension of their care giving roles within the family. All perceive the growing sense of accomplishment and enjoyment of this form of service, though not all reveal their involvement readily to others. Mitra and Van Delinder present us with an excellent example of the kind of exploratory research approach to an area about which much has been discovered in developed countries but little is known in India. May their example and findings inspire the next round of researchers to look at volunteerism as work in other areas of India and within other groups of women.

12

Women, Adivasis, Subalterns

Perspectives on the Empowerment of Santal Women

MARINE CARRIN

In 1942 William Archer was appointed Deputy Commissioner of the Santal Parganas where he continued until 1946 as special officer to record and codify Santal Law. This duty brought him in close contact with the Santals, India's largest tribe[1], who represented for him an image of innocence. Archer loved Santal poetry, which he translated, and enjoyed their hedonistic way of life which he portrayed in his book, *The Hill of Flutes* ... He talks about the standards of charm for women: a girl should be "solid and supple, with small hips and hardly any waist. She may be neither too tall nor too short, neither over large nor too slim. The line of her back should dip at the waist and then swell out in firm magnificent curve. Her buttocks *deke* – should be *samtao* – round, compact and smooth" (1974: 109). Despite this effort to capture the erotic beauty of Santal women, Archer certainly understood the feminine sensitivity expressed in forest songs where a young girl protests that she is still too young for love – until a boy "fills up her mind". Like Elwin (Guha, 1999), Archer idealized tribal societies which they both saw as free from the inhibitions of 'civilized' society. For them, the anthropological quest became like a second birth, a return to nature. When Archer worked in Santal Parganas, some patrilineal norms were becoming contested. He noticed a growing trend where childless widows inherited their late husband's land until they remarried. Besides, some widows managed to transfer their rights to their daughters, sidelining the rights of male agnates (Singh, 1984: IV)[2]. Daughters and widows were increasingly asserting their rights to property. Inspired by the ideas of his friend Elwin, Archer suggested setting up tribal courts as he found the 'modern' law courts unsuitable for tribals. Archer sympathized with women asserting their rights, as he realized that Santal men consider women as property. But, "beyond certain limits", a Santal woman is hardly a property at all. As between the sexes labour is divided but this arrangement is based not on inferiority but on convenience and propriety. For certain acts, men are more fitted than women while in others performance by women would suggest a sexual deviation. Women cannot plough, thatch a roof or use a leveller. All these actions are recognizable diagrams of the male sexual act (Archer 1974: 129).

When I think of my own experience with Santal women what comes to mind is an image of strong personalities, who enjoyed life despite its hardships. For the observer, the most salient point about Santal women is their involvement in labour. While the symbolic value of the female body is present in Santal songs, it is clear that during interviews the construction of femininity seems implicit as if women were shy to talk about their femininity.

Looking at women anointing their body with oil, or combing each other while exchanging jokes about men, a female anthropologist may feel that in a Santal courtyard young unmarried women are seen as the pride of the house. Young women go to the market to meet young boys, or they visit other villages at festivals. Courtship implies an exchange of gifts, poems and songs. Through the latter, we learn that the Santal girl does not want to be married away and that she will return later to the village where she first met her lovers. Romance is described as the awakening of feelings before marriage, which in its turn is often considered as a traumatic event.[3]

Unlike their Hindu counterparts Santal women do not have to assert their place in the parents-in-laws' house, rather their addition to the labour force is highly valued.[4] The young wife does not observe *purdah* before her parents-in-law but on the other hand, she may get sexually harassed by her father-in-law.

The Concept of Pleasure (*raskau*)

The Santals assert that *raskau* (pleasure) implies drinking and having sexual intercourse. There is no ban on premarital sexuality and men as well as women enjoy talking about companionship, romance and sexual pleasure. In a myth, the sexual organs are credited with separate characters and run away because they have not been given names. Later on, people invent names for them which are metaphors of intimacy such as Babu, 'son' for the penis, or Mai, 'daughter' for the vagina. In this way, lovers may refer to them in public without being understood. This openness towards sex is reflected in humorous tales wherein old couples, each finds the other a younger lover so they can enjoy life a last time. This shared intimacy stresses a reciprocal relationship which seems to negate violence. However, images of male violence are sometimes cast into ritual. Thus, when a couple want to get divorced, they take an oath before the village headman, who will allow each of them to speak. But, to close the ritual, the husband kicks an earthen pot, symbol of his wife, and says 'this pot is now broken'. The violence of the metaphor is echoed in narratives of conjugal violence which, however, do not show women as submissive. On the contrary, Santal women resist male dominance in everyday life.

Santal Women and the Bongas

Contrary to caste women Santal women move freely, but their movements are restricted by a number of taboos, excluding women from ritual space. Women are banned from entering the sacred grove alone, especially if they are pregnant or menstruating, as they may pollute the *jaher bonga,* the deities of the grove,[5] and of the Santal creation myth. They are free to go to the forest in groups to dig tubers, pluck edible leaves or gather firewood. Nevertheless, narratives often stress how some of them are caught by the tribal deities *(bongas).*[6] In one such story a pregnant woman is left behind in the forest by her friends. At first, she is afraid when night comes. But suddenly, she grasps a creeper to hold onto, and enters into labour. She gives birth to a child. After resting a while, she finally finds her way out of the forest. At dawn she enters the village, carrying her child on her hip. Her relatives who have been searching for her, welcome her. Then, they notice a halo around her body. Realizing that she has been aided by the *bongas,* they treat her with great respect. In this story, the female link with the deities is not seen as a threat to human masculinity, as it might otherwise be. Here, the woman becomes a sacred figure since she has overcome the dangers of the forest and been able to secure divine aid.

This narrative shows how Santal women are conceptualized as close to the *bongas* and to the forest. This secret connection explains an important taboo preventing women from climbing the roof of the house, since the *bongas* supposed to live there might seduce them.[7]

The Women's Voice

Santal women know myths, riddles and folk-tales, but it is mostly elderly women who are allowed to transmit these oral forms to their grandchildren. Though there is no strict taboo, it is not proper for young women to tell folktales in the presence of elders. As my friend used to say, "it is very difficult to find the proper story as any story might indicate a secret wish". Certainly there are stories that a young woman should not tell in public, such as erotic tales which are generally told by old people, but also those where girls meet with a strange destiny. This is the case in 'the story of an unmarried girl', (*Dangua kuri reak katha*).[8]

> "In a certain village, one old man had many sons but he had only one daughter. This daughter was growing up and she was wearing a blouse. Her father and mother and her brothers said: "Sister, let us go to the bazar and buy bracelets for you". And every year, they talked like that but they did not buy.
>
> And a few days after, the poor girl was taken by the fever. And being with fever, she died. Perhaps it was two weeks since she died; and she went from the place where she had been cremated to the market.
>
> But from the beginning they were acquainted with the owner of the bracelet shop. So the girl said to the owner: "Please, put the bracelets on my hands. But, either my father or my two brothers will pay for it".
>
> But the owner of the shop did not know that the girl was dead. Since he knew her, he put the bracelet on her hand. She said: "if they won't give you money then, tell them which one is your tank. Take me to your tank". And she said these words and went further and vanished. And after some days, the shopkeeper went to them and they placed the *parkom* (bed) on the verandah. The owner of the shop sat and took rest and he started to talk about the bracelets. He started like this: "Where is the daughter? They answered: "Don't you know? Perhaps it was two or three weeks before, that she had fever and she could

> not recover, she died". And this owner of the bracelet shop became pensive. So, he was thinking: who took the bracelets? And he had put bracelets on both her hands and he had asked her: "when will you give the price?" She had answered: "I did not bring the money but either my father or my brothers will pay" he said. "If they don't believe", she said, "tell them to take you to the tank where I was cremated". So, they took him. The shopkeeper called for the girl, that day you put the bracelets but to-day they are not giving the money. But they said: "we do not know, she died". But as you said, I have brought your parents (to the tank)". But when she heard these words, she remembered. And inside the water of the tank, she stretched her hand and they saw the bracelet. So they asked the shopkeeper about the price and said: "it is we who made a mistake. And, for a long time we were thinking to ourselves, therefore we did not give her bracelets. Probably, she wished too much to have the bracelets, that's why she rose from death and went to the bazar. And she was so determined to get the bracelets. Now truly, we have seen the bracelets. Please, tell the price and we will pay. But the shop-owner said: "I will not ask for more, I will take the proper price. Give me one taka and four annas". And the father took money from his house and gave him. And the bracelet shop-owner took the money and went home.
>
> The relatives of the girl returned home and they were sorry and they were thinking in themselves: "to our daughter, we did not give the bracelets: it may be that she died for this reason".

In this story, we see how the unmarried girl manages to make her brothers feel guilty, since they have not offered her the bracelets she wanted so much. We also see that Santal narratives do not deny women the right to use their femininity to manipulate their agnates. Unmarried girls are feared, as their latent reproductive powers are associated with the *bongas.*[9] When the heroine in a story dies unmarried, she becomes a dangerous *preta.* In this story the denied femininity of the girl allows her to become an embodiment of *shakti* – the cosmic energy[10] – after her death when she stretches her arm above the water of the tank. Though the narrative recalls a recurrent Hindu trope, it is expressed here in an entirely Santal idiom and setting (Carrin and Tambs-Lyche, 1993).

Witchcraft as Women's Knowledge

A Santal myth tells us that women listened to Maran Buru – the chief of the *bongas* and creator of the world – who was teaching the art of healing to men. The women were witnessing the scene secretly, but stolen by them, the knowledge became witchcraft (Carrin, 1986). There is an allusion here to the idea that women cannot retain or control any knowledge, just as they also lose menstrual blood. We also find tales which explain why women are unable to perform sacrifices, since they fail to distinguish between the neck and the tail of the sacrificial animal (Bodding, 1925: 229-35). The patrilineal ideology exposes women to taboos which keep them away from ritual life. They are not allowed to watch the killing of sacrificial victims and are not supposed to eat their neck and back.

Santals have different forms of marriage. The most prestigious form involves bride price (*gonon*) which implies an exchange of gifts between wife-givers and wife-takers. Today the bride price is merely nominal, but Santal marriage still excludes hypergamy. Despite the relative equality of wife-givers and wife-takers, the relationship between spouses is often strained. Divorce is quite easy for a man, but more difficult for a woman. Thus a man's extra-marital relations are tolerated, while they are considered as a violation of the husband's rights in the case of a woman. This asymmetrical situation, with the relative dependency it implies for women, may cause resentment.

Let us stress, however, that the wife of the village priest and of the village chief are treated with respect. More specifically, the wife of the priest, the *naeke era,* is considered to form, with her husband, the ancestral couple on earth. She must observe certain taboos on the eve of important festivals, such as sleep on the bare ground, fast, and observe sexual abstinence. She must be pure to broom the sacred grove, as she represents Jaher Era, the most important female *bonga* of the sacred grove, Maran Buru's wife.

Women are not allowed to become priests or chiefs themselves, though exceptions are known. Village hierarchy is clearly reflected in the world of witches (*dain*) who hold assemblies near the shrine (*manjhi than*) which shelters the ancestors of the chief.[11] Ordinary witches take orders from the *dain bonga,* "the chief dain", whose power is almost equal to that of the malevolent *bongas* (Carrin, 1995).

Knowledge is denied to women who, as we have seen, are suspected of having made bad use of 'stolen knowledge' – which became witchcraft. For Santal men, all women are potential witches who may use their menstrual blood, or organic substances taken from their victims' bodies, to do harm. Then women are acknowledged a malevolent power equal to that of the tribal deities. Without entering into detail, we may note that witches enjoy perverse biological functions – they conceive by their anus and excrete through their mouth. Witchcraft stories are short narrations describing masculine characters listening by chance to witch assemblies or being unfortunate witnesses of cannibalistic feasts, where witches cook and eat the liver and heart of their victims.

The anomic body of the witch alludes to the impossibility of controlling feminine sexuality. The most powerful witches are supposed to have a body made of fire (*shakti*).[12] Diviners (*ojhas*) usually say that the *dain* has an unfinished body and that the small finger of each of her hands is spitting fire, a quality she shares with *bongas*. Witchcraft lore describes how women's fertility is transformed into monstrous birth as well as cannibalistic activities.

Women subjected to conjugal violence may try to free themselves by 'eating' (*jom*) their husbands, i.e., by witchcraft. In some cases, a suspicious husband may try to kill his wife. I have seen a case where a man suspecting his wife to 'eat' him took a cloth stained with his wife's menstrual blood and told the village council he had found it under his mattress, a serious accusation of witchcraft. Such accusations could not be brought before the 'modern' panchayat but it had some effect on the Santal elders, who decided to put the woman on trial.

Sometimes, it is the mother or the mother-in-law who teaches witchcraft to the younger woman. To get new recruits, witches induce young girls to eat the liver of their father or husband. In witchcraft stories, novices eat their husbands to take revenge on male domination. But if we look at witchcraft accusations, which are by no means a thing of the past,[13] we find a different picture. The women suspected of witchcraft are often old widows who have land and thus attract the greed of their family. One may even say that witchcraft affairs generally arise from disputes over land and inheritance. If a woman is left a widow without sons, her husband's father or brother will traditionally keep the whole property, except a small plot that she has been given by her brothers called *taben jom*, 'parched rice'. This reference to a 'sweet' clearly indicates that this plot cannot feed the woman. If the widow has a son she will keep the property for herself, but her step-father, or elder brother-in-law, will look after it to see she doesn't waste it. Today, as in Archer's time, there is a tendency for educated widows to go to court and claim the inheritance from their deceased husband. Widows who have land are often molested, psychologically harassed, or indeed accused of witchcraft.

A Santal saying tells us that witches are persons who have not found a place in other people's gaze. They are excluded from other people's attention and even their existence is denied. The Santal conception of witches embodies a negative femininity where cannibalistic compulsions replace sexual desire. In witch stories, women often take away a young boy as a servant to initiate him in the art of witchcraft. In some narratives, the servant is also a kind of sexual toy that the women cajole or even rape, a caricature of the elopment marriage which allows a young man to put *sindur (vermilion)* on the forehead of the girl of his choice, an action which makes her his wife. Today, of course, this elopement marriage is often arranged by the young couple themselves, who want to overcome their parents' refusal or to have a marriage without expenses.

The hierarchical organization of witches seem to reflect the political system of the village, which excludes women, and so we may feel that women take their revenge in shaping the witch assemblies on that model.

In some tales, women are granted religious powers by a yogi. In – 'the good daughter-in-law', a yogi enables a woman to see how the dead are treated in the other world. One day, she sees how a low-caste man is received with honours by Jom raja, the god of death,[14] and she weeps for the death of such a good man. Her family becomes very suspicious at her thus mourning for the death of a stranger from another caste. When her father-in-law dies, she sees three beings dragging him out of the house by his heels – and she laughs to see him so treated for his sins. But the family is shocked by her laughter and concludes that she is a witch. They hold a council and ask the girl why she laughed. They insist until she tells them about the boon the yogi has given to her. And then she lies down on her bed and dies. In this story we see a woman receive religious knowledge by the mediation of a Hindu ascetic. But the Santal family denies her the right to such knowledge. The adjective 'good' in the story's title is ironic, and relates to the compliance of the girl who submits to the family even to the point of dying.

As we have seen, Santal women are barred from the ritual sphere. They are not allowed possession by the *bongas,* since it is perceived as a possibly erotic connection with the tribal deities. However, a few women become priestesses after enduring a personal crisis. They are often the wives or daughters of *ojhas* who for some reason fail to transmit their powers (*siddhi*) to their sons or male disciples. When female possession occurs in Bengal among Santals, it is seen as an exceptional religious experience where the woman is called by the goddess Kali. In most cases the woman has transgressed a sexual taboo and has been excluded from Santal society – or from her caste in the case of Hindu women (Carrin, 1997).

The Story of Parvati

Parvati is the daughter of an *ojha* who was a famous seer. The father could not transmit his knowledge to his sons, but contrary to Santal custom, Parvati got it on dreaming of her father's death. She never married a Santal but fell in love with a degraded Brahman working as a truck driver in the depot where she was employed to carry coal. Formerly, a Santal woman who had any sexual relationship with a *diku* – a non-santal – had to be excluded from Santal society after enduring a terrible rite of ostracism, *bitlaha.*[15] The same rule applied to a Santal who had an affair with a *diku* girl. Today, the agnates of the Santal girl perform a mock funeral for her to show she is no more one of them. Thus, Parvati should be considered as dead by her kin, but her brothers, who are fond of her, have refused to perform the ritual. Parvati and her lover got married before Thakur (Shiva) through a ritual which was not acknowledged by any of the communities. They were married by a *guni,* an ascetic who did not recognize differences between communities. He gave each of them an amulet for their protection.

Parvati settles with her Hindu companion in the suburbs of Bolpur (Birbhum district, West Bengal). But after a while, she fears that she may be sterile, as her menses have stopped. She also realizes the difficulty of being accepted in caste society since it is only at the shrine of their shaktist *guru* that they are recognized as husband and wife. In the region, a number of Santal and low-caste women receive visions of the Goddess when they are undergoing a personal crisis. Theses psychological pressures of the visions impel the devotees to try to catch the message of the goddess. The quest implies a series of obsessions which directly concern their femininity. With Parvati, as with some of the other devotees, we find the idea that Kali stops their menstrual cycle and deprives them of their femininity. Parvati accepts this loss and starts to perform *tapas* (austerities). Then she borrows different Hindu symbols such as the shivaïte trident (*trisul*) to which she offers a *puja*, followed by the matted hair (*joto*). But she feels pain when the *joto* grows in her hair, and is ashamed. She then refuses to hear the warning of the Goddess, and cuts some of the *joto*'s locks which she throws at the feet of the Goddess's statue. Then a miracle occurs. Chand, her husband, sees the locks move by themselves. Neighbours arrive, and a woman who suffers from skin disease rubs her arm on the locks. Her scars disappear. Parvati's therapeutic powers are acknowledged, she utters prophecies, and patients and disciples come to visit the shrine. But Parvati internalizes her devotion by identifying herself with the goddess who, at first, is a punitive figure, before becoming a mother of compassion[16] (Carrin, 1997).

Becoming the Child of the Goddess

The absence of the menstrual cycle is interpreted as the loss of the feminity. Parvati feels depressed, as she wanted to have a child with Chand. During a possession sequence, Parvati sees the Goddess as a mother and declares that she has been born again as the Goddess's child. This second birth implies finding a place in a spiritual lineage, like religious ascetics who become the disciples of a guru and adopt his *parampara*. In Parvati's story, as well as in other Santal female life stories, the *shakti* of the Goddess is seen as a substance transmitted from mother to child. The transmission of the Goddess's powers follows. A mother is generally able to transmit to her daughter her ability to get possessed, as we see from other examples, such as the *matas* of Punjab described by Erndl (1996). In the absence of a mother, it is the priestess who transmits this gift to her disciple.

The Goddess is also supposed to teach her disciple how to acquire the matted hair, encouraging her disciple to leave her hair uncombed. For Obeyesekere (1981) the *joto* is a phallic symbol. Certainly, the *joto* is a masculine symbol but I prefer to stress that for Santal women, its appearance implies the loss of the femininity. What strikes me here is how the matted hair allows a new identity to emerge. When Parvati finally accepts the *joto*, she surrenders to the goddess and is considered as her embodiment. To acquire a *joto* is a long journey which implies sexual ambivalence for the devotee, by accepting the loss of femininity and by practising *tapas* (austerities) which implies fasting and chastity. To surrender to the Goddess implies devotion (*bhakti*) but also allows the devotee to get religious powers as a manifestation of *shakti*. In these stories, Kali wants to remind her disciples that it is not always possible to master one's destiny, rather she offers a redemptive vision (Kinsley, 1986).

Sexual Ambivalence and Priesthood

When a Santal *ojha* is initiated he is feminized. He wears a sari when he walks with the other disciples to sing and beg in the villages. Later, when he is able to exorcize malevolent *bongas*, he prickles his thighs and offers some drops of his blood to them. This offering is called menstrual blood *sitka mayam*. The idea is that he should offer an impure substance to appease malevolent and impure deities. This allows us to understand why the female priestesses lose their menses: the *joto* is identified with the *shakti* and women cannot conciliate the menstrual blood with the fire which the *joto* spits. Women should avoid concentrating fire and blood in their body. A menstruating woman would be too hot to invoke the Goddess, only male *ojha* are allowed to concentrate blood and fire, substances which embody *shakti*, since their menstruation is symbolical.

When the Goddess appears to Santal women she expects from her devotee a religious attitude that Kinsley (1980) defines as a shivaîte and shaktist ethos, which transforms devotion into a quest for religious powers. This religious attitude excludes any worldly attachment and represents an alternative to marriage, as it deprives the woman of her femininity. This kind of elective possession occurs among Santal women deserted by their husbands or who have become widows. Such devotion is expressed through visions and possession episodes, which often occur after the death of kin. Symptoms manifest themselves, but a certain time is required before they are acknowledged as religious expressions. Usually the possessed woman performs a miraculous cure and is thereby ascribed therapeutic powers which are attributed to the *shakti* of the Goddess. Thus the devotee shares that *shakti* and may become a priestess, opening a therapeutic shrine.

Such female careers define marginal forms of priesthood, which are not institutionalized in traditional Santal culture but found at the periphery of tribal society. In these forms of priesthood the symbolism of sexual identity marks different steps of the religious experience. As we have seen, the *ojha* acquires feminine identity at initiation. The new identity is confirmed during a ritual wandering where his guru is supposed to dismember his body and then remember it. This is described in the disciples' songs as a mystic voyage in the sky where they reach the door of the sun. The male disciples return to earth with both a masculine and a feminine identity. But while the male healer is able to retain some femininity which sanctions his initiation to priesthood, the spiritual vocation of a woman often corresponds to a personal crisis sanctioned by the manifestation of masculine corporal symbols, like the matted hair. It is true that the ritual power of the *ojha* is also symbolized by the possession of a *joto*, the mark of the Shivaïte ascetics.

In Parvati's story, possession occurs at the fringes of the caste system allowing a Santal woman to become a priestess. In some cases, the possession implies a social message. This is the story of Asula, a Lohar (blacksmith caste) woman who after separating from her husband receives visions of the Goddess. One tragic event gives her message a political dimension. Her nephew, a boy of thirteen, is beaten to death by his boss, a Marwari[17] merchant. She places the photo of his dead body at the foot of the *murti* (statue) of Kali. People then say they have seen the Goddess moving her arms. Devotees – Maoists among them – come to Asula's shrine imploring the Goddess to take revenge for the unjustice.

We have seen that when Santal women are not witches or *pretas* they may become children of the Goddess.[18] Do Santal women, denied ritual knowledge by the patrilinear ideology, have no other possibility than to escape Adivasi society by joining the path of devotion? To answer, I shall explore the roles that Santal women have taken in tribal movements. Is it possible to define other forms of feminine subaltern agency?

Santal women are excluded from the traditional hunt (*sendera*) which gives Santal men the right to attend the Council of the Hunt (*Lo bir sendera*). Here, men from different villages may demand justice before the *des manjhi*, the chief of the country. Excluded from the hunt, where the ethos of Santal masculinity and discipline was expressed, women used to dress as men, taking bows and arrows to hunt domestic animals in the village. Narratives tell us that some of them ventured into the forest and killed wild animals.

Missionary Influence and Female Education

After the Santal rebellion (1855) various missionary societies established themselves in the Santal Parganas and sustained colonial penetration by developing infrastructures such as schools (Carrin and Tambs-Lyche, 1993). The Adivasi societies allied themselves to missions to use legal channels in their resistance to exploitation. Many Santal women supported the missionary campaign against drink, since drunk husbands were one of their everyday problems (Carrin and Tambs-Lyche, in *press*).

But differences between religious congregations have split some of the pan-tribal political efforts which emerged with the creation of the Adivasi Mahasabha in the 1920s. The proletarization of Adivasis working in industry and the scarcity of land induced the Santals to join the Jharkhand party, started in 1950 by an Oxford-educated Munda, Jaipal Singh.

This was an important step, and the role of the Santals in the movement has been crucial ever since, while reflecting Santal specificity. Since the formation of the party, *adivasis* have claimed a separate Jharkhand state. The sixties brought new political organizations such as the Jharkhand Mukti Morcha (JMM). It supported the claims for a separate state, and adopted a left wing stance to end exploitation of tribals by non-tribals, more specifically the higher castes. The JMM led some agrarian struggles of the 1960s, as the land situation in Chotanagpur deteriorated. The younger generation grew more radical, and, in Bengal, landless Santals participated in the Naxalite struggle in Birbhum. From the late seventies, in Bihar and Orissa, the JMM forged a successful cultural revival known as Sarna Dhorom. Shibu Soren, the founder of the JMM, became a quasi-divine hero, compared by Santals to Chando bonga, one of their main deities. From 1978, the Jharkhand grew in the wake of the ecological movement (Jangal Andolan) which burst out in Singhbhum. The JMM launched a programme to recover tribal land from moneylenders and farmers in the north of Chotanagpur, and tried to obtain waste lands and irrigation for tribals. But during the 1990 elections the JMM joined the BJP – the Hindu fundamentalist party, which is powerful in South Bihar – in order to get non-*adivasi* support, accepting the party's proposal to limit the creation of a Jharkhand State to Chotanagpur and the Santal Parganas. This state was finally created in November 2000.

Women's Agency in Jharkhand

We know that women participated in the Santal insurrection of 1855, though historians have not done justice to their courage. We know from a text from the Oslo archives (*Hul reak katha*)[19] – written by a Santal witness to the events – that the charismatic leaders of the rebellion, Sidhu and Kanhu, sometimes raped women. We also know that they believed it was necessary to eliminate some women as potential witches (Guha, 1983). Much later, in the Tebhaga movement of 'forcible harvesting',[20] women stood in the forefront. They were guarding the village, alerting men by signalling danger, and they were also the major harvesting force. Bimla Manjhi, a widow in Midnapur, acted as a local leader in the Tebhaga movement. She organized several processions against the money-lenders and succeeded in getting the paddy under peasant control. Later, she was arrested (Sahu, 1996:115). In the Tebhaga movement, women were facing several types of oppression – at home they were oppressed by their men and in the fields by the landlords. The exploitation of female labour within the family is often accompanied by control of female sexuality along with the use of violence.

Christian missionaries and Hindu sanskritizers more or less consciously fostered the practices of the patrilineal society. After Independence, the Indian Constitution supposedly guaranteed equality for men and women. But despite many legal reforms women continued to be oppressed. Feminist movements emerged in India in the mid-1970s. Urban educated women from middle and upper middle classes raised their voices to protest against atrocities on women. Before and during the emergency in 1975, when Jayaprakash Narayan mobilized the youth, he took up several issues such as the anti-dowry campaign. Women groups emerged and some are still active like the Bodh Gaya land struggle (Sahu, op.cit.:117).

In 1980 the forest movement got strengthened with the involvement of *Jharkhand Mukti Andolan*. Three thousands women gathered at a single public meeting to show their grievances against illicit cutting of the forest. The police fired and killed fifty five adivasis, some of them women. People protested against the displacement of villages due to the building of the Subarnarekha Dam which started in 1974. Women participated in the movement though they were not in a leading position.

Women's position in Jharkhand varies according to regions and the social classes. Santal women may involve themselves in different organizations but the exploitation of female labour within the family remains and the question of land rights is still problematic.

It should be stressed that JMM policy has sometimes been coercive to women, thus the party insisted that separated or divorced women should remarry to prevent the "sexual and moral corruption of tribal women by non-tribal men". If they refused, they were sometimes beaten up or married off to someone chosen by the cadres, being sent away from their home and worksite to distant areas where the new 'husbands' resided (Kelkar and Nathan, 1991:157). There were also instances, however, where the JMM in Singbhum defended women branded as witches.

Later, women organized themselves inside the JMM. These groups have worked mainly in order to change the power relations between women and men in rural areas. The role of women militants has been acknowledged, but as yet they have not produced a political message regarding the specificity of feminine subaltern agency.

Adivasi students had been always been active in the movement. In 1986 they formed *All Jharkhand Students Union.* From that time, Santal women were more and more present in the processions. Soon separate women's wings of All Indian Students' Union emerged in colleges and universities.

Literacy and Female Agency

The participation of women in spreading literacy is not new as we know from the Lutheran missionaries, who write about Santal women who became teachers (Bodding, 1919; Carrin and Tambs-Lyche, *in press*). In Mayurbhanj (Orissa) in the thirties, Ragunath Murmu, a Santal teacher, invented a new alphabet, reacting against the idea of writing Santali in different Indian scripts. Ragunath Murmu is a reformer who dreams of another age when the Santals were not corrupted by drink and led a spartan life. He argues that they have a glorious past and that their decline was due to the negative influence of neighbouring caste society . He feels women should help reform the Santals and keep their husbands from alcohol. In one of his plays, it is the girl who discovers the hidden script, and his female characters generally influence men to develop literacy.[21]

Women who have studied only at the primary level may still be able to develop their own agency in concrete situations. This is the case of my friend Lokhi who has always impressed me by her own way to develop her own agency. Wherever she worked she used to resist the contractors by her abusive humour. One day, in a private house where she was employed in Shantiniketan, she was assaulted by her boss, a Bengali Babu. She threw a big pot of water at him – which cooled him down, as she said. Similarly, whenever her husband returned home late and drunk, she used to shut her door till the next morning. Very courageous, Lokhi has no illusions about the different political parties. She once 'took a card' from the communist party to get, as she said, 'a sewing machine', and started making children clothes. She also taught other women to use the machine. Later, she had the idea of cooking for some Japanese students who did not like the canteen at Shantiniketan. When other Santal women were suffering, whenever there was no more rice at home, Lokhi had always a solution. She did not trust the Santal elite who, she felt, were too keen to imitate the well-to-do Bengalis. She was not impressed by women possessed by the Goddess, as she felt it was too much display. And she used to tell me that when she felt discouraged she used to go to a small temple dedicated to Shiva and pray there for a few minutes. It was enough, she said, just enough to start struggling again for her children and herself. When I used to ask her what she valued in life she used to answer "to laugh with people".

Illiterate women cannot compete for jobs in the public sector, they have to engage in casual labour in the informal sector and are often the prey of dishonest contractors who abuse them. Still, women have played an important role as nurses, teachers or even writers. They have also developed a concern for environmental issues, like protesting against the illicit cutting of trees or fighting against the building of mega dams which reduce thousands of adivasis to precarity. If Baviskar(1995:189) is right to underline the role of activists who worked among adivasis in rural areas, I feel that the change of consciousness results also from the fact that Santal women have realized that these projects would have a dramatic impact on their lives. Taking part in demonstrations in rural areas as well as in cities, Santal women have united with other adivasis women and participated in a culture of protest where they are gaining more and more self-reliance. Of course, the women who have been engaged in mining have a long experience of struggle as the conditions of domination have shaped the present-day lives of Santals as well as other adivasis in the hills.

In the 1980s some women groups started to create awareness of the cultural role of women in the Jharkhand. The *Jharkhand Mahila Sammelan* met for the first time in 1987, in Ranchi. They tried to redefine the role of women in history and raised different issues, such as their presence in the village panchayat, their role in protecting the environment, to reform Santal custom and obtain full right of heritage for daughters. They also wanted to link up with other women's organizations in Jharkhand. One main problem is that the *Sammelan* was led by educated women who did not always succeed in rallying the rural and illiterate women who are the most exploited. The movement failed to involve women from different ideological backgrounds. One of the issues which was shared by almost all women's wings was the issue of land rights and the reform of inheritance. But the growing participation of women in panchayats has been accepted by Jharkhandi leaders.

Recently however, with a growing consciousness of Adivasi cultural specificity and with the emergence of Jharkhandi's women's voices a new picture has started to emerge. The Jharkhand movement has started to address the problem of strengthening the position of women in the movement.

The educated Santal women who involve themselves in the new wings of the Jharkhand movement try to organize illiterate women in order to define a feminine version of Santal identity refusing the traditional image of Santal women as a potential witches or as ignorant. Some women have become writers. Criticizing witchcraft beliefs, they are anxious to reconciliate Santal identity and modernity. They want by their writing to reform aspects of Santal marriage and inheritance.

Conclusion

Traditional knowledge is denied to Santal women who are still considered as potential witches. The empowerment of rural women often uses the idea of *shakti.* They may succeed like Parvati in becoming the devotee of the Goddess and be empowered through *shakti.* This means that the empowerment of Santal women often takes place in a symbolic way. When Santal women who trangress the taboo of endogamy get possessed by the Goddess Kali, we see how they try to follow a spiritual path at the fringes of the tribal society. This religious quest is marked by a series of trials where the devotee gets to accept her call. The Goddess denies femininity to Santal devotees who become priestesses and perform miracles who get acknowledged by male as well as female disciples .When Santal women become children of the Goddess they do not only produce a female version of the *ojha* priesthood, tinged with shaktist elements but perform miracles and are able to convey a social message as well.

The path of devotion allows Santal women to survive between Adivasi society and Hindu castes. It seems more difficult for Santal women to assert themselves through modernity. The process of exploitation of women within the family is accompanied by a corresponding control on female sexuality along with the use of violence. The subaltern agency of Santal women who fought during the Santal Hul in the Tebagha movements and rural uprisings is largely anonymous. Literacy and involvement in social affairs have allowed Santal women from urbanized areas to play an important role in Jharkhand in reformulating the need for female education, and for female representation in local political groups. Education is important, but we must not forget that women like Lokhi perpetuate a tradition of resistance in their daily life. In the past, resistance to domination took the form of frequent uprisings, today, local struggles get incorporated in larger movements such as the Jharkhand or the local Andolan. The Adivasi communities, however, get transformed by their involvement in local politics. In these transformations everyday resistance for women implies shaping new solidarities. This new knowledge cannot be denied to them as they are, as workers, more and more engaged in private as well as public claims.

Notes

1. Today, the Santals number some five million. They speak an Austro-Asiatic language and are concentrated in the states of Jharkhand, Bengal, Bihar and Orissa, with important settlements in Bangladesh, Assam and Nepal.
2. Singh explains that the settlement officers had sometimes recorded women as owners of land, in defiance to local custom (1984: xiv).

3. Santal girls may marry in another village and leave their first lover. They usually come back to their natal village to attend festivals.
4. Boys, too are welcome in this way, if they join their wife's household. This may happen when a family is sonless, and especially if they own land. The boy will be given wood to cut, and the girl will comment on his efficiency. Such marriage, called 'ghar jawaen' – 'bought husband' – allows the groom to dispense with the bride price.
5. The sacred grove (*jaher*) is the ritual centre of every Santal village. Santals and other Austro-Asiatic speaking groups, as well as some other tribal groups in India, define their religion as the 'religion of the sacred grove' (Sarna Dhorom).
6. The Santals have innumerable deities. Beside the deities of the sacred grove, these include spirits of the boundaries and of the forest. The latter are the most dangerous, and they seduce both men and women. While the former sometimes return to the human world, bestowed with therapeutic powers, the encounter with *bongas* is often fatal to women (Carrin, 1996).
7. On the taboos imposed on women, see Carrin 1986 and *forthcoming*.
8. This story comes from the Santal archives the University Library, Oslo (Santalia, I469 sm). I am grateful to Santosh Soren, who helped me translate this story. It will be included in Andersen, Carrin and Soren (*forthcoming*).
9. When referring to the female reproductive powers, the term *bonga* is used metaphorically.
10. *Shakti* – the cosmic energy, is female in Hinduism and generally associated with the Goddess, though inherent in all females. Santals do not necessarily use this concept, but in this story the parallel to Hindu representations, where the woman's vengeance is conveyed by her inherent female energy, is evident.
11. Generally, the village is seen to have been founded by the chief's ancestors. Thus, his shrine is also a village shrine.
12. *Shakti* is closely associated with fire, which again is clearly connected in some narratives with the idea of tapas (austerities) of the Hindu god Shiva.
13. In some areas – such as in Malda, Bengal, and in Dinajpur, Bangladesh, witchcraft accusations seem actually to be on the rise.
14. Jom raja is clearly a Santal equivalent of the Hindu god of death, Yama.
15. The *bitlaha* is like a hunt, and often both the girl and her lover were killed. Archer (1984: 531-73) describes and analyses actual cases of bitlaha from the 1940s.

16. In Bengal, this dual aspect of the Goddess is often expressed in the mystic songs of Ramprasad.
17. Marwari is the term generally used for the merchants (Jain or Hindu) who have spread over most of India, and who have often come from Marwar, Western Rajasthan. In popular parlance in Bengal, the term is often pejorative, and used to indicate excessive greed.
18. Sometimes, girls who die before marriage are called *juguni* and are supposed to abuse men near the cremation ground. Pregnant women who die are called *curin* and are considered the most dangerous spirits.
19. In Oslo archives, this story is found under the reference (1969).
20. For descriptions of forcible harvesting in Chotanagpur see Devalle (1992) and in Bengal, see Duyker (1987).
21. In Orissa, female literacy is 10.8 per cent against 37.6 per cent for males. Andersen (2005:62) notes that this proportion is almost recurrent in other states.

References

Andersen, P. (2005) Santals: Glimpses of Culture and Identity, Dr. Ambedkar Memorial Lectures, NISWASS, Bhubaneswar.

Archer, W. (1974), *The Hill of Flutes, Life, Love and Poetry in Tribal India: A Portrait of the Santals*, London: George Allen and Unwin.

— (1984), *Tribal Law and Justice*, New Delhi: Concept.

Baviskar, A. (1995), *In the Belly of the River: Tribal Conflicts over Development in the Narmada Valley*, Delhi: Oxford University Press.

Bhatty, K. (1998), Educational Deprivation in India, A Survey of Field Investigations, *Economical and Political Weekly*, July 4, 1731-1740.

Bodding, P. O. (1925-1929), *Santal Folk Tales*, Oslo: Aschehoug, 3 Vols.

— (1932-1936), *A Santal Dictionary*, Oslo: i kommisjon hos Jacob Dybwad, 5 Vols.

Carrin-Bouez, M. (1986), *La fleur et l'os: symbolisme et rituel chez les Santal*, Paris: EHESS.

Carrin, M. (1995), Des récits tenus pour réels, les *bonga*, alibi du désir», *Traditions Orales dans le Monde Indien*, Etudes réunies par C. Champion, *Purusartha*, 18, 367-381.

— (1996), Celles qui sont sorties du regard. Histoires de sorcières en pays santal», Autres mondes, numéro coordonné par G.Calame-Griaule et al., *Cahiers de Littérature Orale*, 39-40, 157-174.

— (1997), *Enfants de la déesse: dévotion et prêtrise féminine au Bengale,* Paris: Editions du CNRS et Maison des Sciences de l'Homme.

— (2002), Le retour du bosquet sacré. Réflexions sur la reinvention d'une culture Adivasi, In M.Carrin et C.Jaffrelot (eds) *Résistance et autonomie dans la société indienne, Purusartha* 23.

Carrin, M. and H. Tambs-Lyche (1993), – «La vengeance des femmes dans ce monde et dans l'Autre. Quelques exemples de l'Inde» (en collaboration avec H.Tambs-Lyche) *Cahiers de Littérature Orale,* n°34, Paris, 48-75.

— (in press), *A Peripheral Encounter Santals and Missionaries 1867 to 1900,* New Delhi: Manohar.

Devalle, S. (1992), *Discourses of Ethnicity: Culture and Protest in Jharkand,* New Delhi and London: Sage.

Duyker, E. (1987), *Tribal Guerrillas: The Santals of West Bengal and the Naxalite Movement,* New Delhi: Oxford University Press.

Erndl, K. (1996), Seranvali: The Mother who Possesses, In J. Hawley and D.M. Wulff (eds.), *Devi: Goddesses of India,* 173-194, Berkeley: University of California Press.

Guha, Ramachandra (1999), *Savaging the Civilized Verrier Elwin, His Tribals and India,* Chicago: Chicago University Press.

Guha, Ranajit (1983), *Elementary Aspects of Peasant Insurgency in Colonial India,* New Delhi: Oxford University Press.

Hawley, J.S. and D.M. Wulff (eds.) (1996), *Devi: Goddesses of India,* Berkeley: University of California press.

Kelkar, G. and Nathan, D. (1991), *Gender and Tribe Women, Land and Forests,* New Delhi: Kali for Women.

Kinsley, D. (1980), Devotion as an Alternative to Marriage in the Lives of Some Hindu Women Devotees, *Journal of Asian and African Studies,* XV, 1-20.

— (1986), *Hindu Goddesses. Visions of the Feminine Divine in the Hindu Religious Tradition,* Berkeley: University of California Press.

Obeyesekere, G. (1981), *Medusa's Hair: An Essay on Personal Symbols and Religious Experience,* Chicago: University of Chicago Press.

Sahu, C. (1996), *The Santhal Women A Social Profile,* New Delhi: Sarup and Sons.

Singh, K.S. (1984), Introduction to Archer, *Tribal Law and Justice,* 1-XXIII, New Delhi: Concept.

13

Women's Empowerment and Self-Help Groups

An Overview of Strategies and Initiatives

B. SUGUNA AND G. SANDHYA RANI

Women and children, who represent more than two-thirds (67.7%) of the country's total population, constitute the most important target groups in the context of the present day developmental planning. Therefore, their concerns are placed on the priority list of the country's developmental agenda.

For more than a decade, the term 'empowerment' has been widely used in relation to women as well as marginalized communities in India. Today one hears this term much more often than terms like 'women's welfare', 'upliftment', 'development' or 'awareness rising'. However, in spite of the growing popularity and widespread usage of the term, there have been few conceptual explorations of what exactly empowerment means, and even more, what the empowerment of women implies in social, economic and political terms. Women's empowerment is a global issue today and discussions on women's political rights are at the forefront of many formal and informal campaigns worldwide.

The concept of women's empowerment is the outcome of several important critiques and debates generated by the women's movement throughout the world, particularly by the Third World feminists. Its source can be traced from the interaction between feminism and the concept of 'popular education' developed in Latin America in the 1970s.

Empowerment in its simplest form means "the manifestation of redistribution of power that challenges patriarchal ideology and the male dominance". 'Becoming powerful' is the literal meaning of the term 'empowerment'. This is being used today in all spheres of life as a process to strengthen the elements of society. It is both a process and the result of the processes. It is transformation of the structures or institutions that reinforces and perpetuates gender discrimination. Empowerment is a process that enables women to gain access to and control of material as well as information resources. The 'empowerment approach', was first clearly articulated in 1985 by Development Alternatives with Women for a New Era (DAWN). This term received prominence in early nineties in western countries.

While discussing empowerment the following four different forms of power can be identified:

- Power over – control or influence over others which is an instrumentation of domination.
- Power to – generate or productive power which creates new possibilities and actions without domination.
- Power with – a sense of the whole being greater than the sum of the individuals, especially when a group tackles problems together.
- Power from within – the spiritual strength and uniqueness that resides in each one of us and makes us truly human. Its basis is self-acceptance and self-respect which extend in turn, respect for and acceptance of others as equals.

Though the interpretation of 'power to' and 'power with' empowerment is concerned with the process by which people become aware of their interests and how these relate to the interests of others but also participate in decision-making and influence such decisions.

Empowerment is also the process of challenging existing power relations and of gaining greater control over the sources of power. The goals of women's empowerment are to challenge patriarchal ideology to transform the structures and institutions that reinforce and perpetuate gender discrimination and social inequality and to enable poor women to gain access to and control of both material and informational resources. It can change existing power relations by addressing itself to the three dimensions of material, human and intellectual resources. Empowerment cannot occur as a revolution but only as evolution.

Empowerment is a 'process' and not an event: It is, therefore, time consuming and may have several phases. Each phase or step may be an effort by itself. It can be built only gradually by constructing each step solidly. The progress of the 'whole' depends on various environmental factors in a given society in which such a process of empowerment is trying to take place. It can be both self initiated or initiated by others. Generally, development with justice is experienced to generate the forces that lead to empowerment of various sections of population in a country and to raise their status.

In today's global society pressures for empowerment are growing. The empowerment theme runs strongly through all the literature, policy documents, planned initiatives, etc., of the Third World countries especially in the context of women. Most of the modern democracies and developing nations are already fascinated with this theme and have a public agenda for the process of empowerment of women. It is more or less a kind of 'national commitment' which is prevalent in these countries including India. This favourable environment to a great extent is the creation of the series of World Women's Conferences held in the last two decades with the UN support. Within the women's movement too, empowerment has been given considerable attention.

Components of Empowerment

The components of empowerment are as follows:

- Women's and men's sense of internal strength and confidence to face life.
- The right to make choices.
- The power to control their own lives within and outside the home.
- The ability to influence the direction of social change towards the creation of a more just social and economic order nationally and internationally.

Strategies for Empowerment

As stated there have been significant shifts in the approach towards the well-being of women from 'welfare' during fifties to 'empowerment' during nineties. In the post-independent India the government's concern and sensitivity to the issue is reflected in many ways. The first serious attempt to better their lot was perhaps taken through assessing their 'existing status'. This was done by way of appointing a Committee on the Status of Women in India in 1971, the report of Towards Equality (1974), which finally led to the preparation of the National Perspective Plan for Women 1988 – 2000. This plan puts together almost all that women have aspired for and what has been formally promised to them. Though the plan claimed to provide an alternate strategy of National development, so far as upliftment of women and their emancipation are concerned, it was admitted that no additional financial outlays were proposed for programmes specifically designed for upliftment of women, who are supposed to be woven into the social fabric in what was called an Integrated National Development Strategy. In the then prevailing social, economic and political environment when there was no commitment on the part of the political and administrative machinery such a tall claim and any expectations on that basis appeared to be misplaced.

The report of the National Commission for Self-Employed Women and Women in the Informal Sector also authenticated many realities about the conditions and contributions of women in this sector. NGO's working with women gained much strength and confidence from this report. The appointment of the National Commission for Women (NCW) in 1992 and the Rashtriya Mahila Kosh (RMK) in 1993 are part of the overall strategy of an integrated approach to empowerment of women adopted by the government in the nineties.

Human resource development has been taken up as one of the major thrust areas by the government of India during the eighth plan and efforts were directed towards mainstreaming men, women and children into the national development on equal footings. While the main thrust in respect of children was to ensure their "survival" with special focus on the girl child, the emphasis in respect of women was to make them economically independent and self–reliant. Empowerment of women is one of the major objectives of the ninth plan, too. The plan reiterates goals to create an enabling environment with requisite policies and programmes, legislative support, exclusive institutional mechanisms at various levels, and adequate financial and manpower to achieve this objective. The strategy is to adopt an integrated approach towards empowering women encompassing all fronts like social, economic, political and legal. The government of India has also prepared a National Policy for the Empowerment of Women in 1996, which reflects all the above measures in detail and the ninth plan recommendations of expeditious adoption of this policy along with a well defined gender development index to monitor the same. Further, a special strategy of earmarking of funds as 'women component' has also been adopted with a close vigil to ensure flow of funds and benefits for women in all developmental sectors both at central and state levels.

Approaches to Women's Empowerment

Women's empowerment according to Kamala Bhasin involved the transformation of power relations at six different levels, namely individual, family, group, organization, village, community and society. In order to empower the rural poor especially the women, female workers must first empower themselves. Batliwala has identified three approaches to women's empowerment: the integrated development approach, which focused on women's survival and livelihood needs; the economic development approach, which aimed to strengthen women's economic position; and the consciousness approach, which organized women into collectives that address the sources of oppression.

The consciousness raising approach asserts that women's empowerment requires awareness of the complex factors causing women's subordination. This approach organized women into collectives that tackle the sources of subordination (ASTHA, Deccan Development Society, Mahila Samakhya, WOP in India, Nigera Kori in Bangladesh).

The female empowerment approach stresses the capacity of women to increase their self reliance and internal strength. The empowerment approach to women's advancement in developing countries recognizes that the patriarchal structure of subordination must be addressed through women's organizations at the grass-root level. Such local groups can facilitate bottom up change by providing a social mechanism to raise women's consciousness about their subordination.

Broad Categories of Empowerment

Empowerment can be broadly categorized as:

- Economic empowerment

- Political empowerment
- Social empowerment

Economic Empowerment

Economic empowerment is undoubtedly the key, and may lead to all other kinds of empowerment. This is truer in the context of women. A major cause of woman's subordination is said to be her economic dependence. In the event of a social crisis, a woman is unable to express or decide for herself mainly because she has no means to support herself and her children. It is precisely because of this that many women development programmes either emphasize fully or have a component on the income generation activity, so that there is money available in women's hand and she moves towards economic independence and takes the first step towards empowerment.

Economic empowerment endorses women's sense of work, the right to determine choices, the power to control their own lives within and outside home and their ability to influence the direction of social change and to create a just social and economic order nationally and internationally. Economically empowered women contribute to the wealth and wellbeing not only of their families but also of their nations.

Economically rural women are in a state of drastic poverty. Rural females are considered as consumers and not producers. They have no occupation, property, education or skills. A majority of women are at a disadvantage in gaining admittance to professional training because of unequal access to education of preparatory levels. As a result they hardly get into the formal sector of employment. They are, however, a major work force in the informal sector but suffer from wage discrimination. Women also have unequal control and access to health.

Many micro studies have demonstrated the inverse relationship between income level of household and women's labour participation. In the last forty years very little structural changes have taken place in female employment. Hence skill development, income generation and credit availability are the main planks of economic empowerment of women. Heavy domestic chores allow women little leisure to invest in other activities.

Serious efforts have taken place for the economic development of women in 1980 with the sixth Five-Year Plan and after the report of the committee on the status of women was published providing a lot of information on the multiple roles of women and their developmental needs. The major thrust of the Sixth Plan was "economic upliftment of women" through greater opportunities for employment imparting new skills and upgrading existing skills. As a result today there are 27 programmes involving 6 ministries and 8 departments of the government of India, which focus on women in forms of training, skill development, wage employment and income generating activities.

The Integrated Rural Development Programme (IRDP) which is the main plank of poverty alleviation provides for 40 per cent beneficiaries as women. The Programme of Training of Rural Youth for Self Employment (TRYSEM) again provides for 40 per cent trainees to women. Wage employment programmes such as Jawahar Rozgar Yojana (JRY) and Employment Assurance Scheme (EAS) have also provided wage employment to women to the extent of 40 per cent. Then the exclusive programme on Development of Women and Children in Rural Areas (DWCRA) provides income generating activities to women.

The level of self-employment among women is also quite low as they have very little control on the productive resources and production process. Some steps are taken to ensure greater accessibility of women to credit though schemes like financing of self-help groups and institutions like Rashtriya Mahila Kosh (RMK). The government is also promoting local Women's Self-Help Groups in a big way under the umbrella of Indira Mahila Yojana (IMY). Another scheme of economic empowerment of women, i.e., Mahila Samriddhi Yojana (MSY) was introduced in 1993.

In spite of these interventions, the basic problem that affects women's roles and opportunities still remains to be tackled in a big way. This problem springs from their lack of independence, caused by their limited skills, illiteracy, restricted mobility and lack of autonomous status. None the less some non-governmental organizations such as Self-Employed Women's Association (SEWA), Ahmedabad; Community Health and Development (CHD), Vellore; All India Women's Conference (AIWC), New Delhi; Working Women's Forum (WWF), Chennai; and Young Women's Christian Association (YWCA); etc., are successfully operating various programmes for economic development of women.

Political Empowerment

Till the end of the nineteenth century women in India were crushed under the weight of evil customs. They were socially suppressed, economically dependent and politically powerless. Politically women were less conscious, less articulate, and less active. They were basically apathetic and indifferent towards the political process. However, women with elite background and political families always found it easy and had a smooth entry in politics. Women's traditional role demanded full attention to home. This domestic focus combined with modesty as a primary virtue kept other women away from politics in general. Their economic dependence and the prohibitive election expenses were also hurdles.

The Constitution of India opened a new chapter in the matter of equality of women. Article 15(3) empowers the states to make any "special provision for women and children" even in violation of the fundamental obligation of the fundamental of non-discrimination among citizens inter-alia of sex. Reservation of seats for women in local or educational institutions has been held to be valid in view of these provisions. Ever since the first general elections in 1952, women voters' participation in various elections has been increasing. But their representation in National Parliament has never crossed 10 per cent. Keeping this in view a modified strategy to increase the women's participation in political decision-making by way of adopting a "quota system to women" in the legislative bodies was adopted. The seventy-third constitutional amendment providing for one-third of the seats to women members in all the rural local self-government institutions (Panchayat Raj Bodies) is considered as landmark attainment towards political empowerment of women. A similar provision for one-third reservation to women in the Lok Sabha and in the legislative assemblies of the states by way of constitutional amendment is under consideration of the Parliament, which could not be placed in the monsoon session of the Parliament in 2005 due to lack of consensus among the political parties. However, these provisions are basically to create more consciousness among women and to strike a greater gender balance in the decision-making. For the first time opportunity to share power with the elite is ensured constitutionally. These acts are expected to bring in a silent revolution in the gender constitution of political structures in India. Amendment is a progressive landmark in the history of political empowerment and will enhance their status and development.

Social Empowerment

Social empowerment is by far the most difficult and long-term goal to attain, because social equality includes equality of treatment, equality of respect, equality of opportunity, equality of recognition, and above all equality of status. It basically entails a change in perception, attitudes and values which are hard to achieve.

In terms of rights and privileges, Indian women not only enjoy constitutional protection but also special legislative enactment. The Constitution of India grants equality to women and also empowers the states to adopt measures of positive discrimination in favour of women for neutralizing the cumulative socio-economic, educational and political disadvantages faced by them. Fundamental rights among others ensure equality before law, equal protection of law, prohibits discrimination against any citizen on grounds of religion, race, caste, sex or place of birth, and guarantees equality of opportunities to all in matters relating to employment. Articles 14, 15, 15(3), 16, 39(A), 39(B), 39(C) and 42 of the Constitution are of specific significance in this regard. Several important social legislations are also enacted which aim at social empowerment of women that include:

- The Hindu Widows Remarriage Act 1856;
- The Child Marriage Restraint Act 1929;
- The Hindu Marriage Act 1955;
- The Hindu Adoption and Maintenance Act 1956;
- The Inheritance and Guardianship Act 1956;
- The Dowry Prohibition Act 1961;
- The Maternity Benefits Act 1981;
- The Factories Act 1948 (Provisions Relating to Creches);
- The Equal Remuneration Act 1976;
- The Medical Termination of Pregnancy Act 1971;
- The Immoral Traffic (Prevention) Act 1986;
- The Indecent Representation of Women (Prohibition) Act 1986 and Rules 1987;
- The Commission of Sati (Prevention) Act 1987.

In addition, in the field of social and criminal justice too, a few changes have been brought about by way of either amending the existing Acts or by way of fresh enactment with the objective of providing greater gender justice and to improve the social and legal status of women. Some of these measures are:

- Amendments to the Indian Evidence Act 1872 in 1983 as part of the judicial reforms;
- Amendments to the Indian Penal Code (IPC) and additions of several new clauses during 1983 and 1986 as part of judicial reforms. (This includes introduction of the concept of custodial rape, redefining of dowry death elaborating the term 'Cruelty' etc.);
- The Family Courts Act 1984 to expedite disposal of select family disputes;
- The Pre-natal Diagnostic Techniques (Regulation and Prevention of Misuse) Act 1994 to prevent the increasing incidence of female foeticide.

Women are still oppressed in many spheres of life and need to be empowered in all walks of life. All aspects of society have to be restructured. The empowerment mechanism is easily enumerated. All agree that women should have:

- Higher literacy and education;
- Better health care;
- Higher age at marriage;
- Better skills and better work participation;
- Economic independence;
- Advancement into higher positions of power and decision-making;
- Self-reliance, self-respect and dignity;
- Better conditions of living with leisure.

Empowerment of Women in India

The Indian Constitution in its fundamental rights has provisions for equality, social justice and protection of women. These goals are yet to be realized. Women still continue to be discriminated against, exploited and exposed to inequalities at various levels. So the concept of empowerment as a goal of development projects and programmes has been gaining wider acceptance.

By empowerment women would be able to develop self-esteem, confidence, realize their potential and enhance their collective bargaining power. Women's empowerment can be viewed as a continuum of several interrelated and mutually reinforcing components, such as:

- Awareness building about women's situation, discrimination and rights and opportunities as a step towards gender equality. Collective awareness building provides a sense of group identity and the power of working as a group;
- Capacity building and skill development, especially the ability to plan, make decisions, organize, manage and carry out activities to deal with people and institutions in the world around them;
- Participation and greater control and decision-making power in the home, community and society;
- Action to bring about greater equality between men and women.

Thus empowerment is a process of awareness and capacity building leading to greater participation, greater decision-making power and control and transformative action. The empowerment of women covers both an individual and collective transformation. It strengthens their innate ability through acquiring knowledge, power and experience.

The Ninth Plan (1997-2002) had made its commitment to the objective of 'empowering women' as the agents of social change and development. The twelve salient strategies spelt out focused on empowering women by making women economically independent and self reliant. It was being hoped that the strategies would be realized through the National Policy for Empowerment of Women. Remarkably, self-help groups were considered to be one of the strategies to mark the beginning of major process of empowering women.

Committee on the Empowerment of Women was constituted in April 1997 to improve the status of women. It consisted of 20 members of Lok Sabha and 10 members of Rajya Sabha of the Indian Parliament. The functions of the committee included examining the measures to secure women's equality, status and dignity in all matters and considering the reports of National Commission for Women.

The Planning Commission in 1999-2000 had given specific emphasis on empowerment of women, besides the continuation of the important initiative programmes like Rural Women's Development and Empowerment Project (RWDEP), which was introduced in the states of Uttar Pradesh, Madhya Pradesh, Bihar, Haryana, Karnataka and Gujarat for a period of five years. The overall objective of the project is to enable empowerment of women by establishing self-help groups which will improve the quality of their lives through greater access to and control over resources.

Emergence of Self-Help Groups: The New Women's Movement

All over the world, there is a realization that the best way to tackle poverty and enable the community to improve its quality of life is through social mobilization of poor, especially women, into self-help groups. Ever since Independence, a number of innovative schemes have been launched for the upliftment of women in India. Indian Government has taken a lot of initiatives to strengthen the institutional rural credit system and development programmes. However, formal sector credit agencies find it difficult to reach the vast majority of rural people. The problem highlighted above required a complete paradigm shift where the flexible and responsive system meets the needs of the rural poor. Viewing it in the welfare programmes of ninth Five-Year Plan (1997-2000) and shifting the concept of 'development to empowerment', the Indian Government adopted the approach of Self-Help Groups (SHGs) to uplift the rural poor women focusing on the following aspects:

- Direct involvement of women in programming and management,
- Effective collaboration with community organization,
- Organizing and strengthening of women's self-help groups,
- Sensitization and advocacy of gender just society,
- Organizing women in different groups to undertake certain productive activities to earn their livelihood and to develop rural community.

Empowerment of women through self-help groups would lead to benefit not only the individual woman and women groups, but also to the families and community as a whole through collective action for development. These groups have a common perception of need and impulse towards collective action. Empowering women means not just for meeting their economic needs but also through more holistic social development.

Origin of Self-Help Group (SHG)

The concept of SHG follows the principle, "by the women, of the women and for the women". The origin of SHG is the brainchild of

Grameena Bank of Bangladesh, which was found by the economist, Prof. Mohammad Yunus of Chittagong University in the year 1975.

Self-help group is a small, economically homogeneous, affinity group of rural poor which is voluntarily ready to contribute to a common fund to be lent to its members as per group decision, which works for group solidarity, group awareness, and social and economic empowerment in the way of democratic functioning. The SHG movement became a silent revolution within a short span of time in the rural credit delivery system in many parts of the world. It has been documented that nearly fifty-three developing countries, including India, have taken up SHG movement on a large scale. In 1997, World Micro Credit Summit at Washington converged the developed and the developing countries to tackle the serious problem of poverty by using micro credit as a tool to empower the poorest sections. A global movement has been launched to reach 100 million of the world's poorest families by the year 2006.

Concept of Self-Help Group

'All for all' is the principle behind the concept of self-help group (SHG). It is mainly concerned with the poor and it is for the people, by the people and of the people. SHG, a mini voluntary agency for self-help at the micro level, has been a focus for the weaker sections particularly women for their social defence. Self-help group has got great potential in increasing awareness on day-to-day affairs, promoting in savings habit, developing self and community assets, increasing the income level, increasing the social power, etc. The concept of SHG generates confidence, self-security and self-reliance.

Objectives of Self-Help Groups

The following are the main objectives of self-help groups:

- To inculcate the habit of saving and banking habit among the rural women.
- To build up trust and confidence between the rural women and the bankers.
- To develop group activity so that various welfare and developmental programmes can be implemented in a better way with the participation of these groups.
- To achieve Women and Child Welfare Programme goals by actively involving these women groups in Universal

Immunization Programme, Pulse Polio, small family norm, Universal Elementary Education Programmes etc.

Characteristics of Self-Help Groups

- Small size.
- Identical interest/social heritage/common occupation, homogeneity, affinity.
- Flexible and responsive.
- Intimate knowledge of members of intrinsic strength, needs and problems.
- Democratic in operations.
- Simple documentation.
- Collective leadership, mutual discussions.
- Group solidarity, self-help, awareness, social and economic development.

Benefits of Self-Help Groups

- A via-media for development of savings habit among the poor,
- An access to large quantum of resources,
- A window for better technology / skill upgradation,
- Availability of emergent, consumption/production credit at the door step,
- Access to various promotional assistance, and
- Assurance of freedom, quality, self reliance and empowerment.

Self-help groups also promote democratic culture and provide women with opportunities to imbibe norms of behaviour that are based on mutual respect. Hence they were able to foster concern even in internal lending of loans based on the individual needs and priorities. It provided a firm base for dialogue and cooperation in programmes with other institutions like government departments, cooperatives, financial and Panchayat Raj Institutions.

The self-help groups engaged not only in productive economic activities but also in social empowerment and capacity building of rural women. Health education, medical facilities, literacy, alternative agriculture practices, leadership qualities and team building are other activities of self-help groups. Various studies have revealed that SHGs ensured 'we feeling' among the members achieving the group cohesiveness and accorded a social identity to the rural women. It also enabled them for collective bargaining while keeping up their dignity.

Empowerment, therefore, is closely linked to economic independence. Nothing succeeds better than the self-help group. And when efforts are supported by the government and private agencies the results could be extremely gratifying. Today there are more than three lakh SHG women focused around economic activities like savings, collective marketing, promotion of individual enterprise and in the process of moving into the main stream of society. In the process, leadership qualities blossom, discipline prevails and true democracy begins to function. This also helps add value to the work they do, their families and their communities.

A social movement has thus began wherein rural women started saving money by forming themselves into small groups and come together to decide all issues which affect their life. During the last 5-6 years a saving movement caught up the imagination of women as a means of self-help groups through which they are trying to mould their destiny. It may be rated as the most successful anti-poverty programme and contribution to women's empowerment and the expectation continue to be high, the need for taking a look at the present status has been felt. Thus women empowered by economic independence can contribute to society and at the same time improve their standard of living. Their self-esteem can be demonstrated and taken to logical conclusion where empowered women folk will take their rightful place in the path of progress.

In promoting self-help groups both Governmental and non-Governmental agencies are involved. Self-help groups have been designed to benefit women especially in rural belt towards providing them social status and identity. Hence, the Central Government had invited the State Government to become involved in the SHG movement. In India, Tamil Nadu and Andhra Pradesh had been successful in the SHG movement. Therefore, the Central Government has asked the State Governments of Orissa, Bihar, Jharkhand, Chattisgarh, MP and UP to provide the same momentum for the development and promotion of SHGs.

Self-Help Groups in Andhra Pradesh

The Government of Andhra Pradesh has taken up women's empowerment as one of the main strategies to tackle socio-economic poverty. SHG movement through savings has been taken up as mass movement by women, a path chosen by them to shape their destiny for the better. Development agenda of the state in the last few years of placing the people, especially women, in the forefront has enabled the formation of a large number of self-help groups through out the state where women are saving one rupee per a day. The state is making efforts to assist SHGs by providing revolving fund under various programmes.

There are about 4,36,579 women self-help groups in Andhra Pradesh covering nearly 65,48,685 of rural poor women. Andhra Pradesh alone has about half of the SHGs existing in the country. Socio-economic survey of self-help groups conducted by District Rural Development Agency (DRDA) in different districts has indicated that the scheme has helped women to earn additional monthly incomes ranging from Rs 1,500 to Rs 1,800 depending upon the economic activities taken up. In addition, women have taken up initiatives in improving their socio-economic status by participating in Governmental programmes such as family planning, pulse polio, AIDS awareness, small family norm, promoting nutritional and educational status, awareness on environment, public health through sanitation and clean drinking water, etc.

Table 13.1

Status of Self-Help Groups in Andhra Pradesh

	1999-2000	*2002-2003*
Total Groups (Nos.)	3,73,044	4,36,579
Women covered members (in lakhs)	50.65	58.50
Women Savings (Rs in crores)	420.45	780.20
Govt. Assistance (Rs in crores)	404.54	630.16
Total Corpus (Rs in crores)	824.99	1413.36
Loan mobilized from banks under SHG linkage programme (Rs in crores)	886.28	931.81
Average savings per groups (Rs)	11258.00	17939.00
Average credit per group (Rs)	23750.55	29261.00
Average corpus per groups (Rs)	22088.85	32376.00
SHGs up to year 1994 (Nos.)	10,000	—
SHGs initiated in 1999-2000 (Nos.)	95,000	—
SHGs initiated in 2000-2001 (Nos.)	60,000	—

Source: MCID, NABARD, 2002

Due to this massive self-help movement, there is a perceptible improvement in the socio-economic status of the rural women. From persistent efforts of the government, women have become very active, assertive and are concerned with the issues relating to themselves and their surroundings. Right from the beginning non-governmental organizations in Andhra Pradesh are working for the cause of women and more than 200 committed NGOs have become involved in facilitating the formation of self-help groups and efforts for their sustenance.

Table 13.2

District-wise cumulative progress of SHGs in Andhra Pradesh through March 2002

Sl. No.	*Name of the District*	*Cumulative No. of SHGs provided with Bank loans up to 31 March 2002*	*Cumulative Bank loans disbursed up to 31 March 2002*
1.	Adlabad	6,806	145.00
2.	Anantapur	6,984	232.72
3.	Chittoor	11,982	344.60
4.	Cuddapah	2,680	154.65
5.	East Godavari	34,765	805.86
6.	Guntur	7,981	189.55
7.	Karimnagar	14,480	206.02
8.	Khammam	13,141	192.92
9.	Krishna	14,852	237.58
10.	Kurnool	6,399	144.52
11.	Mahaboob Nagar	11,653	318.23
12.	Medak	11,832	217.17
13.	Nalgonda	8,032	186.90
14.	Nellore	6,203	205.73
15.	Nizamabad	7,953	144.93
16.	Prakasam	7,077	175.49
17.	Ranga Reddy	8,152	217.50
18.	Sri Kakulam	19,722	332.41
19.	Visakhapatnam	12,635	265.43
20.	Vizinagaram	4,459	67.80
21.	Warangal	18,848	211.91
22.	West Godavari	7,078	215.65
	Total	2,43,714	5,212.57

Source: MCID, NABARD 2002

The Government of Andhra Pradesh has taken up the theme of women's empowerment as one of the main agenda items to tackle rural poverty and socio-economic issues. Self-help movement through thrift and savings has been taken up as a mass movement by women – a path chosen by the women to shape their destiny. Development agenda of the state in the last few years has been to place the poor especially the women (below poverty line) in the forefront. This has facilitated formation of a large number of self-help groups throughout the length and breadth of the state. There are more than 30 lakh women from weaker sections of society who have become members of these groups and saving one rupee a day and rotate the money through a group interaction which starts as a process of empowerment.

All over the world there is a realization that the best way to tackle poverty and enable the community to improve its quality of life is through social mobilization of the poor, especially women, into self-help groups.

Self-Help Groups in Tirupati of Andhra Pradesh

Rayalaseems Seva Samithi (RASS) in Tirupati (AP) is one of the non-governmental organizations promoting thrift among women. The income generating programme by RASS is operated for initiating savings among women through self-help groups. The women of 10-15 members form into a group. Every month they meet and a deposit small amount of money, Rs 20-50 or above in the form of savings. If they have taken a loan from the group, they pay a part of loan amount every month as agreed before, with interest. The amount of interest is decided during the formation of group by the members. RASS also provides the loan amount of double the savings of the group which is shared by 2 or 3 members of the group depending on their need. Many of the group women started self-employment ventures like milk business, tailoring shops, small tea canteens, textile business, etc., by utilizing the money taken as loans.

Objectives of the Study

- To study the functioning of self-help groups.
- To analyse the role of self-help groups in the social, economic and political empowerment of women.

- To understand the nature of participation of Women in self-help groups.
- To understand the future plan of women with regard to their savings.

Methodology

Area of Study

The present Research study was conducted in a voluntary organization, i.e., RASS which is covering the entire Rayalaseema region in Andhra Pradesh with its services Jeevakona, which is situated in Tirupati town, is taken for selecting the sample as the oldest groups are operating in this area from the starting of the project.

Selection of Sample

The income generating scheme in Tirupati urban is running effectively. Out of ten groups fifty per cent of groups have been selected, i.e., five groups and from each group ten women beneficiaries were selected and altogether fifty women beneficiaries were selected by adopting the method of simple random sampling.

Tools of Data Collection

The data was collected with the help of an interview schedule to measure the socio-economic background of the respondents, income levels, expenditure and savings and involvement of women in SHGs and future plans with special reference to self-help groups under RASS.

For the purpose of the study the interview schedule was developed with open and closed questions which were compiled in English. The information was collected from the respondents through the interview method in Telugu as the respondents were Telugu speaking people and analysed manually.

Major Findings of the Study

The typical respondents, 24 per cent, belong to the age group of 25 to 29 years and their family members (32%) main occupation is business. The modal respondents in 24 per cent of the family members are earning in the range of Rs 500 to Rs 1,000 per month. Most of them, 34 per cent, have petty businesses. The majority of respondents, 86 per cent, utilize savings from SHGs when in urgent need. All the respondents replied that they are saving from their earnings through self-help groups.

Most of the respondents took the loans from the group fund. Over two-fifths, 41.6 per cent, took loans for the purpose of business. Almost one-fourth, 24.9 per cent who are illiterates, took loans for the purpose of sheep/goat/cattle rearing. The rest of them have taken loans for cultivation, petty shops, tailoring, etc. Nine in ten respondents are properly repaying their debts.

From the study it is clear that women were very active in participating in the group and in saving money. Frequent meetings of women as a routine exercise of self-help groups enable them besides setting the business matters, to interact and communicate with each other and share their problems and suggest solutions which tend to boost their confidence. This in turn will have manifest and latent consequences on the interpersonal relations both in the family and community.

Impact of SHGs on Empowerment of Women

All the members of the groups are asked to state the changes and improvements they have achieved as a result of their association with SHG. The vast majority, 90 per cent, appreciated and acknowledged the all-round benefits of SHG.

The Achievements of SHG Women are:

- Economic empowerment and improvement in economic status.
- Social mobility increased through exposure to the outside world.
- Awareness on small family norm and adoption of family planning increased.
- Developed team spirit.
- Nutrition and health status improved through greater awareness and better utilization of health services.
- Interaction with the government officials and started questioning the government agencies to get their rights.
- In the family decision-making capacities increased and fairly attained equality in family matters.
- Awareness of age at marriage law increased.
- Social mobility and free movements within and outside the village increased.
- Habit of reading newspaper and watching television increased to get more information about day-to-day affairs and government programmes and policies.

Strategies for the Sustainability of SHGs

The following are some of the strategies to ensure the sustainability of SHGs.

- Effective participation of all members and making decisions democratically on consensual basis after in-depth discussions in the group meetings.
- High level of motivation of members and group has internalized the essential concepts of self-help and mutual help as building blocks of the group.
- To evolve and introduce appropriate savings products for regular and special savings are used for internal lending for consumption and /or production needs.
- Group is able to screen the loan requests and approves loans based on the individual needs.
- Collateral consists of mutual confidence and trust.
- To decide upon appropriate market related interest rate and facilitate the process of internal capitalization.
- Enforce repayment of loans through peer pressure and group dynamics.
- To participate in social issues of mutual interests like literacy, health care and family planning, immunization, enrolment of children in schools, participation in community works and others.
- Improvement in access to credit.
- Creation of common and community assets.
- Greater awareness of the need to higher economic operations.
- To provide favourable climate for conscious leadership development, decentralized decision-making, peer pressure and sustainability of group action.

Suggestions for the Improvement of SHGs

- Adult and continuing education programmes can be conducted for illiterate women workers.
- Women should undergo vocational training programmes to utilize the money in a proper way.
- The members may be given training on managerial and leadership skills and may be motivated to present themselves in Panchayat elections and to take part in the political activities.

- The SHG members may be motivated to prepare annual action plans in their group which will be useful in planning their activities efficiently.

Conclusion

The self-help groups (SHGs) are informal voluntary associations of people formed to attain a collective goal of people who are homogenous with respect to social background, heritage, caste or traditional occupations came together for a common cause to raise and manage resources for the benefits of group members. 'All for all' is the principle behind the concept of self-help groups. SHGs, a mini voluntary organization for self-help at the micro level has been a focus of programmes for the weaker sections particularly women for their social defence. SHGs are fast emerging as a 'women's movement' throughout the nation and especially in Andhra Pradesh, where 50 per cent of India's self-help groups have been formed. This activism within the women's movement has influenced policy and planning of the government for development and empowerment of women.

Select References

Boserup, Ester (1970), *Women's Role in Economic Development,* New York: St. Martins' Press, New York.

Devasia, Leelamma and V.V. Devasia (1994), *Empowering Women for Sustainable Development,* New Delhi: Ashish Publishing House.

Hall, Margaret C. (1992), *Women and Empowerment,* Washington: Hemisphere Publishing Corporation.

Karmakar, K.G. (1999), *Rural Credit and Self Help Groups,* New Delhi: Sage Publications.

Kurtz, L.F. (1997), *Self Help and Support Groups,* New Delhi: Sage Publications.

Pillai, J.K. (1995), *Women and Empowerment,* New Delhi: Gyan Publishing House.

Singh, Arun K. (2000), *Empowerment of Women in India,* New Delhi: Manak Publications Pvt. Ltd.

Suguna, B. (2001), Women's Empowerment: Concept and Framework, *Social Welfare,* 48 (9), December.

— (2002), Strategies for Empowerment of Rural Women, *Social Welfare*, 49 (5), August.

— (2003), An Evaluation of Self Help Groups in Savings and Credit, *Journal of Sri Aurobindo Anusilan Society*, May.

— (2004), Empowerment of Rural Women through Self Help Groups: A Perspective, In R. Venkata Ravi (ed.), *Empowerment of People*, New Delhi: Kanishka Publishers.

Sunder Raj, D. (2004), SHGs and Women's Empowerment, *Social Welfare*, 50 (10), January.

14

An Examination of Empowerment of Women

A Study of Women in Kerala and India

SAJINI SHAJY AND SHAJY ISAC

In the Indian society and elsewhere women are mostly confined within the four walls of the home and dismissed as a 'second sex'. They have little voice in decision-making in the family. However, this is gradually changing and women's movements have developed to fight for the rights of women. The struggle for legal equality has been one of the major concerns of the women's movements all over the world whether it is in the internal situation of women's position in the parental or matrimonial home or in the external situation of acquiring education, skills, profession, employment, government and other activities.

As the saying 'charity begins at home' suggests if the woman has a voice in decision-making in her family, then it is easier to enforce the law and bring about changes. Attempts at bringing about changes in the status of women through either legislation or judicial activism can achieve little success without a simultaneous movement to change the social and economic structures and the culture (values, ideologies and attitude) of society.

Neglect of woman power in our society is perhaps the most important cause of our backwardness. According to the Census 2001, 46 per cent of the women in India are illiterate, most of them live in the remote parts of the country, and are not even aware of their rights. Therefore, they do not demand the enforcement of their rights within the family, community, or nation.

Only a few women have left the sheltered and protected life of home and managed to venture into the wider world. A literate and working woman cannot only minimize the wasteful expenditure on marriage and population growth but also plan the family budget and nutrition in a better way. She can break the barriers of superstition and evil customs and help to create a new society where women play a vital role. Though women constitute half of India's population, without proper education and training they can hardly become part in the development process. Education to a woman means educating the whole family. This results in eradication of poverty as well as removal of inequalities between men and women. On the other hand, suppression of women leads to suppression of progressive ideas.

It is an acknowledged fact that the roles of women as wives and mothers are associated with less power and prerogatives than the roles of men in the family with the result that there is a wide disparity.

Role of Women in the Development of the Nation

India is a developing country, which depends very much on its vast potential of human resources. If these resources are properly tapped, the country is bound to progress efficiently, effectively and rapidly. Women form the most important part of the human resources of the nation and they may contribute very substantially in building a strong, powerful and affluent nation. They can make their best contribution when they are properly educated and are able to explode the myths which have kept them in a state of backwardness and neglect.

The outlook of the women has changed considerably during the last four decades. Much of this is due to the expansion of education that has taken place in the country. The young women of today are neither afraid to move out of their homes nor as dependent on their parents or husbands as were their mothers and grandmothers. The woman wants to be economically independent. She has realized the importance of education and is quite conscious of the need of raising the standard of living of the family through her engagement in the world of work. The most striking fact given these changes is that women still play the subordinate role in family decision-making.

Meaning of Empowerment

Empowerment can be defined as the process by which the powerless gain greater control over the circumstances of their own lives; control relating to both resources and ideology. The power relation that has to be transformed includes women's lives at multiple inter-linked levels; the household/family, the community, the market and the state. Empowering women is important in securing their reproductive and sexual rights which are universally valid. Paula England and George Farkas (1986) offers a model where women's empowerment is based on social and economic conditions. Women's empowerment is the actor's self-interest defined as "anything the woman might want – food, medical care, shelter, income, respectful treatment for herself, a job, property, freedom from violence, sexual pleasure, the family size she desires and so on". Acting in one's self-interest is influenced by the use of power, which in turn has two interacting components: objective power (economic resources, laws and institutional rules and norms held by others) and subjective power (self-efficacy and entitlement).

Empowerment also means the 'ability to assert oneself' striving for upward mobility or attaining the psychological state of being powerful. But ability to assert one's self or to do things is dependent on cultural norms and institutional arrangements that regulate their lives. The social rules and roles keep women's needs and achievements outside the purview of the public world. The emphasis on women's rights to move around freely, to work outside the home, to bodily integrity and freedom from violence, to vote and to education are all crucial for women's empowerment. Emphasis is laid on equal rights in the practical sphere and also in challenging the patriarchal structure of society.

But the idea of empowerment through gaining equal rights has been challenged by radical feminists who feel that separate sets of rights are required for the full empowerment of women (Jones, 1985; Shiva, 1988; Gilligan, 1982). According to this view equal rights simply allow women the right to compete for masculine achievements. Equal rights do not attend to the rights necessary for pursuing activities, which are traditionally associated with women's roles. It can only enable women to get the same education, apply for the same jobs and vote, but 'family' issues such as childbirth, childcare, support, nurturing, and sustenance of less able members of the family are all left outside the purview of 'real' work and 'real' social needs. Thus women's rights need to be redefined as 'human rights', which are specifically women's concern.

The Indian Situation

Women in much of the world lack support for fundamental functions of a human life. They are less well nourished than men, less healthy, more vulnerable to physical and sexual abuse. They are much less likely than men to be illiterate; and still less likely to have professional or technical education. Should they attempt to enter the workplace, they face greater obstacles including intimidation from family or spouse, sex discrimination on hiring and sexual harassment in the workplace – all frequently without effective legal recourse. Similar obstacles often impede their effective participation in political life. In many nations, women are not full equals under the law; they do not have the same property rights as men, the same rights to make a contract, the same rights of associations, mobility and religious liberty. Burdened often with the 'double day' of taxing employment and full responsibility for housework and childcare, they lack opportunities for play and the cultivation of their imaginative and cognitive faculties. All these factors take their toll on emotional well-being. Women have fewer opportunities than men to live free from fear and to enjoy rewarding types of love – especially when, as often, they are married without choice in childhood and have no recourse from a bad marriage. In all these ways, unequal social and political circumstances give women unequal human capabilities.

The work a woman does at home or outside is often monotonous and of a nagging nature. Women's health is very much neglected in village society. It is true that among poor people where bare subsistence is difficult, better health care and medical aids belong to the category of luxury for both men and women. The only luxury the men in such a situation may have is taking rest at home without doing any manual work. Women in general are denied even such rest. The workload and responsibilities of women of the well-off section is not that hard compared to that of poor women. But by and large their lifestyle is culturally circumscribed. Women of relatively higher castes and higher income group do not go for manual jobs. Their life is relatively comfortable but social position remains almost the same. The women of lower castes and lower income groups mostly go for wage labour. This suggests that when there is no other means of subsistence than human labour, cultural impediments or constraints do not seem to be at work. Women put their entire labour for survival of the group.

Women's employment as agricultural or casual labour is almost pan-Indian in nature. Women workers primarily depend on agriculture. Agarwal in this context comments "while the dependence on wage work has been increasing for both men and women, the influence has been greater for women; by census figures, in 1961, 25.6 per cent rural female workers and 16.2 per cent of rural male workers were agricultural labourers; by 1981 the figures for women and men had increased to 49.6 per cent and 24.3 per cent respectively, namely agricultural wage work as their main source of earnings" (1992:37). This suggests that women have very little choice or scope for employment beyond their immediate surrounding. Due to higher domestic responsibility, they prefer to work near their home even with less wage. Another important finding is that if women spend their earnings for the family and for spending money on themselves they are required to ask for permission from their respective husbands or heads of household. Conversely, men particularly from poor households, spend at least one-third of their earning if not more, for their personal amusement, including indulgence in various kinds of addiction. Among the low-income category, the family is benefited where women go out for work. Their children get better nourishment. But it cannot be said that as the women earn they enjoy relatively better treatment. Often women are found malnourished because priority in terms of food and rest go in favour of the males.

The process of socialization too helps to perpetuate the system based gender inequality. The girl child is a victim of unequal treatment and many other forms of discrimination. Even the well-off families do not encourage expenditure on girls' education. Among the poor from the age of five, girls are supposed to help their mothers in the work of baby-sitting. At the age of ten they behave like grown-up girls, sharing the same load of poverty as their mothers do. On the other hand boys of that age roam freely, can attend school and learn any trade. The sharp gender inequality gets reflected in the high infant mortality for girls and skewed sex ratio of the country.

Women in the rural areas in general are not aware of their rights and privileges. Their attitude is fatalistic and they have accepted their subservient position. The gender-based process of socialization creates a sense of inferiority among women. It sets two norms – one is for making a person who is useful to society, the other is merely a mode of sexism, which dictates the gender role for women and creates a gender bias in the society. A boy, irrespective of his economic or caste background grows up as an individual with dignity and respect. He can think for himself, he is for the society and the society is for him. On the other hand, women live for others, their survival depends on the mercy of others. They themselves do not honour their being, as if they are born to be ill-treated. Development activities have not done any major good to the life of rural women; at least women have been exposed to the outside world through some general development programmes implemented in their respective villages or due to improved communication network or electronic media. They can perceive a way beyond their own village – a society where women are better placed. They also vaguely aspire for that sort of life for their children. It is almost universally observed that poor women earnestly plead for employment opportunities through which they can provide some comfort to themselves and their family members. This demonstrates that women in general are more concerned about the well-being of their families.

The outside employment gives women some freedom and some sort of self-confidence though it does not ensure better status in society. Hence it is expected that if women folk can develop themselves, the overall development of society may be enhanced at a much faster pace. The development of women does not depend solely on the role that women play in the development process. Nevertheless gender inequality acts as a great barrier to women's development. A shift is necessary in the development perspective and women's development as such should be integrated to the overall structure and functioning of the society.

Rationales and Objective of the Study

As stated, the low social and economic profile coupled with the cultural set-up in India often determined low status of women in India. Therefore, the present study aims to understand the status of women in two contrasting populations, viz., Kerala and India. The Kerala model has been the focus of international attention for its success in several areas including education, health and family planning. The state is often mentioned as a good example to show that the lives of people can be significantly transformed through public action, especially through government policies and programmes.

The state has achieved international fame for its success in controlling deaths, especially infant deaths and unwanted deaths (Bhat and Irudaya Rajan, 1990; Irudaya Rajan, et al., 1996). Kerala's family planning programme, maternal and child health (MCH) programme and adult literacy programme have been acclaimed as model programmes by the World Bank, UNICEF, and other international organizations and bodies.

On the other hand, India as a whole, being an agrarian society with majority being rural and illiterate, has women with much lower social status. The demographic trends seen in Kerala and India as a whole can be found in Table 14.1.

Table 14.1

Development Indicators: Kerala and India

Indicator	*Period*	*Kerala*	*India*
Expectation of life at birth			
Female	1995-96	72.4	61.7
Male		67.2	60.6
Birth rate	2000**	17.9	25.8
Death rate	2000**	6.4	8.5
Exponential growth rate	2001*	0.9	1.9
Sex ratio (No. of females per 1000 males)	2001*	1058	933
Infant mortality rate (per 1000 live birth)	2000**	13.9	67.8
Maternal Mortality rate (per 1000 live birth)	1990	1.3	5.7
Literacy rate	2001*		
Female		87.9	54.0
Male		94.2	75.6
Scheduled caste	2001*	9.8	16.2
Scheduled tribe		1.1	8.2
Age at marriage	2000***		
Female		21.5	19.7

* Census of India, 2001; ** SRS Bulletin, April 2002; *** IIPS 2000.

The present study examines the status of women in these two populations, Kerala and India, through a set of indicators. Our prime focus is:

(i) To examine the status of women in various population under a single law

(ii) To examine the key variables that determine the status of women

(iii) To analyse subpopulations on the basis of status of women

In order to achieve the stated objectives, we identified the proxy variables as (i) How far the women need permission to visit friends/relatives, (ii) If the women are allowed to keep money at their side, and (iii) if the women are permitted to go to market.

Data and Methodology

The data used for this study is the NFHS (National Family Health Survey) conducted in 1998-1999. The survey covered a representative sample of 89,199 eligible women (currently married women) aged 15-49 years from 26 States that existed at the time of the survey. In Kerala a sample of 2,884 eligible women were covered for the survey. For the present study as mentioned, Kerala and India have been selected to understand the differences that exist in the empowerment of the women. In order to understand the suitable indicators of women's empowerment, this study examines two sets of indicators in these different socio-cultural settings.

- The first category is referred to as indirect indicators of empowerment and includes education, age difference between spouses, education of spouse, and exposure to mass media. These characteristics have relevance in influencing a woman's access to control over resources.
- The next three indicators used for measuring empowerment of women are the direct indicators, which involve indicators such as involvement in decision-making, freedom of movement and access to money. These indicators tend to provide evidence of empowerment (see Kishore, 1998). Women's autonomy is likely to have a significant impact on the demographic and health seeking behaviour of the couple by altering women's relative control over fertility and contraceptive use, and by influencing their attitudes (for example, attitudes towards the sex composition of children) and abilities (for example, the ability to obtain health services for themselves and their children) (Sen

and Batliwala, 1997). However this aspect has not been covered in this study.

The study also examines the determinants of status of women in the study populations using a multivariate approach and controls for different subpopulations defined by social characteristics.

Analysis and Findings

The following sections discuss the study findings to examine the objectives under study.

Distribution of Women

This section examines the profile of the study sample in both populations. Table 14.1 shows that only 23.1 per cent and 26.2 per cent live in urban areas in Kerala and India, respectively. While the majority of each population belong to Hindu religion (51.3% in Kerala and 81.8% in India), Kerala is more diverse. While only 9.8 per cent of women belong to Scheduled Caste or Scheduled Tribes (SC/ST) in Kerala, 27.3 per cent belong to the same group in India. The age distribution of the women indicates that age at marriage in Kerala is much higher than that in India as only 3.1 per cent women belong to 15-19 years, whereas 9.2 per cent in India marry that young.

Table 14.2

Distribution of currently married women, Kerala and India

Characteristics		*Kerala*		*India*	
		Number	*Per cent*	*Number*	*Per cent*
Place of residence	Urban	667	23.1	23370	26.2
	Rural	2217	76.9	65829	73.8
Religion	Hindu	1478	51.3	72903	81.8
	Muslim	941	32.6	11190	12.6
	Christian	462	16.0	2263	2.5
	Others	2	0.1	2763	3.1
Ethnicity	Scheduled caste	252	8.7	16301	18.5
	Scheduled tribe	32	1.1	7750	8.8
	Other backward caste	1244	43.1	29383	33.3
	None of them	1356	47.0	34904	39.5
Age 5-year groups	15-19	89	3.1	8182	9.2

Contd...

Contd...

	20-24	370	12.8	16389	18.4
	25-29	553	19.2	17745	19.9
	30-34	527	18.3	15094	16.9
	35-39	520	18.0	13089	14.7
	40-44	445	15.4	10521	11.8
	45-49	381	13.2	8179	9.2
Marital duration	0-4	558	19.4	17071	19.1
	5-9	496	17.2	16849	18.9
	10-14	519	18.0	15774	17.7
	15-19	478	16.6	13687	15.3
	20-24	414	14.4	11648	13.1
	25-29	301	10.4	8922	10.0
	30+	118	4.1	5248	5.9
Children Ever Born	0-2	1844	63.9	41278	46.3
	3-4	849	29.4	29255	32.8
	5+	191	6.6	18666	20.9
Household members	0-2	64	2.2	2992	3.4
	3-4	831	28.8	20458	22.9
	5+	1989	68.9	65749	73.7
Education	Illiterate	362	12.6	51871	58.2
	Literate, < middle school complete	871	30.2	17270	19.4
	Middle school complete	493	17.1	7328	8.2
	High school complete and above	1158	40.2	12719	14.3
Husband's education	Illiterate	223	7.7	27449	30.8
	Literate, < middle school complete	1050	36.4	22604	25.3
	Middle school complete	524	18.2	11907	13.3
	High school complete and above	1076	37.3	26973	30.2
Household SLI	Low	448	15.5	29033	32.9
	Medium	1590	55.1	41289	46.8
	High	846	29.3	17845	20.2
Exposure to media	No	343	11.9	36997	41.5
	Yes	2541	88.1	52202	58.5
Total		2884	100.0	89199	100.0

We have noticed that the fertility rate in Kerala is much lower. From Table 14.2 we see 63.9 per cent of women in Kerala have a maximum of 2 children, while only 46.3 per cent in India do. As far as the educational level is concerned, literacy level in Kerala is much higher and only 12.6 per cent women and 7.7 per cent husbands are illiterate. Illiteracy among women in India is 58.2 per cent and that among husbands is also high at 30.8 per cent. Socio-economic status is defined using the index, standard of living index (SLI) and only 15.5 per cent women in Kerala are from low SLI households, but 32.9 per cent of women in India belong to the same.

Women who need Permission to Visit Friends/Relatives

NFHS (1998-99) collected information regarding the freedom of movement for currently married women. Specifically, the survey collected information from women about needing permission to visit friends/relatives. Therefore, one proxy to measure the women's status is this very freedom of movement and shown in Table 14.3.

Table 14.3

Per cent currently married women who need permission to visit friends/relatives

Characteristics		*Kerala*				*India*			
		No	*Yes*	*Not allowed to go*	*Total*	*No*	*Yes*	*Not allowed to go*	*Total*
Place of residence	Urban	44.6	54.4	0.9	667	35.0	64.1	0.9	23370
	Rural	35.8	63.6	0.5	2217	20.6	77.6	1.8	65829
Religion	Hindu	43.0	56.8	0.2	1478	24.6	73.8	1.6	72903
	Muslim	30.7	68.3	1.0	941	19.0	79.3	1.7	11190
	Christian	35.8	62.8	1.4	462	35.6	63.7	0.7	2263
	Others	56.1	43.9	0.0	2	31.2	68.5	0.3	2763
Ethnicity	Scheduled caste	45.8	53.7	0.4	252	23.7	74.7	1.5	16301
	Scheduled tribe	38.7	61.3	0.0	32	26.3	72.9	0.8	7750
	Other backward caste	37.5	62.1	0.4	1244	26.6	71.4	2.0	29383
	None of them	36.7	62.4	0.9	1356	22.7	76.0	1.4	34904
Age 5-year groups	15-19	14.5	85.5	0.0	89	10.2	85.9	3.9	8182
	20-24	24.9	74.2	0.9	370	16.6	81.3	2.1	16389

Contd...

Contd...

	25-29	28.9	70.3	0.8	553	21.1	77.4	1.5	17745
	30-34	38.3	60.9	0.8	527	25.1	73.7	1.2	15094
	35-39	41.8	58.2	0.0	520	29.8	69.3	1.0	13089
	40-44	48.4	50.4	1.1	445	35.1	63.9	1.0	10521
	45-49	50.7	49.1	0.2	381	37.5	61.7	0.8	8179
Marital duration	0-4	22.3	76.6	1.1	558	16.0	81.2	2.8	17071
	5-9	32.1	67.6	0.4	496	19.5	78.7	1.8	16849
	10-14	39.7	59.6	0.6	519	23.1	75.5	1.4	15774
	15-19	41.5	57.8	0.6	478	26.3	72.6	1.1	13687
	20-24	46.8	52.7	0.5	414	31.1	68.0	0.9	11648
	25-29	48.3	51.3	0.4	301	34.2	64.7	1.1	8922
	30+	54.8	44.6	0.6	118	34.8	64.5	0.7	5248
Children Ever Born	1-2	37.5	61.8	0.7	1844	23.6	74.5	1.9	41278
	3-4	38.4	61.1	0.5	849	25.5	73.3	1.2	29255
	5+	39.2	59.9	1.0	191	24.3	74.1	1.5	18666
Household members	1-2	60.0	40.0	0.0	64	39.4	59.5	1.1	2992
	3-4	47.0	52.7	0.2	831	32.1	67.0	0.9	20458
	5+	33.3	65.9	0.8	1989	21.3	76.9	1.8	65749
Education	Illiterate	44.2	55.5	0.3	362	21.6	76.5	1.9	51871
	Literate, < middle school complete	39.3	59.7	1.1	871	24.3	74.4	1.3	17270
	Middle school complete	37.8	62.0	0.2	493	25.6	73.1	1.3	7328
	High school complete and above	34.8	64.6	0.6	1158	35.0	64.1	0.9	12719
Husband's education	Illiterate	38.9	59.9	1.2	223	22.4	76.1	1.6	27449
	Literate, < middle school complete	38.6	60.8	0.7	1050	24.4	74.2	1.5	22604
	Middle school complete	35.3	64.4	0.3	524	21.6	76.5	1.9	11907
	High school complete and above	38.2	61.1	0.7	1076	27.6	70.8	1.6	26973
Household SLI	Low	44.4	55.3	0.2	448	23.0	75.3	1.7	29033
	Medium	34.9	64.3	0.8	1590	22.8	75.5	1.7	41289
	High	40.0	59.6	0.4	846	30.2	68.7	1.1	17845
Exposure to media	No	39.3	58.7	2.0	343	20.0	77.9	2.1	36997
	Yes	37.7	61.9	0.4	2541	27.5	71.3	1.2	52202
Total		37.9	61.5	0.6	2884	24.4	74.0	1.6	89199

In India, only 24 per cent of the women have the freedom to visit their friends or relatives as compared with 38 per cent of the women in Kerala. Freedom of movement increases rapidly with age. For example, only 14 per cent of women aged 15-19 years in Kerala do not need permission to visit their friends or relatives as compared with 51 per cent women in the age group 45-49 years. Similarly, in the country as a whole 10 per cent in the age group 15-19 years does not need permission to visit their friends or relatives as compared with 38 per cent in the higher age group of 45-49 years. A similar trend was noticed as far as the marital duration is concerned. Urban women have more freedom to visit their friends or relatives than their counterparts in the rural areas. This trend can be seen in both the nation and Kerala.

Forty-five per cent of the urban women in Kerala have the freedom to visit their friends or relatives, whereas in the rural set-up only 36 per cent has this freedom. In India, the figures are slightly less with 35 per cent in the urban areas and 21 per cent in the rural areas. As far as the religion is concerned, we find that only 31 per cent Muslims in Kerala have the freedom to visit their friends or relatives, which is lower than that among Hindus (43%). It may be noted that comparison to Kerala women, the women in India all the religious groups have less freedom to go visiting (19%) and 24.6 per cent respectively among Hindu and Muslim religions.

Number of household members may be a determining factor in decision-making in the family. It also may lead to the status of women in various populations. Analysing the table, it is found that while 60 per cent women with at least 2 household members do not need permission to visit friends/relatives, only 33.3 per cent do not need permission if the household has more than 5 members. Though the level is much lower in India, a similar trend could be noticed. Education effect is not noticed in Kerala, but it has a clear indication in India with increasing the proportion of women who do not need permission from 21.6 per cent to 35 per cent from illiterate to literate with more than high school education.

Comparing the state with the nation, women in Kerala have a greater freedom in this aspect. Employment was not considered as the data revealed that housewives were an overwhelming proportion covered in the sample.

Women who are Allowed to Keep Money

Using the information collected in the NFHS, Table 14.4 gives the information with regard to freedom to keep money aside for their personal use.

Table 14.4

Per cent currently married women allowed to keep money set aside

Characteristics		*Kerala*			*India*		
		No	*Yes*	*Total*	*No*	*Yes*	*Total*
Type of place of residence	Urban	28.0	72.0	667	26.3	73.7	23370
	Rural	35.6	64.4	2217	45.2	54.8	65829
Religion	Hindu	27.4	72.6	1478	40.5	59.5	72903
	Muslim	47.4	52.6	941	43.8	56.2	11190
	Christian	26.7	73.3	462	31.2	68.8	2263
	Others	43.9	56.1	2	27.7	72.3	2763
Ethnicity	Scheduled caste	32.6	67.4	252	43.9	56.1	16301
	Scheduled tribe	33.5	66.5	32	49.1	50.9	7750
	Other backward caste	36.4	63.6	1244	37.5	62.5	29383
	None of them	31.7	68.3	1356	38.8	61.2	34904
Age 5-year groups	15-19	49.7	50.3	89	54.4	45.6	8182
	20-24	37.6	62.4	370	45.8	54.2	16389
	25-29	34.6	65.4	553	41.0	59.0	17745
	30-34	31.2	68.8	527	38.7	61.3	15094
	35-39	33.6	66.4	520	35.5	64.5	13089
	40-44	33.2	66.8	445	33.9	66.1	10521
	45-49	30.1	69.9	381	32.2	67.8	8179
Marital duration	0-4	33.4	66.6	558	45.2	54.8	17071
	5-9	33.8	66.2	496	43.0	57.0	16849
	10-14	34.5	65.5	519	41.4	58.6	15774
	15-19	30.1	69.9	478	38.4	61.6	13687
	20-24	36.5	63.5	414	35.8	64.2	11648
	25-29	36.0	64.0	301	35.2	64.8	8922
	30+	34.1	65.9	118	35.2	64.8	5248

Contd...

Contd...

Children Ever Born	1-2	30.3	69.7	1844	39.4	60.6	41278
	3-4	37.1	62.9	849	39.6	60.4	29255
	5+	53.7	46.3	191	43.2	56.8	18666
Household members	1-2	17.1	82.9	64	28.7	71.3	2992
	3-4	25.6	74.4	831	34.1	65.9	20458
	5+	37.8	62.2	1989	42.7	57.3	65749
Education	Illiterate	43.8	56.2	362	47.1	52.9	51871
	Literate,<middle school complete	41.2	58.8	871	38.5	61.5	17270
	Middle school complete	37.0	63.0	493	33.3	66.7	7328
	High school complete and above	23.9	76.1	1158	18.9	81.1	12719
Husband's education	Illiterate	45.1	54.9	223	47.4	52.6	27449
	Literate, < middle school complete	42.6	57.4	1050	43.4	56.6	22604
	Middle school complete	34.3	65.7	524	42.9	57.1	11907
	High school complete and above	22.8	77.2	1076	29.2	70.8	26973
Standard of Living	Low	37.2	62.8	448	47.7	52.3	29033
	Medium	40.0	60.0	1590	41.7	58.3	41289
	High	20.5	79.5	846	24.7	75.3	17845
Exposure to media	No	57.9	42.1	343	50.9	49.1	36997
	Yes	30.6	69.4	2541	32.7	67.3	52202
Total		33.8	66.2	2884	40.3	59.7	89199

In India, only 60 per cent of the women have the freedom to keep money for their personal use as compared with 66 per cent of the women in Kerala. Freedom to keep money for their personal use increases rapidly with age, education, and household standard of living. The minimal differences between Kerala and India are dwarfed by the impact of increasing age, education and standard of living. For example, only 50 per cent of women aged 15-19 years in Kerala keep money for their personal use as compared with 70 per cent women in the age group 45-49 years. Similarly, in the country as a whole, 46 per cent in the age group 15-19 years keep money for themselves as compared with 68 per cent in the higher age group of

45-49 years. Urban women have more freedom to keep some money for their personal use than their counterparts in the rural areas. This trend can be seen in both the Nation and Kerala as well. Seventy-two per cent of the urban women in Kerala have the freedom to save money for their personal use whereas in the rural set-up only 64 per cent has this freedom. In India the figures are just under 74 per cent urban and 55 per cent rural.

As far as the religion is concerned, we find that Muslim women have the least freedom to keep money for their personal use. Comparing the state with the nation, women in Kerala have a greater freedom in this aspect. Education as a variable reveals that as literacy increases the women have more power to keep money aside for their personal use. This can be observed in both the state as well as the national level. The education of the husband also reveals a greater freedom for the women to keep money for their personal use. The status of scheduled caste/tribe women in Kerala seems to be much better than women in the other parts of the nation with regard to the power to keep money for themselves. In most of these statistics, the women in Kerala hold a better position than their counterparts in other states.

Women who need Permission to Go to Market

We also examined how the need for permission to go to market is an indicator of the status of women. Table 14.5 gives the information with regard to the freedom of women to go to the market.

In India, only 32 per cent of the women have the freedom to visit the market as compared with 48 per cent of the women in Kerala. Freedom of movement increases rapidly with age. For example, only 28 per cent of women aged 15-19 years in Kerala do not need permission to visit the market as compared with 57 per cent women in the age group 45-49 years. Similarly, in the country as a whole 14 per cent in the age group 15-19 years does not need permission to visit the market as compared with 45 per cent in the higher age group of 45-49 years. Urban women have more freedom to go to the market without permission than their counterparts in the rural areas. This trend can be seen in both the Nation and Kerala as well. Fifty eight per cent of the urban Kerala women have the freedom to visit the market whereas as in the rural set up only 45 per cent have this freedom. In India the figures are about 47 per cent in urban and 26 per cent in rural have this freedom to visit markets without permission.

Table 14.5
Per cent currently married women permission needed to go to market

Characteristics		*Kerala*				*India*			
		No	*Yes*	*Not allowed*	*Total*	*No*	*Yes*	*Not allowed*	*Total*
Place of residence	Urban	57.7	39.6	2.7	667	46.9	49.8	3.3	23370
	Rural	44.7	51.5	3.7	2217	26.2	66.7	7.1	65829
Religion	Hindu	55.7	42.0	2.3	1478	31.8	62.0	6.2	72903
	Muslim	34.6	60.6	4.8	941	23.4	69.4	7.1	11190
	Christian	48.9	46.5	4.6	462	44.6	53.3	2.1	2263
	Others	100	0.0	0.0	2	47.9	49.1	3.0	2763
Ethnicity	Scheduled caste	58.3	40.4	1.3	252	31.3	63.3	5.3	16301
	Scheduled tribe	59.3	40.7	0.0	32	30.7	64.4	4.9	7750
	Other backward caste	49.0	48.5	2.6	1244	34.7	58.6	6.7	29383
	None of them	44.3	50.8	4.9	1356	29.6	64.2	6.2	34904
Age 5-year groups	15-19	27.5	68.8	3.7	89	13.8	73.7	12.6	8182
	20-24	33.6	60.9	5.5	370	22.0	70.0	8.0	16389
	25-29	39.1	56.8	4.1	553	28.8	65.2	6.0	17745
	30-34	48.5	48.9	2.6	527	34.0	60.8	5.3	15094
	35-39	52.7	45.0	2.3	520	37.9	57.9	4.2	13089
	40-44	59.4	36.2	4.4	445	43.0	52.9	4.1	10521
	45-49	57.1	40.3	2.6	381	45.4	51.2	3.4	8179
Marital duration	0-4	31.8	62.9	5.2	558	22.1	68.9	9.0	17071
	5-9	45.5	50.5	4.0	496	26.3	66.7	7.1	16849
	10-14	48.9	49.5	1.6	519	31.1	63.3	5.6	15774
	15-19	52.3	44.3	3.5	478	34.4	60.2	5.3	13687
	20-24	56.6	39.8	3.7	414	38.8	56.8	4.3	11648
	25-29	53.8	42.8	3.5	301	41.0	54.6	4.4	8922
	30+	61.9	36.5	1.6	118	41.6	54.2	4.2	5248
Children Ever Born	1-2	47.5	48.9	3.7	1844	30.8	62.6	6.6	41278
	3-4	50.2	46.8	3.0	849	33.8	60.7	5.6	29255
	5+	39.0	56.8	4.2	191	29.8	64.2	6.0	18666
Household members	1-2	70.3	29.7	0.0	64	48.4	47.4	4.2	2992
	3-4	57.6	38.9	3.5	831	41.3	54.3	4.4	20458

Contd...

Contd...

	5+	42.8	53.5	3.6	1989	27.8	65.4	6.8	65749
Education	Illiterate	53.1	44.6	2.3	362	27.1	66.1	6.8	51871
	Literate, < middle school	47.9	48.1	4.0	871	32.6	61.1	6.3	17270
	Middle school complete	48.8	49.3	1.8	493	35.9	58.2	5.9	7328
	High school complete and above	45.4	50.3	4.2	1158	46.2	50.5	3.3	12719
Husband's education	Illiterate	49.2	47.7	3.1	223	27.9	66.1	6.0	27449
	Literate, <middle school	47.9	49.4	2.8	1050	31.3	62.5	6.2	22604
	Middle school complete	45.0	52.6	2.3	524	29.2	63.5	7.3	11907
	High school complete and above	48.6	46.5	4.9	1076	36.6	57.8	5.6	26973
Standard of living	Low	55.4	43.6	1.0	448	28.5	65.1	6.3	29033
	Medium	44.8	51.7	3.5	1590	30.0	63.3	6.7	41289
	High	49.2	46.0	4.8	846	40.1	55.3	4.5	17845
Exposure to media	No	45.5	50.3	4.2	343	24.1	68.6	7.3	36997
	Yes	48.0	48.6	3.4	2541	36.9	57.8	5.3	52202
Total		47.7	48.8	3.5	2884	31.6	62.3	6.1	89199

Cultural values are highly influential in the status and religion served as a key variable. We find that only 35 per cent Muslims in Kerala have the freedom to visit the market but in the all India level only 23 per cent have the freedom. For Hindus an even wider gap shows 56 per cent in Kerala versus 32 per cent in the nation as a whole. Comparing the state with the nation, women in Kerala have greater freedom in this aspect. There is less difference among Christian women so they occupy a middle position within Kerala and the lead position in India.

Multivariate Analysis for Permission Needed to Visit Friends/Relatives

In the previous section, we examined the individual effect of various socio-economic and demographic variables on the need for permission to visit friends/relatives. It was hypothesized that women from rural areas, Muslim religion, younger age and recently married, with higher number of children ever born and household members, low or medium standard of living and not exposed to media have less autonomy as compared to their counterparts. In other words, these women need permission from their spouse for visiting friends/relatives to larger extent than their counterparts.

The current section examines the combined effect of various factors on the women's autonomy vis-à-vis permission needed for visiting friends/relatives. A logistic regression approach has been evolved to examine the contributing factors in determining the woman's power. Considering the nature of the variable under examination (permission), bivariate logistic approaches enable us to see how various independent variables are contributing to the need for permission to go out to visit close associates. The variable under examination is defined as a binary variable with 0 if they do not need permission and 1 if they require permission. Table 14.6 provides the odds ratio of various independent variables on the dependent variables. In other words, it explains how the explanatory variables affect the explained variable. Also, a comparison has been made for both populations, namely, Kerala and India.

Table 14.6

Odds ratio of logistic regression for permission needed to visit friends/relatives

Characteristics	*Kerala*	*India*
Place of residence		
Urban	1.0000	1.0000
Rural	1.3293**	1.7192**
Exposure to media		
Not exposed	1.0000	1.0000
Exposed	1.0739	0.8418**
Religion		
Hindu	1.0000	1.0000
Muslim	1.2955*	1.1411**
Christian	1.4077**	0.8237**
Others	1.1150	0.8199**
Ethnicity		
SC	1.0000	1.0000

Contd...

Contd...

ST	1.1492	0.7822**
OBC	1.1961	0.8958**
Others	1.1923	1.3161**
Age		
15-19	1.0000	1.0000
20-24	0.5642	0.6153**
25-29	0.4585*	0.4405**
30-34	0.3132**	0.3394**
35-39	0.2646**	0.2623**
40-44	0.2037**	0.1996**
45-49	0.1819**	0.1799**
Education		
Illiterate	1.0000	1.0000
Literate, < middle school complete	1.0861	0.8712**
Middle school complete	1.0873	0.7633**
High school complete and above	1.3709	0.5720**
Husband's education		
Illiterate	1.0000	1.0000
Literate, < middle school complete	0.8400	0.9572
Middle school complete	0.8815	1.0784*
High school complete and above	0.6826*	1.0459
Children Ever Born		
<3	1.0000	1.0000
3-4	1.1891	1.0568*
5+	1.2362	1.2109**
Household members		
<3	1.0000	1.0000
3-4	1.2720	1.3471**
5+	1.7964*	2.0204**
Standard of living		
Low	1.0000	1.0000
Medium	1.4183**	1.1925**
High	1.1758	1.2335**
Constant	1.4652	3.3484**

* $p<0.05$; ** $p<.01$

The logistic model included place of residence, exposure to media, religion, caste, education of woman and husband, age of the woman, children ever born and household members and standard of living of the household. We expect that these variables could explain a large variation in the woman's autonomy as far as the liberty to visit her friends/relatives. The table shows that only place of residence, age, religion and standard of living of the household is highly significant in Kerala, while all the included variables exerted significance in India as a whole.

It may be noted that the rural-urban difference is significantly higher in India with a rural women 72 per cent higher (odds ratio=1.7192) than urban women in needing permission to visit even after controlling the effect of other variables. Further, the table shows that place of residence is significant in Kerala as between rural and urban areas with 33 per cent higher chance of needing permission to visit friends/relatives after controlling the effect of other variables. Exposure to media does not show any effect in Kerala, while those exposed to media in India require significantly less permission as compared to those not exposed (odds ratio=0.8418). As far as the religion is concerned, more Muslims in both Kerala and India need permission to go out as compared to Hindu religion. It is interesting to note that significantly more Christians in Kerala need permission, but less significant for them in India as compared to Hindus. Though caste is not an important factor in Kerala, it is highly important in India as a whole.

Age of the currently married women is shown to have the most important and significant factor to determine the woman's autonomy in both Kerala and India. As the age increases, more and more women are free to go out to visit friends/relatives. For instance a women in the age 45-49 years require 82 per cent less permission than a women in the age group 15-19 years in both Kerala and India (odds ratio=0.18). Education of both woman and husband did not show any significant effect in Kerala, except that highest educated husbands have wives with more permission. This lack of significance in general is probably due to high literacy and exposure to media. However education level of women in India is a significant factor. In other words, as the education of the woman increases, less and less women need permission from their spouse in India. More importantly, women who are educated high school and above require 43 per cent less permission than illiterate women.

Children ever born or the number of household members are an indication of the social status and home duties. A high socio-economic population always has fewer children. It is clear from the table that as the number of children ever born and household members increases, higher proportion of women require permission to go out and visit their friends/relative. One of the important factors the literature mentioned in determining the women's status is the standard of living of the household. It is interesting to note that higher SLI women need permission more than women in low SLI households. This is significant for middle level Kerala women and both middle and high level Indian women, perhaps reflecting aspirations to middle class values and the status of supporting a wife among higher standards of living in the nation as a whole.

Multivariate Analysis for Allowed to Keep Money Set Aside

Another indicator of women's autonomy is the degree they are allowed to keep money set aside. In other words, in a socio-economically developed society, women either work outside or women are treated equally important as their spouse. In such a scenario, men permit women to keep money at their side for their own use and for household needs. Therefore, we examine the important factors in Kerala and India that determine if the women may keep money aside for personal use.

Table 14.7

Odds ratio of logistic regression for allowed to keep money set aside

Characteristics	*Kerala*	*India*
Place of residence		
Urban	1.0000	1.0000
Rural	1.0136	0.6756**
Exposure to media		
Not exposed	1.0000	1.0000
Exposed	2.0813**	1.4235**
Religion		
Hindu	1.0000	1.0000
Muslim	0.5818**	0.9923
Christian	0.8243	1.1300*
Others	0.2086	1.4195**

Contd...

Contd...

Ethnicity		
SC	1.0000	1.0000
ST	1.1302	0.9003**
OBC	0.9972	1.1767**
Others	1.1010	0.8751**
Age		
15-19	1.0000	1.0000
20-24	1.4386	1.2376**
25-29	1.6276*	1.5278**
30-34	1.9494**	1.7345**
35-39	2.1052**	2.0097**
40-44	2.0656**	2.1565**
45-49	2.4022**	2.3280**
Education		
Illiterate	1.0000	1.0000
Literate, < middle school complete	0.8965	1.1557**
Middle school complete	0.8645	1.3382**
High school complete and above	1.1471	2.1933**
Husband's education		
Illiterate	1.0000	1.0000
Literate, < middle school complete	1.0332	0.9950
Middle school complete	1.2423	0.9549
High school complete and above	1.6638**	1.1884**
Children Ever Born		
<3	1.0000	1.0000
3-4	0.8929	1.0295
5+	0.6665*	0.9656
Household members		
<3	1.0000	1.0000
3-4	0.5780	0.6966**
5+	0.4229*	0.5053**
Standard of living		
Low	1.0000	1.0000
Medium	0.7507*	0.9892
High	1.4611*	1.2481**
Constant	1.2925	1.4540**

*p<0.05; ** p<.01

Table 14.7 present the correlates of women who are allowed to keep money set aside, using the logistic approach. The variable under study, permitted to keep money, is defined as 0 if not permitted and 1 if permitted. An odds ratio of above unity is an indication that the women in that socio-economic or demographic category are more allowed to keep money with them as compared to the reference category.

It may be noted that the exposure to media, religion, age of the woman and education of husband are highly significant factors related the women's autonomy in Kerala, while all the variables except the children ever born are highly significant in India. In other words, though rural-urban difference is noticed in Kerala, a rural woman is significantly less likely allowed to keep money with her in India by 32 per cent (odds ratio=0.6756). Further, exposure to media shown as a key factor both in Kerala and India as evident that an exposed woman is twice as likely to be allowed to keep money in Kerala, whereas 42 per cent higher in India (odds ratio 2.08 and 1.42 respectively in Kerala and India). Religion-wise, though Muslims in Kerala are significantly less allowed to keep money, the difference in India is not significant and Christian and other religions are more allowed to have money at their side as compared to Hindu religion.

As seen in case of permission needed to visit friends/relative, age is a highly significant factor in explaining women being allowed to keep money. As the age of the woman increases, more and more women are allowed to have money with them with those in the age group 35-39 years are twice likely to have money with them as compared to women in the age groups 15-19 years. Educational effect is not observed in Kerala, but as the education increases, more and more women are permitted to keep money in India and a women educated high school and above are 2.2 times more likely to possess money than an illiterate women. As far as the husband's education is concerned, a woman whose husband is educated more than high school is allowed to possess money, which is significant and is as high as 66 per cent and 19 per cent respectively in Kerala and India as compared to women whose husbands are illiterate.

While children ever born is not an important covariate to explain the women's autonomy in either population, number of household members is significant. A woman whose household members are more than 5 members is 58 per cent and 50 per cent, respectively, less allowed to have money in Kerala and India as compared to woman who has less than 3 household members. Standard of living index as defined is an indicator for the socio-economic status. We may expect that a woman from higher SLI household may be allowed to keep money than a woman from low SLI household. The study also recognizes that a woman from high SLI household is 46 per cent (Kerala) and 25 per cent (India) more likely allowed to keep money than their low SLI counterparts.

Women's Status – Exploration of Population Groups

In the previous section we have identified the significant variables affecting the women's autonomy in both Kerala and India. We found that while most of the variables under study are significant as far as India is concerned, only place of residence, religion, exposure to media and age are usually important factors in Kerala. It is, therefore important to identify a set of variables that may operate together to define a risk group to exhibit as a composite index of woman's status. We, therefore, considered four variables taking into account the nature and effect of these variables on various decisions making to define this index. The variables in the model, which we grouped together to examine the status of women in the two populations under study, are place of residence, exposure to media, woman's and her husband's education.

Table 14.8 provides the adjusted mean percentage of women who needed permission to visit their friends/relatives or who are allowed to keep money with them. It should be noted that these are the effect of the population sub-groups after adjusting the effect of age, religion, caste, children ever born, household members and standard of living of the household. The coefficients arrived at the logistic regression model and the mean per cent of each variable are translated into Multiple Classification Analysis (MCA) to derive the adjusted means.

Though education (both women and their husband's) and media exposure is not explaining much variation in Kerala, place of residence is certainly contributing some effect on women's status with urban women needing less permission than rural women. On the other hand, all these variables differentiate the women's status in India. The table shows that women in rural areas, who are not exposed to media and both spouses are illiterate possess a low status, particularly in India, where as high as 92 per cent of women

Table 14.8

Adjusted means for permission needed to visit friends/relatives and allowed to keep money set aside

Place of residence	Exposure to media	Woman's education	Husband's education	Permission needed to visit friends/ relatives		Allowed to keep money	
				Kerala	India	Kerala	India
Rural	Not exposed	Illiterate	Illiterate	64.4	91.8	47.2	48.7
		Illiterate	High school	54.9	69.2	61.2	53.0
		High school	Illiterate	71.3	87.3	50.6	67.5
		High school	High school	64.5	58.0	78.0	77.9
	Exposed	Illiterate	Illiterate	64.4	90.4	47.2	48.7
		Illiterate	High school	55.3	65.4	59.8	53.0
		High school	Illiterate	71.3	85.3	50.6	67.5
		High school	High school	62.9	53.7	63.0	71.2
Urban	Not exposed	Illiterate	Illiterate	57.7	86.8	46.8	58.4
		Illiterate	High school	48.2	56.8	59.4	62.5
		High	Illiterate	65.1	80.2	50.3	75.5
		High school	High school	56.0	44.7	62.7	78.5
	Exposed	Illiterate	Illiterate	59.4	84.7	64.7	66.7
		Illiterate	High school	50.0	52.5	75.3	70.4
		High school	Illiterate	66.7	77.3	67.8	81.4
		High school	High school	57.8	40.5	77.8	83.9

Note: The means are the adjusted means after controlling the effect of age, religion, caste, children ever born, household members and standard of living of the household.

need permission to go out and visit their close friends/relatives. Such women who are exposed to media even need about 90 per cent permission from their spouse. However, if the woman is illiterate and their husbands are literate high school and above, their status is much better as only 69.2 per cent need permission, whereas the group where women are high school literate and husbands are illiterate possess lower status (87.3% need permission). It is interesting to note that even for women from rural areas and not exposed to media, if both the woman and her husband are educated more than high school, only 58 per cent need permission, which is much lower than those women if both are illiterate (91.8%).

We have noticed that women from rural areas who are exposed to media but both spouses are illiterate possess a lower profile (90.4%) as far as the women's status is concerned in India, particularly when compared to the 64.4 per cent in Kerala. However, 53.7 per cent women with spouses, who are literate more than high school education, still need permission to visit friends/relatives in India, even higher in Kerala (62.9%).

Among the urban women who are not exposed to media and both spouses are illiterate, 86.8 per cent need permission in India, but only 57.7 per cent in Kerala. Women in the groups of high education (both spouses), only 44.7 per cent in India and 56 per cent in Kerala are not allowed to go out with permission. Further, among the exposed and illiterate group of women and husbands, 84.7 per cent in India and 56 per cent in Kerala possess a profile which is significantly low, among literate more than high school 40.5 per cent in India and 57.8 per cent in Kerala.

On the whole, though these variables do not significantly differentiate women's status in Kerala, each group under consideration is significant in India with education playing an important role.

Table 14.8 further examines the effect of these factors on the status of women by analysing how far the women are allowed to keep money. It is clear that low social groups are less allowed to keep money, Kerala being no different from India, with 47.2 vs 48.7 per cent. This is true also of women who are from rural areas, not exposed to media and illiterate along with their spouses. Among the group of high school educated women and their spouses, as high as 78 per cent are allowed to keep money in both populations we examined. Similar patterns appear among those from rural areas and exposed to media as well as from urban areas regardless of exposure to media.

Conclusion

A regional divide exits in the level of women's empowerment (Roy and Niranjan, 2004). However it is clear that a woman in Kerala stands in a much better situation than her counterparts in other parts of India in terms of her empowerment with regard to decision-making in issues such as freedom of movement and choice to keep aside money for her personal use. The dramatic decline in fertility in the Kerala society could be attributed this increasing power in decision-making that women in Kerala hold. It is clear from studies that decision-making capacity within family is one of the major reasons of decline in fertility rate in many countries especially for women.

By development we mean the development of all sections of the society and of course across gender. Discrimination across gender is the most distressing fact of such deprivation cutting across caste, class and ethnic composition. Like their male counterpart, women also play their important parts in the social, economic and cultural process directly or indirectly. Even in the traditional tribal societies (as is observed in Meghalaya, Manipur, Kerala, some parts of West Bengal, etc.) women played the dominant role in the social and economic activity excepting the political processes. In spite of this, they are long neglected in the sense of food, and calorie intake, education, health care, political participation and psychologically.

Traditionally women were thought to be the symbol of sacrifice. They play simultaneous roles of a daughter, sister, wife, mother and their activities were mainly confined within the boundaries of four walls. Their main tasks include bearing and rearing of children, the household works, cooking, washing, cleaning etc and above all to satisfy all the members of the family. In most families they take initiative and necessary steps for the beginning of education of their children. In many societies especially in rural area women take the responsibilities of fetching drinking water, collecting fuel wood as well as take part in gardening, and agricultural activities from sowing to harvest. Their role either as a mother or wife in addition to other socio-economic performance has immense importance in the welfare of the society. Sometimes in the very poor (low-income) families they sustain without sufficient food or nutritional intake themselves while trying hard to fulfil the nutritional intake male members in the family.

Presently the women contribute around 50 per cent of the world's food supply and account for 60 per cent of the working force. In India, women constitute a major portion of total workforce. They work for long hours both at house and outside the house. In rural areas, they play a vital role in agricultural production. They account for nearly 50 per cent of the rural labour force in addition to fetching of water, collection of fuel wood and other household activities and maintaining the children. Work participation of female rose from 14.2 per cent in 1971 to 22.3 per cent in 1991 (Census of India 1971, 1991). However, their engagement in the organized sector is very limited and most of them work in the unorganized sector for low pay or no-pay jobs. Despite their important contribution to the society, in earlier days they were not allowed to take part in decision-making.

The year 2001 has been declared as the "International Women's Empowerment Year" by the United Nations. In UNDP South Asia Human Development Report (2000) "empowerment has been defined in women context at comprising increased power in the economic, social and political realms and consider this in conjunction with women identification of their own problems and needs". In the context of a woman's life "empowerment can be considered as a change that enables her increased capacity to lead a fulfilling human life characterized by external qualities such as health, mobility, education and awareness, status in the family, participation in decision-making as well as internal qualities such as self-consciousness and self-confidence" (Ackerley, 1995).

Empowering women does not mean to give them power to dominate others or to use power to establish their superiority over others. Therefore, empowerment of women in reality is to empower themselves. Here, empowerment means empowering the self-recognition of one's own capacities and contribution to the family, community, and society at large in order to create a positive self-image and build confidence.

References

Ackerley (1995), *UNDP South Asia Human Development Report (2000)*, New York: United Nations.

Agarwal (1992), The Gender and Environment Debate Lessons from India, *Feminist Studies* 18, 1, pp. 119-158.

Bhat and Irudaya Rajan (1990), Demographic Transition in Kerala Revisited, *Economic and Political Weekly* 25(35 & 36): 1957-1980.

Census of India 1971, 1991.

England, Paula and George Farkas (1986), *Households, Employment and Gender: A Social, Economic, and Demographic View.* New York: Aldine.

Ghadially, Rehana (1988), *Women in Indian Society – A Reader*, New Delhi: Sage Publications.

Gilligan, Carol (1982), *In a Different Voice – Psychological Theory and Women's Development*, London: Harvard University Press.

Gupta, Mukta (2000), *Issues Related to Women*, Lucknow: Institute of Environment Development Studies, Pages 1-5. Sarup Publications.

International Institute for Population Studies (IIPS) and ORC Macro (2000), *National Family Health Survey (NFHS-2)*.

Jahan, Farhat (2004), *Women in India*, New Delhi: Anmol Publications Pvt. Ltd.

Kelkar, Meena A. (1995), *Subordination of Women: A New Perspective*, New Delhi: Discovery Publishing House.

Kishore (1998), "Empowerment of Women in Egypt and Links to the Survival of Their Infants" in Harriet B. Presser and Gita Sen (eds.), *Womens Empowerment and Demographic Process* by IUSSP, Oxford University Press, pp. 119-156.

Mukerjee, Asha and Kumkum Battacharya (2003), *Conditioning and Empowering of Women – A Multidimensional Approach*, Pages 12, 29, 186-190. Gyan Publications.

Rajan, Irudaya et al., (1996), *Fallacies About the Sex Ratio of the Population of Kerala*. Paper presented at the International conference on Kerala's Development Experience: National and Global Dimensions organized by the Institute of Social Sciences, India International Centre, New Delhi.

Sen and Batliwala (1997), *Empowering Women for Reproductive Rights: Moving Beyond Cairo*. Paper Presented at the Seminar on Female Empowerment and Demographic Process: Moving Beyond Cairo, IUSSP, Lund, Sweden, 21-24 April.

Shiva (1988), *Women and Empowerment: Case Studies from selected villages of Orissa*, New Delhi: Council of Professional Social Workers.

Roy, T.K. and S. Niranjan (2004), "Indicators of Women's Empowerment in India" *Asia-Pacific Population Journal*, Vol. 19, No. 3.

Utpal, Kumar, D. and Bhola Nath Ghosh (2004), *Issues on Empowerment of Women*. Mohit Publications, New Delhi, Page 1, 2, 96, 111.

Vishwanathan, Maithili (1994), *Women & Society*, Vol. 1.

Zachariah, K.C. and Irudaya Rajan S. (1997), *Kerala's Demographic Transition-Determinants and Consequences*, New Delhi: Sage Publications.

15

Elite Women's Roles in Empowering Oppressed Women

Volunteer Work in NGOs in Kolkata, India

ADITI MITRA AND JEAN VAN DELINDER

In this chapter we discuss how upper-class, elite women in Kolkata (formally Calcutta) use their unpaid volunteer work in non-profit Non-Governmental Organizations (NGOs) to empower oppressed women. We argue that even though these women thought they were helping those less fortunate, their own stories reveal how much they are constrained by the trappings of their own advantaged situations. Empowerment is a two-way process; though these women use their volunteer roles in NGOs to help empower other women, they are also constructing their own empowerment with their work. Using data collected from a combination of participant observation and in-depth interviews conducted in Kolkata between December 2003 and March 2004, we discuss how their volunteer roles are an extension of and reinforce their existing status, social class norms, education, upbringing, family values and social networks. Their interviews also reveal the hidden processes of their own empowerment. All of women interviewed self-identified as being upper-middle class or higher; most were highly educated, many with master's degrees. They ranged in age from 40 to 70 years and all were involved in decision-making positions or served on boards of trustees in ten women's NGOs in Kolkata.

Much of the existing literature on women in India concentrates either on the problems facing rural and/or urban lower class women (Narayan, 1997; Shiva, 1988; Mehra, 1997; Gopalan, 1997; Seth, 2001; Rai, 2002, etc.). By studying highly educated elite women volunteers in an urban setting, a different picture of women in India emerges. This study also aids in pointing out the differing perceptions and interests of elite women volunteers in non-Western settings.

Utilizing a similar theoretical framework used by Diana Kendall (2002) in her study of the social elite women volunteers in America, we argue that though many NGOs in Kolkata, were founded to facilitate empowerment of less fortunate women through consciousness-raising, social change and economic independence by attempting to modernize India, many elite women volunteers, either intentionally or unintentionally, perpetuate the glorification of unpaid volunteer work as an ideal alternative to paid work, adopt conservative (traditional establishment-oriented) approaches and work more toward reproducing existing gender role-expectations, norms, and traditional family values. These women are helping less fortunate women to break out of the cycle of patriarchal domination, yet most of these women chose to distance themselves from what they perceived were 'angry' feminist activists. All preferred to remain within their conventional gender roles, guided by the same ethic of compassion that initially drew them into their NGO work.

Unpaid Work as Philanthropy

The private pursuit of public purpose is a unique feature of civil society, and the non-profit sector remains crucial in addressing problems facing modern, industrializing communities (Markham and Bonjean, 1995). Though many citizens willingly and unselfishly volunteer their efforts in communities, non-profit organizations depend disproportionately on wealthier, more prestigious citizens for financial support, legitimacy and unpaid labour (Hodgkinson and Weitzman, 1992). Many times it is the upper class and higher status women who have the leisure and financial resources to work without pay (Daniels, 1988). In addition, it is these same women who play key roles in many community organizations and have a strong voice in defining community problems (Domhoff, 1983). Research indicates that though paid work is regarded as a disgrace to women, unpaid volunteer or 'charity' work is seen as a virtue of the ideal woman (Plemper, 1996).

In the United States, this small group of elite women having the necessary financial resources to engage in philanthropic work often find themselves as valuable participants at charitable events and fund-raisers (Daniels, 1985: 363). Those who are successfully involved in this type of volunteer work gradually generate community renown and are called upon for advice and assistance for other projects. Through their unpaid labour for 'charity' these women gradually become civic leaders, are often called upon to serve on non-profit boards of directors and news of their activities appear in local news media as their expertise in volunteer work attract attention from communities. Although their leadership has been the most vital resource in the establishment of empowerment groups, scholars have also noted that because of their economic resources and social connections, elite women are able to perform 'good deeds' that benefit diverse categories of women while, at the same time, maintaining their own upper class lifestyle and enhancing their social power through connections with other elite women volunteers (Kendall, 2002:19).

Similarly in India, elite women play a leadership role helping poor and illiterate women who cannot sustain an organization without the help of educated and influential activists (Calman, 1992). Like in other parts of the world, volunteer work for elite Indian women is an ideal alternative to paid work "as a strategy to gain prestige, enhance status and maintain social contracts without breaking social, religious and community norms" (Plemper, 1996; Daniels, 1998).

Kendall's (2002:19) work in the United States discusses the significance of upbringing, home atmosphere and neighbourhoods where elite women grow up, in creating the typical elite community volunteer. Once these women are grown up and married they reproduce their social class by raising their children in much the same way: carefully selecting their friends, teaching 'appropriate' behaviours and beliefs, and carefully selecting their educational experiences. This process of social reproduction ensures that the next generation of elites will come to see their privilege not only as natural but as justified.

In a related vein, we may ask why do women from upper classes and with high educational backgrounds choose to work in the NGO[1] sector in India? A study of social class norms, upbringing, education, family values and social networks on the role of women in society and their role as social workers may help shed light on the their personal and societal motivations (Ostrander, 1980) as to why elite women take up unpaid volunteer work in NGO settings in India. Additionally, in the age of transnational feminisms, the way these women define feminism and construct the image of a feminist based on their appeal to feminist ideas helps to analyse the discourse of feminism in the post-colonial context.

Women's Movement in India

In the twentieth century were several cycles or 'waves' of social reform movements in India that addressed women's issues (Gandhi and Shah, 1991:21). The roots of the most recent phase or wave of the women's movement lie in the mass struggles and agitations of middle class and working class women during the 1960s and 1970s (Kumar, 1993). This wave of the feminist movement seeks to "understand the oppressive, hierarchical relationship between men and women and societal systems in order to introduce changes and a new society" in which women are liberated from oppression (Gandhi and Shah, 1991:21). There is also a self-conscious attempt to create organizational forms in which women become empowered psychologically and socially. Participating in decision-making and in the implementation of decisions, raising consciousness about the situation of women, creating mutual interdependence and group solidarity, developing skills, self-confidence and assertiveness are all seen as integral to the process of empowerment in the Indian women's movement.

Calman (1992) points out two major ideological and organizational tendencies within India's women's movement. One, which is largely urban-based, focuses on issues of rights and equality while the other emphasizes empowerment and liberation and has both urban and rural components. The two wings of the movement share a desire to transform the consciousness of women and men. One seeks to raise awareness that women in contemporary India occupy an inferior position to men economically, socially and politically. While the other seeks to make them realize that this position is unjust, unacceptable and alterable.

Those who advocate rights over empowerment see women's concerns as issues of human rights within the secular democracy that India's Constitution proclaims. Their demand is for equality within the law; they see themselves as modernizers and social democrats seeking basic human rights rather than as feminists pressing a radical social agenda (ibid.). The rhetoric of the rights group refrains from positing a conflict between women and men; it does not even present itself as a challenge to gender roles, fearing that such an attack would mark the movement overly influenced by the West, and as attacking the family (which, in India, is almost sacred). They are determined to be in the mainstream of an attempt to modernize India without sacrificing essential Indian culture or values except insofar as those values violate women's rights as human beings and as equal citizens (ibid.).

However, in the current phase of the Indian women's movement, some new issues have been raised, some of which parallel those of Western feminism, such as the assertion of women's rights over their own bodies. Although these are difficult subjects to analyse specifically given the scope of this study, it should suffice to mention that the new understandings of Indian women's lives incorporate new tropes such as 'empowerment', 'globalism', 'modernization' and 'individual rights'. The issues arising from the current Indian women's movement are complex, and this is reflected in its fragmented and diffused organization of today's Indian women's movement (Gandhi and Shah, 1991:22-23).

Women's NGOs in Kolkata

Non-governmental organizations (commonly referred to as NGOs) are involved in programmes, projects and campaigns related to women's social problems. While NGOs propose to raise women's awareness and empower them, we address some problematic aspects of the role of elite women volunteers, both as volunteers with decision-making authority (involved in women's development) and women from upper classes of the Indian society.

There are few ethnographic studies on Indian women's lives which explore the role of elite women volunteers in specific organizational settings. There is a substantial body of literature dealing with women's issues in India including grass-roots studies on rural women, debates surrounding legislation that effects women, and on controversial acts such as sati and dowry-death, women's poverty and health issues (Narayan, 1997; Shiva, 1988; Mehra, 1997; Gopalan, 1997; Seth, 2001; Rai, 2002, etc.). Though there is research on women volunteers and activists in Europe and the United States (see Rothschild, 1979; Daniels, 1985; Metzendorf and Cnaan, 1992; Markham and Bonjean, 1995, 1996; Plemper, 1996; Donner, 1997; Caputo, 1997) there is little available on elite women volunteers from urban India.

Despite the paucity of previous research, Kolkata provides an interesting case for our current investigation. As a city located on India's north-eastern coast,[1] it is a region characterized by growing divide between the rich and the poor, high levels of poverty, illiteracy and gender inequality. These conditions are compounded further by the impact of globalization, conflict between modern and traditional gender norms based on class, education, age, Indian family value-systems, social and religious mores and political ideologies. These problems make the organization of women urgent if they are to achieve equality, but also make it that much more difficult.

Although increasing numbers of governmental and non-governmental institutions are attempting to introduce modernization and developmental programmes to intervene, the policies, procedures and practices of these institutions often reflect and perpetuate existing unequal hierarchies in their organizational set-up. Despite heightened concern about gender inequalities and the espousal of gender training by both governmental and non-governmental institutions in the 1990s, developmental programmes vary widely in terms of their vision and goals as well as their understanding of gender as an operational objective.

As in other countries in developing areas, the population of India is not all poor. Indeed, the divide between those of middle-class standing and above, with their access to most of the consumer goods the world economy has to offer, and the majority who are desperately poor is becoming deeper and more painful. As in other cultures, although many women, especially from the lower classes continue to work to support their families and themselves, the majority of women in India are housewives and mothers (Plemper, 1996). Many women from upper middle and upper classes work as unpaid volunteers because they have the financial means to delegate housework and childcare to their paid servants (ibid.). In their spare time, they can distinguish themselves from labouring women by philanthropic activities (Kooymans, et al., 1983). It has also been suggested that volunteer work offers upper-class women status; hence, they are proud they do not work for money (Van Daal, 1994).

Women of different classes experience different problems and of course have different opportunities and political agendas. Organized attempts to introduce social reforms on behalf of women are, of course, not unique to India. However, the women's movement in India is sufficiently broad based that it tackles problems of different classes of women though opportunities for unity are limited by these same distinctions (Calman, 1992). Neither are the deep social and cultural divisions in India unique, but studying India can provide us with instructive material from which to compare non-Western settings. Additionally, the Indian population, in many ways, is similar to other developing nations at a time of globalization, when social and religious mores still limit the activities of women in politics and the economy. In India, it is the particular effects of Hinduism and Indian-based Islam that must be the focus of analysis, rather than those of Christianity, Judaism and Islam as practiced and adjudicated in other parts of the world (ibid.). Still, the fact of having underlying patriarchal socio-religious traditions that relegate women to a secondary status is common to most developing countries and must be with specificity in each instance, taken into account in understanding the status of women and the limits of and possibilities for change.

Women's organizations in Kolkata have been divided into three types in a recent study by Ray (1999): (1) politically affiliated, (2) autonomous from state and national politics; and, (3) subordinate. This study concerns itself with subordinate organizations. The autonomous organizations are what might be called 'social work' agencies and are headed by highly respected elite women who publicly eschew politics (Ray, 1999:58), while the politically affiliated organizations are the women's wings of political parties. However, Ray mentions another type which she characterizes as 'subordinate' within the political field of Kolkata. This label grows out of her analysis of Kolkata's political culture in which state politics is dominated by the Communist Party of India and is therefore strongly Marxist, commonly referred to as CPI (M), which is the hegemonic institution in the political field. According to Ray (1999), the autonomous women's organizations which have arisen from the second and third waves of the Indian women's movement are in a subordinate position, unable to compete with the politically affiliated organizations, since they do not have the hegemonic CPI (M) party on their side.

Not surprisingly then, it appears that class is a major aspect of activism due to Kolkata's longstanding communist political culture, which "has for years been more open to the borrowed ideologies of class struggle than the borrowed ideologies of feminist struggle" (Ray, 1999:69). Moreover, Kishwar (1990) has pointed out that the word 'feminism' evokes western stereotypes for many Indians. Coinciding with these facts, the current movement is so fragmented that there is no unified attitude towards the patriarchal structure of society or any agenda to deal with it (Ford, 2001).

In Kolkata, the leadership of NGOs remains dominated by middle or upper class women, a situation which is frequently criticized (Gandhi and Shah, 1990:283). Although some branches of the women's movement are focused through NGOs, it is important to attend to class differences which may affect women's choices in building a career as a volunteer with women's NGOs at Kolkata. Feminist theorists have argued that elite women – like those in other classes – remain subordinate to men when power is viewed solely in that context. However, elite women do have power. Their power is based on a combination of the economic power that they hold either individually or jointly with other members of their families and social power that they derive from influential social connections and prestigious organizational affiliations (Kendall, 2002). Privilege advantages elite upper class women over others in that they have greater control over their life chances including opportunities for themselves, their children and other members of their family (Kendall, 2002).

On a more speculative note however, Fernandes (1997) claims that a sense of ambiguity surrounds the attitudes held towards working women in Kolkata, not only in this but also women's own opinion about working outside the home. At the same time Banerjee, et al. (n.d.: 39-40) claim that most middle class (and upper class) households aspire to follow social norms in which it is a mark of status if women do not work outside the home. The Indian women's movement also diverges from the equivalent movements in the West with respect to the notion of sexual difference. While some feminist's struggles in the West have emphasized equality with man in all spheres, there was a tendency among Indian men and women to dwell on the idea of separate roles for males and females (Kumar,

1993). Although women's organizations in Kolkata may have the potential to facilitate change through their support of women's resistance to societal attitudes, the consequences of these changes are quite likely to be complicated (Ford, 2001).

The need for radical change in the Indian society is asserted by most women's groups, yet there is a paradox confronting women's activism. Those who espouse causes akin to Western feminism or who propose radical solutions to women's issues may find themselves accused of trouble-making and derogatorily labelled as 'feminists' (Ray, 1999: 77,97). Women working in politically affiliated groups may be unable to address the underlying sources of the problems women face, and may be distanced from women at the grass-roots level, due to their positions (Ray, 1999:91-92). Other organizations that are purposefully autonomous from government and NGO funding (especially Western) can be criticized for merely doing charity and social work (Ray, 1999:58).

Perhaps as a result of these challenges, some autonomous women's groups in Kolkata focus on different areas ranging from health care to consciousness raising (Ford, 2001). Interestingly, Ray, (1999:78, 97) points out the existence of a few rare autonomous groups who do not hesitate to use explicitly feminist approaches. However, feminism is a contentious stance which is associated with both British imperialism and decadence in Kolkata, i.e., 'western' and therefore non-Indian. While Kolkata has a history of women's organizations involved in social welfare projects, the Indian women's movement has undergone great changes (Gandhi and Shah, 1991), though not without retaining some continuity. Yet in important ways, the Indian women's movement has addressed some shortcomings of their predecessors, responding to critiques of earlier positions, embraced new issues and incorporated new structures such as network of groups and cooperative models which is likely to have impacted even the role of elite women volunteers in the NGOs in the developmental sector (ibid.).

Volunteering as 'Work'

Historically, volunteerism in the United States[2] emerged as a significant activity for women during the industrial revolution, when higher status women, largely excluded from paid work, were encouraged to make voluntary activity as key part of their lives (Harris, 1978). As volunteers, they developed and used their hidden talents for planning, leadership, and administration in ways that posed no threat to patriarchal family roles; in this way they used their socializing with peers as a way to validate their status through community service for those who were less fortunate (Ostrander, 1984).

In more recent times, the participation of women in community activism or volunteer work, especially through NGOs, still outnumber the participation of men. There are, of course, several reasons that can be put forth to understand this dynamic, albeit with several inherent dichotomies. To start with, engaging in community activism through NGOs has had several positive implications for women. Women's NGOs can act as independent social service agencies, interest and self-help groups designed to pressure the government to change laws or implement existing laws for the empowerment of women; thereby, creating a parallel power structure in the public sphere (Plemper, 1996).

However, in addressing these issues, other related concerns arise concerning the variables of social class standing, gender, education level, employment status, power relations and member selectivity to organizations run by women for oppressed women further complicates the dynamics which affect feminist theory and praxis. Moreover, in cultures where women are ideally not supposed to join the labour force but instead become caring mothers and housewives, women's empowerment and a career based on feminist activism can, indeed, be a difficult proposition. Significantly, volunteering for community service or philanthropy has been the privileged position of only middle and upper class women volunteers which, in many ways, typically serve to continue to disadvantage subsequent generation's working-class and poorer beneficiaries.

To maintain social contacts and to gain prestige without abrogating social, religious and community norms, upper-class (usually married) women have been known to turn to philanthropic and volunteer organizations, especially in social services, welfare and health care (ibid.). As alluded to earlier, although many of the upper class women have found a lifetime occupation in volunteering, there are some associated problems. Reviews on literature on women's volunteerism suggest several typologies based on roles played by individual workers. Two main typologies as suggested by Metzendorf and Cnaan (1992) are service and policy volunteers.

Based on these categories, the nature of power relations within and without the organization can perpetuate social inequality and gender oppression. Moreover, privilege advantages of elite women can also lead them to exert social control over those in other classes, whom they help with their volunteer efforts, hire as their household workers, or who serve in staff positions in non-profit organizations (Kendall, 2002). From this, certain core assumptions can be made as to the problems of elite women volunteers engaged in women's empowerment and development.

Discussion of the Data

The interview data on these Kolkata women' confirm what the literature states about elite women using volunteer roles as an extension of and reinforce their existing status, social class norms, education, upbringing, family values and social networks. All eleven of the respondents in this study identified themselves as being at least from the upper-middle class. Because of their relatively uniform class background, all but one of these women had mothers or mothers-in-law, aunts, grandmothers, who served as role models in terms of what was considered appropriate work for women in their family.

Not surprisingly, many respondents described their unpaid labour as an extension of their own social class or their husband's family. Many women wanted to do more than be a housewife and found volunteering as a way to have a 'career' without violating gender norms. One woman, married and in her late 60s discussed her entry into an NGO involved in community-development and water sanitation:

> It was never-never a paying job, instead I had to spend money…in fact a lot of money daily every month to come and go….I had to spend money all my life to do this work, so it was not easy… I wanted to give reign to my natural inclination; just living in a social/socialite environment and interaction was not me.

Another woman, age 55, married with two children found that her privileged situation elicited both envy and admiration for her social position that allowed her to do volunteer work:

> At a superficial level, there are two types of reactions that I have found – one is that they say that "Oh, she belongs to a higher economical background family, so she can afford to do

this work, she just wiles away her time." Another reaction is appreciative in that – in spite of her education and opportunities when she could have earned money but she has opted out for doing voluntary work.

A 60 year old married woman and now president of a NGO was initially drawn into volunteer work through her husband's family, and an extension of her care giving role as a wife and mother:

> After my marriage, my mother-in-law who was an eminent social worker told me that she gets a lot of satisfaction doing this sort of social work. She is one of the founders of Calcutta Social Project, which largely dealt with women in slums. It was kind of a….It wasn't like there was official work; it was meeting and doing things together. I was also accompanying her to remote villages to teach them and make them aware of their social condition, health and hygiene, basic education and all that. Basically, India is a country of poor people, and so many are illiterate or half-literate. So if we can make time to go to the remote villages and teach them, then it is a tremendous satisfaction for fruitfully spending your time.

Another respondent was drawn into volunteer work after her children were older and no longer needed her as much. She is now 65 and a widow:

> I have done my college education, I am an honours graduate (B.A) in Philosophy…Then I got married and had three children – one daughter and two sons. I basically didn't do anything in the first ten years of my married life, but then I got involved with... and did voluntary work for them, but not for any remuneration.

An interesting theme that kept coming up in the interviews was whether or not doing charitable work was really 'work' or 'useful':

> My daughter thinks this is important. My husband's side of the family has always done this type of work, but my paternal family is not very sure whether I am doing something useful.

A 51 year old married woman observed that volunteer work was starting to be recognized as a 'real' job:

> Many of friends would say "Oh you are working for an NGO", so they assume it is social work where you have nothing much

> to do because you come from well-to-do families and you are bored (you need to be occupied with something). Like in our Mother's time, many women used to do charity work, you know. So there is no identifiable difference between charitable work and developmental work. But today, the charitable work and developmental work both are becoming more and more professionalized, I must say.

This same respondent also admitted that volunteering in an NGO gave her a second chance at finding meaningful work:

> Yes, the goal was to carve out a career for myself. It took me quite a while to find out what I really wanted to do. At first I was a little confused I must confess. There were different things I wanted to do; I was looking at various options because I come from a family of lawyers, my father is a lawyer and politician. But that didn't work out for me because I found that to be a little boring. Then I had the option of going into the Indian Administrative Service, which I missed it.

Several women thought of volunteer work as an escape from being a housewife:

> I always wanted a pursue career, I did not want to remain in the household only.

The youngest woman in the study (40) was very curious about other people and knew that she did not want to be confined as a housewife.

> Since my very childhood, I wanted to mix with other people, I want to know other's problems, I am inquisitive about other's lives, I was a bit analytical...I wanted to go to the villages. I want to know about them because it's only my luck that I was born in a family (of wealth), but I am curious about the lives of others (who are not wealthy). My family was able to provide me a lot many facilities, but that is by luck and it is not my achievement. However, I never thought that I would establish an NGO. But I love this work. I love to do research, I want to know more about new things, find new angles to a work, and that I am doing here.

This 60 year old woman thought of social class and her volunteer work in terms of social responsibility or philanthropy and her responses were similar to elite women pursuing similar activities in the United States:

> I do feel that we here in India, particularly women in India who have had the good life, at least a life much better than the average woman, we have some responsibility to give something back to our society and I do feel that we should be doing something (about it).

The oldest woman in the study, 70, described her volunteer work as being seamlessly connected with her social status and well within family expectations:

> My family maintains me; I am well-secured with my finances. We are all voluntary workers. This is the only place where only women work only voluntarily. We get only tea and biscuits, and we have to spend fifty per cent of it ourselves. We are part of the managing committee; at first we become life-members, and then we have an election and a general committee formed; all the like-minded people from the general committee work here, they don't work for payment but they work to have the pleasure of service (of doing social work). Only the staff are paid.

One woman was conscious of contradictions regarding the social acceptance for women of her class to engage in volunteer work even though doing NGO work is considered less desirable:

> Indian society at some point of time can be very callous. For the upper middle class, priorities are very different. As you know we are going through this transition (globalization) in (urban) India, which is a strictly consumerist society; people are so caught up with their own materialistic needs and ethos, that they are not very responsive to where and what kind of work that is being done by the developmental sector....And NGOs, I am sorry to say, have carved a very bad image for themselves. Whenever they think of work done by an NGO, they think it is a scam, like getting money from a foreign donor agency and misusing it. That is the general image of an NGO that most people in this country have. I am not trying to be judgmental, but that's the image they have in their minds without going into much details.

Consistent with the literature, many women described their labour in terms of being unthreatening to patriarchy:

> I've had a tremendous partnership with my husband because he has given me endless freedom to find my salvation or

> destiny or whatever. I just gave you an idea about my work schedule, so you can imagine you much time I spend outside the home.
>
> I was married (my husband took care of me). He never grudged that.
>
> Unless they (family) are supportive, we wouldn't be able to work here, they think we are doing some good work. In helping these underprivileged women and children we are sort of helping ourselves as well because we are gaining lot of experience and insight and understanding.

One respondent described the difficulties she encountered when her family did not support her desire to do volunteer work:

> Firstly, if my family did not give me proper support I wouldn't be able to do this job, because I use the family car, I give a lot of donations from lot of money that is earned by my husband.

However, once she showed them that her volunteer work would not detract from her familial duties, they were much more accepting and she continued to work outside the home:

> That way since I am looking after the household and everybody's need, and then I am doing this social work, my family is giving me full support (as a result of my looking after them). Apart from doing my family duties, I am also getting a lot of satisfaction for this sort of job.

Another woman also initially encountered resistance from her husband's family. However, once she started to receive public recognition for her efforts they were more accepting:

> Family thinks this kind of work does not bring in any kinds of rewards – monetary or any kind. Initially, my in-laws were not at all approving but now.....when I was always being quoted in the newspapers and was being interviewed and all that, then they started saying "oh, we are so proud of our daughter-in-law!!".

Many women interviewed described their volunteer work as an extension of their care giving role as mothers:

> I will tell you how I got into social work...I told my Mom that I think I seem to have lost my mission in life somewhere (in the

> process)....the goal, you know (sighs). And then suddenly I started thinking that I care for children a lot, even before I had my own children...quite early on behind my house were slums...poor..poor slums. I thought " My God! here I am hanging a chandelier and those people don't have enough to eat, their kids are not going to school.....I got so concerned (about them).
>
> I am attached to the children but otherwise no (I wouldn't have been here). Whatever little time I have throughout the day I will spend for them, the most distressed human beings – these children and women – whatever age they may be. I always try my best to help the parents or the guardians with what they need. People come to me for help and information. It's not that I am talking about my abilities, but I would love for someone to come and ask me for information on whatever, like finding a good doctor for a woman who has been detected with cancer.

All of the women mentioned the importance of social connections in getting involved in volunteer work and all of their responses included a reference to either a relative or friend who drew them in. This type of volunteer recruitment is similar to elite women in more developed countries.

Even though many women felt validated by society for their volunteer work, some respondents mentioned that women's volunteer work was devalued:

> Because of my background, I am not a typical NGO women activist, which I am also.....but not just that....Even though it is run by women it is "professional" I mentioned the word "professional" several times because women's NGOs...and I have faced this. Because this whole perspective of women's NGOs being just do-gooders and welfarists (sic) with no conception of what "development" is. These are the catch-words that catch us unawares and we get marginalized. We share evidence of proper systems of monitoring, evaluation, having documentation, which is very clear-cut and organized.
>
> It's a mixed response. Many people view as a work which is not a career per say. It is more to keep yourself occupied rather than anything else, and it's not a profession. It's an extension of charity.

Some women also expressed dissatisfaction with more traditional women's organizations and this eventually led her to work as a volunteer in a NGO:

> Since I was interested in women's work, I joined an association which I thought would give me scope to do this kind of volunteer work — but I was very disillusioned because it was a glorified women graduate ladies club (laughs). They had the "do-gooding" attitude – they would take fruits on Christmas Day and occasionally they had seminars etc...There were one or two women's groups formed in Calcutta, so I met them. They said "Yes we will give you the information you want, but you must join us". So I joined [an NGO]. And I will tell briefly about the rewards, it's not that I will be marked out for a "Padmashree" (National Award) or anything, but as a person I have expanded beyond my imagination – I could never think that doing this kind of volunteer work would be so emotionally fulfilling and satisfying. I think it was that which has made me improve as a human being. I learnt to relate with people better, till then I was a little snooty about women because (other) women were not intelligent and they were only interested in the kitchen, so I related much better with men. But I soon came out of that "honorary men syndrome" and I started relating with women much better and feeling comfortable with them, and realizing their plight as to why their horizons were limited. It gives your personality a different texture.

Even though some of the respondents were conscious of their work being under-valued, many respondents noted they found their work deeply satisfying.

> You know, let us face it in the present society around the world if you don't earn too much, then your work is not seen as important. In my family, everybody is earning in five figures. Because of this (low) earning possibly, there is little contempt I can feel, although people don't tell me. But also they think that I am doing important, at least somewhat they accept and my daughters also think that this work is important.

> [But] there is a plus point of this work; where I work there my work is very much appreciated. As I said, starting at such an old age, I found it difficult to be accepted in other places, including one women's NGO, but here I have been very well accepted. The girls I work with I feel they love me, they love

> me....and that is a very great thing. Outside the NGO, yes in the Maitreyi they like me, they did not say anything (directly) but I noticed some of them had doubts when I started that I have suddenly started working in an old age and from a conservative family.

Some even go so far as to avoid mentioning their work:

> Well, I don't introduce myself as an NGO-worker. Moreover, I only meet those who are working for others (social work). I never tell anybody what I am doing.

We expected to find responses about volunteer work being about empowerment for others and many women took satisfaction in helping others:

> If we help them, they are happy but even if we can't they are just happy that they could share their problems with us. Most of the time, we really can't help them. Sometimes they are not satisfied, but overall they are very satisfied.

> They show their appreciation in various ways. There have been times when I have thought of moving on and doing something else because after a certain point of time what I can give to an organization, I can give but after that I feel the need to move on and start a different project. My job strictly is not so much implementation, but (rather) planning and setting up the job; and day to day implementation at this particular age in my life, I do not much enjoy. But I have not been able to move on because there is a failing of the way we work. I feel NGOs in India do not know how to withdraw from a particular project. The result is you are tied down, and the dependency of the women you are helping increase; they are emotionally as well as economically depending on you (NGO).

> Some of the members who joined were in appreciation of the work that we had done for their cousin, or their friend. But there were some women who we helped to go back to their in-laws and repair the rift, those women were taken back to their families in the condition that they should not have anything to do with women's groups (laughs), and they have not kept in touch with us. But in our forum, we are only twenty members but we have some clout, which we feel embarrassed about because we are respected and recognized (by the general society) To the women and children for whom we work, they

> are very appreciative. When I go to the school, the children absolutely adore me, and the women are also very nice.
>
> When they find that my child got raped by someone, and that we are the persons who are coming to us and going with us to the court, we are taking initiative with the police follow up, talking to the public prosecutor, and local people, they automatically see the value. When the (rescued) trafficked girl is sent to her home by the police, the court is not willing to hand her over to her parents because her parents are not equipped to support or feed her. We take care of her, give her shelter and open a rehabilitation centre and vocational training unit in that specific village, and take care of her education and medical needs, then it is very visible that we are valuable to them.

One of the most interesting findings was how volunteer work was a source of self-empowerment for most of these women.

> This is my life. If one gives me the choice.....it gives my life some meaning.
>
> They definitely respect my work. Many of them have come to me saying that they want to become a member or join this type of organization that helps others.
>
> There is such a crying need I guess; the distress level is so high amongst women. Apart from this NGO there are lots of networks of women's organizations. One of the first organizations we started in the early eighties...I was a founder member of that, I was still in advertising at that time. It was also a gut-level reaction to what was wrong with the system.
>
> Yes, it is very fulfilling that much I can (definitely) say because I've always been interested in women's welfare, women's empowerment, women's emancipation.
>
> It is partly that it is my profession, and also partly the cause. I haven't been working for money all my life, (as I mentioned) the first eight years of this work I was just working as a volunteer for two reasons – a) I wanted to get experience and b) it was because I felt very strongly about the cause, to be able to do something for society, something for these women. I did get a lot of learning experience.

> I have so many works. I want to live meaningfully, it's a meaningful life otherwise it is of no use to live like others. I don't like living like the others (regular people's lifestyle). I am doing for someone else, some other work. If I am not there by the side of these girls, they won't get justice, they are denied their basic rights. So whatever time I devote for them means a better living for someone, for someone's survival, for someone's protection, for someone's development. That is my motivation.
>
> Now I am happy that I am working with women's issues. Yes, I am satisfied with my work. As you know, this type of work was not available in my time (youth) and people did not even think in the feminist way, it was totally like out of the planet in this part of the world.

Though some respondents were aware of the women's movement, they were careful to define their emerging feminist consciousness in terms of universal rights rather than radical activism:

> Coming out of the social stereotype that has been assigned to us in terms of women's roles and taking their place beside the males. I use the word "beside" as equal partner and I think that is the biggest challenge of this century where women have to define their roles as mothers and wives, on the other hand as women who are contributing, who are earning…..this status definition is going to be a huge role. I don't think that has happened worldwide in fact. We still have the glass ceiling and the glass wall.
>
> I am a feminist and I am really deeply into women's problems in India, specifically West Bengal, which is increasing everyday – molestation, sexual harassment, rape etc. My whole life has been geared to working for women's lives and problems. When I talk to people I get into a lot of arguments, even in my close family, my brother and other relations because my views don't match with theirs. It's a life-style with me, not just I just come here to work and go back. … my immediate family but with my relatives – well, most of them they are not at all happy with my feminist views. Generally among the middle class or lower middle class, the work I do they don't see it in any good light at all, because they see it as "feminist" quote unquote organizations are simply creating problems in the happy families, they

> are going and giving wrong ideas to these women. That is the attitude of the society, they don't like feminists. This is something that I have faced from my extended family, from outside, from everywhere.

> Yes. A lot of women, intellectuals, go all out to say "I am not really a feminist in that sense", you know. In fact the last time when this NGO completed twenty years, we put out a competition asking "Why I am not a feminist?" and we gave out prizes (laughs).

When asked "What does being a feminist mean to you?" many thought it was a Western concept and not applicable to women in India.

> The word feminism is a problematic and negative word for some reason in India.

> I never do use the word feminist, but others use the word for me (to describe me). Feminist or activist, and that is my image. But I never saw myself as just that, but I care for the underdog if you see what I mean, so women appear to be the underdogs, to me women are in a very deprived situation, therefore, you might say 'yes' I am a feminist. At present I am a feminist but I may not always be.

One woman responded to this question about feminism as making possibilities for her to forge a separate identity other than wife, mother or daughter:

> I feel that women need to have a space for themselves. I myself have many times felt, even before I worked with this organization, as just a housewife I think we don't have any individual space for ourselves in any household. We are either mothers, or wives or daughters'-in-law etc. But as an individual you do need your own space to do your own thing, which in Indian households......even though my husband's family was quite forward looking, not really conservative but even then I felt the need of having my own space which they don't allow.

Though some women thought of feminism as empowerment, they separated it from the idea of being an activist.

> Feminism means empowerment, if a woman cannot take decisions of her own life then no matter how much the concept

> of feminism is thrown around it's a waste, you know. To my mind, it (feminism) is superficial. For example, bra burning, scandal marching, I find that too symbolic (simplistic). And frankly speaking I am not an activist.

For many, feminism meant simply "equality" and "respect" for difference:

> For me, Feminism means relating better to other women and also understanding diverse views of women and men, in other words, seeing the other person's point of view. If I find that I disagree, I try to understand why I disagree....you know being more tolerant. We feminists are human beings basically, and we want to be bridges of communication.

One woman distanced herself from feminism as conflicting with her family obligations:

> But no, I would not consider myself a feminist, not in the true sense of the term. A feminist, at least according to my conception, would be a little more activist which I am not. I don't consider myself an activist. I am too entangled with the family, and also there are some family values and social values which I quite adhere to, so I don't want to break out of that .

Finally, one woman came to an understanding of feminism for her own lived experience:

> I am a hundred per cent feminist. Why not? Women are so oppressed; I feel every woman should be a feminist. I feel very strange why so many women are not. I have had no formal education in Feminism or theory, but I know from my own life.

Summary and Conclusion

One striking similarity between the women volunteers interviewed in this study and those in Western countries such as the United States, Canada and Britain, is that they used their upper-class status to seek work outside the home. As the literature pointed out, though upper-class women are more likely not to pursue professional paid careers, even though in their capacity as volunteers they are often in decision-making positions (Lubove, 1975; McCarthy, 1990; Metzendorf and Cnaan, 1992; Markham and Bonjean, 1995; Kendall, 2002). The eleven women discussed in this chapter were all performing duties and responsibilities comparable to business and government professionals, but they were careful to describe their work within the context of their traditional roles as wives and mothers.

Though the practice of categorizing theories as a method of enquiry into feminist projects is more common in the West than in India (Kachuck, 2003), the need to better understand volunteer work has been recognized by some Indian authors, especially with issues related to women's empowerment (Gandhi and Shah, 1991). Studying Third World women requires a special theory and method that will do justice to their lived experiences. This study is intended to begin to fill the gap between the existing literature on elite women in Western society and those living in less developed countries like India. It is beyond the scope of this study to generalize about the problems and prospects of elite women volunteers in an area as vast and distinct as India. Instead we explored the day-to-day lived experience of upper class, elite women working in NGOs in Kolkata. By having them speak about their own lives in connection with trying to empower other women we found that they were just as concerned with empowering themselves. All of the women involved in this study either had no children or their children were adults. Many of them were widowed, indicating that their traditional roles as wives and mothers were no longer relevant and they sought fulfilment and meaning through unpaid work in women's NGOs.

Though many of the women were consciously aware that they wanted to empower women who were less fortunate than they were, many of them revealed their own process of empowerment in their volunteer work. Many rejected the Western definition of feminism as being in conflict with their identities as wives and mothers. However, their stories show their own longings for recognition of their work not only as unpaid volunteers, but also in their daily lives as women.

Notes

1. Kolkata (formally named Calcutta) was the capital of British India for 200 years. Contemporary Kolkata is also a city that has had the reputation of being politically tempestuous (Ray, 1999) and

passionate with the Marxist ideology, amidst forces of globalization and a fairly recent liberalized economy.

2. According to Hodgkinson and Weitzman (1994), higher status women continue to be greatly over-represented among numerous Americans who participate in voluntary activities and belong to volunteer organizations.

References

Banerjee, Himani, J. Bagchi, D. Bhandar, B. Cranney, K. Banerjee, A. Chanda, P. Banerjee, N. Chakraborty, S. Acharya and S.N.U. Khondakar (n.d), *Modernization, Poverty, Gender and Women's Health: An Action Research in Development among Poor Women in Khidirpur (Ward 78 and 79) Slum of Calcutta.* Kolkata: School of Women's Studies, Jadavpur University.

Calman, Leslie J. (1992), *Toward Empowerment: Women and Movement Politics in India,* San Francisco: Westview Press.

Caputo, Richard K. (1997), "Women as Volunteers and Activists", *Nonprofit and Voluntary Sector Quarterly,* 26: 156-174.

Daniels, Arlene Kaplan (1985), "Good Times and Good Works: The Place of Sociability in the Work of Women Volunteers", *Social Problems,* 32: 363-374.

— (1988), *Invisible Careers: Women Civic Leaders from the Volunteer World,* Chicago: University of Chicago Press.

Domhoff, G. William (1983), *Who Rules America Now?* New York: Prentice Hall.

Donner, Henriette (1997), "Under the Cross: Why V.A.Ds Performed the Filthiest Task in the Dirtiest War: Red Cross Women Volunteers 1914-1918", *Journal of Social History,* 30: 687-705.

Fernandes, Leela, (1997), *Producing Workers: The Politics of Gender, Class and Culture in the Calcutta Jute Mills,* New Delhi: Vistaar Publications.

Ford, Laura (2001), *Like a Fish Out of Water: Gender and Space in Calcutta,* Ph.D. Dissertation, Department of Sociology, University of Regina, Regina, Sask.

Gandhi, Nandita and Nandita Shah (1991), *The Issues at Stake: Theory and Practice in the Contemporary Women's Movement in India,* New Delhi: Kali for Women.

Gopalan, Pritha (1997), "The Trust Factor in Participation and Social Education", *Annals of the American Academy of Political and Social Science,* 554:178-192.

Harris, B.J. (1978), *Beyond Her Sphere: Women and the Professions in American History*, Greenwich CT: Greenwood Press.

Hodgkinson, Virginia A. and Murray S. Weitzman (1992), *Giving and Volunteering in the United States: Findings from a National Study*, Washington, D.C.: Independence Sector.

Kachuck, Beatrice (2003), "Feminist Social Theories: Theme and Variations" pp. 53-87 in *Sociology of Gender: The Challenge of Feminist Sociological Knowledge*, edited by S. Rege, New Delhi and Thousand Oaks, CA: Sage Publications.

Kendall, Diana (2002), *The Power of Good Deeds: Privileged Women and the Social Reproduction of the Upper Class*, New York: Rowman and Littlefield.

Kishwar, Madhu (1990), "Why I Do Not Call Myself a Feminist" *Manushi* (Nov/ Dec): 2-8.

Kooymans, C. Velthius, M. and Vonk, E. (1983), *Volunteering: A Women's Matter?: An Analysis of the Position of the Women Volunteers and a First Impulse to Improve Disposition*, Wageningen, NL: Agricultural School, Household Guild and Project Group Women Studies.

Kumar, Radha (1993), *The History of Doing: An Illustrated Account of Movements for Women's Rights and Feminism in India 1800-1990*, London: Verso.

Lubove, R. (1975), *The Professional Activist*, New York: Atheneum.

Markham, William T. and Charles M. Bonjean (1995), "Community Orientations of Higher Status Women Volunteers", *Social Forces*, 73 (4): 1553-1571.

McCarthy, Kathleen D. (1990), "Parallel Power Structures: Women and the Voluntary Sphere" pp. 1-31, in *Lady Bountiful Revisited: Women, Philanthropy and Power*, edited by K.D. McCarthy, New Brunswick, NJ: Rutgers University Press.

Mehra, Rekha (1997), "Women, Empowerment and Economic Development", *Annals of the American Academy of Political and Social Science*, 554: 136-149.

Metzendorf, D. and Ram A. Cnaan (1992), "Volunteers in Feminist Organizations", *Nonprofit Management and Leadership*, 2: 255-269.

Narayan, Uma (1997), *Dislocating Culture: Identities, Traditions and Third World Feminism*, New York: Routledge.

Ostrander, Susan A. (1980), "Upper-Class Woman: The Feminine Side of Privilege", *Qualitative Sociology*, 3:23-42.

Plember, Esther (1996), "Women's Strategies in Dutch Philanthropy", *Voluntas: International Journal of Voluntary and Non-Profit Organizations*, 7:365-382.

Rai, Shirin M. (2002), *Gender and the Political Economy of Development: From Nationalism to Globalization,* Malden, MA: Polity Press.

Ray, Raka (1999), *Fields of Protest: Women's Movement in India,* University Press Minnesota Press: Minneapolis, MN.

Rothschild, Mary Aickin, (1979), "White Women Volunteers in the Freedom Summers: Their Life and Work in a Movement for Social Change", *Feminist Studies,* 5:466-494.

Seth, Mira (2001), *Women and Development: The Indian Experience,* New Delhi: Sage Publications.

Shiva, Vandana, (1988), *Starving Alive: Women, Ecology and Development,* New Delhi: Kali for Women.

Van Daal, H.J. (1994), "Contemporary Volunteering: Shapes, Identity and Attractions" in P. Dekker (ed.), *Civil Society and Volunteering, Part 1: Civil Society: Explorations of a Perspective on Volunteering; Social and Cultural,* Rijswijk: Planbureau.

Part IV

Women in New Roles

Our collection closes with the pioneers, women stepping into new arenas of public life. From the emerging entrepreneurs among the Orissa *Kela,* to the few scientists in Tamil Nadu to the newly elected female reservation cohort in Panchayati Raj politics of Maharashtra, we begin to see the new challenges facing women across India.

With Mohanty's study of *Kela* women in Chapter 16 we have yet another exploration of a nomadic group which contradicts some of our cultural expectations. Not only does this study reveal significant details of women's contribution to the family management and sustenance, but it also uncovers the extent to which women have begun to modify their role in response to changing physical and social environments that are transforming their community's very definition as snake-charmers. In addition to the traditional census we have numerous tables of the decision-making and economic variation among the over 250 households of the one *Kela* community in Orissa.

Ravikumar invites us into the sparsely populated world of the woman scientists in Chapter 17. Through a survey of scientists and extensive interviews she contrasts the few women with the many men in two research organizations, one a university and one an institute. Though the numbers are small, there are some definite contrasts between the women and the men scientists. Percentages can be misleading, so they are only presented with the frequencies to avoid exaggerating the differences. The educational profile of spouses is a clear contrast and the interaction of productivity and marital status. The women's advantages in urban background and educated parents also seem to set up a contrast with their male peers. However, the over productivity is equal. Analysing what science demands of a person, she claims many of the qualities revealed are associated with the feminine and suggests that marital expectations in the broader society may be interfering at the critical career launching time, particularly with migration for work, as well as the choices women feel compelled to make in prioritizing their family responsibilities. She concludes with some implications for developing this human resource for future science.

Our final Chapter 18, presents a study by Aparna Thomas who gives us insight about the reality of political reform and women's reservation implementation for local politics. Her careful research of three levels shows the delicate interplay of parties, elites, and women beginning to participate in village and district decision-making. It is not as simple as we might think and the way she pays attention to structural features along with personal qualities reveals the complicated world we all recognize if we pursue such rigorous observation and spend the time it takes to reach more of an insider's understanding of our social world.

16

The *Kela* Women of Orissa and the Changing Entrepreneurship

JYOTSNA MOHANTY

The snake-charmers, popularly known as *Kela,* is a nomadic community of Orissa. The community is well known for their profession and acquaintance with snakes, which the people perceive as dangerous creatures. These dangerous creatures become their sole asset on which they depend, in order to eke out a living. For the people who enjoy snake charming, the variety of snakes constitutes a mobile zoo for them.

The *Kela* have been pursuing this occupation for generations together, wandering from place to place. They are known for their quarrelsome nature. At the same time they are viewed as harmless, adventurous and highly adaptable to any trying situation. They follow their folk traditions. Although ordinary people are acquainted with the profession and behaviour of the snake-charmers, there is hardly any information systematically available which can throw some light on the lifestyle and culture of such a dwindling wandering community. The information available is only piecemeal without any scientific approach to the study of their culture and habitat. Authorities who have made some attempts to look at this community are amateurs. Although they have attempted to visualize and interpret the *Kela* people, they have not succeeded in presenting them scientifically and systematically. As a consequence, the snake-charmers community continues to remain as a lesser known community for the anthropologist and others.

The *Kela* is a small community, small in terms of its number and also of identity. Even though it has a small population, which is hardly seen in the village excepting for a few months, has succeeded in establishing its identity. Although, it enjoys a lower position among the local caste groups, the migratory habitat of its members due to occupational compulsions has not affected their autonomous character.

The *Kelas* along with their family members move from place to place to ply their occupational craft. Such nomadism compels them to adapt to the local environments. In camp life, the selection of campsite, adjustment to the local resources, occasional rains, storms, cyclones, etc., are the main threats. Apart from these hindrances of nature, their presence in the outskirts of the village raises suspicion among the native residents. But such difficulties are usually overcome because of their high degree of adaptability to the work environment and society, which is a striking feature of this community.

The community solely depends on nature for its sustenance. From catching of snakes, to collecting herbal medicines against snake bites, from kitchen to thatching of roof and from cradle to pyre, they depend on local environment. Snake catching is the most hazardous work in their life. The identification of locations, knowledge in the type of snakes and probable behaviour of snakes are their personal acumen. The frequency of attack by snakes during the course of catching and charming makes their profession all the more challenging. The treatment of snakebites through herbal medicines is another challenging occupation of the *Kelas*.

In the traditional context, *Kela* women are indispensable for the camp life. The income from snake-charming is augmented by the tattooing skill of the females. Tattoos of different deities marked on the hands of rural women are the insignia of the skills of *Kela* women. The snake-charmer's woman shoulders the responsibility of judicious management of the household economy. She is the mistress of the kitchen. Their amicable behaviour with the villagers helps them to share village resources like water, firewood, etc. Her familiarity with the villagers in course of pursuing her occupation provides an access to the village fishing ground, forest, nests, which are trapped for the kitchen. Their main economy, however, revolves around the snakes. The women-folk make tattoo to supplement the income. Such being the economy, they remain away from their homes and lead a camp life for about eight months in a year.

In the present context the meager income from snake charming is not sufficient to maintain one's family. Loss of interest among the rural women for tattooing has made the snake-charmer women jobless. Further, loss of natural resources in the rural areas and growth of 'rural cosmopolitanism' have reduced the participation of *Kela* women in the traditional occupations. The interferences of environmentalists have minimized the scope of snake catching and charming. As a consequence, the *Kela* women have been struggling hard to retain their earlier position in the family economy. They no longer accompany their husbands to the camps. The traditional knowledge has lost its glamour. Encouragement by the Government through sponsoring of different alluring schemes for the economic development of the weaker sections of the society has made some contribution in restricting women's mobility in the society. The shift of attention and emphasis from traditional economy to modern has provided a challenge to the *Kela* women to adjust with the changing scenario. They are compelled to pursue an occupation which is little known to them. The society, as it appears, has the potential to keep the women-folk in the forefront of the household economy by providing them adequate support by relaxing the traditional rules and regulations. The spread of education and development of communication facilities have made the *Kela* women more dynamic and prominent in the family economy.

Objectives

Against this background the present chapter makes a humble attempt to empirically study the snake-charmer community by highlighting some of their traditions and crafts. To understand the nature of women folk in any society, it is essential to focus on the cultural expression concerned. The pivotal task of this paper is, therefore, to determine the socio-cultural image of the *Kela* women according to their ideological beliefs and practices. The paper analyses participation of the snake-charmer women in various works and the extent of their contribution to the family economy. On the basis of empirical study it evaluates the nature of the work of the snake-charmer women in contrast to women of the neighbouring community. The study also aims at evaluating the nature of entrepreneurial potential of the snake-charmer women, both in traditional and changing context. Finally, it proposes some measures for encouraging snake-charmer women for furthering their entrepreneurial habits and practices.

Methodology

Keeping in view the aforesaid objectives, the only *Kela* village of Orissa inhabited by the snake-charmers was selected. The preliminary survey conducted through door-to-door household census enumeration. The study was holistic in character and intensive in nature. Data were collected both from primary and secondary sources. Structured and semi-structured interviews were conducted to elicit most of the primary data. All information, particularly about the involvement of men and women in varieties of works, was collected through interviews and group discussions. Since *Kela* males were not available all the time in the village, obviously most of the information was collected from the women.

Landscape and the People: An Interlinked History

In the outskirts of Bhubaneswar, the State Capital of Orissa, the village Padmakesharipur is situated with all its charm and glory. The fringe village is exclusively inhabited by the snake-charmers, popularly known as the *Kela*. The *Kela* as per their myth have migrated from Midnapore district of West Bengal to finally settle in the village Padmakesharipur due to the blessings and patronage of the then king of Kanika. Although previously they were staying in the village Patia, which is about 3 km away from their present homeland, they were forced to quit Patia, because of a feud between the *Kela* and the *Zamindar* (landlord) of Patia.

The *Kela* settlement pattern in Padmakesharipur is linear. The houses are constructed on the one side of the main road and sub-roads. Some houses face the street while others are opposite to it. The houses are mostly rectangular in shape having side verandahs and a single door opening to the courtyard. Such houses have two sloped roofs thatched with straw supported by wooden pillars and mud walls. There are some houses which have pucca walls and asbestos roofs. The interior room is unpartitioned and used as bed room, dining room and also for the domestic animals. The snakes are also kept there in baskets in this room. The hearth is located at the right corner of the entrance of the verandah. The *Kelas* are generally of medium stature and dark brown in complexion. They are dolicocephals with oval face, black or brown eyes having black hair, whereas women possess long flowing wavy hair. Both men and women are strongly built and quite stalwart and are capable of much endurance.

Snake charming is an art and a skill that has been recognized as a very popular tradition of the *Kela*. The tradition of displaying snakes of various types amidst different charms and spells constitutes its complex form, which has been adopted by the *Kela* as their main occupation and the major source of their livelihood. The snake-charmer families used to make seasonal migration to different places of the State of Orissa and quite often beyond it, to ply their occupational craft. Thus snake-charmers of village Padmakesharipur could be considered as transhumants.

Settling in the village Padmakesharipur was a turning point in their life and occupation. As Table 16.1 reveals, the total population of the village is 1,047 comprising of 254 families at the time of this survey. The sex ratio (number of females per thousand males) is 970 which is almost the same as the state's sex ratio (1971) but more than the country's sex ratio, i.e., 927 females per 1,000 males, as per the 1991 census. The male literacy rate is not much higher in comparison to the female literacy.

Table 16.1

Demographic Profile of Padmakesharipur

Parameters	*Number*
Number of household	254
Number of population	1047
Male	530
Female	517
Sex ratio	970
Male literacy rate (percentage)	58.58
Female literacy rate (percentage)	41.42

Snake-charmer Community and their Tradition

There are five categories of *Kelas* housed in Orissa. They have emigrated from different states of the country, viz., Andhra Pradesh, West Bengal, Uttar Pradesh and eventually settled in Orissa. *Kela* group is divided into the following five sub-groups depending on their occupation and food habits:

(1) The *Nalua* are the bird catchers by using a *Nala* or a bamboo pole;
(2) The *Sapua* are the snake-charmers;
(3) The *Matia* are the earth workers;
(4) The *Sabakhia* are the omnivorous ones; and
(5) The *Gandia* are hill cultivators.

The *Sapua Kela* or the snake-charmers occupy the highest position among the *Kela* groups because of their proximity to the Hindu caste groups and profession involving snakes. The term *Kela* cannot be taken as a caste name but it can be used as a category label which means a heterogeneous group of people having some common characteristics, identified as *Kela*.

The *Kela* community has four lineage groups, viz., Nandaguru, Paramanik, Nayak, and Prasad, which are called as *Patakas*. Each *Pataka* is called *Bha-a-da*, which means brother. The four *Patakas* are known as *Charibandhu* (four friends). In all life cycle rituals, the presence of *Charibandhu* is essential. The birth pollution in the community continues for three months and final purification is held with the participation of *Charibandhu*. Marriage among the *Kela* are more contractual than sacramental. It is significant for maintaining group solidarity and homogeneity of culture. The snake-charmers constitute an inbreeding endogamous group and marriage takes place between the first cousins and other close relatives.

When they were fully nomads in the past, marriages were celebrated on any day of the year. But subsequently, marriages are solemnized on the auspicious days of 'Raja Sankranti' (in the month of June) or 'Dassehera' (in the month of October), with the exchange of garlands. Though payment of bride price was once practiced, it was stopped due to frequent dissolution of marriages. Dissolution of marriage was mainly due to temperamental differences between the spouses. It was materialized with the approval of the caste council. The divorce was made by the striking of wooden log thrice subsequently replaced by the tearing of straw.

The snake-charmer family is monogamous, nuclear, patriarchal and neolocal. Sometimes their family is extended by the addition of closely related kin members. Though their family structure is very simple, yet the presence of remarriage and frequent practice of divorce complicate the structure of family as well as the kinship relationship. Burial of the dead is still practiced among the *Kela* and the death rite continues up to the ninth day. But in the changing scenario it has been extended to the eleventh day, probably due to the influence of the neighbouring caste groups.

The economic activities of the snake-charmers revolve around the snakes. Apart from snake charming, treatment of persons affected by snakebite, collection and sale of herbal medicines to the rural folk, exhibition of snake catching skills are other dimensions of their life and living. Though, their main occupation is snake charming, most of the times they engage themselves in fishing, catching of birds, collection of forest products, rearing domestic animals, etc., to supplement their main income.

The snake-charmers start their journey after the festival of lights, Diwali, celebrated during the months of October-November. The outgoing group is divided into four or five batches, while each batch consists of twenty-five to thirty persons. Each batch is led by a leader *Saibandha,* who is more experienced, brave and has fairly good knowledge of the foreign land. The snake-charmers make their temporary settlement in open meadows nearer to water resources. They exhibit snake charming preferably at market places and places of large gathering. During snake charming they explain their expertise in snake catching, miraculous power of chanting, efficacy of drug and utility of herbal medicines. The snake-charmer women move from door-to-door for tattooing by narrating different designs and significance of tattoo marks in a poetic manner.

They being a nomadic community of Orissa, most of their places of visit come within the State of Orissa. They cover almost all areas and occasionally camp in some places up to one month, depending on the extent of income in the locality. Snake catching is the most important and hazardous part in snake-charmers' life and living. On the onset of rainy season during the months of June and July, which is the breeding season of the snakes, and during the months of October-November, when the baby snakes are found in large numbers, the snake-charmers mainly set out for catching snakes. The identification of habitat of snakes is the personal acumen of theirs. During the period of snake catching the miraculous power of chanting and *gada* (herbal medicine for snakebite) provide psychological support to deal with these venomous creatures.

The community has a caste council – *panch,* headed by the *Behera*. In olden days the post of *Behera* was hereditary; subsequently it has become a selective one. The *Kela* caste council meets twice a year, i.e., during Raja Sankranti (June-July) and during the Dassehera festival (September-October). It decides all important matters relating to the community. The interesting aspect of their community is the enforcement of 'Siddi' and 'Sudamanta'; the former is about the responsible behaviour of the general public and latter dealing with the obligations of sons towards their old and ailing parents. The caste council imposes fines on the villagers for various offences, the highest amount of fine of Rs 20 being collected from the person who has failed to reach the village on 'Raja Sankranti' festival. The snake-charmers are animatists. They worship the village deity, *Champanahakani,* and *Gaudiya Thakura* for the prosperity of the village and to protect them against diseases and evil sprits.

Status of Women: A Socio-Cultural Category

The women form an integral part of the *Kela* society. In every sphere of activity, the active participation of women along with men reflects the cultural necessity of women. Their association and active participation in all important spheres like social, political, religious and economic, make their status and position more meaningful.

In the socialization of the female child, the mother along with other female relatives takes maximum care. At an early age the mother trains the daughters in different designs of tattoo marks and to assist her in the household work. She also trains her daughter to make herself attractive and beautiful. On the whole, the socialization of female children in the community is a marked phenomenon which shows that the girls are trained with qualities and skills to become good household managers, efficient mothers and good entrepreneurs.

Sharing of responsibility among the women is quite spectacular. In household activities, vending, and also on the festive occasions sharing of responsibility, strengthen the network of solidarity and group behaviour.

Being a nomadic community, the *Kela* male members enjoy the least opportunity in decision-making process. The women of the snake-charmers constitute an integral part in the decision-making process. In every sphere and almost in all issues the women take an active role. So decision-making in the snake-charmers' household is a major factor to consider regarding the involvement of husband and wife in day-to-day activities. Following Tables reflects the decision-making in the household.

Table 16.2

Decision-Making in Kela Households (Social Issues)

Decision Maker	*Nature of Decision*		
	Marriage of Children (%)	*Education of Children (%)*	*Health Care (%)*
Wife alone	1.18	72.83	66.14
Joint decision	64.96	26.38	27.95
Husband alone	33.86	0.79	5.91
Total	100.00	100.00	100.00

Table 16.3

Decision-Making in Households (Economic Issues)

Decision Maker	*Nature of Decision*			
	Food Budget (%)	*Clothing Expenditure (%)*	*Social/ Ceremonial Expenditure (%)*	*Repair & Maintenance (%)*
Wife alone	87.40	74.41	1.18	6.69
Joint decision	11.81	24.80	98.03	87.40
Husband alone	0.79	0.79	0.79	5.91
Total	100.00	100.00	100.00	100.00

On a comparative analysis it is evident that the women possess almost sole authority pertaining to economic expenditure in the household which signifies their status in the society along with their managerial skills. On the other hand, although 33.86 per cent of husbands decide about the marriage of their offspring, in reality, it is a joint decision by both the parents. This reveals that the *Kela* women are the major decision makers in comparison to their male counterparts.

Not only in socio-economic issues but also in religious and political issues the women also take a vital role in decision-making. In traditional societies the women were allowed to sit in the *Sabha* (meeting of village council where major decisions are taken). But in the changing circumstances women are directly participating in the village council and expressing their opinion pertaining to the community problems. The present day Panchayati Raj system also shows the active participation of women in the political field with a raised level of political awareness.

The snake-charmer women, therefore, occupy a significant position in the *Kela* social life and culture, although it is not easy to ascertain social and economic status of the women, particularly in a nomadic community like that of the snake-charmers. The wandering habit of the male folks compels their women to manage their home and hearth. It is significant to note that the moral standards of the *Kela* women do not decline whether they are barren, divorced or widows. The economic status of the women does not decline, rather they invest more time in their productive works to augment their family economy in a respectful manner.

Work Participation of *Kela* Men and Women: An Asymmetrical Distribution

The human way of life is characteristically the thinking patterns of the males, though females constitute half of the total population in a community. The beginning of the world historic defeat of the female sex is the dichotomization of subsistence activities and establishment of culturally defined division of labour that created two genders – men and women. Gender virtually creates outer and inner operational spaces. The cultural construction of gender itself has led to a gender based asymmetrical society. With the advent of the concept of private property, men attempt to control women's labour by engaging themselves in farming activities. Significant economic contribution by men and secondary contribution like childcare and household work by women pave way for the inner and outer spaces in the gender relations.

Work schedule and participation of men and women is quite interesting in the snake-charmers community. It is noticed that women are the main workforce of the community. Table 16.4 depicts that 81.63 per cent of men usually undertake snake charming and snake catching as the main occupation, while 75.26 per cent of women is engaged in household work with the rest 25 per cent undertaking different income generating activities, viz. shop-keeping and vending, Government service and other work like tattooing and begging.

Table 16.4

Distribution of Working Population in Different Categories

Type of Occupation	*Men %*	*Women %*
Snake charming & catching	81.63	–
Wage labour	2.29	2.10
Shopkeeping & vending	8.20	20.90
Household work	–	75.26
Government service	4.60	0.70
Others	3.28	1.04
Total	100.00	100.00

Due to their migratory habit of the *Kelas* the nature of labour is assessed under the following two broad categories: the nature and type of work in permanent settlement; and the nature and type of work in temporary settlement or in the camp.

Table 16.5

Average Daily Working Hours of Adult Kela Women

Nature of Work	*Permanent Settlement*	*Total*	*Temporary Settlement*	*Total*
Household work	12 hours	12 hours	–	–
Household work+ Wage Labour	6 hours + 8 hours	14 hours	–	–
Household work + Government service	6 hours+ 8 hours	14 hours	–	–
Household work+ Shop-keeping or vending	7 hours+ 4 hours	11 hours	6 hours+ 8 hours	14 hours
Household work+ Tattooing	–	–	7 hours+ 6 hours	13 hours
Household work+ Fishing	–	–	9 hours+ 2 hours	11 hours

Table 16.5 shows that in permanent settlement the women make themselves busy in household work for about 12 hours a day. The longest period of working hours, i.e., 14 hours per day is being spent by women, those who are engaged in wage labour and Government and private sector services. Women engaged in shop-keeping and vending have least number of working hours, i.e., 11 hours. The working hours in camp sites are different from the working hours in the village. In the camp the women spend more time in shopkeeping and vending for about 14 hours daily.

Nowadays the snake-charmer women do not accompany their male counterparts during seasonal migration. During the period of my research, interview was made among adult females aged 15-59 years to evaluate their average daily working hours for different types of work in various months.

Table 16.6

Average Daily Working Hours of Adult Women Over the Year

Nature of Work	*Average Daily Working Hours by Months of the Year*											
	J	*F*	*M*	*A*	*M*	*J*	*J*	*A*	*S*	*O*	*N*	*D*
Domestic work	10	10	10	10	10	12	12	10	10	12	12	10
Shop keeping & vending	4	4	4	4	1	—	—	4	6	6	4	4
Wage Labour	8	8	8	—	—	—	—	—	—	—	8	8
Government service	7	7	7	7	7	7	7	7	7	7	7	7
Community work	—	—	1	1	—	2	—	—	—	—	—	—

Table 16.6 indicates that the snake-charmer women spend more hours in the months of June, July and October in domestic work, as husbands are at home having returned from the camps. Before the approach of rainy season they thatch and repair their houses which keep the women at work for more hours. Shopkeeping and vending attracts the snake-charmer women. They spend four hours daily in this work. 'Raja Sankranti' is celebrated by the snake-charmers with full participation of all members of the village. Each member of the house remains present in the village, so the women have to suspend vending work and give more time to household work. But in the month of September and October they spend six hours to sell the

items which provide them double the income compared to other months.

Cooperation and conflict in work is also noticed in their community. Cooperation in work is mainly seen among the spouses, the parents and children, and among fellow members. Conflict in work is mainly noticed between the husband and wife, and among the fellow members. The main causes of conflict among the couple are based on casual misunderstanding, whereas among fellow beings it is primarily because of professional enmity.

Kela Women's Contribution to Family Economy

Snake-charmer women constitute a very significant component of their population. The most explicit role of the women in the *Kela* society is their contribution to their household economy in addition to managing the household work and childcare at home. It is seen that 39.37 per cent of the total household's average annual income is Rs 11,000, 52.75 per cent of the total household's average annual

Figure 16.1

Annual Per Capita Expenditure of the Snake-Charmers

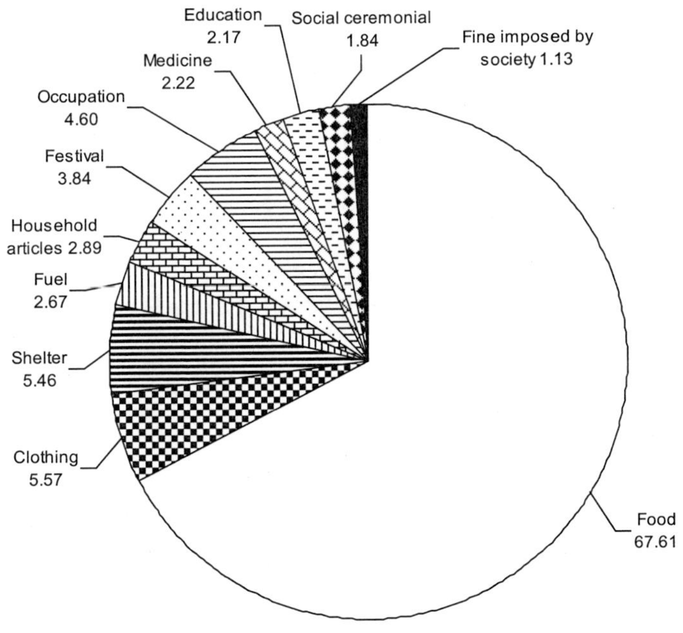

income ranges from Rs 12,000 to Rs 33,000 (Table 16.7). So far as women's earning in household is concerned, 81.69 per cent of them earn between Rs 10,000 to 15,000 per annum (Table 16.8). Major sources of earning for both males and females are snake charming, shopkeeping, vending, wage labour and service in private and Government agencies. From the analysis of data pertaining to economic life, it is revealed that the male-folk prefer the traditional occupations whereas the women prefer work which is remunerative. Women contribute 43.54 per cent to their family income, where as males contribute 56.46 per cent, which is evident from the Table 16.9. Their annual per capita expenditure reveals that food is the major source of expenditure, constituting 67.60 per cent of the total expenditure. Expenditure in clothing and repairing is almost the same. A nominal percentage of expenditure incurred in fines shows that the anchorage of society is still strong among the people (Figure 16.1).

Table 16.7

Average Income of the Kela Household

Income Group	*% of Households*
Up to 11,000	39.37
11,000-22,000	22.83
22,000-33,000	29.92
33,000-44,000	5.12
Rs 44,000 +	2.76

Table 16.8

Average Earning of the Kela Women

Average Earning	*% of Women*
Up to 5,000	8.45
5,000-10,000	7.04
10,000-15,000	81.69
15,000-20,000	1.41
Rs 20,000 +	1.41

Table 16.9

Average Annual Income of Working Kela Men and Women

Sources of Income	*Average Earning*		
	Male %	*Female %*	*Total %*
Wage labour	3.51	2.58	6.09
Shopkeeping and vending	12.20	13.04	25.24
Services	21.93	18.55	40.48
Snake charming	9.71	—	9.71
Others	9.11	9.37	18.48
Total	56.40	43.54	100.00

Kela Women vis-à-vis the Women in the Neighbouring Farming Communities

The status and role of women in the farming community are considered to be sacred, because of their association with the farm and farm products. Working in the field in different seasons for production of varieties of crops not only provide them with a psychological satisfaction for implementing the orders of the divine, but also they feel proud of themselves for supplying food to mankind. Agriculture being the mainstay of the rural economy the involvement of people in agriculture easily secures their position. However, the women who work in the field directly are said to be having a lower economic status in comparison to the women working in the household and with the finished products of agriculture.

The women in the farming community living around the village Padmakesharipur perform varieties of work in different seasons. Apart from being directly involved in agriculture, they also take care of the domestic animals. Livestock plays an important role in rural economy and social life in Orissa. The women prepare cow-dung cake for fuel, plaster the walls by using cow-dung water justifying the involvement of cattle population in peasant life. Celebration of 'Raja' festival in the month of June marks the beginning of the agricultural season and the observance of 'Manabasa puja' in honour of Goddess Lakshmi after the harvesting marks its ending. The beginning and the end of agrarian rituals are celebrated and organized by the women only. This shows the involvement of women both physically and psychologically in the rituals associated with agriculture.

The snake-charmer women, although they do not own much agricultural land, associate themselves in a variety of occupations to supplement their family economy. After harvesting, they roam from village to village along with their tattooing box, containing stationary articles, metal amulets and herbal medicines and return to the village with a handful of rice, paddy and allied agricultural products in exchange of their items. The women of the farming community do not treat them as parasites but enjoy their skill by paying them in kind for their tattooing or entertaining services.

The roaming habit of snake-charmer women has nothing to do with local agricultural operation and also the farming community does not depend on them for agricultural labour. As a consequence, they are not offered either grains or eatables during social ceremonies and rituals, although other low caste people are invited for the same purpose. For the women in the farming community, the role of snake-charmer women is that of an entertainer and is not economically dependable.

Occupational Shift and New Modes of Earning

Snake-charmer women have a significant role in managing their family economy as discussed earlier. Traditionally, the women of the community were accompanying the men during seasonal migration. When the male members were busy in snake charming, the women were also keeping themselves busy in tattooing and vending. Selling of herbal medicines, particularly 'gada' (a type of tuber for protection from snake biting), to the villagers was the business practiced by them for supplementing the family income.

Snake charming as an art and skill has been recognized as a very popular tradition of the snake-charmers' community. The *Kela* men were exclusively dependent upon snake charming. With the passage of time, it has become less remunerative. On the other hand, tattooing, which was the main occupation of the women, became unpopular. Consequently, the *Kela* society passed through economic hardship which forced the women to shift their traditional occupation and create new avenues for new modes of earning. Primarily they have shifted their modes of earning to shopkeeping, vending, wage labour and employment in Government and private organizations. The striking feature is that the women have given up peddling and instead have started doing shopkeeping that has made them stationary. The customers come to their shops instead of their moving to the customers' doorsteps.

The Enterprising *Kela* Women and their Problems

Entrepreneurship is a skill of discovering new opportunities, managing the business, taking risks by introducing new innovations. Basically the women entrepreneurs in small-scale trading do not have education or any formal training in management but they rely on utilizing the skills with which they already have some familiarity. The skill of vending by the snake-charmer women in the village highlights their enterprising quality.

It is reported that the snake-charmer women have acquired the skill of vending from another *Kela* group called *Nalua Kela*. With the advancement of time, the former could realize the importance of utilitarian and fashionable cosmetic items among the rural people, particularly the women. They buy these items in bulk at a reasonable rate and sell to the customers in the nearby villages at a higher price. Vending became a lucrative business as it required low investment and had good marketability. However, to carry out the business, arrangement of capital was always a difficult task on their part. They being a wandering community do not have any agricultural land or even ownership right over their habitation site. Unfortunately, none of the financial institutions agree to provide economic assistance to these highly enterprising *Kela* women, as they possess no immovable property to offer to the financier as a mortgage.

The customer-vendor relationship is also an important factor in the arena of small-scale trading. Some of the snake-charmer women are well versed in mobilizing the support of the customers. They establish good rapport with the people during their visit to their villages. Such skill of mobilization helps them to develop almost a permanent relationship with their customers.

In the process of change and development, the women have adopted new occupations and have developed a new trend of entrepreneurial relationship. They consider presentation and physical capabilities as the qualities of enterprising women. The quality of expression in women is another enterprising quality. Some women snake-charmers are more vocal than others which help them in persuading the customers to buy their goods. Emotional black-mailing the customer is another enterprising quality in them. It is especially required while selling the herbal medicines and metal amulets. During the course of selling, they highlight the tedious process of preparation of amulets which are specially designed to solve critical problems. They go to great extent in narrating different mythical inauspicious events and the power of their charms in warding off the evil and bringing in peace and prosperity. By narrating many such beneficial effects they usually tempt the customers to purchase their items. Making friendship bonds with the customers is another enterprising quality with the snake-charmer women. During their regular visit to the villages, they tend to develop friendships with the women of rich families in order to establish a permanent customer-seller relationship. Such friendship bonds also become a medium of faith and security for the items they transact and the persons they encounter.

The above qualities are the most enterprising ones possessed by the snake-charmer women. Although some of the above said qualities can be acquired, others are inherited. Every snake-charmer woman tries her best to be a good entrepreneur by using these qualities which make her a successful entrepreneur. Her decent earning goes into the maintenance of her family in a better fashion. Of late, some Government and non-government organizations (NGOs) have encouraged the snake-charmer women by implementing various income generating schemes for them. These schemes not only train them in the skill but also render financial support to carry out their entrepreneurial activities.

Conclusion

Padmakesharipur, the homeland of snake-charmers in Orissa, is a small hamlet of the main village, Patia. Though *Kelas* are categorized under Scheduled Caste (SC) or 'Harijan' communities, their small number and migratory habits never restricted their identity and participation in inter-village activities. Their proximity to the erstwhile king of the region had helped them to have a distinctive status in the region for their expertise in snake charming. With the trend of downplaying of untouchability in recent times and the efforts made by the Government to bridge the gap between high and low caste people, the snake-charmers find themselves in the mainstream of the rural society in their region of habitation. These have brought about marked changes in the interpersonal relationships in the villages.

The work of women in traditional societies has been considered as confined to mere household work rather than anything remunerative or income generating. My observation of the *Kela* women seems to make a departure from the above statement. There is no denying the fact that in the changing perspective the women have adopted remunerative jobs and in the process have become more enterprising, but the key point is that the tradition of small-scale entrepreneurship of the *Kela* women has always been there even in the past. In fact, the *Kela* women had a major stake in their traditional economy. This has placed the *Kela* women in relatively higher position compared to the women in the neighbouring farming communities. With the shifting of their attention to more entrepreneurial activities like small-scale trading and vending, the *Kela* women occupy almost an equal status in their society, despite an intense intellectual debate over the dependent status of women in India and elsewhere.

Select References

Aiyappan, A. (1944), *Irvas and Culture Change,* Madras: Madras Government Museum.

Amsden, A. (1980), *The Economics of Women and Work,* Harmondsworth: Penguin.

Anna, V. and N.C. Pillai (1990), Women Entrepreneurs in Kerala, *Social Change,* 20 (2), June, 32-37.

Arora, S. and A.K. Haldar (1994), Economy of the Nomadic Communities of India, *Man in India,* 74 (2).

Bhattacharya, A. (1908), The Bengali Snake Charmers and their Profession, *Indian Folklore,* I, 3-10.

Bujra, J. (1989), Women Entrepreneurs of Early Nairobi, *Canadian Journal of African Studies,* 9 (2).

Das, Shivatosh (1990), *Nomadas: A Study of the Bay of Islanders,* Delhi: Penman Publishers.

Deolanker, V. (1985), Status of Women Entrepreneurs, *Khadi Gramudyog,* 31(8), May, 331-35.

Elsun, D. and Ruth Pearson (1983), The Subordination of Women and the Internationalization of Factory Production, In K. Young,

C. Wolkwitz and R. McCullagh (eds.), *Of Marriage and Market*, 18-40, London: CSE Books.

Joshi, V. (1995), Anthropological Studies of Kalberia (Snake Charmers) Tradition, *Shodhak*, 20.

Marriot, M. (1955), Little communities in an Indigenous Civilization, In McKim Marriott (ed.), *Village India: Studies in the Little Community*, 171-222, Chicago and London: University of Chicago Press.

Melvin, L.P. (1966), The changing status and role of women in Toro (Uganda), *Cahiers d' Etudus Africanes*, XIV (3), 113-120.

Kumari, R. (ed.) (1992), *Women in Decision Making*, New Delhi: Vikas.

Mishra, P.K. and K.C. Malhotra (1982), *Nomads in India*, Kolkata: Anthropological Survey of India.

Mohanty, U.C. (1960), The *Kela*, Unpublished M.A Dissertation, Bhubaneswar: Utkal University.

Nadkarni, S.A. (1982), Women Entrepreneurs: A Socio-Economic Study with Reference to Pune, Unpublished Doctoral Dissertation, Pune: Institute of Management, Development and Research.

Reiter, R. (1975), *Towards an Anthropology of Women*, New York: Monthly Review Press.

Vinze, M.D. (1987), Women *Entrepreneurs in India: A Socio-economic Study of Delhi, 1975-85*, New Delhi: Mittal Publications.

Whitehead, A. (1984), Women's Solidarity and Divisions among Women, In C. Pelzer, White and K. Young (eds.), *Research on Rural Women: Feminist Methodological Question*, Sussex: IDS Publication.

White, C.P. (1984), Rural Women: Issue for Research, Policy and Organization for Gender Equality, In C. Pelzer, White and K. Young (eds.), *Research on Rural Women: Feminist Methodological Question*, Sussex: IDS Publication.

17

Women Scientists in India

A Socio-Economic Survey

ROOPA RAVIKUMAR

Robert K. Merton (1976) recognized the mutual interdependence between science and society. He saw scientific organizations as a reflection of the social environment. There has been an increasing enrolment of women into higher education to pursue graduate and undergraduate studies. In the past much of higher education was closed to Indian women. However, the market has brought in a change and the necessity for women's skills in the areas of health, information technology and computer science. This trend has encouraged women to enter into professional education.

Table 17.1

Indian Men and Women in Higher Education

Age in Years	*Graduates*		*Engineering/ Technology*		*Teaching*	
	Males	*Females*	*Males*	*Females*	*Males*	*Females*
20-24	39,12,315	28,56,492	4,31,378	1,66,606	60,160	66,966
25-29	49,02,358	29,93,483	4,20,647	1,32,396	1,31,761	1,31,657

Source: Census 2001, Government of India.

One observes from the statistics given in Table 17.1 that the ratio of men to women in all streams in the academia is higher. An equal proportion of males and females are seen in the teaching profession indicating that the teaching job is gender neutral and more feminine prone.

Science has a special place in today's world denoting the frontier of modernization of a society. Science is also considered as an agency of social change and social control. The sociological question at the macro level, which is raised here interrogates the significance women have derived from their experience of science education and the significance of being placed or employed in a scientific environment.

In this context a research study was conducted in two research organizations to explore the social background of the scientists. The investigator studied the scientists in Madurai Kamaraj University and The Central Electro Chemical Research Institute, Karaikudi, both in the State of Tamil Nadu in India. Only the science departments of the university were included in the sample, but at the research institute all the departments are science-based and, therefore, all were included. This method was followed as all the respondents held a graduate degree in science and the results of the study could be comparable. Therefore, scientists from the humanities departments were excluded for the sample selection. The researcher employed a structured interview schedule as the main tool to collect primary data and supplemented it with uncontrolled non-participant observation and case studies. The scientific approach adopted to collect data enabled the researcher to collect relevant information. The term scientist was operationally defined in the study as a permanent employee of the research organization. The sampling technique adopted was proportionate stratified sampling. This sampling technique further facilitated the comparison of the scientists in their respective organizations. The study is qualitative and the findings are valuable because of the in-depth interviews made by the investigator and the rapport established with the respondents. The total size of the sample in the research study was one hundred and thirty-one.

Every culture has its own traditional conception of the jobs meant for both the sexes. The pursuit of science, especially serious and original investigation, has not been one of the traditionally accepted pursuits for every one in this country. This study, therefore, of men and women involved in serious scientific work in research organizations is of immense sociological relevance. It could show us the social perspective of the status of scientific work.

Of the people engaged in scientific research and development in India, women form a mere 6% (Data Book on Science and Technology, 1995). At the Council of Scientific and Industrial Research (CSIR) Laboratories in India, only 7.55% of the scientists were women. A similar picture emerges from the study conducted by the researcher in these organizations. The Central Electro Chemical Research Institute has a mere 7.3% women and the Madurai Kamaraj University has 14.6% women on their rolls. Out of the total sample size in the research study 89.3% (n=117) are men and only 10.75% (n=14) are women. The ratio of male-female in the total sample is roughly 9:1. In the university, the male –female ratio is 7:1 whereas in the Research Institute the ratio is 14:1. Radha Chakravarthy, et al., (1988) in their study show that men scientists outnumber women in Indian organizations and their performance and status are in a number of ways related to gender differences reflecting the notions of patriarchy.

The numerical advantage that the males enjoy is a reflection of other male dominated occupations in the Indian society. Traditional thinking expects women to get married early, and expects men to be more career oriented which forces many women to get a general education rather than a highly specialized education that leads to independent or corporate projects of study and experimentation.

The distribution of women scientists in the research organizations is not an indicator of the number of women employed in research organizations. A distribution of the total workforce reveals that almost 50 per cent of the employees are women. These women participate in indirect, sometimes invisible and uncounted for jobs. Women are employed for various jobs such as posts of research scholar, research assistant, laboratory assistant, teaching assistant, and as library assistant, secretary, attender, sweeper, etc. An indirect method of participating in scientific activities is to assist in research projects as research scholars or research assistants. It was observed that in both the research organizations there were quite a few women working as research assistants, but they could not make their way into the cadre of the teaching staff or scientists. Only these persons are entitled and eligible to conduct independent research work. Moreover, the mundane and routine tasks are carried out by women, ignoring the remarkable skills of women in planning and development. The share of women in decision-making is denied by placing them in subordinate positions. This is an indirect way that reduces the developmental potential of the women as a whole. Women get married and have to keep moving according to the plans of their husbands. Such movements might curb the continuity and stability of a job.

Another interesting distinction in the distribution of women scientists is explained below. The Annual Report, 2000 of the Madurai Kamaraj University shows that the number of women in the university science departments has not increased. There are 88 male scientists against 8 female scientists, and in the humanities and social sciences division there are 29 women scientists against 9 men. Whereas the social science and humanities derive a third of their strength from the female sex the science departments draw only a tenth of their strength from the female sex. Three of the women in the social sciences and humanities departments head their departments. In contrast no woman in science is heading any department in the science department.

Another observation is that there are more women scientists in the department of biological sciences than in the department of physical sciences. This seems to confirm the findings of Balasubramanian that there is a great 'mathematical divide' based on the traditional bias of putting women in medical and related fields rather than in the study of physical and mathematical sciences.

Marital Status

Two of the women scientists were unmarried in the sample. It is interesting to note that proportionately fewer men remained unmarried and they considered themselves as prospective bridegrooms whereas the single women had ruled out marriage as an option. It is also interesting to note that the women who were unmarried belonged to the upper caste. Women seem to have peculiar problems about marriage when they acquire higher academic degrees like a post-graduate degree or a doctorate degree. When a girl is highly qualified academically, she prefers to marry a person who is more qualified or at least have an equal qualification as her. This is one of the reasons why the choice of a bridegroom is limited. Another difficulty is the problem of finding suitable bridegrooms whose horoscopes match those of the girls. These problems affect the women of upper (forward) castes more than they affect women of other castes. One of the respondents said that she had to reject proposals because the proposed grooms happened to be settled in other parts of the country. The groom was unwilling to migrate and she was unwilling to give up a government job.

A study conducted by Krupalini and Bhat regarding the desired level of education between life partners upheld the common sense notion in the Indian society that it is desirable for husbands to be more educated than their wives or have an equal or comparable education. The respondents opined that this was important for a stable, happy and healthy family set-up. The data in Table 17.2 indicates the educational qualification of the spouses.

Table 17.2

Educational Qualification of the Spouse of the Respondents

Educational Level of the Spouse	*University*		*Research Institute*		*Total N (%)*
	Male	*Female*	*Male*	*Female*	
Not applicable	2(4.7)	-	4(5.4)	2(18.2)	9(6.9)
Primary	2(4.7)	-	5(6.8)	-	7(5.3)
High School	9(20.9)	-	16(21.6)	-	25(9.1)
Pre-University	6(14.0)	-	12(16.2)	-	18(13.7)
Graduate	13(30.2)	-	24(32.4)	2(18.2)	38(29)
Post-Graduate	9(20.9)	1(33.3)	9(12.2)	2(18.2)	31(23.7)
Professional	2(4.7)	2(66.7)	4(5.4)	5(45.5)	13(9.9)
Total	43(100.0)	3(100.0)	74(100.0)	11(100.0)	131(100.0)

Note: Figures in parentheses indicate the percentage of respondents.

While the male scientists have married women who belong to varying levels of education, the female scientists have been restricted to the higher levels.

With regard the marital status of the scientist, it has been found that all over the world marriage has a negative impact on productivity and participation in a demanding and career oriented job. Cole and Zuckerman say that there is a negative correlation between marriage and motherhood on the one hand and women's labour force participation on the other.

At the Central Electro Chemical Research Institute, there were 3 scientist-couples working. The women had entered into the profession as research scholars but had found a mate of their choice from the same institute. It is interesting to note that the spouse spoke the same language and belonged to the same caste and religion.

Nativity – Rural and Urban Origin

Historically, modern educational opportunities were first available in urban centres. However, in recent decades rural students have found their way into institutions of higher learning.

While many of the male scientists in the research sample hailed from the rural areas, it was observed that all female scientists hailed from the urban areas. Women from urban areas had an edge over their rural counterparts for access to higher education. It appears that a rural background causes problems that are too difficult for rural women to overcome. The study found that the family background of the women scientists included that their parents were educated, either professionals or scientists or teachers. Their families also had a reasonably good economic standing.

Educational Background

Half of the women scientists said that they were toppers in the schools; they had availed regular government scholarships for higher studies and support of their family members encouraged them to pursue higher education and get the job of a scientist.

Only one in five of the women scientists (3/14) compared to three in eight of the male scientists (36.7%) in the research organizations did not enter their fields of specialization as a matter of their choice. For the women, to be a doctor was their first choice. However, they did not get admission into these courses either because of caste considerations or family circumstances. Whatever may be the reason for their initial failure they were happy to have attained the status of being a scientist now.

Hobbies and Recreation

Scientific research is an exhausting work, which calls for concentration for hours. Such work cannot be carried out mechanically. One needs to have a break and change of routine. There should be provision for this in the busy life of the scientist. The researcher conducted a survey of such interests and activities of scientists and these are presented in Table 17.3.

It was noted that not many of the scientists were seriously involved in leisure and social activities. Some of them considered their involvement in academic work in other institutions as a means of entertainment because they were taken out of their usual environment. Academic work includes interacting with the peers from other colleges as a member on the Board of Examinations or a member of the Academic Council. But many scientists felt that they could not afford any leisure time activities.

Table 17.3

Leisure Time Activities of the Respondents

Nature of Leisure Activity	*University*			*Research Institute*			*Grand Total*
	Male	*Female*	*Total*	*Male*	*Female*	*Total*	
Not involved	21 (41.8)	1 (33.3)	12 (26.1)	24 (32.4)	5 (45.4)	29 (34.1)	51 (38.9)
Intellectual Pursuits	9 (20.9)	1 (33.3)	10 (21.7)	15 (20.3)	3 (27.3)	18 (21.2)	28 (21.4)
Aesthetics	11 (25.6)	-	11 (23.9)	29 (39.2)	1 (9.1)	30 (35.3)	41 (31.3)
Politics	-	-	-	1 (1.3)	-	1 (1.2)	1 (0.8)
Religious Pursuits	2 (4.7)	1 (33.3)	3 (6.5)	5 (6.7)	2 (18.2)	7 (8.2)	10 (7.6)
Total	43 (100.0)	3 (99.9)	46 (100.2)	74 (99.9)	11 (100.0)	85 (100.0)	131 (100.0)

Note: Figures in parentheses indicate the percentage of respondents.

Quite a number of scientists were interested in reading; some of them were very much interested in serious reading which eventually brought them back to their professional interests. Others were interested in light reading, watching television, viewing films, and listening to music. Only one respondent in the research organization was involved in some political pursuits. One of the remarkable facts about Indian politics is that the intellectuals keep away from practical politics. The codes of conduct for scientists, especially for those working in public organizations like the University and the Research Institute, do not permit them to be actively involved in politics. But it cannot forbid them from articulating their considered opinions on political issues. If the scientists were involved in politics, then the politicians probably might have restrained from reckless adventurism. But not many scientists were seen to be seriously involved in recreational activities, which could provide them with a healthy break from their routine. In fact, it is unfortunate that almost 50 per cent of the scientists (n=63) in the research organizations did not engage themselves in any kind of socializing activity. They were all wedded to science. One of them said, "Science is My First Wife".

Factors of Scientific Productivity

The research study looked into factors of scientific productivity. Some of the factors comprising research output are number of publications in international journals, number of books published, number of citations, membership in professional bodies, having gone abroad, attending seminars, number of projects undertaken, awards received, number of patents taken, amount of royalty received, number of processes developed, etc.

Women scientists made comparable contributions to science as the men scientists. While the study revealed that around 10% of the men scientists spent their time in an indifferent manner, which did not lead to scientific productivity, all the women (100%) had a high sense of commitment to their task. In fact, one woman scientist claimed that if people utilized their working hours prescribed by the government (i.e., from 9.00 a.m. to 5.00 p.m.) seriously, there would be visible research output for the scientists. Women scientists were rated as high as the men scientists for all the factors of scientific productivity mentioned above.

Obstacles faced by the scientists during the research activity were common to both the sexes. Women scientists claimed that there was no sex-wise discrimination within the scientific environment. They said that the male colleagues were cooperative and the problems mentioned by the scientists, namely the difficulty in getting a project sanctioned or for a book to be published could not be termed as gender specific.

Job satisfaction is a multi-dimensional concept. The study included four variables, namely, job involvement, collegiality, reward system, job security and job mobility. Most of the women scientists (11/14) said that they had a feeling of involvement in the activities of the research organization. They were invited for all the meetings held at various levels: the research team level, department level, divisional and organizational level. They were not excluded based on their sex. Almost all the women scientists (13/14) expressed that they had a 'we–feeling' towards the research organization where they were employed. They considered their research organization as their Alma Mater because they were the products of the very same university or had worked as research scholars before getting employment in the research organization.

To be involved in decision-making and participation in the policy formation of the research organization enhances job satisfaction for an employee. To have healthy interpersonal relationships within the organization furthers the job satisfaction of the scientists. A conducive work environment contributes to effective communication and directly influences better research output. Collegiality is the capacity of the co-workers to recognize the worth of one's colleagues transcending a natural feeling of jealousy and envy against those whom one considers an equal, intellectually, if not socially, economically or in terms or organizational status. This concept was enunciated by Argyris (1957) in his study on the scientists of a research organization. He stressed on healthy working situations to be created which would lead to self-actualization and better job involvement for the employees.

The reward system in the form of promotions was based on seniority and confidential reports. The scientists were not happy about the undue weight given to the confidential reports. It was suggested that increments be given to achievers.

Another factor which enhances job satisfaction is the 'job security' that scientists have in their research organization. They were content with their income and made no complaints about their standard of living.

Constraints that Women Face to Become Scientists

1. The state and the institutions of a country impinge on scientific pursuits so palpably that traditional ideas of the universality and the absolute objectivity of scientific pursuits have to be abandoned. Robert K. Merton says that the ethos of science consists of universalism, communism, objectivity and ethical neutrality. These are terms that are gender neutral. The qualities required of a scientist in order to pursue science are patience, curiosity, perseverance, determination, and faithfulness. These terms have a feminine connotation in all societies. An analysis of gender socialization practices for women in both developed as well as developing societies

encourage women to take on roles that require patience, endurance, commitment, seriousness, etc. However, the scientific environment is rigid and authoritative which is non-feminine. Therefore, the question raised here is could this be one of the reasons that women though possess inherent characteristics for the making of a scientist are pushed out or suffocated in the scientific environment? This could one of the reasons why women are less represented in scientific environment and women opt not to do research.

2. The median age at marriage for an Indian woman is 24 years and this coincides with the entry into starting a career in science. When a student completes post graduation degree in straight course, she is approximately 23 years old and the next milestone is to be settled in life, which means a search for a prospective groom in the Indian context. Therefore, in order to have a wider selection of spouse, women generally prefer to take up jobs that are transferable.
3. Women prefer teaching jobs to research due to flexible teaching hours and adaptable demands on one's energy and time. A teaching job enables women to meet multiple familial role expectations and poses less role strain on them. Moreover, the objective and purpose of higher education is also achieved through teaching. Women do not perceive the task of a researcher as conducive as it involves physical and strenuous work outside home that requires long time absence from home, even extending to the nights.
4. To be a scientist, one needs to be career oriented. To be a professional scientist, one needs to be single-minded. Then only the women scientist can stand in the platform of competition among scientists. Scientific discoveries and developments are taking place at a very fast rate and if one wants to participate in the race, women scientists who are productive, have expressed that their domestic front took a back lashing. In the research study, the productive scientists were women who were single. The married women scientists have an encouraging and supportive social system that enables them to do well and concentrate on their work. Due to gender socialization, women have perceived and also given primary preference to their role in the domestic sphere, and secondarily to their career. Any job undertaken is seen as only next to the home front.

Select References

Argyris, C. (1975), *Personality and Organization: The Conflict between the System and the Individual*, New York: Harper and Row.

Balasubramanin, D. (1993), Women Scientists Knocking at the Glass Ceiling, *The Hindu* (Madurai), Nov. 17, 1993, Vol. CXVI, 19.

Chakravarthy, R., et al. (1988), Women Scientists at Work: An International Comparative Study of Six Countries, *Scientometrics*, XIV (1-2), 43-74.

Cole, R.J. and Zuckerman Harriet (1983), The Structure of Scientific Careers: Are Marriage and Family Incompatible with Research Productivity? Paper read at the American Sociological Association Conference, New York.

Government of India (1997), *Pocket Data Book*, New Delhi: Ministry of Science and Technology, Govt. of India.

International Institute for Population Sciences (2001), National Family Health Survey (2001), Mumbai.

Jessie, Bernard (1974), *Academic Women*, USA: Meridian Books.

Maithreyi, Krishnaraj (1991), *Women and Science: Selected Essays*, Bombay: Himalaya Publishing House.

Merton, R.K. (1976), *Sociological Ambivalence and Other Essays*, New York: The Free Press.

Reskin, Barbara F. (1978), Sex Differentiation and the Social Organization of Science, *Sociological Inquiry*, XLVIII, 3-37.

Ruth B. Kundsin (ed.) (1974), *Women and Success: The Anatomy of Achievement*, New York: Morrow Paperback Edition.

Sundaramony, Roopa (1999), Research Output of Scientists in a University and a Research Institute in Tamil Nadu: A Study in Sociology of Science, Unpublished Ph.D. Dissertation, Madurai: Madurai Kamaraj University.

Violet, B. Haas and Carolyn C. Perucci (eds.) (1987), *Women in Scientific and Engineering Professions*, Ann Arbor: University of Michigan Press.

18

Parties, Patronage and Gender in the *Panchayati Raj*

APARNA THOMAS

With the implementation of the 73rd Amendment, Indian states began to rethink the relationship between state and local governments. A renewed emphasis on decentralization of economic and political functions was evident in the changes and reforms initiated by states, especially Maharashtra, which was the first state to implement the reforms outlined in the 73rd Amendment. The local government or *panchayati raj* is a three-tiered institution, with the district level or *zilla parishad* at the top, followed by the intermediate/block or *panchayat samiti* level, and the village or *gram panchayat* level at the bottom. Elected members in turn elect a president to chair each of the levels.

Commenting on the role of the state, Pradeep Chhibber (2002:48) argues that the state in India occupies a primary role in the economic and social transformation of the nation. State governments have been key players in the political process. Local governments have no real power and owe their existence to the state governments (Chhibber, 2002: 49). As a result, local governments are unable to make decisions because they lack authority and financial resources. Chhibber argues that the nature and structure of the state has influenced the development of the party system, which emerged as an executive-centred, state-based system in which the national party could influence the states and state parties controlled local parties.

This argument is applicable to state and local level politics in Maharashtra. Until the 1990s, the dominance of the Congress Party throughout the state provided the basis for most of the policy creation and implementation at the state as well as the *panchayat* levels. This is particularly true in the Sangli District, considered a traditional Congress stronghold. The fact that one of the most prominent chief ministers of the state was from Sangli further consolidated the relationship between the Congress at the state level and the three levels of the *panchayati raj* in the district. In addition, other factors such as the influence of the political elites and party leaders also influence decisions and policies in the district. Women are not exempt from these influences. Rather, women's participation at all three levels is influenced by their party affiliation and relationships with the local elite.

However, since 1995, other parties such as the BJP and the Shiv Sena have also been influential in *panchayati raj* politics in the district, as they have to some extent weakened the Congress hold. The split within the Congress Party has also created space for other parties to claim their stakes in *panchayat* politics.

In this paper, I discuss the role of parties in local politics; specifically, the nature of the relationship between party leaders and policy-making in the Sangli District at all three levels of the *panchayat* system, the site of my case studies. By presenting evidence from interviews and proceedings of meetings, I argue that decisions are commonly made along party lines and that party leaders, both elected and informal, strongly influence policy. Women are thereby constrained in their ability to successfully participate in decision-making unless they follow the party line.

However, party competition can also work in favour of women. In instances where intense party competition and rivalry exist, women have been successful in making their voices heard, and men have taken them seriously. On the other hand, in some instances where one party dominates the *gram panchayat, panchayat samiti* or *zilla parishad,* women have been less successful in influencing policy, while in other instances of one-party domination, women have had more success. What this suggests is an interesting relationship between parties and women's participation. While women benefit from the support of the party, they also seem to be more effective at times when they are not part of the majority. Thus I argue that parties and the influence of political elites can both foster as well as hinder women's participation.

First, I discuss the emergence of the major political parties active in *panchayat* politics in Maharashtra. Next, I discuss the historical role of the Congress Party in India and specifically in Maharashtra. The Congress dominated *panchayat* politics throughout the Sangli district until the early 1990s, and although other parties have since gained greater influence in the area, the Congress influence continues in direct and sometimes indirect ways. Third, I discuss the role of political elites, both formal/elected and informal elites in *panchayat* politics. Finally, I discuss specific cases and instances in which parties and elites have influenced women's participation at all three levels. Field research for this project was conducted during 2001-2002.

Party Politics and the Political Atmosphere in India

In recent years, tensions both within Indian politics and between India and neighbouring Pakistan have escalated sharply; domestic and international politics in India are tightly intertwined. Domestic politics in India had become so tense by late 2001 that India's highly popular Prime Minister Vajpayee offered to resign in August of that year due to his inability to lead the coalition government and his own BJP party.

The Hindu-Muslim conflict that is symbolized by the long-running violence in Kashmir is the main reason for tensions in the region. Tensions with Pakistan over the war in Kashmir continued to climb through 2001 and reached a crisis following a terrorist attack on the Indian Parliament. India and Pakistan were on the verge of war, with conventional and nuclear forces placed on the borders, and it was only through international efforts that the crisis was diffused. Another domestic crisis erupted during 2002 when Hindu-Muslim riots paralyzed Gujarat state beginning in late February and continuing through April, as many as 2000 people lost their lives.

India is a parliamentary democracy in which citizens have the right to select their chief executive through electoral mechanisms. During the first three decades after achieving independence from England, the Congress Party dominated both the Federal and regional governments of India. Congress achieved this success by drawing on its nationalist legacy, the extensive use of state patronage, and the accommodation of numerous class and communal interests inside the party structure (Chhibber, 2002). The Congress Party suffered its first electoral defeat in 1977 following the two-year state of emergency declared by Prime Minister Indira Gandhi. During the past twenty years the hegemony of the Congress Party has weakened. While Congress still remains a primary force in Indian politics, non-Congress prime ministers have governed this country on seven different occasions since the lifting of the state of emergency in 1977. In 1999 Atal Vajpayee led a 25-party coalition (headed by his Hindu nationalist BJP) to electoral victory over the Congress Party and numerous other class- and regional-based parties.

Under the Indian Constitution executive power is formally vested in the president but, in reality the prime minister who holds these powers. As is the case in most parliamentary systems, the prime minister is directly accountable to the national assembly. In an effort to hold together the fragile coalitions that have characterized India politics in the last 20 years, India's prime ministers have been forced to compromise on major issues in order to maintain the confidence of a majority faction in the Lok Sabha (Chhibber, 2002).

Parties in Maharashtra

Like most other Indian states, the state of Maharashtra encompasses a wide range of political opinions and ideologies represented in the form of political parties. The parties are national, regional and caste based. The Congress, including both the Congress I, and the Nationalist Congress Party, and the Bharatiya Jananta Party (BJP) are the dominant national parties represented in Maharashtra, while the Shiv Sena is the largest regional party in the area. Caste-based parties such as the Dalit party are also present. Religious based organizations such as the Vishwa Hindu Parishad (VHP) and the Rashtriya Swayamsevak Sangh also influence parties. The BJP in particular is closely allied with both these religious organizations, and all three have interlocking leadership making the relationship even stronger.

While the Congress party has dominated both national and regional politics, a dramatic shift occurred in 1996, with the rise of the BJP, a right wing religious party. Another significant event was the formation of a series of coalitions among parties that began in the late 1990s and continue to exist today. After 1996, various regional political parties have governed India and are key elements of the coalition that brought the BJP into power in 1998. Caste-based parties have also played an important role in creating the coalition. As Chhibber (2002:1) writes, it was the first time since independence that the Indian party system, which had been dominated by the Congress Party, was fractured along regional, caste and religious lines.

The Congress Party

The Congress party remains one of the most, if not the most influential parties in Indian political life. No discussion of parties is complete without an understanding of the origins and structure of the Congress party. Much of the literature on the nature of the Congress Party prior to the 1990s focused on its 'all encompassing' qualities (Kothari, 1964; Joshi, 1968). This body of literature emphasized the party's strengths based on the fact that it began as a nationalist movement and thus had a built in philosophy that included secularism. It was able to promote itself as the alternative to the religious movements emerging at the time of independence. Another source of strength of the Congress Party came in the form of its original founders and leaders like Jawaharlal Nehru, who continued to emphasize the inclusive nature of the party in an effort to win over Muslim votes.

Currently, the Congress party consists of two major branches: the Congress I and the Nationalist Congress Party (NCP). The Congress I is part of the original Congress Party founded by Nehru and others and later led by Indira Gandhi and her son Rajiv. The split within the Congress occurred in the mid 1980s, due to a power struggle for leadership positions. This was further intensified in the 1990s, after the death of Rajiv Gandhi, when a vacuum in leadership was created. One of the major points of contention among members was support of or opposition to Sonia Gandhi, Rajiv's widow, an Italian-born woman who is now the leader of the Congress I.

The Congress Party Rule in Maharashtra

Since 1935, the Congress has dominated politics in both urban and rural areas. Congress was successful also in part because of the strategies employed by leaders to co-opt members of different castes and the sugar cooperatives in the state. The first chief minister of

Maharashtra, Y.B. Chavan, was instrumental in strengthening the relationship between the Congress and the majority of rural Maharashtra. As a Maratha from Kolhapur (the adjacent district to Sangli) and a prominent leader of the then Nationalist Congress Party, Chavan was seen as one of the original 'sons of the soil', a term indicating his caste and hence close ties to the region, destined to take Maharashtra to new heights. It is interesting to note that early on Chavan was aware of the caste dynamics within the emerging political elite. He built up the Congress Party with non-Brahmin elites and as a result acquired the support from other caste groups as well (Rosenthal, 1977). Thus the party was viewed as one representing various groups, keeping in line with the secularist agenda of the Congress Party at the national level.

The Congress has also had a long-standing relationship with the *panchayati raj* in Maharashtra. Singh, Lele, Sathe, et al. (1992) argue that, through the control of rural areas, the Congress has successfully dominated institutions of local government. This is evident through their control and influence over the sugar cooperatives. Often the Chairman of the cooperative is also the Chairman of the *zilla parishad* or *panchayat samiti,* and in most cases is also a local Congress leader (Singh, Lele, et al. 1992: 66). For example, Vasantdada Patil, another key figure in both the Congress Party and Maharashtra State politics, effectively combined the offices of the President of the Maharashtra State Congress Committee and the chairmanship of the Maharashtra State Cooperative Bank for several years.

Additionally, various boards related to the major cooperative credit institutions were also reorganized in such a manner that top positions were taken by the leading actors in the Congress Party (Rosenthal, 1974). Since then, holding an office position in these cooperative structures has been seen as a prize and a matter of prestige in Maharashtra. Rosenthal further suggests that almost by definition, the successful rural politician is likely to hold a seat on a major credit institution (Rosenthal, 1974: 421).

Thus the Congress Party consolidated its power in the state by achieving both economic and political control. Economic power was gained through the control of the cooperative sector. Similarly, political power was consolidated through the control of *panchayat* institutions in the state. This has proved to be a successful strategy for the party overall.

However, the elections of 1990 changed the power structure of the Congress in Maharashtra. The alliance between the BJP and Shiv-Sena (the regional, Hindu, Maratha caste based party from Maharashtra) resulted in the entry by opposition parties into *panchayat* politics for the first time. Also for the first time, there were more competition, more takers for the political space and more opportunities at the rural level in the district. However, before launching into an analysis of elite influences, a discussion of precisely who constitutes the elite is in order.

Political Elites in the Sangli District

The Congress Party played an important role in enhancing the interests of the political elites. By providing them with economic and political opportunities, the party received loyalty and the political support of the rural masses. This relationship is also very useful for the elites. The power of the ruling elites is enhanced by the fact that the Congress ideology of secularism provides them with an effective political formula (Sirsikar, 1995: 133). The elites were able to convince the people that their welfare was safe as long as it was in Congress hands. This ideology was firmly rooted in rural Maharashtra until the 1990s.

For this study, I define elites to include both political elites and bureaucrats. Within the category of political elites, I include elected officials both at the state level (including members of parliament and members of the legislative assembly), political party leaders (again at all levels), and informal elites. The category of informal elites includes local village leaders, as defined by their socio/economic status, and also the traditional *goondas* (local ruffians, often on the payroll of the informal elite, to enforce authority when needed).

Although this definition of elites is fairly narrow, there is a clear hierarchy within it, with the state-level elected politicians at the top and the informal village elite at the bottom. Moreover, the hierarchy also exists at all three levels of the *panchayati raj*, with the state-level elites exercising power over the *zilla parishad*, and the district-level elites in turn exercising power over the *panchayat samitis*, and so on. The hierarchy is seen in all the major political parties such as the Congress I, Nationalist Congress, the BJP and Shiv Sena, perhaps in varying degrees, but nevertheless always present, orchestrating nominations, elections, agendas and most importantly policies.

Village elites in their turn exercise control over the lower orders through the customs of establishing patron-client relationships, money-lending, sharecropping, wage labor, and dominance over institutions of local self-government (Rosenthal, 1974). In the villages surrounding Sangli, the village elites usually belong to the Maratha caste, because it is the majority caste in the area. They are always men, from landed families or from political families. Due to the fact that the area was home to two of Maharashtra and Congress prominent leaders, the extended families of Y.B. Chavan and Vasantdada Patil are very powerful and command respect and authority in the political functioning of the *panchayats*. For example, it is very common to find members of these political families invited to sit in on *panchayat* meetings, otherwise restricted only to the elected members and the *gram sevak*. In other instances, informal political leaders, or party leaders at the local level, also manipulate their way into the meetings.

Typically, at each level of the *panchayati raj*, a government appointed bureaucrat facilitates meetings. At the *panchayat level*, it is the *gram sevak*, at the *panchayat samiti*, it is the block development officer (BDO), and at the *zilla parishad* level, it is the chief executive officer (CEO). The responsibilities of these bureaucrats are limited to non-partisan coordination of the meetings, providing explanations of the rights and responsibilities of the elected members, and record keeping, among other duties. Although the rules are clear about participation in meetings limited to only the elected members and bureaucrats, in reality, local political elites representing various political parties, as well as other prominent members in the villages attend and participate in meetings, especially at the *gram panchayat* level.

Role of Parties and Elites at the Gram Panchayat Level

For this project, I studied three *gram panchayats*: Bharatpur, Bhimagaon, and Kapsewadi.[1] Among the *gram panchayats* studied, party leaders played an important role in decision-making and influenced women's participation most clearly in three cases: Kapsewadi, Bhimagaon, and Bharatpur. In Kapsewadi, one party, Shiv Sena, dominated the *gram panchayat*, Bhimagaon was evenly divided between two parties, while in Bharatpur, Congress I dominated. The picture that emerges from these three villages is one that suggests that in these cases of one-party domination, it was easier for women to initiate and implement policies favourable to them, while in other cases where intense party competition exists, women had a more difficult time initiating policy.

Kapsewadi is a small village with a population of 6,000. It lies on the outskirts of the town of Malegaon, which is also the closest *panchayat samiti*. Most of the people in Kapsewadi work in the service industry. The village is located within the larger Maharashtra Industrial Developmental Corporation (MIDC) area; a government undertaking that assists industries, so a number of people are employed in the factories. In fact, the village itself was created as the result of a relocation programme when the Koyna dam was built on the Krishna River. The government compensated people with a plot of land in order to relocate them to this area in the 1960s. At that time, about 80 families moved there.

The composition of the Kapsewadi *gram panchayat* is very homogenous along party lines. It is virtually controlled by the Shiv Sena. With a total of seven members, including five men and two women, it is one of the smaller *gram panchayats*. One of the two women belongs to the dominant Maratha caste, while the other belongs to the *Kumbhar* caste (a scheduled caste). The male *sarpanch* (president) also belongs to the Maratha caste. The Kapsewadi *gram panchayat* is also one of the more organized in terms of record keeping and holding regularly scheduled meetings. I was welcomed at the first *gram panchayat* meeting that I attended and promised 'full cooperation' during the course of my research.

Observations based on attendance at *gram panchayat* meetings in Kapsewadi for six months and on interviews with all the *gram panchayat* members and some of the local informal political elites indicate that decision-making and policy-making at the *panchayat* are determined along party lines, and most often according to the wishes of the informal elites. This became evident when I analysed records of the meetings that would document decisions not taken at *panchayat* meetings. Additionally, since it was a gram panchayat dominated by one party, the voices of dissent were few and soft. Members of the dominant party were united in their agenda for both the party and the village. On more than one occasion, I was informed about the positive changes the party had implemented since taking power. The unanimous decision-making along party lines was also seen as an asset. Moreover, Party officials from the *taluka* level would sit in on meetings and ensure that appropriate decisions were being taken.

Party dominance affected women's participation as well. Although one of the women members was very active, she also belonged to the dominant caste and was recruited by the Shiv Sena to run for elections. She won virtually unopposed. She was the female deputy *sarpanch* and was one of the most active and articulate women in the *gram panchayat*. She single-handedly started a *balwadi* (a kind of a pre-school often assisted by the government) in the village and currently worked there as well. She convinced the rest of the *gram panchayat* that the village needed the *balwadi* and campaigned vigorously for it. She was educated, having completed high school and also a one-year teacher-training course and outspoken on issues during meetings.

This deputy *sarpanch* came from a family with political ties to the Shiv Sena party. Her brother-in-law had been the *sarpanch* in Kapsewadi for the past five years. When he finished his term, in her words, "it was decided that I should be nominated for the post of the deputy-*sarpanch*, since my husband was not interested in getting involved". Although her husband is not formally involved in the *gram panchayat*, he did attend some of the meetings during my time there, and was initially always present when I met her. Also, the *sarpanch* of Kapsewadi is a good friend of her husband and I often witnessed the husband accompanying the *sarpanch* on his trips to the *panchayat samiti* or *zilla parishad* offices.

As the deputy *sarpanch*, she took her job seriously. She was proud of her achievements that including both the *balwadi* and the creation of two bore wells in the village. Securing water is a problem that she was concerned about and towards that end; she successfully allocated funds so that additional wells could be built in Kapsewadi. While clearly she was a motivated and dynamic personality in her own right, the political backing she experiences from the Shiv Sena was also crucial to her success. The fact that the Shiv Sena dominated the entire gram panchayat made it easier for her to speak up, given her political affiliation and background. Although her husband and brother-in-law were never far from the scene, she was considered one of the success stories of the party in the area.

The other female member in the Kapsewadi *gram panchayat* belonged to the *kumbhar* caste. The *kumbhars* are traditional potters. They make various pots and other household items from clay and mud. One of the specialties is making mud statues of Hindu gods and goddesses. This is a particularly lucrative business during the festival season. When I first visited their home, she showed me the statues that her husband was getting ready for the up coming Diwali season, which began in early November.

This representative came from a different socio-economic background than the deputy *sarpanch*. Her house was very modest, consisting only of two rooms, with very sparse furniture. But she and her husband owned a small plot of land outside their house, where they grew vegetables. Her husband worked in a garment factory as a line supervisor. They had been married for the past eleven years and had two children, both girls, age nine and seven. The mother-in-law also lived with them. She moved to Kapsewadi with her husband nine years earlier.

She has served on the Kapsewadi *gram panchayat* for almost five years now. She recalls the time that she was first approached to contest the elections: "the *sarpanch* and two other men from the village came to meet with my husband. They told him that I should enter my name on the ballot, as they needed a woman from our caste to fill the seat. They assured my husband that I would not have to do anything. They would take care of all the formalities. All I needed to do was place my thumbprint on the papers that they would send".

The *kumbhar* representative rarely attended *panchayat* meetings, and when she did, she usually sat on the floor in a corner (to maintain her caste status). She only attended a couple of meetings when I was present. Both times she did not speak, and interestingly, was not asked to vote. During one of the meetings, a vote was taken on the decision to hold a special *gram sabha* to discuss the village cleanliness campaign. Kapsewadi had been a strong contestant the previous year, and enthusiasm was high to do better this time around. As various options were being deliberated, the deputy *sarpanch* and the men made the decisions, while the kumbhar representative remained silent. When I brought it up with her in a later interview, her response was: "but how can I speak? I am a *kumbhar*, they are all Marathas. If I say the wrong thing, the Shiv Sena *goondas* will hurt my family".

The Shiv Sena recruited both the female representatives. Hence on paper, it would seem that both would be given equal opportunities. However, in reality, the deputy *sarpanch* has successfully used her party connections to achieve results, while the *kumbhar* representative remains bound by her caste and economic status. The Kapsewadi *gram panchayat* presents a case in which one-party dominance creates for a very amicable atmosphere. Alternatively, from another perspective, it represents a *panchayat* where the party and party leaders control the decision-making and the opposition is almost invisible. The one opposition member in the *gram panchayat* belonged to the Congress I and on several occasions, when he tried to question a decision, he was silenced both by the *sarpanch* and the *gram sevak.*

Similarly, Bharatpur also represents a case of one-party dominance in the *gram panchayat*. This village is outside Sangli, in the heart of the sugar belt, close to one of the major sugar factories. Bharatpur has a unique political history and is known as the hometown of Vasantdada Patil, one of the most prominent ex-chief ministers of Maharashtra. In fact, he was referred to merely as 'dada' (which means older brother in Marathi). The village population is used to being in the political limelight, as they have been exposed to numerous television and newspaper interviews. As such, the villagers are politically aware and actively support Congress I campaigns throughout the district.

Within the extended family of Vasantdada Patil there are two factions. These factions are directly linked to the personal life of the famous leader. Vasantdada Patil was married with children in the 1970s when be became acquainted with another woman, also an activist for Congress I. Their friendship over the years resulted in his companion adopting Vasantdada's last name (for all practical purposes, she became known as his second wife, although they did not formally marry). She moved into Bharatpur and the couple has one son. Although Vasantdada recently passed away, his former companion and his son are active member of the Congress I, while Vasantdada's son from his wife is also in politics, in the opposition Nationalist Congress Party.

Thus Bharatpur is divided between people who are loyal to his companion and her son and people loyal to his first wife. Yet, while the two political factions have serious differences, they also come together and unite against what they see as any outside opposition. As a result, they have successfully prevented any other political party from entering into the *gram panchayat* politics.

The *gram panchayat* in Bharatpur also has the unique distinction of being the only all-women's *panchayat* in the district. It is made up of nine women, all from the Congress I party. While the phenomena of all-women's *panchayats* is not new to Maharashtra, it is new to the

Sangli District.[2] Moreover, it is also a *panchayat* with no opposition member. It was created directly by the Congress Party. In an effort to promote Bharatpur in the district and the state, the local Congress I leaders, i.e., members of Vasantdada's extended family, decided to nominate an all-women's panel for the 2000 elections. The women were carefully chosen from the prominent families in the village and the announcement was made that this was the panel endorsed by Congress I.

The panel won an uncontested election. Bharatpur not only became the first village in the Sangli District to boast an all-women's *panchayat*, but it was also the first all-women's *gram panchayat* to be nominated, created and supported solely by a political party. Studies on all women's *panchayats* in Maharashtra indicate that in most cases, social movements, women's organizations and semi-political groups such as the Shetkari Shramik Sanghatana have been instrumental in the creation of *panchayats* (Datta, 1998; Singh, Lele, et al., 1992). Other research also demonstrates the impact of influential individuals such as in the case of Ralegaon Siddhi, the native village of the famous social activist, Anna Hazare (Omvedt, 1990).

However, in Bharatpur, the creation of the all-women's *panchayat* was a carefully deliberated choice by the ruling party in order to support the party position on the women's reservation bill and the general party position on women's participation in politics. In other words, the *panchayat* did not come to power on the initiative of women. With the Congress I traditionally considered as the moderate, progressive, secular and inclusive party in India (Chhibber, 2002; Sirsikar, 1995; Rosenthal, 1974), the all-women's *panchayat* in Bharatpur portrays the image that party leaders were attempting to promote in the district.

Bharatpur had a female *sarpanch*.. I first met with her in her home one evening. First impressions indicate that she comes from a well-to-do family, evident from the location of her house, the nicest one on the block. She belonged to a politically connected family. Her husband is the nephew of Vasantdada Patil, and is currently MLA from the Rashtrawadi Congress party. Her husband was the *sarpanch* for the previous 10 years.

She was articulate about the issues facing the *gram panchayat*, stating that water was the primary concern for women in the village, as there is only one tank and it was not enough for the village. As *sarpanch*, she had also initiated a plan to increase the water supply to the village, by reallocating to the village some of the water supply intended for the nearby sugar fields.

She was quite enthusiastic about the all-women's *panchayat* and also about the fact that its members won the election unopposed. She also mentioned that prior to that *panchayat* elections were usually not contested. The women worked closely with the *gram sevak*, as I observed from the meetings. The *gram panchayat* meetings in Bharatpur operated under a power dynamic completely different from that of Kapsewadi. With the *gram sevak* being the only male present in the room, he was usually the one sitting in a corner, answering questions, as theoretically required of this role. All nine members attended meetings most of the time. The women were all vocal and deliberated on whatever issue was being discussed.

When asked why Bharatpur had an all-women's *panchayat*, she responded that "the men wanted to give us an opportunity to participate in politics". When asked about women's participation in the *gram sabha* (village meetings) she said that women did not attend the meetings. They did, however, attend the monthly meetings. Although the *gram sabha* was designed to include and increase citizen participation in politics through deliberation, in reality, women tend to be absent from most *gram sabhas*. The *gram sabhas* are held in the evenings, when most women are busy cooking the evening meal. Furthermore, *gram sabhas* are seen as meeting where men get together, sometimes drunk. They often lead to shouting matches and fights among different political groups in the village. In other words, a *gram sabha* is not seen as a place where women feel comfortable, as they would be exposed to such situations. Most of the other women members are older than her and less educated.

The issues discussed at the *gram panchayat* meetings reflect the gender composition and interests of the members. More time and sensitivity was given to women-centred problems such as day care and solving domestic disputes. One of the members recalled a recent incident in which the *gram panchayat* had successfully intervened and solved a domestic dispute.

One of the young, newly married brides in the village had been requesting her in-laws to allow her to visit her parents in the neighbouring village. For various reasons, the in-laws and her husband refused to let her go. Finally, frustrated, she decided to run away on her own. A male acquaintance agreed to give her a ride on a two-wheeler (the most common mode of transportation in urban areas). However, some people saw her with this man. Upon her return from her parents' village, her in-laws refused to accept her into the family, accusing her of having an affair with the man who gave her the ride. They physically removed her out of the house and humiliated her in front of the entire village.

Several members of the *gram panchayat* heard about the incident and decided to help out the young girl. They summoned an emergency *panchayat* meeting and decided to pay a visit to the in-laws. According to witnesses, the in-laws were given a harsh warning that criminal charges for harassment would be launched unless they agreed to take back the daughter in-law. According to the *sarpanch*, a male *gram panchayat* would not have been as successful in handling this case because "men do not understand the pressures that women face". Another member also aptly summarized women's positions in the villages when she stated, "Village women have a tough life. They have to take care of the house, family, and animals, get firewood, water, cook, clean, wash. Where is the time to have an affair?"

The situation in Bhimagaon is different from those of both Kapsewadi and Bharatpur. First, Bhimagaon has a larger *gram panchayat* with 17 members, including six women. Second, it has also a *gram panchayat* that is divided almost equally between two political parties, thus creating a different political scene overall, especially regarding women's participation. Third, although Bhimagaon also has a female *sarpanch*, her role in *panchayat* activities can be described at best as minimal.

The two major parties represented in the Bhimagaon *gram panchayat* are the Nationalist Congress (also known as the Rashtrawadi Congress) and the Vikas Aghadi Party (an opposition party). Members from both parties are in constant conflict with each other and as a result the *gram panchayat* meetings are quite chaotic. Most of the meetings I attended in Bhimagaon can be described as shouting matches among the members. Also, the *gram sevak* was in control of the agenda, and not the *sarpanch* – unlike the meetings in Kapsewadi and Bharatpur, at Bhimagaon, the *gram sevak* ran the show.

The Bhimagaon female *sarpanch* belonged to the Nationalist Congress Party. She too had political connections. Her husband was the personal assistant to the local MLA from the Nationalist

Congress Party. She rarely attended meetings, and when she did, she was a silent member. On one occasion, she spent the entire time reading the newspaper. At another time, she answered phone calls throughout the meeting.

The Bhimagaon *gram panchayat* had another active female member. She and her husband owned a piece of land and both worked on the farm. She had completed high school. Like most village women, she was married at an early age and came to Bhimagaon as a bride. Our first meeting was at her house. She spoke to me as she covered the floor with cow dung. This method used by the rural poor in India to cover floors, is often an indication of the economic status of a family. Although her family owns land, they were not among the upper classes in Bhimagaon.

There is a tremendous contrast between these two women. As a *sarpanch,* one was in a position of considerable power. The other female representative was a member of the opposition party, constantly at odds with the majority party. However, she was the more active member of the *panchayat,* constantly questioning, challenging, initiating, and demanding. According to her, all the decisions in the village were made from the outside. Nothing happened inside. Previously people were ignorant about the *gram panchayat*. She argued that the *sarpanch* had a lot of power and was aware of what went on. The previous *sarpanches* of Bhimagaon came from rich families. This representative was the one who had also accused the previous *sarpanch* of corruption.

An analysis of the proceedings of the Malegaon *Panchayat Samiti* also indicates that, on more than one occasion, both the *sarpanch* and the *gram sevak* from Bhimagaon were summoned and questioned about misappropriating funds allocated for specific development schemes. For example, they were charged with forging names and signatures on beneficiary lists to entitle people below the poverty line. However, according to the records, they were only warned and no further action was taken.

Decisions were often predetermined at meetings. The *gram sevak* would read out an issue during a meeting. If opposed, the issue would be tabled for later. But then a different decision would be taken by the *gram sevak* and the *sarpanch*. Moreover, if a decision was taken during a meeting, it would often be changed later. This was due to the fact that the political parties would order the *sarpanch* and the *gram sevak* to change the decision according to their wishes. The majority party's decisions would ultimately hold up. It was also common to see the local Nationalist Congress Party leaders attend the meetings and support their party members.

The cases of Kapsewadi, Bharatpur and Bhimagaon suggest various ways in which parties and elites have influenced women's participation both in positive and negative terms. In Kapsewadi, Shiv Sena provided space and opportunity for one woman leader to succeed, while in Bharatpur, Congress put up an all-women's *panchayat*. Whatever the motives behind these actions, the results have been favourable (at least to some extent) to women members in these villages. However, in Kapsewadi, the situation is complicated due to the lack of participation by the female *panchayat* member from the lower caste.

In Bhimagaon, on the other hand, party rivalry and competition also show mixed results. One female member uses her position in the *panchayat* to question alleged misdoings. However, the party is clearly using the female sarpanch as a proxy. The members of the Bhimagaon *gram panchayat* are strictly divided along party lines for all decisions. A similar outcome is seen at the next level, in the Malegaon *Panchayat Samiti*.

Role of Parties and Elites at the Panchayat Samiti Level

The Malegaon *Panchayat Samiti* represents the strongest case for party involvement in the functioning of the committee. Over the years, it has acquired the reputation of being one of the more corrupt and politically unstable institutions. The record for women's participation is also not positive. In fact, during my case selection process, bureaucrats at the Sangli *Zilla Parishad* discouraged me from choosing this particular *panchayat samiti*, stating, "it was not the best case, given its history and the level of outside influence on it". However, since my cases at the *gram panchayat* level were part of this particular block, I did not have much choice. This was also the only place where I had to show documentation regarding my credentials as well as an introduction letter from the chief executive officer of the *zilla parishad*.

The *panchayat samiti* and the *zilla parishad* also differ in the types of women members represented from the gram *panchayats*. Although *gram panchayats* also favour women from certain castes and family backgrounds, there is more room for other women to contest elections, if supported by the 'right' party. However, at the other two levels, factors such as political involvement in local and state level politics become more crucial.

The composition of the female members in the Malegaon *panchayat samiti* reflects the political party in power at the time and also reflects the influence of other political elites. For example, the *sabhapati* (chair) of the *panchayat samiti* was the wife of a prominent member of a nearby village. Her husband often accompanied her to the *samiti* meetings and although a silent member during the meetings, he was nevertheless a source of influence.

My several attempts to interact with the *sabhapati* proved to be less than successful. At first, she was cautious to the extent of being suspicious about my motives for talking to her and studying the functioning of the *panchayat samiti*. Later, she requested that I hand her written questions to study, and then she agreed to talk to me. Our interview was short, and the picture that emerged was that she was chosen for this position by the party and was fulfilling her role according to the party's wishes. This experience was in sharp contrast with my usual interviews with women. For the most part, women were eager and enthusiastic to talk and our sessions would last more than an hour each time (of course, some of our time together was spent discussing other aspects of their lives, and mine). *Gram panchayat* representatives were the most accessible, as I would go to their homes, or to the fields where they worked, to meet with them. Representatives at the other two levels came to the *taluka* and *zilla* for the meetings, so these interviews were more planned. Women at both the upper levels of the *panchayati raj* were more vocal about their roles as representatives. I observed this at meetings as well. Women at the *zilla* level, in particular were vocal at meetings. I was never asked to submit my questions. On the other hand, the women were more than eager to talk. I make this comparison to illustrate the fact that the female president at the *taluka* level was an exception with regards to the manner in which she perceived my motives. It was also an indication of the intense party politics and factions that existed at the *samiti*, characterized by suspicion.

The block development officer, who is the government civil service appointee at the *panchayat samiti* level, has an important role in the functioning of the committee. Although he or she is supposed to remain neutral and objective, and merely to assist in administrative matters, the story in Malegaon suggests otherwise. The block development officer exemplified the stereotype of a seedy, corrupt government official. This characterization was confirmed by the number of corruption allegations against him currently under investigation at the *zilla parishad* level. He remained very powerful in the Malegaon *Panchayat Samiti,* as was evident from observing their monthly meetings.

For example, according to the State Act, all cheques issued, deposited, or cashed require two signatures, one from the elected official and one from the appointed official. On several occasions, I watched elected officials ask the block development officer to sign certain cheques, along with overt hints of benefits he could derive as a result of it. Bank accounts are also in the names of the government official and the elected official. While this system was designed to provide checks and balances, it is blatantly misused at the *samiti* level. Attempts by certain female members in requesting his transfer were met with resistance from other male members of the *samiti,* as well as from local politicians.

Another female member of the *panchayat samiti* recalled the problems she faced during her election campaign. "There were numerous difficulties I had to face. The family members of the previous *sabhapati* (chair of the *panchayat samiti*) made an all out effort to stop me from contesting. Just a week before the election, some other contestants framed a false case against my husband for illegal possession of *ganja* (marijuana), and he was imprisoned. I had to run around to resolve the matter. Besides being a psychological shock, this incident had severe financial implications. I had to take a loan from my relatives and friends to bail him out."

According to her, most opposition comes from other male members of the *panchayat samiti,* who conspire to gain personal benefit from government funds. When she tries to question their activities, they indulge in activities to undermine and defame her. For example, during a recent construction of a link road to a village, there was disagreement about who should acquire the tender for the construction contract. This happens to be a very important issue, as construction companies do their best to promote their cases in order to acquire government contracts. She claimed that the block development officer gets a hefty commission for promoting certain companies and ensuring that they get contracts for construction.

Women's voices are rarely heard at the *panchayat samiti* meetings. The block development officer in this particular case clearly ran the show. The members of the committee were equally divided among the Congress I, Nationalist Congress, BJP and Shiv Sena. The *panchayat samiti* represents a case in which political elites and male party members make decisions, and women's seats are considered as necessary quotas to be filled in order to ensure the party majority. It is interesting to note that while party elites influence decisions, the role of the block development officer at this level was also important.

Role of Parties and Elites at the Zilla Parishad Level

In Maharashtra, the *zilla parishad* is the most powerful of the three levels in the *panchayati raj.* As a result of various factors, the *zilla parishad* has dominated *panchayati raj* politics throughout the state. The Maharashtra Zilla Parishad and Panchayat Samiti Act of 1961 differed from the provisions of the Mehta Committee with regards to the specific powers and functions allocated to the *zilla parishads* (Shrader and Joshi, 1964). One such break with the recommendations made by the Mehta Committee concerns the role of the president of the *zilla parishad*. According to the Maharashtra *Zilla parishad* and *Panchayat Samiti* Act, district political leadership is provided with the Chief Executive Officer (a civil service ranked officer) as the chief administrative aide, responsible in most matters to the president, although a member of the state's civil service (Shrader and Joshi, 1964: 145). This provided the president with greater power and flexibility to act independently of political pressures from above.

Theoretically, this empowers the presidents of the *zilla parishads* and protects them from party pressures. However, in reality, party leaders, and more importantly, the MLAs and MPs maintain close ties with the presidents of *zilla parishads* and their chief executive officers, thus creating a relationship among the *zilla parishad* leadership different from that originally envisioned by the framers of the State Act.

The Sangli *Zilla Parishad* had had a female president since 1999. Prior to this, she was a member of the *zilla parishad*. She belongs to the Congress I Party and she is also a close political ally of the Minister of State for Education, having been born and raised in his native village. She also spoke of him as her mentor. She represents a case of a strong and effective female leader, who is nonetheless not independent in most of the choices and decisions she makes. In order to illustrate this complexity, it is necessary to discuss her achievements while in office.

For the past two years, the government of Maharashtra has implemented a cleanliness programme in the villages called the "*Sant Gadge Baba Gram Shwachetha Abhiyaan* (Gadge Baba Village Cleanliness Campaign)". The basic goals of the programme were to provide an incentive for the villagers to come together and participate in the cleanliness programme as well as to educate and increase awareness about cleanliness and hygiene in the villages.

A unique aspect of this programme was the fact that it was self-financed by the village *panchayats.* Village members raised funds through contributions. People eagerly donated both money and, more importantly, their time and efforts, to improve the cleanliness in their villages. It was an example of true "team spirit" and community participation.

The *zilla parishad* president believed in allocating greater powers to the lower levels of the *panchayati raj* institutions, as well as to the *gram sabhas.* The idea that rural problems are to be solved at the rural level was also important to her. Towards this end, she organized various workshops for newly elected *sarpanches,* women representatives, *anganwadi* workers, etc., to educate them about their rights and responsibilities.

She encouraged people to participate in *gram sabhas.* Specifically she emphasized women's roles in *gram sabhas,* and has presided over numerous *gram sabhas* held only for women in a number of villages. Additionally, she also reminded *sarpanches* and *gram sevaks* of different villages to encourage women to attend *gram sabhas,* so much so that she warned them that they would be held responsible if women did not attend and participate in *gram sabhas.*

She also initiated and set up a centre at the *zilla parishad* office to assist women with issues relating to any form of abuse. The centre has a full staff of two female social workers, with masters' degrees in social work. The centre also works closely with the police department and seeks their help when necessary. Such a centre provides a safe and confidential place for women to report abuse, at times when it might be difficult for them to speak to anyone else.

While the above description of her achievements is important, it is also equally important to note is that she was carefully chosen and groomed for this post by the Congress I and particularly by the local MLA. Her decisions are in line with the general Congress I perspective. At times, her actions have directly reflected the power hierarchy within the party structure. In one instance, the above-mentioned MLA influenced a decision regarding the suspension of one of the *sarpanches* in the district on corruption charges. He made a personal visit to the *zilla parishad* office to meet with the president to request her not to suspend the *sarpanch* in question. She complied, although the official reason given was the lack of evidence to prove his involvement in corruption activities. Moreover, her husband, also a member of the Congress I and a local informal political elite in their native village, was closely involved in the MLAs re-election campaign and viewed her position in the *zilla parishad* as a means for gathering support for the Congress I.

The relationship between the president and the chief executive officer of the Sangli *Zilla Parishad* illustrates the links to the party and political elite. In an attempt to maintain objectivity and non-partisanship, the chief executive officer often found himself at odds with the majority party. It was a common sight to see local politicians barge into his office, uninvited, and demand that he change a particular decision. I witnessed several of these meetings, where politicians would make a case for a particular issue or person, and attempt to pressure the chief executive officer to change his mind. The issues were most often related to allocation of funds for developmental activities. Since the *zilla parishad* controls the budgets for the other two levels of the *panchayati raj*, this is perhaps one of the most contentious issues.

My analysis based on observing *zilla parishad* monthly meetings for six months and reading through the proceedings dating to the start of the term of the committee reveals less than democratic scenarios. Issues raised in the meetings, especially monetary issues, almost always resulted in very contentious debate, shouting matches, among men and women. Decisions were often made without a vote, with the chief executive officer exercising his rights to take matters into his hands. However, the proceedings do not capture the full picture of the debates and the deliberations. Much of the evidence regarding the influence of party leaders and other elites comes from my interactions with and observations of *zilla parishad* members. This is not surprising considering that it is at this level that decisions affecting the other two levels are made.

The *zilla parishad* level in Maharashtra is the most important of the three levels. Control over the members and policies of the *zilla parishad* are a goal that all major political parties strive towards. It is an avenue for politicians to exercise power, to strengthen their vote base and sometimes also to gain personal benefits. However, this also works to the advantage of women. Members like the President of the *zilla parishad* discussed above, although considered protégés of a party or a politician, have managed to carve a space for themselves and have succeeded in effective policy making.

Conclusion

Parties play a crucial role in *panchayat* politics at all three levels. According to the *Panchayati Raj* Act, the *gram panchayat* level, elections are not supposed to be contested along party lines. However, the majority of the members who contested and won filed their nomination papers with the support of political parties. I observed several instances of resistance to women's entry into politics. Party members would throw lavish parties or openly offer monetary support to candidates and woo them to their side. Thus women running on an independent ticket had almost no chance of winning.

Parties also play an important role in another very popular practice-passing 'no confidence' motions to remove *sarpanchs* from their posts. This is often seen in cases where members are divided into groups along party lines (Bhimagaon's example). This affects women, as they become easy targets for rival party members. Moreover, it is one of the reasons for lack of cooperation among members.

Furthermore, political leaders are also involved in *panchayati raj* politics at all three levels. They use their influence to nominate members for positions, as well as to remove them. Political leaders also influence government officials such as civil servants to pass certain bills or resolutions. This contradicts the Maharashtra State Panchayati Raj Act, which prohibits direct influence of MLAs (member of legislative assembly) from intervening in *panchayat* politics. In reality, members vote along party lines, parties control nominations and MLAs have considerable influence in *panchayat* politics.

As seen through the example of the Sangli Zilla Parishad, the MLAs continue to monitor closely decisions made and the elected members of the *zilla parishad*, particularly the president, continue to maintain close ties with the state level politicians. This contradicts the original intent of the state-level act, which was designed to isolate the MLAs from the *panchayati raj* institutions in the state.

The Congress party in particular has been influential in *panchayat* politics in Maharashtra. From its inception, the party has successfully penetrated into rural areas and has established a firm base due to two major factors. First, with its links to the sugar cooperatives, the party at the state level has created loyal leadership at the local levels. As office holders of the cooperatives are also often involved – directly or indirectly – in *panchayat* politics, the Congress has solidified its position in the area.

Second, the influence of individual Congress leaders such as Y.B. Chavan and Vasant Patil also continue to generate a loyal Congress following. The influence extends beyond the members of their extended families participating in *panchayati raj* politics. New and emerging leaders at the local level desire to be associated with these political families and thus a new form of patronage is created, with the older more experienced political leaders and families providing the support to the newer leaders.

Since the 1990s, opposition parties have also started the process of consolidating their power base in the area. With the rise of the BJP and the Shiv Sena, and the Nationalist Congress, the original Congress I faces serious competition in an area where it previously enjoyed an unchallenged monopoly. This has the potential to produce in a change in the power structure within the Congress. One the one hand, it could result in greater involvement by political elites into the affairs of the *panchayati raj*, or it could also result in greater decentralization of actual decision-making abilities of leaders, especially women, and eventually create a new group of leadership.

Political parties in Maharashtra can be generally categorized as highly fragmented and competitive. The split within the Congress Party began a trend that continues with the emergence of other smaller, regional parties. Party competition is also evident in *panchayat* politics, at all three levels. Parties recruit and nominate candidates for elections and once elected, members are expected to vote along party lines. The consequences of dissent can sometimes be harsh, and can include social and political isolation, and even violence.

Although it is difficult to measure the exact linkages between political parties and violence, the role played by some of the informal political elites, the *goondas,* indicate that physical threats and violence is sometimes used as a tool to achieve desired political results. As noted in interviews with several female members, especially at the *gram panchayat* level, and especially those from lower castes, this type of threat is quite real. I commonly heard phrases indicating the fear, such as, "but if I go against the wishes of the party, the *goondas* can hurt my family," or "they will ruin my reputation and the reputation of my family".

However, along with the fractional and competitive approach to party politics, there also exists some room for accommodation of different interests that is absent in the more vicious 'winner take all' politics. In Maharashtra political winners are expected to reserve some share of rewards for losers, or at least to keep the losers working within the system. Winners in Congress Party factional struggles do not try to eliminate losers from all rewards of political life, because today's losers are expected to stay in the game, and maybe even to win later on. For example, in 1985, the main political issue of the time centred on Sharad Pawar, a former chief minister who had earlier left the Congress to form his own party, a group which had lost badly in the parliamentary and assembly polls. Instead of trying to eliminate him completely from political life, the winners in Maharashtra were negotiating with him on the terms of his re-admission to the Congress Party. This eventually occurred in late 1987, but did not last long, as Pawar eventually split again from the Congress I to form the Nationalist Congress Party. An episode such as this could be a measure of the strength of the Congress Party in the area, where it was comfortable with the idea of trying to make deals with dissidents.

Party fragmentation both works to the benefit of and becomes an obstacle to female members in the *panchayati raj* at all three levels. On the one hand, as seen through the example in Bhimagaon, it was the female member from the opposition party that held the rest of the *panchayat* accountable for certain actions and demanded transparency and openness. However, in Kapsewadi and Bharatpur, both places with a clear majority of one party, women from the dominant party were more successful. This was certainly the case also at the other two levels, particularly in the Sangli *Zilla Parishad.*

Moreover, the cases under study suggest that party fragmentation is also a variable that works more to women's advantage at the higher levels in the *panchayati raj* . Although Bhimagaon presents a clear example of this at the *gram panchayat* level, women at the *taluka* and *zilla* level from opposition parties were in a better position to negotiate and discuss issues.

The nature of political participation in India is complex. The influences of class, caste, religion, language, and regional identity are constantly creating cross-pressures that threaten to bring down the institutions of democratic governance. While the secular and inclusive nature of the Congress initially served to strengthen the institutions of democracy in this society, during the last twenty years the weakening of Congress influence has been associated with the increasing factionalization of both the party system and the society at large (Hasan, 2002).

So long as the Congress Party was able to integrate the diverse interests of Indian society into a centralized institutional framework, the democratic system was able to operate in a highly regulated manner. The locus of political power was at the federal level and class-based politics were institutionalized through party competition. While the institutions of Indian democracy remain strong, nevertheless, in recent years they have been increasingly challenged. Hence decentralized political competition, serious and recurring political violence, the rise of Hindu nationalism and caste politics is more prominent today.

Notes

1. The names of the *gram panchayats* have been changed.
2. For a detailed discussion on all women's *panchayats* in Maharashtra, see Datta, Bishaka (1998). *And Who Will Make the Chapatis*?' Kolkata: Stree Publications.

Select References

Aggarwal, J.C. and N.K. Chowdhry (1998), *Elections in India 1998,* New Delhi: Shipra Publications.

Attwood, Donald W. and B.S. Baviskar (1988), *Who Shares?: Cooperatives and Rural Development,* New Delhi: Oxford Univ. Press.

Bavadam, Lyla (2002), "A Campaign for Clean Villages," *Frontline,* 19(23).

Baviskar, B.S. (1980), *Politics of Development: Sugar Co-operatives in Rural Maharashtra*, New Delhi: Oxford University Press.

Beteille, Andre (1969), *Castes: Old and New. Essays in Social Structure and Social Transformation*, Bombay: Asia Publishing House.

Brass, Paul (1984-1985), *Caste, Faction and Party in Indian Politics*, Vol. I (1984); Vol. II (1985), Delhi: Chanakya Publications.

— (1994), *The Politics of India Since Independence*, Cambridge: Cambridge University Press.

— (1984), National Power and Local Politics in India: A Twenty year Perspective, Modern Asian Studies XVIII, No. 89-118.

Buch, Nirmala (2000), Women's Experience in New Panchayats: The Emerging Leadership of Rural Women. Occasional Paper # 35. New Delhi: Centre for Women's Development Studies.

Carras, Mary (1970), Congress Factionalism in Maharashtra: A Case Study of the Akola Zilla Parishad, *Asian Survey*, 10 (5), 410-426.

— (1972), *The Dynamics of Indian Political Factions: A Study of District Councils in the State of Maharashtra*, London: Cambridge University Press.

Carter, Anthony T. (1974), *Elite Politics in Rural India: Political Stratification and Political Alliances in Western Maharashtra*, London: Cambridge University Press.

Chandra, Kanchan (2000), The Transformation of Ethnic Politics in India: The Decline of the Congress and the Rise of the Bahujan Samaj Party in Hoshiarpur, *Journal of Asian Studies*, 59 (1), 26-61.

Chatterji, P.C. (1996), Reservation: Theory and Practice, In T.V. Sathyamurthy (ed.), *Region, Religion, Caste, Gender and Culture in Contemporary India*, New Delhi: Oxford University Press.

Chhibber, Pradeep K. (1999), *Democracy Without Associations: Transformation of the Party System and Social Cleavages in India*, Ann Arbor: University of Michigan Press.

— (2002), Why Are Some Women Politically Active? The Household, Public Space and Political Participation in India, *International Journal of Comparative Sociology*, 43 (3).

Cornwall, Andrea (2000), Making a Difference? Gender and Participatory Development, IDS Discussion Paper 378, Brighton: Institute of Development Studies.

Datta, Bishaka (ed.) (1998), *And Who Will Make the Chapatis? A Study of All-Women's Panchayats in Maharashtra*, Kolkata: Stree Publications.

D'Lima, Hazel (1983), *Women in Local Self-Government: A Study of Maharashtra*, New Delhi: Concept Publishing Company.

Dreze, Jean and Amartya Sen (1997), *Indian Development: Selected Regional Perspectives,* Delhi: Oxford University Press.

Everett, Jana, M. (ed.) (1979), *Women and Social Change in India,* New Delhi: Heritage Publications.

— (1996), Reservation of Seats for Women in India: Toward the Engendering of Politics? Prepared for delivery at the 1996 annual meeting of the American Political Science Association, The San Francisco Hilton and Towers, August 29-September 1.

Feldhaus, Anne (ed.) (1998), *Images of Women in Maharashtrian Society,* Albany: State University of New York Press.

Frankel, Francine R., Hasan Zoya, *et al.* (eds.) (2000), *Transforming India: Social and Political Dynamics of Democracy,* New York: Oxford University Press.

Gavankar, Rohini (1993), Role of Women in Panchayati Raj, In Sushila Kaushik (ed.), *Women's Participation in Politics,* New Delhi: Vikas Publishing.

Government of India (1950), *Constitution of India,* Part IV: Articles 36-51. New Delhi: Govt. of India Publications.

— (1952), *Report of the Planning Commission,* New Delhi: Govt. of India Publications.

— (1974), *Towards Equality: Report of the Committee on the Status of Women in India,* New Delhi: Ministry of Education and Social Welfare.

— (1978), *Report of the Committee on Panchayati Raj Institutions,* New Delhi: Ministry of Rural Development.

— (1991), *Census Report,* New Delhi: Office of the Registrar General.

— (1991), *Lok Sabha, The Constitution: 72nd Amendment Bill,* New Delhi: Ministry of Rural Development.

— (1992), *The Constitution: 73rd Amendment Act on the Panchayats,* New Delhi: Ministry of Rural Development.

— (1995), *Lok Sabha Debates*: Session XV, November 27 – December 22.

— (1996), *Lok Sabha, The Constitution: 81st Amendment Bill,* New Delhi: Ministry of Rural Development.

— (2001), *Census Report,* New Delhi: Office of the Registrar General. Available at http://www.censusindia.net/

Government of Maharashtra (1961), *Report of the Committee on Democratic Decentralization,* Bombay: Department of Cooperation and Rural Development.

Hasan, Zoya (ed.) (2002), *Parties and Party Politics in India,* New Delhi: Oxford University Press.

Institute of Social Sciences (1995), *Panchayati Raj Development Report.*

— (1999), *State and Union Territories Panchayati Raj Acts,* New Delhi: Institute of Social Sciences.

Jain, Devaki (1985), *India: A Condition Across Caste and Class,* London: Penguin Books.

Jalvaani (2000), *Newsletter on Rural Water and Sanitation in India* 3 (4), February.

John, Mary E. (1999), Democracy, Patriarchies and Reservations for Women: A Note, *Indian Journal of Gender Studies* 6 (1).

Joshi, Ram (1968), Maharashtra. In Myron Weiner (ed.), *State Politics in India,* New Jersey: Princeton University Press.

Joshi, S.D. and N.P. Mitragotri (1994), Maharashtra, In George Matthew (ed.), *Status of Panchayati Raj in the States of India,* New Delhi: Institute of Social Sciences.

Kak, Subhash (1990), The Politics of Quotas in South Asia, *Journal of Social, Political, and Economic Studies,* 42.

— (1994), *India At Century's End: Essays on History and Politics,* New Delhi: Voice of India.

Kaviraj, Sudipta (ed.) (1997), *Politics in India,* New Delhi: Oxford University Press.

Keya, Acharya (1999), Rights-India: Once Organized, Rural Women Realize Their Power, Inter Press Service, 25 November.

Kincaid, C.A. and Rao Bahadur D.B. Parasnis (1968), *A History of the Maratha People,* New Delhi: S. Chand and Co.

Kohli, Atul (1987), *The State and Poverty in India: The Politics of Reform,* Cambridge: Cambridge University Press.

— (1990), *Democracy and Discontent: India's Growing Crisis of Governability,* Cambridge: Cambridge University Press.

— (ed.) (2001), *The Success of India's Democracy,* Cambridge: Cambridge University Press.

Kolenda, Pauline (1978), *Caste in Contemporary India: Beyond Organic Solidarity,* Prospect Heights: Waveland Press.

Kothari, R. (ed.) (1970), *Caste in Indian Politics,* New York: Orient Longman.

— (1967), *Party System and Election Studies,* Mumbai: Allied Publishers.

Kumar, Ashok (1990), *Rural Development in India: Dimensions of Its Planning,* New Delhi: Inter-India Publications.

Kumar, Dharma (1992), The Affirmative Action Debate in India, *Asian Survey,* 32 (3), 290-302.

Maheshwari, Shriram (1979), New Perspectives on Rural Government in India: The Ashok Mehta Committee Report, *Asian Survey,* 19 (11), 1110-1125.

Manikyamba, P. (1989), *Women in Panchayati Raj Structures*, New Delhi: Gian Publishing House.

Manor, James (1990), How and Why Liberal Representative Politics Emerged in India, *Political Studies*, 38, 20-38.

Matthew, George (1994), *Panchayati Raj in India: From Legislation to Movement*, New Delhi: Institute of Social Sciences.

— (ed.) (1994), *Status of the Panchayati Raj in the States of India*, New Delhi: Institute of Social Sciences.

— (1999), *Panchayati Raj Factors*, New Delhi: Institute of Social Sciences.

— (ed.) (2000), *Status of the Panchayati Raj in the States and Union Territories of India*, New Delhi: Institute of Social Sciences.

Mitra, Subrata K. (1991), Room to Maneuver in the Middle: Local Elites, Political Action and the State in India, *World Politics*, 43, April, 390-413.

— (1992), *Power, Protest and Participation: Local Elites and the Politics of Development in India*, London: Routledge.

Ministry of Agriculture and Irrigation (1978), *Report of the Committee on Panchayati Raj Institutions*, New Delhi: Government of India.

Ministry of Rural Development (2001), *Panchayati Raj Institutions*, New Delhi: Government of India.

Mitra, Sumit and Javed Ansari (1998), Women's Bill: Ladies Seat, *The Nation*, July 20.

Mohanty, Bidyut (1999), Panchayat Raj Institutions and Women, In Aparna Basu and Bharata Ray (eds.), *From Independence Toward Freedom: Essays on Indian Women Since 1947*, New Delhi: Oxford University Press.

Muralidharan, Sukumar (1997), A Bill in Vain, *Frontline*, January 10.

Nanda, B.R. (ed.) (1976), *Indian Women from Purdah to Modernity*, New Delhi: Concept Publishing House.

Nanivadekar, Medha (1998), Reservation for Women, *Economic and Political Weekly*, July 11.

— (2003), Partners in Politics, Competing in Crime: Growing Importance of Independents and Rebels in Local Elections, *Manushi*, 137, 26-34.

Nath, Meenakshi (1996), Cutting Across Party Line: Women Members of Parliament Explain their Stand on Reservation Quotas, *Manushi*, 96, 15.

Omvedt, Gail (1980), *We Will Smash This Prison: Indian Women in Struggle*, London: Zed Press.

Patnaik, Biju and Shivraj Patil (1994), *Panchayati Raj, Parliamentarians and Legislators*, New Delhi: Institute of Social Sciences.

Phillips, Anne (1991), *Engendering Democracy*, University Park: The Pennsylvania State University Press.

— (1994), Must Feminists Give Up On Liberal Democracy?, *Political Studies*, XL, 5, 93-111.

— (1995), *The Politics of Presence*, Oxford: Clarendon Press.

Panda, Snehalata (1990), *Determinants of Political Participation: Women and Public Activity*, New Delhi: Ajanta Publishers.

Parikh, Sunita (1997), *The Politics of Preference: Democratic Institutions and Affirmative Action in the United States and India*, Ann Arbor: The University of Michigan Press

Rai, Shirin M. (1997), Gender and Representation: Women in the Indian Parliament, 1991-1996, In A. M. Goetz (ed.) *Getting Institutions Right for Women in Development*, London: Sage.

— (1999), Democratic Institutions, Political Representation and Women's Empowerment: The Quota Debate in India, *Democratization*, 6 (3), 84-99.

— and Kumud Sharma (2000), Democratizing the Indian Parliament: the 'Reservation for Women' Debate, In Shirin M. Rai (ed.), *International Perspectives on Gender and Democratization*, New York: St. Martin 's Press.

— (2002), *Gender and the Political Economy of Development: From Nationalism to Globalization*, Malden: Blackwell.

— (ed.) (2003), *Mainstreaming Gender, Democratizing the State?: Institutional Mechanisms for the Advancement of Women*, New York: Manchester University Press.

Rajput, Pam (1993), Women Leadership at the Grassroots Level in Punjab, In Susheela Kaushik (ed.) *Women's Participation in Politics*, 31-44, New Delhi: Vikas Publishing House.

Raman, Vasanthi (2001), The Women's Question in Contemporary Indian Politics, *Asian Journal of Women's Studies*, 7 (2), 39.

Revankar, Ratna (1971), *The Indian Constitution: A Case Study of Backward Classes*, Madison: Fairleigh Dickinson University Press.

Rosenthal, Donald B. (1974), Making it in Maharashtra, *Journal of Politics*, 36 (2), 409-437.

— (1977), *The Expansive Elite: District Politics and State Policy-Making in India*, Berkeley: University of California Press.

Shah, A.M., B.S. Baviskar, E.A. Ramaswamy, and M.N. Srinivas (1996), *Women in Indian Society*, New Delhi: Sage Publishing.

Sharma, Kumud (1998), Power vs. Representation: Feminist Dilemmas, Ambivalent State and the Debate on Reservation for Women in India, Occasional Paper No. 28. New Delhi: Centre for Women's Development Studies.

Sharma, Miriam (1978), *The Politics of Inequality: Competition and Control in an Indian Village*, Hawaii: University Press of Hawaii.

Shrader, Lawrence L. and Joshi, Ram (1963), Zilla Parishad Elections in Maharashtra and the District Political Elite, *Asian Survey*, 3 (3), 143-156.

Singh, Smrita Gopal, Medha Kotwal Lele, and Nirmala Sathe, et al. (1992), Participation of Women in Electoral Politics in Maharashtra, In *Women in Politics: Forms and Processes*, New Delhi: Friedrich Ebert Stiftung.

Sirsikar, V.M. (1964), Leadership Patterns in Rural Maharashtra, *Asian Survey*, 4 (7), 929-939.

— (1995), *Politics of Modern Maharashtra*, New Delhi: Orient Longman.

Sooryamoorthy, R. (2000), Political Participation of Women: The Case of Women Councilors in Kerala, India, *Journal of Third World Studies*, 17, 45-60.

Srinivas, M.N. (1962), *Caste in Modern India and Other Essays*, Bombay: Asia Publishing House.

Spear, Percival (1965), *A History of India, Volume II*, New Delhi: Penguin Books.

Stree, Aadhar Kendra (1995), *Women in Decision Making: A Study of Gram Panchayats in Maharashtra*, Bangalore: Institute of Social Studies Trust.

Tekchandani, Bharti, Jyoti, Kiran and Priti Sharma (1997), *They Call Me Member Saab: Women in Haryana Panchayati Raj*, New Delhi: Multiple Action Research Group.

Unnithan Kumar, Maya (1997), *Identity, Gender and Poverty: New Perspectives of Caste and Tribe in Rajasthan*, Oxford: Berghahn Books.

Contributors

Aditi Mitra is Assistant Professor of Sociology and Women's Studies at University of Colorado at Colorado Springs. She is a British Chevening Scholar with her masters (Mass Communication) from University of Leicester (UK) and doctorate (Sociology) from Oklahoma State University (USA). Her research interests include Gender/Race Inequality, Globalization, Non-Governmental Organizations, International Relations and Social Psychology.

Aparna Thomas is Assistant Professor of Politics and Women's Studies, at Cornell College, in Iowa. She received her Ph.D. in Political Science from Western Michigan University, Kalamazoo, MI. Her areas of interest include Comparative Politics, South Asian politics, Gender and Development, Gender and Politics and Feminist Theory.

Arima Mishra is Research Associate in the Department of Sociology, Delhi School of Economics, University of Delhi. She teaches Industrial Sociology and Population and Society. Her research addresses Tribal Studies, Folk Culture, Sociology of Poverty and Medical Sociology. She has previously worked on several international research projects.

B. Suguna is Associate Professor in the Department of Women's Studies, Sri Padmavathi Mahila Visvavidyalayam, Tirupati, Andhra

Pradesh. She received her M.A. and Ph.D. in Sociology from Sri Venkateswara University, Tirupati. Later she took an M.A. in Women's Studies from Mother Theresa Women's University, Kodaikanal. She has vast research experience, completing projects funded by the University Grants Commission, DoEN, UGC, and CIIL. Besides wide teaching experience, she has published a book on Working Women and Religion. Her interests include Women's Studies, Sociology of Women and Empowerment of Women.

Celine Augustine is Lecturer in Sociology at St. Teresa's College, Ernakulam, Kerala, where she teaches graduates and undergraduates. She earned her Masters from Loyola College of Social Sciences, Thiruvananthapuram. She served as Secretary and President of the Kerala Sociological Society. The real emancipation of women is her active interest through issues in development. Despite hailing from Kerala, a state highly educated and developed, she continues to encounter conservative, male-dominated outlooks while working assertively but quietly for women's empowerment. Social response to HIV/AIDS is a recent focus of her work.

D. Radha Devi retired from the International Institute for Population Sciences (IIPS), Mumbai, India as Professor in 2002 after more than 35 years of teaching and research in the field of Demography. Prior to this she served as Senior Social Scientist in the Gandhigram Institute of Rural Health and Family Welfare Trust, Madurai, Tamil Nadu and as Senior Research Assistant in the Department of Statistics, Kerala University, Thiruvananthapuram. She earned a B.A. & M.A. in Economics and M.Sc. in Demography from the University of Kerala, an M.A. in Sociology emphasizing demography from the University of North Carolina-Chapel Hill and she worked for her Ph.D. in Economics at the Institute for Social and Economic Change (ISEC), Bangalore. She has published over 40 papers in National and International journals and presented in both national and international seminars/conferences about the same number of papers. Among these are papers on family planning, aging, women's labour force participation, fertility, and manpower issues. She co-authored the book, *Role of Education in Shaping Fertility in India: Evidences from National Family Health Survey*. She completed over a dozen research projects while at IIPS and continues with demographic projects from her home in Thiruvananthapuram, Kerala.

G. Sandhya Rani has been working as Associate Professor in the Department of Women's Studies, Sri Padmavathi Mahila Visvavidyalayam, Tirupati. She obtained her first Post Graduate Degree in Economics from Sri Krishnadevaraya University, Anantapur in Andhra Pradesh. She was awarded M.Phil. and Ph.D. in the field of Economics of Sericulture also from SKU. She also obtained Post Graduate Degrees in Women's Studies from Mother Teresa Women's University, Kodaikanal and in Education from University of Madras. Besides 12 years of P.G. teaching she has written a book, *Sericulture and Rural Development*, completed one Major Research Project funded by UGC on "Employment to Rural Women Through Sericulture", has published 24 research papers and presented papers in 48 national and international conferences. Her academic interests include Women's Studies, Women and Entrepreneurship, Women and Education and Rural and Agricultural Economics.

Janet Huber Lowry is Associate Professor of Sociology and former Dean of Social Sciences at Austin College, in Sherman, Texas, USA. She had her academic training in Mathematics at Hanover College in Indiana and Sociology for both M.A. and Ph.D. at UNC-Chapel Hill where she specialized in research methods and demography. As a teacher of undergraduates she has offered courses in aging, demography, gender, Indian society, marriage and family, research methods, statistics, and work. Most of her research has been in community service and social gerontology, including dissertation research on retirement. Her publications include numerous local survey reports, chapters in *Normal Aging III: Reports from the Duke Longitudinal Studies, 1975-1984* (Duke University Press 1985), *Faith and Families* (Westminster Press 1986), and *Challenges of Multicultural Education: Teaching and Taking Diversity Courses* (Paradigm 2005), syllabi and assignments in teaching resource guides for Sociology of Aging and Research Methods, articles in *Research on Aging* and *Discourse(s) – a journal for multidisciplinary studies.*

Jean Van Delinder is Associate Professor of Sociology and Director of Women's Studies at Oklahoma State University. She received an undergraduate degree in Humanities from the University of Minnesota-Twin Cities, masters in American Studies and doctorate in Sociology from the University of Kansas. Her research interests are interdisciplinary and include Culture, Theory, Gender and Globalization.

Jyotsna Mohanty is Lecturer in the Department of Anthropology, Kamala Nehru Women's College, Bhubaneswar, Orissa. She has obtained her Doctorate in Anthropology from Utkal University, Bhubaneswar, Orissa. She has worked in the Norwegian Agency for Development Cooperation (NORAD) on various projects concerning Environmental Pollution. Her areas of interest include Gender Issues, Eco Tourism, Tribal Studies, and Environment and Development.

Kamal K. Misra is Professor of Anthropology at the University of Hyderabad, Hyderabad. He has authored *Social Structure and Change among the Ho of Orissa* (Gian, 1987), *Tribal Elite and Social Transformation* (Inter-India, 1984), *Text Book of Anthropological Linguistics* (Concept, 2000), *Indigenous Knowledge, Natural Resource Management and Development* (Pratibha Prakashan, 2005), co-edited *Peoples and Environment in India* with M.L.K. Murty (Discovery, 2001), and edited *Anthropology, New Global Order and Other Essays* (Concept, 2005). A former Commonwealth and Fulbright Fellow, his academic interests include Culture, Ecology and Development; Culture, Language and Cognition; Anthropological Theories; and Anthropology of Gender.

Marine Carrin is Director of Research, CNRS, at the Centre d'Anthropologie, Toulouse. She is the author of *La Fleur et l'Os: symbolisme et rituel chez les Santal* (EHESS, Paris 1986). *Enfants de la Déesse: prêtrise et dévotion féminine au Bengale* (CNRS and MSH, Paris 1997), and has edited *Managing Distress: therapeutic cults in South Asia* (Manohar, Delhi 1999) and with C. Jaffrelot *Tribus et Basses castes. Résistance et Autonomie dans la Société Indienne,* (EHESS, Paris 2002). With H. Tambs-Lyche she has written*: A Peripheral Encounter; Santals, Missionaries and their Changing Worlds, 1867-1900* (Manohar, Delhi, in press), and edited *People of the Jangal: Reformulating Identities and Adaptations in Crisis* (Manohar, Delhi in press). A book on Santal Ritual Discourse is in preparation. She has also published several articles on the Bhuta Cults of South Canara.

Michael P. Johnson is Associate Professor of Sociology, Women's Studies, and African and African-American Studies at Penn State. He received his Ph.D. in sociology from the University of Michigan, Ann Arbor. His major areas of research are intimate partner violence and commitment to personal relationships. Recent papers are available at his Web site at www.personal.psu.edu/mpj.

Niveditha Menon is a doctoral student pursuing her degree in Sociology and Demography, with a minor in Women's Studies at Penn State University. Her major areas of research are Violence against Women, Feminist Family Sociology, and Global Feminism.

N. Sudhakar Rao is Professor in the Department of Anthropology at the University of Hyderabad, Hyderabad. Earlier he was Professor of Sociology at Assam University, Silchar and an Associate Professor at TALEEM Research Foundation, Ahmedabad. Before that, he was a Visiting Research Fellow at Centre for Development Studies, Department of Anthropology, University of Bergen, Norway. He has an extensive field work experience and carried out several anthropological and sociological researches. He has co-authored *Yanadi Response to Change: An Attempt in Action Anthropology* (1985) and has authored *Organised Power and Unorganised Resistance* (1998) and *Ethnography of a Nomadic Tribe* (2002). He has also contributed several research papers in journals of Anthropology and Sociology.

Ramola B. Joseph is Reader and Head of the Department of Sociology, St. Teresa's College, Ernakulam, Kerala. She holds Masters Degrees in Sociology and History from University of Kerala and a Doctorate from Loyola University of Chicago. She has served as Visiting Lecturer to the Government of Kerala Personnel and Indian Civil Service candidates. Dr. Joseph has also presented papers and chaired sessions at several Sociological Conferences. She has co-authored *Hardship and Support Systems in Chicago* (1986) along with Dr. Kristen A. Gronbjerg, et al., in the United States. She has also co-edited *Sociology for Social Development* (1998), and edited *Sociology of Education: Potentials and Prospects* (2000), *An Introduction to Sociology* (2001) and *Indian Society and Social Change* (2001). She has contributed several articles to professional journals. She served as the President of Kerala Sociological Society from 1998-2000.

Richa Chauhan is Adjunct Professor at Widener University in Pennsylvania. She received her Ph.D. in Sociology from State University of New York at Stony Brook. Her research interests are Gender and Development, and Gender and Family. Currently she is working on an introductory text for Gender and Development.

Roopa Ravikumar teaches in the Department of Social Sciences in Lady Doak College in Madurai, Tamil Nadu. She graduated from Madurai Kamaraj University in Madurai where she was awarded the Wilhelmson Prize for the best outgoing student in undergraduate studies in Social Sciences as well as the Gold Medal for M.A. Sociology. She is involved in extension activities and currently serves as President of the YWCA, Madurai.

Sachidananda Mohanty is Professor of English at the University of Hyderabad. He was a British Council Scholar in U.K. (1990), Fulbright Post-doctoral Fellow at Texas and Yale (1990-91) and Salzburg Fellow, Austria (1996). He received the Katha Award for outstanding translation from the President of India, the Katha British Council Translation Prize (1994) and University Grants Commission's "Career Award" (1994-97). He was a Senior Academic Fellow at the American Studies Research Center, Hyderabad (1999); Fellow, Cambridge Seminar on the Contemporary British Writer, 1999; and a Fulbright Visiting Professor in the U.S. in 2005. Dr Mohanty has published thirteen books in English and in Oriya. His essays and articles have appeared in some of the leading journals and forums in the country including India Today, The Hindu, The Indian Express, Span Magazine, The India International Center Quarterly, PEN, India, The Aligarh Journal of English Studies, New Quest, and The Economic and Political Weekly.

Sajini Shajy had two years of professional working experience and is now finishing her Masters in Sociology from the Mahatma Gandhi University, at St. Teresa's College in Ernakulam, Kerala. She also completed her Diploma in Population Sciences from International Institute for Population Sciences, Mumbai during the period 1998-99 and was awarded the gold medal and the J.R. Rele medal for the best term paper.

Shajy Isac is presently working as Deputy Research Director at TNS India, New Delhi. He has got more than 8 years of professional working experience in various national and international organizations. He completed his Ph.D. in Population Studies in the year 1999 from the International Institute for Population Sciences, Mumbai. Prior to this, he did his Masters in both Statistics and Population Studies.

Sheela Prasad is Professor in the Centre for Regional Studies, University of Hyderabad. Her basic training has been in the discipline of Geography earning her doctoral degree from Jawaharlal Nehru University, New Delhi. Her research interests are in Urban and Regional Studies, Women's Health, and Environmental Studies. She has taught in the University of Pittsburgh, USA and served as faculty on its Semester at Sea Program. She has authored *Urban Health Care: Public and Private Hospitals in Hyderabad* and co-edited a volume *The Third World City: Emerging Contours*. She is involved with local NGOs working in the areas of Health and Environment. She is an Executive Member of Anveshi, a research centre of women's studies in Hyderabad.

Subhadra Mitra Channa is Professor of Social Anthropology at the University of Delhi. She holds a Ph.D. from University of Delhi and has been interested in the study of Marginal Groups in Indian Society, including those belonging to the Dalits, tribes and women as a category. Her specialization ranges over Gender Studies, Religion and Ecology along with Anthropological Theory and Methodology. She has been the recipient of several international fellowships. She was a Charles Wallace Fellow to U.K., a Visiting Professor to MSH, Paris and a Fulbright Visiting Lecturer. She has widely travelled and has been invited to Japan, South Africa, Italy, East Africa and Oxford University to present papers and attend various seminars. She has written about fifty scholarly papers published in reputed journals and books across the world, including one in the Japanese language. She is the author of four books (two edited) and has edited two encyclopedias. She was the President of the Indian Anthropological Association and currently is editor of the *Indian Anthropologist*, the journal of the Association. She is also co-chair of the Commission on the Anthropology of Women, an international body.

Index